The Disinherited: Plays

The Disinherited: Plays

ABE C. RAVITZ
California State College, Dominguez Hills

MYRNA J. HARRISON
ROBERT J. GRIFFIN
Consulting Editors

Dickenson Publishing Company, Inc.
Encino, California and Belmont, California

ISBN-0-8221-0048-7

Library of Congress Catalog Card Number: 72-90247

Printed in the United States of America

Printing (last digit): 9 8 7 6 5 4 3 2 1

FOR MY MOTHER

Acknowledgments

Contents

The Disinherited: Plays

Introduction

Historically cut off from full pursuit of the beguiling, nebulous American dream, the disinherited of our country have at crucial moments emerged from invisibility to challenge the consciousness of us all. From the settling of the earliest colonies, human exploitation, social violence, and ideological dispute have been notoriously evident in America's development: New England Puritan versus Quaker, Southern Cavalier versus Slave—the elect always opposed to the alleged unregenerate. While proclaiming principles of democracy, equality, and social progress, both the frontier communities and the growing cities evolved tightly restrictive political and social hierarchies. Moreover, heresy-hunting "Saints" were forever intent on pursuing the outcasts of the land, for the Bible advised "Thou shalt not suffer a witch to live."

In Bret Harte's famous tale "The Outcasts of Poker Flat," for instance, one can see a realistic picture of social discrimination emerging from the supposedly democratic frontier. Law and justice were haphazard and weak; the code of the people frequently became the code of the jungle. A "spasm of virtuous reaction" among the citizens of Poker Flat in the 1850's vindictively singled out for exile and certain death a gambler (who had fairly won the townspeople's money), a prostitute (who had outraged the respectable) and an accused thief (whose closest ally was "Demon rum"). The sanctimonious crusade, led by a secret committee of vigilantes, was directed toward ridding the community of "improper persons." And in all the Poker Flats and Sandy Bars dotting the middle border of America, similar arbitrary purges often took place. The gambling-hall proprieter, the doctor, and the minister were quickly identified in the prairie towns as being socially and morally superior to the fallen in their midst: particularly symbolic of all the "depraved" were the slave, the sharecropper, and the squatter. The coming of the railroad brought with it a spurious geographical separation, clearly marking off the sheep (God's Chosen) from the goats (the Devil's own); "the wrong side of the tracks" located one's inescapable place in the established order of class and caste.

Contrary to the vigorous assertions of democracy and equality, the mainstream of American life tended to be exclusive; whole segments of the population were effectively blocked from assuming responsible roles in molding the shape of the nation. Whether such discrimination stemmed from motives which were conscious or unconscious, racial or ethnic, idiosyncratic or economic, scapegoats were identified and forced into frustrated lives of desperation, alienation, and anger. Quaker and Mormon, Black and Oriental, Jew and Italian, Indian and Latino, farm hand and factory worker, woman and drop-out all must be brought into focus for a full and faithful picture of the disinherited.

The theater has reflected with nightmare accuracy the distrust and mistreatment of these American disinherited. The social conditions that spawn disaffiliates, the political prejudices that hinder upward mobility, and the general injustices that confront "underdogs" and outsiders have been examined by playwrights who offer their audiences, among other theatrical possibilities, either a social mirror, an open forum, or a psychological escape. The raw materials of life have supplied the often explosive details of art and polemic.

This book offers a profile of the disinherited through a selection of plays that range in time from life in the ante-bellum slave quarter to confrontations in the streets of our contemporary cities, and in style from the superficiality of vaudeville to the complexity of avant-garde expressionistic fantasy. Many American dramatists have pictured the rigidly puritan society of the frontier, the hopelessness of Appalachia, and the dilemmas of the ghetto. Other playwrights have dealt with the plight of American workers caught in technological change, the know-nothing attitudes toward American immigrants, and the controversial double standard applied to American women. Disinherited all.

The plays in this anthology comprise a theatrical spectrum: they are variously comical, experimental, farcical, realistic, and romantic; each, however, manages to show some aspect of America's social and spiritual malaise. The selections have been chosen for their relevance in illuminating this part of the record of our national experience.

The playwright sets it on the stage for all to see. This is how we look. This is the way things were. This is the way things are. After the final curtain, life in America waited, and continues to wait, outside.

The Slave

William Wells Brown

(c1816–1884)

His mother was Elizabeth, a field-working slave; his father was George Higgins, a prominent slaveholder of Lexington, Kentucky. Given the slave name William, he was taken with his mother by their master to St. Louis. She was immediately "hired out." When the boy had barely reached puberty, he was "hired out" too. William first worked in a "public house," then on a steamboat, and finally as a printer's aid to the noted abolitionist editor Elijah P. Lovejoy, an outspoken reformer who was murdered by a mob for publishing antislavery articles. When the young slave was about sixteen, he escaped to Ohio with the intention of crossing Lake Erie to seek his freedom in Canada. A stopover on this journey caused a fundamental change in William's image of himself. At the home of Wells Brown, a Quaker Samaritan, the runaway learned a new and vitally important lesson: a slave is a man, not a chattel. He subsequently adopted the name of the philanthropist who had helped him toward this understanding of his own value and identity.

When William Wells Brown published his personal narrative in 1847, he wrote a moving dedication to his benefactor:

> *Thirteen years ago, I came to your door, a weary fugitive from chains and stripes. I was a stranger, and you took me in. I was hungry and you fed me. Naked was I, and you clothed me. Even a name by which to be known among men, slavery had denied me. You bestowed upon me your own. Base indeed should I be, it I ever forget what I owe to you, or do anything to disgrace that honored name.*

This self-educated man who at one time bore only the name "Elizabeth's son" was to become a leading Negro historian, writer, physician, and spokesman for the black man in nineteenth-century America. His literary accomplishments were many. In addition to a graphic account of the slave's life as field hand, house boy, and fugitive, Brown published *The Black Man: His Antecedents, His Genius and His Achievements* (1863), a work directed specifically at "the calumniators and traducers of the Negro. . . . " His book *Clotelle; or, The Colored Heroine. A Tale of the Southern States* is the first known novel by a black man in America. In it Brown vividly illustrates the hideous disinheritance of his people:

> *Notice.—Seventy-nine negroes will be offered for sale on Monday, September 10, at 12 O'clock, being the entire stock of the late John Graves. The negroes are in excellent condition, and all warranted against the common vices. Among them are several mechanics, able-bodied field hands, ploughboys, and women with children, some of them very prolific, affording a rare opportunity for any one who wishes to raise a strong and healthy lot of servants for their own use. Also several mulatto girls of rare personal qualities,—two of these very superior.*

The novel ranges from such clinically excerpted reality to outrage:

> *This was a Virginia slave auction, at which the bones, sinews, blood and nerves of a young girl of eighteen were sold for $500; her moral character for $200; her superior intellect for $100; the benefits supposed to accrue from*

> *her having been sprinkled and immersed, together with a warranty of her devoted Christianity, for $300; her ability to make a good prayer, for $200; and her chastity for $700 more.*

For the first time in American fiction, the passion in these words came not from sympathetic antislavery white authors but from an incensed, angry black man.

Brown's drama *The Escape; or, A Leap for Freedom* (1858) explores the institution of slavery in America, whose conditions the author knew first hand. Despite unrealistic dialogue scattered throughout the play, a balance of comedy and pathos reveals an artist behind the crusader. Brown easily integrates satiric motifs into the action: the stupidity of class pride, the hypocrisy of religion, the zeal of certain medical men for making money rather than helping humanity. He knew how to adjust language to denote character and class, and shrewdly incorporated into his play "The Fugitive Slave's Apostrophe to the North Star," a popular poem written by the Reverend John Pierpont of Boston, a fiery antislavery preacher; sympathetic audiences quickly recognized and responded to the touching lyric. The playwright aimed his thrusts simultaneously at the head and heart.

Essentially serious but using humor at crucial instances to highlight the natural foibles of mankind, *The Escape* dramatizes black awareness, anger, and incipient violence. Two men were at combat within William Wells Brown: the dedicated literary craftsman and the ex-slave who remembered the past with bitterness. "I heard that my master was sick," he wrote in his *Narrative,* "and nothing brought more joy to my heart than that intelligence. I prayed fervently for him—not for his recovery, but for his death." These conflicting forces—his essential compassion and his understandable hostility—generated the tension of his literary career. From both personal experience and creative imagination, William Wells Brown dramatized the life and dreams of the slave, who was the epitome of the disinherited American.

Author's Preface

This play was written for my own amusement, and not with the remotest thought that it would ever be seen by the public eye. I read it privately, however, to a circle of my friends, and through them was invited to read it before a Literary Society. Since then, the Drama has been given in various parts of the country. By the earnest solicitation of some in whose judgment I have the greatest confidence, I now present it in a printed form to the public. As I never aspired to be a dramatist, I ask no favor for it, and have little or no solicitude for its fate. If it is not readable, no word of mine can make it so; if it is, to ask favor for it would be needless.

The main features in the Drama are true. GLEN and MELINDA are actual characters, and still reside in Canada. Many of the incidents were drawn from my own experience of eighteen years at the South. The marriage ceremony, as performed in the second act, is still adhered to in many of the Southern States, especially in the farming districts.

The ignorance of the slave, as seen in the case of "BIG SALLY," is common wherever chattel slavery exists. The difficulties created in the domestic circle by the presence of beautiful slave women, as found in DR. GAINES'S family, is well understood by all who have ever visited the valley of the Mississippi.

The play, no doubt, abounds in defects, but as I was born in slavery, and never had a day's schooling in my life, I owe the public no apology for errors.

W. W. B.

The Escape; or, A Leap for Freedom

Characters Represented

DR. GAINES, *proprietor of the farm at Muddy Creek.*
REV. JOHN PINCHEN, *a clergyman.*
DICK WALKER, *a slave speculator.*
MR. WILDMARSH, *neighbor to Dr. Gaines.*
MAJOR MOORE, *a friend of Dr. Gaines.*
MR. WHITE, *a citizen of Massachusetts.*
BILL JENNINGS, *a slave speculator.*
JACOB SCRAGG, *overseer to Dr. Gaines.*
MRS. GAINES, *wife of Dr. Gaines.*
MR. and MRS. NEAL, and DAUGHTER, *Quakers, in Ohio.*
THOMAS, *Mr. Neal's hired man.*
GLEN, *slave of Mr. Hamilton, brother-in-law of Dr. Gaines.*
CATO, SAM, SAMPEY, MELINDA, DOLLY, SUSAN, and BIG SALLY, *slaves of Dr. Gaines.*
PETE, NED, and BILL, *slaves.*
OFFICERS, LOUNGERS, BARKEEPER, &c.

ACT I

Scene I

A Sitting-Room.

MRS. GAINES, *looking at some drawings*—SAMPEY, *a white slave, stands behind the lady's chair.*

Enter DR. GAINES, R.

DR. GAINES: Well, my dear, my practice is steadily increasing. I forgot to tell you that neighbor Wyman engaged me yesterday as his family physician; and I hope that the fever and ague, which is now taking hold of the people, will give me more patients. I see by the New Orleans papers that the yellow fever is raging there to a fearful extent. Men of my profession are reaping a harvest in that section this year. I would that we could have a touch of the yellow fever here, for I think I could invent a medicine that would cure it. But the yellow fever is a luxury that we medical men in this climate can't expect to enjoy; yet we may hope for the cholera.

MRS. GAINES: Yes, I would be glad to see it more sickly here, so that your business might prosper. But we are always unfortunate. Every body here seems to be in good health, and I am afraid that they'll keep so. However, we must hope for the best. We must trust in the Lord. Providence may possibly send some disease amongst us for our benefit.

Enter CATO, R.

CATO: Mr. Campbell is at de door, massa.

DR. G.: Ask him in, Cato.

Enter MR. CAMPBELL, R.

DR. G.: Good morning, Mr. Campbell. Be seated.

MR. CAMPBELL: Good morning, doctor. The same to you, Mrs. Gaines. Fine morning, this.

MRS. G.: Yes, sir; beautiful day.

MR. C.: Well, doctor, I've come to engage you for my family physician. I am tired of Dr. Jones. I've lost another very valuable nigger under his treatment; and, as my old mother used to say, "change of pastures makes fat calves."

DR. G.: I shall be most happy to become your doctor. Of course, you want me to attend to your niggers, as well as to your family?

MR. C.: Certainly, sir. I have twenty-three servants. What will you charge me by the year?

DR. G.: Of course, you'll do as my other patients do, send your servants to me when they are sick, if able to walk?

MR. C.: Oh, yes; I always do that.

DR. G.: Then I suppose I'll have to lump it, and say $500 per annum.

MR. C.: Well, then, we'll consider that matter settled; and as two of the boys are sick, I'll send them over. So I'll bid you good day, doctor. I would be glad if you would come over some time, and bring Mrs. Gaines with you.

DR. G.: Yes, I will; and shall be glad if you will pay us a visit, and bring with you Mrs. Campbell. Come over and spend the day.

MR. C.: I will. Good morning, doctor.

Exit MR. CAMPBELL, R.

DR. G.: There, my dear, what do you think of that? Five hundred dollars more added to our income. That's patronage worth having! And I am glad to get all the negroes I can to doctor, for Cato is becoming very useful to me in the shop. He can bleed, pull teeth, and do almost any thing that the blacks require. He can put up medicine as well as any one. A valuable boy, Cato!

MRS. G.: But why did you ask Mr. Campbell to visit you, and to bring his wife? I am sure I could never consent to associate with her, for I understand that she was the daughter of a tanner. You must remember, my dear, that I was born with a silver spoon in my mouth. The blood of the Wyleys runs in my veins. I am surprised that you should ask him to visit you at all; you should have known better.

DR. G.: Oh, I did not mean for him to visit me. I only invited him for the sake of compliments, and I think he so understood it; for I should be far from wishing you to associate with Mrs. Campbell. I don't forget, my dear, the family you were raised in, nor do I overlook my own family. My father, you know, fought by the side of Washington, and I hope some day to have a handle to my own name. I am certain Providence intended me for something higher than a medical man. Ah! by-the-by, I had forgotten that I have a couple of patients to visit this morning. I must go at once.

Exit DR. GAINES, R.

Enter HANNAH, L.

MRS. G.: Go, Hannah, and tell Dolly to kill a couple of fat pullets, and to put the biscuit to rise. I expect brother Pinchen here this afternoon, and I want every thing in order. Hannah, Hannah, tell Melinda to come here.

Exit HANNAH, L.

We mistresses do have a hard time in this world; I don't see why the Lord should have imposed such heavy duties on us poor mortals. Well, it can't last always. I long to leave this wicked world, and go home to glory.

Enter MELINDA

I am to have company this afternoon, Melinda. I expect brother Pinchen here, and I want every thing in order. Go and get one of my new caps, with the lace border, and get out my scolloped-bottomed dimity petticoat, and when you go out, tell Hannah to clean the white-handled knives, and see that not a speck is on them; for I want every thing as it should be while brother Pinchen is here.

Exit MRS. GAINES, L, HANNAH, R.

Scene II

Doctor's shop—CATO *making pills.*

Enter DR. GAINES, L.

DR. G.: Well, Cato, have you made the batch of ointment that I ordered?

CATO: Yes, massa; I dun made de intment, an' now I is making the bread pills. De tater pills is up on the top shelf.

DR. G.: I am going out to see some patients. If any gentlemen call, tell them I shall be in this afternoon. If any servants come, you attend to them. I expect two of Mr. Campbell's boys over. You see to them. Feel their pulse, look at their tongues, bleed them, and give them each a dose of calomel. Tell them to drink no cold water, and to take nothing but water gruel.

CATO: Yes, massa; I'll tend to 'em.

Exit DR. GAINES, L.

CATO. I allers knowed I was a doctor, an' now de ole boss has put me at it, I muss change my coat. Ef any niggers comes in, I wants to look suspectable. Dis jacket don't suit a doctor; I'll change it. [*Exit* CATO—*immediately returning in a long coat.*] Ah! now I looks like a doctor. Now I can bleed, pull teef, or cut off a leg. Oh! well, well, ef I aint put de pill stuff an' de intment stuff togedder. By golly, dat ole cuss will be mad when he finds it out, won't he? Nebber mind, I'll make it up in pills, and when de flour is on dem, he won't know what's in 'em; an' I'll make some new intment. Ah! yonder comes Mr. Campbell's Pete an' Ned; dems de ones massa sed was coming'. I'll see ef I looks right [*Goes to the looking-glass and views himself.*] I em some punkins, ain't I? [*Knock at the door.*] Come in.

Enter PETE and NED, R.

PETE: Whar is de doctor?

CATO: Here I is; don't you see me?

PETE: But whar is de ole boss?

CATO: Dat's none you business. I dun tole you dat I is de doctor, an dat's enuff.

NED: Oh! do tell us whar de doctor is. I is almos dead. Oh me! oh dear me! I is so sick. [*Horrible faces.*]

PETE: Yes, do tell us; we don't want to stan here foolin'.

CATO: I tells you again dat I is de doctor. I larn de trade under massa.

NED: Oh! well, den, give me somethin' to stop dis pain. Oh dear me! I shall die. [*He tries to vomit, but can't—ugly faces.*]

CATO: Let me feel your pulse. Now put out your tongue. You is berry sick. Ef you don't mine, you'll die. Come out in de shed, an' I'll bleed you.

Exit all—re-enter

CATO: —Dar, now take dese pills, two in de mornin' and two at night, and ef you don't feel better, double de dose. Now, Mr. Pete, what's de matter wid you?

PETE: I is got de cole chills, an' has a fever in de night.

CATO: Come out, an' I'll bleed you.

Exit all—re-enter

Now take dese pills, two in de mornin' and two at night, an' ef dey don't help you, double de dose. Ah! I like to forget to feel your pulse and look at your tongue. Put out your tongue. [*Feels his pulse.*] Yes, I tells by de feel ob your pulse dat I is gib you de right pills.

Enter MR. *Parker's* BILL, L.

CATO: What you come in dat door widout knockin' for?

BILL: My toof ache so, I didn't tink to knock. Oh, my toof! my toof! Whar is de doctor?

CATO: Here I is; don't you see me?

BILL: What! you de doctor, you brack cuss! You looks like a doctor! Oh, my toof! my toof! Whar is de doctor?

CATO: I tells you I is de doctor. Ef you don't believe me, ax dese men. I can pull your toof in a minnit.

BILL: Well, den, pull it out. Oh, my toof! how it aches! Oh, my toof! [*Cato gets the rusty turnkeys.*]

CATO: Now lay down on your back.

BILL: What for?

CATO: Dat's de way massa does.

BILL: Oh, my toof! Well, den, come on. [*Lies down, Cato gets astraddle of Bill's breast, puts the turnkeys on the wrong tooth, and pulls—Bill kicks, and cries out*]—Oh, do stop! Oh! oh! oh! [*Cato pulls the wrong tooth—Bill jumps up.*]

CATO: Dar, now I tole you I could pull your toof for you.

BILL: Oh, dear me! Oh, it aches yet! Oh me! Oh, Lor-e-massy! You dun pull de wrong toof. Drat your skin! ef I don't pay you for this, you brack cuss! [*They fight, and turn over table, chairs and bench—Pete and Ned look on.*]

Enter DR. GAINES, R.

DR. G.: Why, dear me, what's the matter? What's all this about? I'll teach you a lesson, that I will. [*The doctor goes at them with his cane.*]

CATO: Oh, massa! he's to blame, sir. He's to blame. He struck me fuss.

BILL: No, sir; he's to blame; he pull de wrong toof. Oh, my toof! oh, my toof!

DR. G.: Let me see your tooth. Open your mouth. As I live, you've taken out the wrong tooth. I am amazed. I'll whip you for this; I'll whip you well. You're a pretty doctor. Now lie down, Bill, and let him take out the right tooth; and if he makes a mistake this time, I'll cowhide him well. Lie down, Bill. [*Bill lies down, and Cato pulls the tooth.*] There now, why didn't you do that in the first place?

CATO: He wouldn't hole still, sir.

BILL: He lies, sir. I did hole still.

DR. G.: Now go home, boys; go home.

Exit PETE, NED and BILL, L.

DR. G.: You've made a pretty muss of it, in my absence. Look at the table! Never mind, Cato; I'll whip you well for this conduct of yours to-day. Go to work now, and clear up the office.

Exit DR. GAINES, R.

CATO: Confound dat nigger! I wish he was in Ginny. He bite my finger and scratch my face. But didn't I give it to him? Well, den, I reckon I did. [*He goes to the mirror, and discovers that his coat is torn—weeps.*] Oh, dear me! Oh, my coat—my coat is tore! Dat nigger has tore my coat. [*He gets angry, and rushes about the room frantic.*] Cuss dat nigger! Ef I could lay my hands on him, I'd tare him all to pieces,—dat I would. An' de ole boss hit me wid his cane after dat nigger tore my coat. By golly, I wants to fight somebody. Ef ole massa should come in now, I'd fight him. [*Rolls up his sleeves.*] Let 'em come now, ef dey dare—ole massa, or any body else; I'm ready for 'em.

Enter DR. GAINES, R.

DR. G.: What's all this noise here?

CATO: Nuffin', sir; only jess I is puttin' things to rights, as you tole me. I didn't hear any noise except de rats.

DR. G.: Make haste, and come in; I want you to go to town.

Exit DR. GAINES, R.

CATO: By golly, de ole boss like to cotch me dat time, didn't he? But wasn't I mad? When I is mad, nobody can do nuffin' wid me. But here's my coat, tore to pieces. Cuss dat nigger! [*Weeps.*] Oh, my coat! oh, my coat! I rudder he had broke my head den to tore my coat. Drat dat nigger! Ef he ever comes here again, I'll pull out every toof he's got in his head—dat I will.

Exit, R.

Scene III

A Room in the Quarters.

Enter GLEN, L.

GLEN: How slowly the time passes away. I've been waiting here two hours, and Melinda has not yet come. What keeps her, I cannot tell. I waited long and late for her last night, and when she approached, I sprang to my feet, caught her in my arms, pressed her to my heart, and kissed away the tears from her moistened cheeks. She placed her trembling hand in mine, and said, "Glen, I am yours; I will never be the wife of another." I clasped her to my bosom, and called God to witness that I would ever regard her as my wife. Old Uncle Joseph joined us in holy wedlock by moonlight; that was the only marriage ceremony. I look upon the vow as ever binding on me, for I am sure that a just God will sanction our union in heaven. Still, this man, who claims Melinda as his property, is unwilling for me to marry the woman of my choice, because he wants her himself. But he shall not have her. What he will say when he finds that we are married, I cannot tell; but I am determined to protect my wife or die. Ah! here comes Melinda.

Enter MELINDA, R.

I am glad to see you, Melinda. I've been waiting long, and feared you would not come. Ah! in tears again?

MELINDA: Glen, you are always thinking I am in tears. But what did master say to-day?

GLEN: He again forbade our union.

MELINDA: Indeed! Can he be so cruel?

GLEN: Yes, he can be just so cruel.

MELINDA: Alas! alas! how unfeeling and heartless! But did you appeal to his generosity?

GLEN: Yes, I did; I used all the persuasive powers that I was master of, but to no purpose; he was inflexible. He even offered me a new suit of clothes, if I would give you up; and when I told him that I could not, he said he would flog me to death if I ever spoke to you again.

MELINDA: And what did you say to him?

GLEN: I answered, that, while I loved life better than death, even life itself could not tempt me to consent to a separation that would make life an unchanging curse. Oh, I would kill myself, Melinda, if I thought that, for the sake of life, I could consent to your degradation. No, Melinda, I can die, but shall never live to see you the mistress of another man. But, my dear girl, I have a secret to tell you, and no one must know it but you. I will go out and see that no person is within hearing. I will be back soon.

Exit GLEN, L.

MELINDA: It is often said that the darkest hour of the night precedes the dawn. It is ever thus with the vicissitudes of human suffering. After the soul has reached the lowest depths of despair, and can no deeper plunge amid its rolling, foetid shades, then the reactionary forces of man's nature begin to operate, resolution takes the place of despondency, energy succeeds instead of apathy, and an upward tendency is felt and exhibited. Men then hope against power, and smile in defiance of despair. I shall never forget when first I saw Glen. It is now more than a year since he came here with his master, Mr. Hamilton. It was a glorious moonlight night in autumn. The wide and fruitful face of nature was silent and buried in repose. The tall trees on the borders of Muddy Creek waved their leafy branches in the breeze, which was wafted from afar, refreshing over hill and vale, over the rippling water, and the waving corn and wheat fields. The starry sky was studded over with a few light, flitting clouds, while the moon, as if rejoicing to witness the meeting of two hearts that should be cemented by the purest love, sailed triumphantly along among the shifting vapors.
Oh, how happy I have been in my acquaintance with Glen! That he loves me, I do well believe it; that I love him, it is most true. Oh, how I would that those who think the slave incapable of the finer feelings, could only see our hearts, and learn our thoughts,—thoughts that we dare not utter in the presence of our masters! But I fear that Glen will be separated from me, for there is nothing too base and mean for master to do, for the purpose of getting me entirely in his power. But, thanks to Heaven, he does not own Glen, and therefore cannot sell him. Yet he might purchase him

from his brother-in-law, so as to send him out of the way. But here comes my husband.

Enter GLEN, L.

GLENN: I've been as far as the overseer's house, and all is quiet. Now, Melinda, as you are my wife, I will confide to you a secret. I've long been thinking of making my escape to Canada, and taking you with me. It is true that I don't belong to your master, but he might buy me from Hamilton, and then sell me out of the neighborhood.

MELINDA: But we could never succeed in the attempt to escape.

GLEN: We will make the trial, and show that we at least deserve success. There is a slave trader expected here next week, and Dr. Gaines would sell you at once if he knew that we were married. We must get ready and start, and if we can pass the Ohio river, we'll be safe on the road to Canada.

Exit, R.

Scene IV

Dining-Room.

REV. MR. PINCHEN *giving* MRS. GAINES *an account of his experience as a minister*—HANNAH *clearing away the breakfast table*—SAMPEY *standing behind* MRS. GAINES' *chair.*

MRS. GAINES: Now, do give me more of your experience, brother Pinchen. It always does my soul good to hear religious experience. It draws me nearer and nearer to the Lord's side. I do love to hear good news from God's people.

MR. PINCHEN: Well, sister Gaines, I've had great opportunities in my time to study the heart of man. I've attended a great many camp-meetings, revival meetings, protracted meetings, and death-bed scenes, and I am satisfied, sister Gaines, that the heart of man is full of sin, and desperately wicked. This is a wicked world, sister Gaines, a wicked world.

MRS. G.: Were you ever in Arkansas, brother Pinchen? I've been told that the people out there are very ungodly.

MR. P.: Oh, yes, sister Gaines. I once spent a year at Little Rock, and preached in all the towns round about there; and I found some hard cases out there, I can tell you. I was once spending a week in a district where there were a great many horse thieves, and one night, somebody stole my pony. Well, I knowed it was no use to make a fuss, so I told brother Tarbox to say nothing about it, and I'd get my horse by preaching God's everlasting gospel; for I had faith in the truth, and knowed that my Savior would not let me lose my pony. So the next Sunday I preached on horse-stealing, and told the brethren to come up in the evenin' with their hearts filled with the grace of God. So that night the house was crammed brim full with anxious souls, panting for the bread of life. Brother Bingham opened with prayer, and brother Tarbox followed, and I saw right off that we were gwine to have a blessed time. After I got 'em pretty well warmed up, I jumped on to one of the seats, stretched out my hands, and said, "I know who stole my pony; I've found out; and you are in here tryin' to make people believe that you've got religion; but you ain't got it. And if you don't take my horse back to brother Tarbox's pasture this very night, I'll tell your name right out in meetin' to-morrow night. Take my pony back, you vile and wretched sinner, and come up here and give your heart to God." So the next mornin', I went out to brother Tarbox's pasture, and sure enough, there was my bob-tail pony. Yes, sister Gaines, there he was, safe and sound. Ha, ha, ha.

MRS. G.: Oh, how interesting, and how fortunate for you to get your pony! And what power there is in the gospel! God's children are very lucky. Oh, it is so sweet to sit here and listen to such good news from God's people! You Hannah, what are you standing there listening for, and neglecting your work? Never mind, my lady, I'll whip you well when I am done here. Go at your work this moment, you lazy huzzy! Never mind, I'll whip you well. [*Aside.*] Come, do go on, brother Pinchen, with your godly conversation. It is so sweet! It draws me nearer and nearer to the Lord's side.

MR. P.: Well, sister Gaines, I've had some mighty queer dreams in my time, that I have. You see, one night I dreamed that I was dead and in heaven, and such a place I never saw before. As soon as I entered the gates of the celestial empire, I saw many old and familiar faces that I had seen before. The first person that I saw was good old Elder Pike, the preacher that first called my attention to religion. The next person I saw was Deacon Billings, my first wife's father, and then I saw a host of godly faces. Why, sister Gaines, you knowed Elder Goosbee, didn't you?

MRS. G.: Why, yes; did you see him there? He married me to my first husband.

MR. P.: Oh, yes, sister Gaines, I saw the old Elder, and he looked for all the world as if he had just come out of a revival meetin'.

MRS. G.: Did you see my first husband there, brother Pinchen?

MR. P.: No, sister Gaines, I didn't see brother Pepper there; but I've no doubt but that brother Pepper was there.

MRS. G.: Well, I don't know; I have my doubts. He was not the happiest man in the world. He was always borrowing trouble about something or another. Still, I saw some happy moments with Mr. Pepper. I was happy when I made his acquaintance, happy during our courtship, happy a while after our marriage, and happy when he died. [*Weeps.*]

HANNAH: Massa Pinchen, did you see my ole man Ben up dar in hebben?

MR. P.: No, Hannah; I didn't go amongst the niggers.

MRS. G.: No, of course brother Pinchen didn't go among the blacks. What are you asking questions for? Never mind, my lady, I'll whip you well when I'm done here. I'll skin you from head to foot. [*Aside.*] Do go on with your heavenly conversation, brother Pinchen; it does my very soul good. This is indeed a precious moment for me. I do love to hear of Christ and Him crucified.

MR. P.: Well, sister Gaines, I promised sister Daniels that I'd come over and see her this morning, and have a little season of prayer with her, and I suppose I must go. I'll tell you more of my religious experience when I return.

MRS. G.: If you must go, then I'll have to let you; but before you do, I wish to get your advice upon a little matter that concerns Hannah. Last week, Hannah stole a goose, killed it, cooked it, and she and her man Sam had a fine time eating the goose; and her master and I would never have known a word about it, if it had not been for Cato, a faithful servant, who told his master. And then, you see, Hannah had to be severely whipped before she'd confess that she stole the goose. Next Sabbath is sacrament day, and I want to know if you think that Hannah is fit to go to the Lord's supper after stealing the goose.

MR. P.: Well, sister Gaines, that depends on circumstances. If Hannah has confessed that she stole the goose, and has been sufficiently whipped, and has begged her master's pardon, and begged your pardon, and thinks she'll never do the like again, why then I suppose she can go to the Lord's supper; for

"While the lamp holds out to burn,
The vilest sinner may return."

But she must be sure that she has repented, and won't steal any more.

MRS. G.: Now, Hannah, do you hear that? For my own part, I don't think she's fit to go to the Lord's supper, for she had no occasion to steal the goose. We give our niggers plenty of good wholesome food. They have a full run of the meal tub, meat once a fortnight, and all the sour milk about the place, and I'm sure that's enough for any one. I do think that our niggers are the most ungrateful creatures in the world, that I do. They aggravate my life out of me.

HANNAH: I know, missis, dat I steal de goose, and massa whip me for it, and I confess it, and I is sorry for it. But, missis, I is gwine to de Lord's supper, next Sunday, kase I ain't agwine to turn my back on my bressed Lord an' Massa for no old tough goose, dat I ain't. [*Weeps.*]

MR. P.: Well, sister Gaines, I suppose I must go over and see sister Daniels; she'll be waiting for me.

Exit MR. PINCHEN, M. D.

MRS. G.: Now, Hannah, brother Pinchen is gone, do you get the cowhide and follow me to the cellar, and I'll whip you well for aggravating me as you have to-day. It seems as if I can never sit down to take a little comfort with the Lord, without you crossing me. The devil always puts it into your head to disturb me, just when I am trying to serve the Lord. I've no doubt but that I'll miss going to heaven on your account. But I'll whip you well before I leave this world, that I will. Get the cowhide and follow me to the cellar.

Exit MRS. GAINES and HANNAH, R.

ACT II

Scene I

Parlor.

DR. GAINES *at a table, letters and papers before him.*

Enter SAMPEY, L.

SAMPEY: Dar's a gemman at de doe, massa, dat wants to see you, seer.

DR. GAINES: Ask him to walk in, Sampey.

Exit SAMPEY, L.

Enter WALKER

WALKER: Why, how do you do, Dr. Gaines? I em glad to see you, I'll swear.

DR. G.: How do you do, Mr. Walker? I did not expect to see you up here so soon. What has hurried you?

WALK.: Well, you see, doctor, I comes when I em not expected. The price of niggers is up, and I em gwine to take advantage of the times. Now, doctor, ef you've got any niggers that you wants to sell, I em your man. I am paying the highest price of anybody in the market. I pay cash down, and no grumblin'.

DR. G.: I don't know that I want to sell any of my people now. Still, I've got to make up a little money next month, to pay in bank; and another thing, the doctors say that we are likely to have a touch of the cholera this summer, and if that's the case, I suppose I had better turn as many of my slaves into cash as I can.

WALK.: Yes, doctor, that is very true. The cholera is death on slaves, and a thousand dollars in your pocket is a great deal better than a nigger in the field, with cholera at his heels. Why, who is that coming up the lane? It's Mr. Wildmarsh, as I live! Jest the very man I wants to see.

Enter MR. WILDMARSH

Why, how do you do, Squire? I was jest a thinkin' about you.

WILDMARSH: How are you, Mr. Walker? and how are you, doctor? I am glad to see you both looking so well. You seem in remarkably good health, doctor?

DR. G.: Yes, Squire, I was never in the enjoyment of better health. I hope you left all well at Licking?

WILD.: Yes, I thank you. And now, Mr. Walker, how goes times with you?

WALK.: Well, you see, Squire, I em in good spirits. The price of niggers is up in the market, and I am lookin' out for bargains; and I was jest intendin' to come over to Lickin' to see you, to see if you had any niggers to sell. But it seems as ef the Lord knowed that I wanted to see you, and directed your steps over here. Now, Squire, ef you've got any niggers you wants to sell, I em your man. I am payin' the highest cash price of any body in the market. Now's your time, Squire.

WILD.: No, I don't think I want to sell any of my slaves now. I sold a very valuable gal to Mr. Haskins last week. I tell you, she was a smart one. I got eighteen hundred dollars for her.

WALK.: Why, Squire, how you do talk! Eighteen hundred dollars for one gal! She must have been a screamer to bring that price. What sort of a lookin' critter was she? I should like to have bought her.

WILD.: She was a little of the smartest gal I've ever raised; that she was.

WALK.: Then she was your own raising, was she?

WILD.: Oh, yes; she was raised on my place, and if I could have kept her three or four years longer, and taken her to the market myself, I am sure I could have sold her for three thousand dollars. But you see, Mr. Walker, my wife got a little jealous, and you know jealousy sets the women's heads a teetering, and so I had to sell the gal. She's got straight hair, blue eyes, prominent features, and is almost white. Haskins will make a spec, and no mistake.

WALK.: Why, Squire, was she that pretty little gal that I saw on your knee the day that your wife was gone, when I was at your place three years ago?

WILD.: Yes, the same.

WALK.: Well, now, Squire, I thought that was your daughter; she looked mightily like you. She was your daughter, wasn't she? You need not be ashamed to own it to me, for I am mum upon such matters.

WILD.: You know, Mr. Walker, that people will talk, and when they talk, they say a great deal; and people did talk, and many said the gal was my daughter; and you know we can't help people's talking. But here comes the Rev. Mr. Pinchen; I didn't know that he was in the neighborhood.

WALK.: It is Mr. Pinchen, as I live; jest the very man I wants to see.

Enter MR. PINCHEN, R.

Why, how do you do, Mr. Pinchen? What in the name of Jehu brings you down here to Muddy Creek? Any camp-meetins, revival meetins, death-bed scenes, or any thing else in your line going on down here? How is religion prosperin' now, Mr. Pinchen? I always like to hear about religion.

MR. PIN.: Well, Mr. Walker, the Lord's work is in good condition every where now. I tell you, Mr. Walker, I've been in the gospel ministry these thirteen years, and I am satisfied that the heart of man is full of sin and desperately wicked. This is a wicked world, Mr. Walker, a wicked world, and we ought all of us to have religion. Religion is a good thing to live by, and we all want it when we die. Yes, sir, when the great trumpet blows, we ought to be ready. And a man in your business of buying and selling slaves needs religion more than any body else, for it makes you treat your people as you should. Now, there is Mr. Haskins,—he is a slave-trader, like yourself. Well, I converted him. Before he got religion, he was one of the worst men to his niggers I ever saw; his heart was as hard as stone. But religion has made his heart as soft as a piece of cotton. Before I converted him, he would sell husbands from their wives, and seem to take delight in it; but now he won't sell a man from his wife, if he can get any one to buy both of them together. I tell you, sir, religion has done a wonderful work for him.

WALK.: I know, Mr. Pinchen, that I ought to have religion, and I feel that I am a great sinner; and whenever I get with good pious people like you and the doctor, and Mr. Wildmarsh, it always makes me feel that I am a desperate sinner. I feel it the more, because I've got a religious turn of mind. I know that I would be happier with religion, and the first spare time I get, I am going to try to get it. I'll go to a protracted meeting, and I won't stop till I get religion. Yes, I'll scuffle with the Lord till I gets forgiven. But it always makes me feel bad to talk about religion, so I'll change the subject. Now, doctor, what about them thar niggers you thought you could sell me?

DR. GAINES: I'll see my wife, Mr. Walker, and if she is willing to part with Hannah, I'll sell you Sam and his wife, Hannah. Ah! here comes my wife; I'll mention it.

Enter MRS. GAINES, L.

Ah! my dear, I am glad you've come. I was just telling Mr. Walker, that if you were willing to part with Hannah, I'd sell him Sam and Hannah.

MRS. G.: Now, Dr. Gaines, I am astonished and surprised that you should think of such a thing. You know what trouble I've had in training up Hannah for a house servant, and now that I've got her so that she knows my ways, you want to sell her. Haven't you niggers enough on the plantation to sell, without selling the servants from under my very nose?

DR. G.: Oh, yes, my dear; but I can spare Sam, and I don't like to separate him from his wife; and I thought if you could let Hannah go, I'd sell them both. I don't like to separate husbands from their wives.

MRS. G.: Now, gentlemen, that's just the way with my husband. He thinks more about the welfare and comfort of his slaves, than he does of himself or his family. I am sure you need not feel so bad at the thought of separating Sam from Hannah. They've only been married eight months, and their attachment can't be very strong in that short time. Indeed, I shall be glad if you do sell Sam, for then I'll make Hannah *jump the broomstick* with Cato, and I'll have them both under my eye. I never will again let one of my house servants marry a field hand—never! For when night comes on, the servants are off to the quarters, and I have to holler and holler enough to split my throat before I can make them hear. And another thing: I want you to sell Melinda. I don't intend to keep that mulatto wench about the house any longer.

DR. GAINES: My dear, I'll sell any servant from the place to suit you, except Melinda. I can't think of selling her—I can't think of it.

MRS. G.: I tell you that Melinda shall leave this house, or I'll go. There, now you have it. I've had my life tormented out of me by the presence of that yellow wench, and I'll stand it no longer. I know you love her more than you do me, and I'll—I'll—I'll write—write to my father. [*Weeps.*]

Exit MRS. GAINES, L.

WALK.: Why, doctor, your wife's a screamer, ain't she? Ha, ha, ha. Why, doctor, she's got a tongue of her own, ain't she? Why, doctor, it was only last week that I thought of getting a wife myself; but your wife has skeered the idea out of my head. Now, doctor, if you wants to sell the gal, I'll buy her. Husband and wife ought to be on good terms, and your wife won't feel well till the gal is gone. Now, I'll pay you all she's worth, if you want to sell.

DR. G.: No, Mr. Walker; the girl my wife spoke of is not for sale. My wife does not mean what she says; she's only a little jealous. I'll get brother Pinchen to talk to her, and get her mind turned upon religious matters, and then she'll forget it. She's only a little jealous.

WALK.: I tell you what, doctor, ef you call that a little jealous, I'd like to know what's a heap. I tell you, it will take something more than religion to set your wife right. You had better sell me the gal; I'll pay you cash down, and no grumblin'.

DR. G.: The girl is not for sale, Mr. Walker; but if you want two good, able-bodied servants, I'll sell you Sam and Big Sally. Sam is trustworthy, and Sally is worth her weight in gold for rough usage.

WALK: Well, doctor, I'll go out and take a look at 'em, for I never buys slaves without examining them well, because they are sometimes injured by overwork or underfeedin'. I don't say that is the case with yours, for I don't believe it is; but as I sell on honor, I must buy on honor.

DR. G.: Walk out, sir, and you can examine them to your heart's content. Walk right out, sir.

Scene II

View in Front of the Great House.

Examination of SAM *and* BIG SALLY.—DR. GAINES, WILDMARSH, MR. PINCHEN *and* WALKER *present.*

WALK: Well, my boy, what's your name?

SAM: Sam, sir, is my name.

WALK: How old are you, Sam?

SAM: Ef I live to see next corn plantin' time, I'll be 27, or 30, or 35, or 40—I don't know which, sir.

WALK: Ha, ha, ha. Well, doctor, this is rather a green boy. Well, mer feller, are you sound?

SAM: Yes, sir, I spec I is.

WALK: Open your mouth and let me see your teeth. I allers judge a nigger's age by his teeth, same as I dose a hoss. Ah! pretty good set of grinders. Have you got a good appetite?

SAM: Yes, sir.

WALK: Can you eat your allowance?

SAM: Yes, sir, when I can get it.

WALK: Get out on the floor and dance; I want to see if you are supple.

SAM: I don't like to dance; I is got religion.

WALK: Oh, ho! you've got religion, have you? That's so much the better. I likes to deal in the gospel. I think he'll suit me. Now, mer gal, what's your name?

SALLY: I is Big Sally, sir.

WALK: How old are you, Sally?

SALLY: I don't know, sir; but I heard once dat I was born at sweet pertater diggin' time.

WALK: Ha, ha, ha. Don't know how old you are! Do you know who made you?

SALLY: I hev heard who it was in de Bible dat made me, but I dun forget de gentman's name.

WALK: Ha, ha, ha. Well, doctor, this is the greenest lot of niggers I've seen for some time. Well, what do you ask for them?

DR. GAINES: You may have Sam for $1000, and Sally for $900. They are worth all I ask for them. You know I never banter, Mr. Walker. There they are; you can take them at that price, or let them alone, just as you please.

WALK: Well, doctor, I reckon I'll take 'em; but it's all they are worth. I'll put the handcuffs on 'em, and then I'll pay you. I likes to go accordin' to Scripter. Scripter says ef eatin' meat will offend your brother, you must quit it; and I say, ef leavin' your slaves without the handcuffs will make 'em run away, you must put the handcuffs on 'em. Now, Sam, don't you and Sally cry. I am of a tender heart, and it allers makes me feel bad to see people cryin'. Don't cry, and the first place I get to, I'll buy each of you a great big *ginger cake,*—that I will. Now, Mr. Pinchen, I wish you were going down the river. I'd like to have your company; for I allers likes the company of preachers.

MR. PINCHEN: Well, Mr. Walker, I would be much pleased to go down the river with you, but it's too early for me. I expect to go to Natchez in four or five weeks, to attend a campmeetin', and if you were going down then, I'd like it. What kind of niggers sells best in the Orleans market, Mr. Walker?

WALK: Why, field hands. Did you think of goin' in the trade?

MR. P.: Oh, no; only it's a long ways down to Natchez, and I thought I'd just buy five or six niggers, and take 'em down and sell 'em to pay my travellin' expenses. I only want to clear my way.

Scene III

Sitting-Room—Table and Rocking-Chair.

Enter MRS. GAINES, R, *followed by* SAMPEY.

MRS. GAINES: I do wish your master would come; I want supper. Run to the gate, Sampey, and see if he is coming.

Exit SAMPEY, L.

That man is enough to break my heart. The patience of an angel could not stand it.

Enter SAMPEY, L.

SAMP: Yes, missis, master is coming.

Enter DR. GAINES, L.

The Doctor walks about with his hands under his coat, seeming very much elated.

MRS. GAINES: Why, doctor, what is the matter?

DR. GAINES: My dear, don't call me *doctor.*

MRS. G.: What should I call you?

DR. G.: Call me Colonel, my dear—Colonel. I have been elected Colonel of the Militia, and I want you to call me by my right name. I always felt that Providence had designed me for something great, and He has just begun to shower His blessings upon me.

MRS. G.: Dear me, I could never get to calling you Colonel; I've called you Doctor for the last twenty years.

DR. G.: Now, Sarah, if you will call me Colonel, other people will, and I want you to set the example. Come, my darling, call me Colonel, and I'll give you any thing you wish for.

MRS. G.: Well, as I want a new gold watch and bracelets, I'll commence now. Come, Colonel, we'll go to supper. Ah! now for my new shawl. [*Aside.*] Mrs. Lemme was here to-day, Colonel, and she had on, Colonel, one of the prettiest shawls, Colonel, I think, Colonel, that I ever saw, Colonel, in my life, Colonel. And there is only one, Colonel, in Mr. Watson's store, Colonel; and that, Colonel, will do, Colonel, for a Colonel's wife.

DR. G.: Ah! my dear, you never looked so much the lady since I've known you. Go, my darling, get the watch, bracelets and shawl, and tell them to charge them to Colonel Gaines; and when you say "Colonel," always emphasize the word.

MRS. G.: Come, Colonel, let's go to supper.

DR. G.: My dear, you're a jewel,—you are! [*Exit,* R.]

Enter CATO, L.

CATO: Why, whar is massa and missis? I tought dey was here. Ah! by golly, yonder comes a mulatter gal. Yes, it's Mrs. Jones's Tapioca. I'll set up to dat gal, dat I will.

Enter TAPIOCA, R.

Good ebenin', Miss Tappy. How is your folks?

TAPIOCA: Pretty well, I tank you.

CATO: Miss Tappy, dis wanderin' heart of mine is yours. Come, take a seat! Please to squze my manners; love discommodes me. Take a seat. How, Miss Tappy, I loves you; an ef you will jess marry me, I'll make you a happy husband, dat I will. Come, take me as I is.

TAP: But what will Big Jim say?

CATO: Big Jim! Why, let dat nigger go to Ginny. I want to know, now, if you is tinkin' about dat common nigger? Why, Miss Tappy, I is surstonished dat you should tink 'bout frowin' yousef away wid a common, ugly lookin' cuss like Big Jim, when you can get a fine lookin', suspectable man like me. Come, Miss Tappy, choose dis day who you have. Afore I go any furder, give me one kiss. Come, give me one kiss. Come, let me kiss you.

TAP: No you shan't—dare now! You shan't kiss me widout you is stronger den I is; and I know you is dat. [*He kisses her.*]

Enter DR. GAINES, R, *and hides.*

CATO: Did you know, Miss Tappy, dat I is de head doctor 'bout dis house? I beats de ole boss all to pieces.

TAP: I hev hearn dat you bleeds and pulls teef.

CATO: Yes, Miss Tappy; massa could not get along widout me, for massa was made a doctor by books; but I is a natral doctor. I was born a doctor, jess as Lorenzo Dow was born a preacher. So you see I can't be nuffin' but a doctor, while massa is a bunglin' ole cuss at de bissness.

DR. GAINES, (in a low voice.) Never mind; I'll teach you a lesson, that I will.

CATO: You see, Miss Tappy, I was gwine to say ——Ah! but afore I forget, jess give me anudder kiss, jess to keep company wid de one dat you give me jess now,—dat's all. [*Kisses her.*] Now, Miss Tappy, duse you know de fuss time dat I seed you?

TAP: No, Mr. Cato, I don't.

CATO: Well, it was at de camp-meetin'. Oh, Miss Tappy, dat pretty red calliker dress you had on dat time did de work for me. It made my heart flutter—

DR. G. (low voice.) Yes, and I'll make your black hide flutter.

CATO: Didn't I hear some noise? By golly, dar is teves in dis house, and I'll drive 'em out. [*Takes a chair and runs at the Doctor, and knocks him down. The Doctor chases Cato round the table.*]

CATO: Oh, massa, I didn't know 'twas you!

DR. G.: You scoundrel! I'll whip you well. Stop! I tell you.

Curtain falls.

ACT III

Scene I

Sitting-Room.

MRS. GAINES, *seated in an arm chair, reading a letter.*

Enter HANNAH, L.

MRS. GAINES: You need not tell me, Hannah, that you don't want another husband, I know better. Your master has sold Sam, and he's gone down the river, and you'll never see him again. So, go and put on your calico dress, and meet me in the kitchen. I intend for you to *jump the broomstick* with Cato. You need not tell me that you don't want another man. I know that there's no woman living that can be happy and satisfied without a husband.

HANNAH: Oh, missis, I don't want to jump de broomstick wid Cato. I don't love Cato; I can't love him.

MRS. G.: Shut up, this moment! What do you know about love? I didn't love your master when I married him, and people don't marry for love now. So go and put on your calico dress, and meet me in the kitchen.

Exit HANNAH, L.

I am glad that the Colonel has sold Sam; now I'll make Hannah marry Cato, and I have them both here under my eye. And I am also glad that the Colonel has parted with Melinda. Still, I'm afraid that he is trying to deceive me. He took the hussy away yesterday, and says he sold her to a trader; but I don't believe it. At any rate, if she's in the neighborhood, I'll find her, that I will. No man ever fools me.

Exit MRS. GAINES, L.

Scene II

The Kitchen—Slaves at Work.

Enter HANNAH, R.

HANNAH: Oh, Cato, do go and tell missis dat you don't want to jump de broomstick wid me, —dat's a good man! Do, Cato; kase I nebber can love you. It was only las week dat massa sold my Sammy, and I don't want any udder man. Do go tell missis dat you don't want me.

CATO: No, Hannah, I ain't a gwine to tell missis no such thing, kase I dose want you, and I ain't a-gwine to tell a lie for you ner nobody else. Dar, now you's got it! I don't see why you need to make so much fuss. I is better lookin' den Sam; an' I is a house servant, an' Sam was only a fiel hand; so you ought to feel proud of a change. So go and do as missis tells you.

Exit HANNAH, L.

Hannah needn't try to get me to tell a lie; I ain't a-gwine to do it, kase I dose want her, an' I is bin wantin' her dis long time, an' soon as massa sold Sam, I knowed I would get her. By golly, I is gwine to be a married man. Won't I be happy! Now, ef I could only jess run away from ole massa, an' get to Canada wid Hannah, den I'd show 'em who I was. Ah! dat reminds me of my song 'bout ole massa and Canada, an' I'll sing it fer yer. Dis is my moriginal hyme. It comed into my head one night when I was fass asleep under an apple tree, looking up at de moon. Now for my song:—

AIR—"*Dandy Jim.*"

Come all ye bondmen far and near,
Let's put a song in massa's ear,
It is a song for our poor race,
Who're whipped and trampled with dis-
grace.

CHORUS.

My old massa tells me, Oh,
This is a land of freedom, Oh;
Let's look about and see if it's so,
Just as massa tells me, Oh.

He tells us of that glorious one,
I think his name was Washington,
How he did fight for liberty,
To save a threepence tax on tea.
[*Chorus.*]

But now we look about and see
That we poor blacks are not so free;
We're whipped and thrashed about like
fools,
And have no chance at common schools.
[*Chorus.*]

They take our wives, insult and mock,
And sell our children on the block,
They choke us if we say a word,
And say that "niggers" shan't be heard.
[*Chorus.*]

Our preachers, too, with whip and cord,
Command obedience in the Lord;

They say they learn it from the big book,
But for ourselves, we dare not look.
[*Chorus.*]

There is a country far away,
I think they call it Canada,
And if we reach Victoria's shore,
They say that we are slaves no more.

Now haste, all bondmen, let us go,
And leave this *Christian* country, Oh;
Haste to the land of the British Queen,
Where whips for negroes are not seen.

Now, if we go, we must take the night,
And never let them come in sight;
The bloodhounds will be on our track,
And wo to us if they fetch us back.

Now haste all bondmen, let us go,
And leave this *Christian* country, Oh;
God help us to Victoria's shore,
Where we are free and slaves no more!

Enter MRS. GAINES, L.

MRS. GAINES: Ah! Cato, you're ready, are you? Where is Hannah?

CATO: Yes, missis; I is bin waitin' dis long time. Hannah has bin here tryin' to swade me to tell you dat I don't want her; but I telled her dat you sed I must jump de broomstick wid her, an' I is gwine to mind you.

MRS. G.: That's right, Cato; servants should always mind their masters and mistresses, without asking a question.

CATO: Yes, missis, I allers dose what you and massa tells me, an' axes nobody.

Enter HANNAH, R.

MRS. GAINES: Ah! Hannah; come, we are waiting for you. Nothing can be done till you come.

HANNAH: Oh, missis, I don't want to jump de broomstick wid Cato; I can't love him.

MRS. G.: Shut up, this moment. Dolly, get the broom. Susan, you take hold of the other end. There, now hold it a little lower—there, a little higher. There, now, that'll do. Now Hannah, take hold of Cato's hand. Let Cato take hold of your hand.

HANNAH: Oh, missis, do spare me. I don't want to jump de broomstick wid Cato.

MRS. G.: Get the cowhide, and follow me to the cellar, and I'll whip you well. I'll let you know how to disobey my orders. Get the cowhide, and follow me to the cellar.

Exit MRS. GAINES *and* HANNAH, R.

DOLLY: Oh, Cato, do go an' tell missis dat you don't want Hannah. Don't you hear how she's whippin' her in de cellar? Do go an' tell missis dat you don't want Hannah, and den she'll stop whippin' her.

CATO: No, Dolly, I ain't a-gwine to do no such a thing, kase ef I tell missis dat I don't want Hannah, den missis will whip me; an' I ain't a-gwine to be whipped fer you, ner Hannah, ner nobody else. No, I'll jump de broomstick wid every woman on de place, ef missis wants me to, before I'll be whipped.

DOLLY: Cato, ef I was in Hannah's place, I'd see you in de bottomless pit before I'd live wid you, you great big wall-eyed, empty-headed, knock-kneed fool. You're as mean as your devilish old missis.

CATO: Ef you don't quit dat busin' me, Dolly, I'll tell missis as soon as she comes in, an' she'll whip you, you know she will.

Enter MRS. GAINES *and* HANNAH, R.

Mrs. G. fans herself with her handkerchief, and appears fatigued.

MRS. G.: You ought to be ashamed of yourself, Hannah, to make me fatigue myself in this way, to make you do your duty. It's very naughty in you, Hannah. Now, Dolly, you and Susan get the broom, and get out in the middle of the room. There, hold it a little lower—a little higher; there, that'll do. Now, remember that this is a solemn occasion; you are going to jump into matrimony. Now, Cato, take hold of Hannah's hand. There, now, why couldn't you let Cato take hold of your hand before? Now get ready, and when I count three, do you jump. Eyes on the *broomstick!* All ready. One, two, three, and over you go. There, now you're husband and wife, and if you don't live happy together, it's your own fault; for I am sure there's nothing to hinder it. Now, Hannah, come up to the house, and I'll give you some whiskey, and you can make some apple toddy, and you and Cato can have a fine time. [*Exit* MRS. GAINES *and* HANNAH, L.]

DOLLY: I tell you what, Susan, when I get married, I is gwine to have a preacher to marry me. I ain't a-gwine to jump de broomstick. Dat will do for fiel' hands, but house servants ought to be 'bove dat.

SUSAN: Well, chile, you can't speck any ting else from ole missis. She come from down in Carlina, from 'mong de poor white trash. She don't know any better. You can't speck nothin' more dan a jump from a frog. Missis says she is one of de akastocacy; but she ain't no more of an akastocacy dan I is. Missis says she was born wid a silver spoon in her mouf; ef she was, I wish it had a-choked her, dat's what I wish. Missis wanted to make Linda jump de broomstick wid Glen, but massa ain't a-gwine to let Linda jump de broomstick wid anybody. He's gwine to keep Linda fer heself.

DOLLY: You know massa took Linda 'way las' night, an' tell missis dat he has sold her and sent her down de river; but I don't b'lieve he has sold her at all. He went ober towards de poplar farm, an' I tink Linda is ober dar now. Ef she is dar, missis'll find it out, fer she tell'd massa las' night, dat ef Linda was in de neighborhood, she'd find her.

Exit DOLLY *and* SUSAN.

Scene III

Sitting Room—Chairs and Table.

Enter HANNAH, R.

HANNAH: I don't keer what missis says; I don't like Cato, an' I won't live wid him. I always love my Sammy, an' I loves him now.

Knock at the door—goes to the door.

Enter MAJ. MOORE, M. D.

Walk in, sir; take a seat. I'll call missis, sir; massa is gone away.

Exit HANNAH, R.

MAJ. MOORE: So I am here at last, and the Colonel is not at home. I hope his wife is a good-looking woman. I rather like fine looking-women, especially when their husbands are from home. Well, I've studied human nature to some purpose. If you wish to get the good will of a man, don't praise his wife, and if you wish to gain the favor of a woman, praise her children, and swear that they are the picture of their father, whether they are or not. Ah! here comes the lady.

Enter MRS. GAINES, R.

MRS. G.: Good morning, sir!

MAJ. M.: Good morning, madam! I am Maj. Moore, of Jefferson. The Colonel and I had seats near each other in the last Legislature.

MRS. G.: Be seated, sir. I think I've heard the Colonel speak of you. He's away, now; but I expect him every moment. You're a stranger here, I presume?

MAJ. M.: Yes, madam, I am. I rather like the Colonel's situation here.

MRS. G.: It is thought to be a fine location.

Enter SAMPEY, R.

Hand me my fan, will you, Sampey? [*Sampey gets the fan and passes near the Major, who mistakes the boy for the Colonel's son. He reaches out his hand.*]

MAJ. M.: How do you do, bub? Madam, I should have known that this was the Colonel's son, if I had met him in California; for he looks so much like his papa.

MRS. G. [*To the boy.*] Get out of here this minute. Go to the kitchen. [*Exit* SAMPEY, R.] That is one of the niggers, sir.

MAJ. M.: I beg your pardon, madam; I beg your pardon.

MRS. G.: No offence, sir; mistakes will be made. Ah! here comes the Colonel.

Enter DR. GAINES, M. D.

DR. GAINES: Bless my soul, how are you, Major? I'm exceedingly pleased to see you. Be seated, be seated, Major.

MRS. G.: Please excuse me, gentlemen; I must go and look after dinner, for I've no doubt that the Major will have an appetite for dinner, by the time it is ready. [*Exit* MRS. GAINES, R.]

MAJ. M.: Colonel, I'm afraid I've played the devil here to-day.

DR. G.: Why, what have you done?

MAJ. M.: You see, Colonel, I always make it a point, wherever I go, to praise the children, if there are any, and so to-day, seeing one of your little servants come in, and taking him to be your son, I spoke to your wife of the marked resemblance between you and the boy. I am afraid I've insulted madam.

DR. G.: Oh! Don't let that trouble you. Ha, ha, ha. If you did call him my son, you didn't miss it much. Ha, ha, ha. Come, we'll take a walk, and talk over matters about old times. [*Exit,* L.]

Scene IV

Forest Scenery.

Enter GLEN, L.

GLEN: Oh, how I want to see Melinda! My heart pants and my soul is moved whenever I hear her voice. Human tongue cannot tell how my heart yearns toward her. Oh, God! thou who gavest me life, and implanted in my bosom the love of liberty, and gave me a heart to love, Oh, pity the poor outraged slave! Thou, who canst rend the veil of centuries, speak, Oh, speak, and put a stop to this persecution! What is death, compared to slavery? Oh, heavy curse, to have thoughts, reason, taste, judgment, conscience and passions like another man, and not have equal liberty to use them! Why was I born with a wish to be free, and still be a slave? Why should I call another man master? And my poor Melinda, she is taken away from me, and I dare not ask the tyrant where she is. It is childish to stand here weeping. Why should my eyes be filled with tears, when my brain is on fire? I will find my wife —I will; and wo to him who shall try to keep me from her!

Scene V

Room in a Small Cottage on the Poplar Farm, (ten miles from Muddy Creek, and owned by Dr. Gaines).

Enter MELINDA, R.

MELINDA: Here I am, watched, and kept a prisoner in this place. Oh, I would that I could escape, and once more get with Glen. Poor Glen! He does not know where I am. Master took the opportunity, when Glen was in the city with his master, to bring me here to this lonely place, and fearing that mistress would know where I was, he brought me here at night. Oh, how I wish I could rush into the arms of sleep!—that sweet sleep, which visits all alike, descending, like the dews of heaven, upon the bond as well as the free. It would drive from my troubled brain the agonies of this terrible night.

Enter DR. GAINES, L.

DR. GAINES: Good evening, Melinda! Are you not glad to see me?

MELINDA: Sir, how can I be glad to see one who has made life a burden, and turned my sweetest moments into bitterness?

DR. G.: Come, Melinda, no more reproaches! You know that I love you, and I have told you, and I tell you again, that if you will give up all idea of having Glen for a husband, I will set you free, let you live in this cottage, and be your own mistress, and I'll dress you like a lady. Come, now, be reasonable!

MELINDA: Sir, I am your slave; you can do as you please with the avails of my labor, but you shall never tempt me to swerve from the path of virtue.

DR. G.: Now, Melinda, that black scoundrel Glen has been putting these notions into your head. I'll let you know that you are my property, and I'll do as I please with you. I'll teach you that there is no limit to my power.

MELINDA: Sir, let me warn you that if you compass my ruin, a woman's bitterest curse will be laid upon your head, with all the crushing, withering weight that my soul can impart to it; a curse that shall cling to you throughout the remainder of your wretched life; a curse that shall haunt you like a spectre in your dreams by night, and attend upon you by day; a curse, too, that shall embody itself in the ghastly form of the woman whose chastity you will have outraged. Command me to bury myself in yonder stream, and I will obey you. Bid me do any thing else, but I beseech you not to commit a double crime,—outrage a woman, and make her false to her husband.

DR. G.: You got a husband! Who is your husband, and when were you married?

MELINDA: Glen is my husband, and I've been married four weeks. Old Uncle Joseph married us one night by moonlight. I see you are angry; I pray you not to injure my husband.

DR. G.: Melinda, you shall never see Glen again. I have bought him from Hamilton, and I will return to Muddy Creek, and roast him at the stake. A black villain, to get into my way in that manner! Here I've come ten miles tonight to see you, and this is the way you receive me!

MELINDA: Oh, master, I beg you not to injure my husband! Kill me, but spare him! Do! do! he is my husband!

DR. G.: You shall never see that black imp again, so good night, my lady! When I come again, you'll give me a more cordial reception. Good night! [*Exit* DR. GAINES, L.]

MELINDA: I shall go distracted. I cannot remain here and know that Glen is being tortured on my account. I must escape from this place,—I must,—I must!

Enter CATO, R.

CATO: No, you ain't a-gwine to 'scape, nudder. Massa tells me to keep dese eyes on you, an' I is gwine to do it.

MELINDA: Oh, Cato, do let me get away! I beg you, do!

CATO: No; I tells you massa telled me to keep you safe; an' ef I let you go, massa will whip me. [*Exit* CATO, L.]

Enter MRS. GAINES, R.

MRS. G.: Ah, you trollop! here you are! Your master told me that he had sold you and sent you down the river, but I knew better; I knew it was a lie. And when he left home this evening, he said he was going to the city on business, and I knew that was a lie too, and determined to follow him, and see what he was up to. I rode all the way over here to-night. My side-saddle was lent out, and I had to ride ten miles bare-back, and I can scarcely walk; and your master has just left here. Now deny that, if you dare.

MELINDA: Madam, I will deny nothing which is true. Your husband has just gone from here, but God knows that I am innocent of any thing wrong with him.

MRS. G.: It's a lie! I know better. If you are innocent, what are you doing here, cooped up in this cottage by yourself? Tell me that!

MELINDA: God knows that I was brought here against my will, and I beg that you will take me away.

MRS. G.: Yes, Melinda, I will see that you are taken away, but it shall be after a fashion that you won't like. I know that your master loves you, and I intend to put a stop to it. Here, drink the contents of this vial,—drink it!

MELINDA: Oh, you will not take my life,—you will not!

MRS. G.: Drink the poison this moment!

MELINDA: I cannot drink it.

MRS. G.: I tell you to drink this poison at once. Drink it, or I will thrust this knife to your heart! The poison or the dagger, this instant! [*She draws a dagger;* MELINDA *retreats to the back of the room, and seizes a broom.*]

MELINDA: I will not drink the poison! [*They fight;* MELINDA *sweeps off* MRS. GAINES,—*cap, combs and curls. Curtain falls.*]

ACT IV

Scene I

Interior of a Dungeon—Glen in Chains.

GLEN: When I think of my unmerited sufferings, it almost drives me mad. I struck the doctor, and for that, I must remain here loaded with chains. But why did he strike me? He takes my wife from me, sends her off, and then comes and beats me over the head with his cane. I did right to strike him back again. I would I had killed him. Oh! there is a volcano pent up in the hearts of the slaves of these Southern States that will burst forth ere long. When that day comes, wo to those whom its unpitying fury may devour! I would be willing to die, if I could smite down with these chains every man who attempts to enslave his fellow-man.

Enter SAMPEY, R.

SAMPEY: Glen, I jess bin hear massa call de oberseer, and I spec somebody is gwine to be whipped. Anudder ting: I know whar massa took Linda to. He took her to de poplar farm, an' he went away las' night, an' missis she follow after massa, an' she ain't come back yet. I tell you, Glen, de debil will be to pay on dis place, but don't you tell any body dat I tole you. [*Exit* SAMPEY, R.]

Scene II

Parlor.

DR. GAINES, *alone.*

DR. GAINES: Yes, I will have the black rascal well whipped, and then I'll sell him. It was most fortunate for me that Hamilton was willing to sell him to me.

Enter MR. SCRAGG, L.

I have sent for you, Mr. Scragg. I want you to take Glen out of the dungeon, take him into the tobacco house, fasten him down upon the stretcher, and give him five hundred lashes upon his bare back; and when you have whipped him, feel his pulse, and report to me how it stands, and if he can bear more, I'll have you give him an additional hundred or two, as the case may be.

SCRAGG: I tell you, doctor, that suits me to a charm. I've long wanted to whip that nigger. When your brother-in-law came here to board, and brought that boy with him, I felt bad to see a nigger dressed up in such fine clothes, and I wanted to whip him right off. I tell you, doctor, I had rather whip that nigger than go to heaven, any day,—that I had!

DR. G.: Go, Mr. Scragg, and do your duty. Don't spare the whip!

SCRAGG: I will, sir; I'll do it in order. [*Exit* SCRAGG, L.]

DR. G.: Every thing works well now, and when I get Glen out of the way, I'll pay Melinda another visit, and she'll give me a different reception. But I wonder where my wife is? She left word that she was going to see her brother, but I am afraid that she has got on my track. That woman is the pest of my life. If there's any place in heaven for her, I'd be glad if the Lord would take her home, for I've had her too long already. But what noise is that? What can that be? What is the matter?

Enter SCRAGG, L., *with face bloody.*

SCRAGG: Oh, dear me! oh, my head! That nigger broke away from me, and struck me over the head with a stick. Oh, dear me! Oh!

DR. G.: Where is he, Mr. Scragg?

SCRAGG: Oh! sir, he jumped out of the window; he's gone. Oh! my head; he's cracked my skull. Oh, dear me, I'm kilt! Oh! oh! oh!

Enter SLAVES, R.

DR. G.: Go, Dolly, and wash Mr. Scragg's head with some whiskey, and bind it up. Go at once. And Bob, you run over to Mr. Hall, and tell him to come with his hounds; we must go after the rascal. [*Exit all except the* DOCTOR, R.] This will never do. When I catch the scoundrel, I'll make an example of him; I'll whip him to death. Ah! here comes my wife. I wonder what she comes now for? I must put on a sober face, for she looks angry.

Enter MRS. GAINES, L.

Ah! my dear, I am glad you've come, I've been so lonesome without you. Oh! Sarah, I don't know what I should do if the Lord should take you home to heaven. I don't think that I should be able to live without you.

MRS. G.: Dr. Gaines, you ought to be ashamed to sit there and talk in that way. You know very well that if the Lord should call me home to glory to-night, you'd jump for joy. But you need not think that I am going to leave this world before you. No; with the help of the Lord, I'll stay here to foil you in your meanness. I've been on your track, and a dirty track it is, too. You ought to be ashamed of yourself. See what promises you made me before we were married; and this is the way you keep your word. When I married you, every body said that it was a pity that a woman of my sweet temper should be linked to such a man as you. [*She weeps and wrings her hands.*]

DR. G.: Come, my dear, don't make a fool of yourself. Come, let's go to supper, and a strong cup of tea will help your head.

MRS. G.: Tea help my head! tea won't help my head. You're a brute of a man; I always knew I was a fool for marrying you. There was Mr. Comstock, he wanted me, and he loved me, and he said I was an angel, so he did; and he loved me, and he was rich; and mother always said that he loved me more than you, for when he used to kiss me, he always squeezed my hand. You never did such a thing in your life. [*She weeps and wrings her hands.*]

DR. G.: Come, my dear, don't act so foolish.

MRS. G.: Yes; every thing I do is foolish. You're a brute of a man; I won't live with you any longer. I'll leave you—that I will. I'll go and see a lawyer, and get a divorce from you—so I will.

DR. G.: Well, Sarah, if you want a divorce, you had better engage Mr. Barker. He's the best lawyer in town; and if you want some money to facilitate the business, I'll draw a check for you.

MRS. G.: So you want me to get a divorce, do you? Well, I won't have a divorce; no, I'll never leave you, as long as the Lord spares me. [*Exit* MRS. GAINES, R.]

Scene III

Forest at Night—Large Tree.

Enter MELINDA, L.

MELINDA: This is indeed a dark night to be out and alone on this road. But I must find my husband, I must. Poor Glen! if he only knew that I was here, and could get to me, he would. What a curse slavery is! It separates husbands from their wives, and tears mothers from their helpless offspring, and blights all our hopes for this world. I must try to reach Muddy Creek before daylight, and seek out my husband. What's that I hear?—footsteps? I'll get behind this tree.

Enter GLEN, R.

GLEN: It is so dark, I'm afraid I've missed the road. Still, this must be the right way to the poplar farm. And if Bob told me the truth, when he said that Melinda was at the poplar farm, I will soon be with her; and if I once get her in my arms, it will be a strong man that shall take her from me. Aye, a dozen strong men shall not be able to wrest her from my arms. [*Melinda rushes from behind the tree.*]

MELINDA: Oh, Glen! It is my husband,—it is!

GLEN: Melinda! Melinda! it is, it is. Oh God! I thank Thee for this manifestation of Thy kindness. Come, come, Melinda, we must go at once to Canada. I escaped from the overseer, whom Dr. Gaines sent to flog me. Yes, I struck him over the head with his own club, and I made the wine flow freely; yes, I pounded his old skillet well for him, and then jumped out of the window. It was a leap for freedom. Yes, Melinda, it was a leap for freedom. I've said "master" for the last time. I am free; I'm bound for Canada. Come, let's be off, at once, for the negro dogs will be put upon our track. Let us once get beyond the Ohio river, and all will be right. [*Exit* R.]

ACT V

Scene 1

Bar-Room in the American Hotel—Travellers Lounging in Chairs, and at the Bar.

Enter BILL JENNINGS, R.

BARKEEPER: Why, Jennings, how do you do?

JENNINGS: Say Mr. Jennings, if you please.

BARKEEPER: Well, Mr. Jennings, if that suits you better. How are times? We've been expecting you, for some days.

JENNINGS: Well, before I talk about the times, I want my horses put up, and want you to tell me where my niggers are to stay to-night. Sheds, stables, barns, and every thing else here, seems pretty full, if I am a judge.

BARKEEPER: Oh! I'll see to your plunder.

1st LOUNGER: I say, Barkeeper, make me a brandy cocktail, strong. Why, how do you do, Mr. Jennings?

JENNINGS: Pretty well, Mr. Peters. Cold evening, this.

1st LOUNG: Yes, this is cold. I heard you speak of your niggers. Have you got a pretty large gang?

JENNINGS: No, only thirty-three. But they are the best that the country can afford. I shall clear a few dimes, this trip. I hear that the price is up.

Enter MR. WHITE, R.

WHITE: Can I be accommodated here to-night, landlord?

BARKEEPER: Yes, sir; we've bed for man and beast. Go, Dick, and take the gentleman's coat and hat. [*To the waiter.*] You're a stranger in these parts, I rec'on.

WHITE: Yes, I am a stranger here.

2d LOUN: Where mout you come from, ef it's a far question?

WHITE: I am from Massachusetts.

3d LOUN: I say, cuss Massachusetts!

1st LOUN: I say so too. There is where the fanatics live; cussed traitors. The President ought to hang 'em all.

WHITE: I say, landlord, if this is the language that I am to hear, I would like to go into a private room.

BARKEEPER: We ain't got no private room empty.

1st LOUN: Maybe you're mad 'bout what I said 'bout your State. Ef you is, I've only to say that this is a free country, and people talks what they please; an' ef you don't like it, you can better yourself.

WHITE: Sir, if this is a free country, why do you have slaves here? I saw a gang at the door, as I came in.

2d LOUN: He didn't mean that this was a free country for niggers. He meant that it's free for white people. And another thing, ef you get to talking 'bout freedom for niggers, you'll catch what you won't like, mister. It's right for niggers to be slaves.

WHITE: But I saw some white slaves.

1st LOUN: Well, they're white niggers.

WHITE: Well, sir, I am from a free State, and I thank God for it; for the worst act that a man can commit upon his fellow-man, is to make him a slave. Conceive of a mind, a living soul, with the germs of faculties which infinity cannot exhaust, as it first beams upon you in its glad morning of existence, quivering with life and joy, exulting in the glorious sense of its developing energies, beautiful, and brave, and generous, and joyous, and free,—the clear pure spirit bathed in the auroral light of its unconscious immortality,—and then follow it in its dark and dreary passage through slavery, until oppression stifles and kills, one by one, every inspiration and aspiration of its being, until it becomes a dead soul entombed in a living frame!

3d LOUN: Stop that; stop that, I say. That's treason to the country; that's downright rebellion.

BARKEEPER: Yes, it is. And another thing,—this is not a meeting-house.

1st LOUN: Yes, if you talk such stuff as that, you'll get a chunk of cold lead in you, that you will.

Enter DR. GAINES *and* SCRAGG, *followed by* CATO, R.

DR. G.: Gentlemen, I am in pursuit of two valuable slaves, and I will pay five hundred dollars for their arrest.

Exit MR. WHITE, L.

1st LOUN: I'll bet a picayune that your niggers have been stolen by that cussed feller from Massachusetts. Don't you see he's gone?

DR. G.: Where is the man? If I can lay my hands on him, he'll never steal another nigger. Where is the scoundrel?

1st LOUN: Let's go after the feller. I'll go with you. Come, follow me. [*Exit all,* L., *except* CATO *and the waiter.*]

CATO: Why don't you bring in massa's saddle-bags? What de debil you standin' dar for? You common country niggers don't know nuffin', no how. Go an' get massa's saddle-bags, and bring 'em in. [*Exit* SERVANT, R.]
By golly! ebry body's gone, an' de bar-keeper too. I'll tend de bar myself now; an' de fuss gemman I waits on will be dis gemman of color. [*Goes behind the counter, and drinks.*] Ah, dis is de stuff fer me; it makes my head swim; it makes me happy right off. I'll take a little more.

Enter BARKEEPER, L.

BARKEEPER: What are you doing behind that bar, you black cuss?

CATO: I is lookin' for massa's saddle-bags, sir. Is dey here?

BARKEEPER: But what were you drinking there?

CATO: Me drinkin'! Why, massa, you muss be mistaken. I ain't drink nuffin'.

BARKEEPER: You infernal whelp, to stand there and lie in that way!

CATO: Oh, yes, seer, I did tase dat coffee in dat bottle; dat's all I did.

Enter MR. WHITE, L., *excited.*

MR. WHITE: I say, sir, is there no place of concealment in your house? They are after me, and my life is in danger. Say, sir, can't you hide me away?

BARKEEPER: Well, you ought to hold your tongue when you come into our State.

MR. WHITE: But, sir, the Constitution gives me the right to speak my sentiments, at all times and in all places.

BARKEEPER: We don't care for Constitutions nor nothin' else. We made the Constitution, and we'll break it. But you had better hide away; they are coming, and they'll lynch you, that they will. Come with me; I'll hide you in the cellar. Foller me. [*Exit* BARKEEPER *and* WHITE, L.]

Enter the MOB, R.

DR. GAINES: If I can once lay my hands on that scoundrel, I'll blow a hole through his head.

JENNINGS: Yes, I say so too; for no one knows whose niggers are safe, now-a-days. I must look after my niggers. Who is that I see in the distance? I believe it's that cussed Massachusetts feller. Come, let's go after him.

Exit the MOB, R.

Scene II

Forest at Night.

Enter GLEN *and* MELINDA, R.

MELINDA: I am so tired and hungry, that I cannot go further. It is so cloudy that we cannot see the North Star, and therefore cannot tell whether we are going to Canada, or further South. Let's sit down here.

GLEN: I know that we cannot see the North Star, Melinda, and I fear we've lost our way. But, see! the clouds are passing away, and it'll soon be clear. See! yonder is a star; yonder is another and another. Ah! yonder is the North Star, and we are safe!

"Star of the North! though night winds drift
 The fleecy drapery of the sky
Between thy lamp and me, I lift,
 Yea, lift with hope my sleepless eye,
To the blue heights wherein thou dwellest,
And of a land of freedom tellest.

"Star of the North! while blazing day
 Pours round me its full tide of light,
And hides thy pale but faithful ray,
 I, too, lie hid, and long for night:

For night: I dare not walk at noon,
Nor dare I trust the faithless moon—

"Nor faithless man, whose burning lust
For gold hath riveted my chain,—
Nor other leader can I trust
But thee, of even the starry train;
For all the host around thee burning,
Like faithless man, keep turning, turning.

"I may not follow where they go:—
Star of the North! I look to thee
While on I press; for well I know,
Thy light and truth shall set me free:—
Thy light, that no poor slave deceiveth;
Thy truth, that all my soul believeth.

"Thy beam is on the glassy breast
Of the still spring, upon whose brink
I lay my weary limbs to rest,
And bow my parching lips to drink.
Guide of the friendless negro's way,
I bless thee for this quiet ray!

"In the dark top of southern pines
I nestled, when the Driver's horn
Called to the field, in lengthening lines,
My fellows, at the break of morn.
And there I lay till thy sweet face
Looked in upon "my hiding place."

"The tangled cane-brake, where I crept
For shelter from the heat of noon,
And where, while others toiled, I slept,
Till wakened by the rising moon,
As its stalks felt the night wind free,
Gave me to catch a glimpse of thee.

"Star of the North! in bright array
The constellations round thee sweep,
Each holding on its nightly way,
Rising, or sinking in the deep,
And, as it hangs in mid heaven flaming,
The homage of some nation claiming.

"*This* nation to the Eagle cowers;
Fit ensign! she's a bird of spoil:—
Like worships like! for each devours
The earnings of another's toil.
I've felt her talons and her beak,
And now the gentler Lion seek.

"The Lion, at the Monarch's feet
Crouches, and lays his mighty paw
Into her lap!—an emblem meet
Of England's Queen, and English law:
Queen, that hath made her Islands free!
Law, that holds out its shield to me!

"Star of the North! upon that shield
Thou shinest,—Oh, for ever shine!
The negro, from the cotton field
Shall, then, beneath its orb recline,
And feed the Lion, couched before it,
Nor heed the Eagle, screaming o'er it!"

With the thoughts of servitude behind us, and the North Star before us, we will go forward with cheerful hearts. Come, Melinda, let's go on. [*Exit,* L.]

Scene III

A Street

Enter MR. WHITE, R.

MR. WHITE: I am glad to be once more in a free State. If I am caught again south of Mason and Dixon's line, I'll give them leave to lynch me. I came near losing my life. This is the way our constitutional rights are trampled upon. But what care these men about Constitutions, or any thing else that does not suit them? But I must hasten on. [*Exit,* L.]

Enter CATO, *in disguise,* R.

CATO: I wonder ef dis is me? By golly, I is free as a frog. But maybe I is mistaken; maybe dis ain't me. Cato, is dis you? Yes, seer. Well, now it is me, an' I em a free man. But, stop! I muss change my name, kase ole massa might foller me, and somebody might tell him dat dey seed Cato; so I'll change my name, and den he won't know me ef he sees me. Now, what shall I call myself? I'm now in a suspectable part of de country, an' I muss have a suspectable name. Ah! I'll call myself Alexander Washington Napoleon Pompey Caesar. Dar, now, dat's a good long, suspectable name, and every body will suspect me. Let me see; I wonder ef I can't make up a song on my escape? I'll try.

AIR—"*Dearest Mae.*"

Now, freemen, listen to my song, a story I'll relate,
It happened in de valley of de ole Kentucky State:
Dey marched me out into de fiel', at every break of day,
And work me dar till late sunset, widout a cent of pay.

Chorus.—Dey work me all de day,
Widout a bit of pay,
And thought, because dey fed me well,
I would not run away.

Massa gave me his ole coat, an' thought I'd happy be,

But I had my eye on de North Star, an' thought of liberty;
Ole massa lock de door, an' den he went to sleep,
I dress myself in his bess clothes, an' jump into de street.

Chorus.—Dey work me all de day,
Widout a bit of pay,
So I took my flight, in the middle of de night,
When de sun was gone away.

Sed I, dis chile's a freeman now, he'll be a slave no more;
I travell'd faster all dat night, dan I ever did before.
I came up to a farmer's house, jest at de break of day,
And saw a white man standin' dar, sed he, "You are a runaway."

Chorus.—Dey work me all de day, &c.

I tole him I had left de whip, an' bayin' of de hound,
To find a place where man is man, ef sich dar can be found;
Dat I had heard, in Canada, dat all mankind are free,
An' dat I was going dar in search of liberty.

Chorus.—Dey work me all de day, &c.

I've not committed any crime, why should I run away?
Oh! shame upon your laws, dat drive me off to Canada.
You loudly boast of liberty, an' say your State is free,
But ef I tarry in your midst, will you protect me?

Chorus.—Dey work me all de day, &c.

Exit, L.

Scene IV

Dining-Room.—Table Spread

MRS. NEAL *and* CHARLOTTE

MRS. NEAL: Thee may put the tea to draw, Charlotte. Thy father will be in soon, and we must have breakfast.

Enter MR. NEAL, L.

I think, Simeon, it is time those people were called. Thee knows that they may be pursued, and we ought not to detain them long here.

MR. NEAL: Yes, Ruth, thou art right. Go, Charlotte, and knock on their chamber door, and tell them that breakfast is ready. [*Exit* CHARLOTTE, R.]

MRS. N.: Poor creatures! I hope they'll reach Canada in safety. They seem to be worthy persons.

Enter CHARLOTTE, R.

CHARLOTTE: I've called them, mother, and they'll soon be down. I'll put the breakfast on the table.

Enter NEIGHBOR JONES, L.

MR. N.: Good morning, James. Thee has heard, I presume, that we have two very interesting persons in the house?

JONES: Yes, I heard that you had two fugitives by the Underground road, last night; and I've come over to fight for them, if any persons come to take them back.

Enter THOMAS, R.

MR. N.: Go, Thomas, and harness up the horses and put them to the covered wagon, and be ready to take these people on, as soon as they get their breakfast. Go, Thomas, and hurry thyself. [*Exit* THOMAS, R.]
And so thee wants to fight, this morning, James?

JONES: Yes; as you belongs to a society that don't believe in fighting, and I does believe in that sort of thing, I thought I'd come and relieve you of that work, if there is any to be done.

Enter GLEN *and* MELINDA, R.

MR. N.: Good morning, friends. I hope thee rested well, last night.

MRS. N.: Yes, I hope thee had a good night's rest.

GLEN: I thank you, madam, we did.

MR. N.: I'll introduce thee to our neighbor, James Jones. He's a staunch friend of thy people.

JONES: I am glad to see you. I've come over to render assistance, if any is needed.

MRS. N.: Come, friends, take seats at the table. Thee'll take seats there. [*To* GLEN *and* MELINDA.] [*All take seats at the table.*] Does thee take sugar and milk in thy tea?

MELINDA: I thank you, we do.

JONES: I'll look at your *Tribune,* Uncle Simeon, while you're eating.

MR. N.: Thee'll find it on the table.

MRS. N.: I presume thee's anxious to get to thy journey's end?

GLEN: Yes, madam, we are. I am told that we are not safe in any of the free States.

MR. N.: I am sorry to tell thee, that that is too true. Thee will not be safe until thee gets on British soil. I wonder what keeps Thomas; he should have been here with the team.

Enter THOMAS, L.

THOMAS: All 's ready; and I've written the prettiest song that was every sung. I call it "The Underground Railroad."

MR. N.: Thomas, thee can eat thy breakfast far better than thee can write a song, as thee calls it. Thee must hurry thyself, when I send thee for the horses, Thomas. Here lately, thee takes thy time.

THOMAS: Well, you see I've been writing poetry; that's the reason I've been so long. If you wish it, I'll sing it to you.

JONES: Do let us hear the song.

MRS. NEAL: Yes, if Thomas has written a ditty, do let us hear it.

MR. NEAL: Well, Thomas, if thee has a ditty, do let us hear it.

THOMAS: Well, I'll give it to you. Remember that I call it, "The Underground Railroad."

AIR—"*Wait for the Wagon.*"

Oh, where is the invention
 Of this growing age,
Claiming the attention
 Of statesman, priest, or sage,
In the many railways
 Through the nation found,
Equal to the Yankees'
 Railway under-ground

Chorus.—No one hears the whistle,
Or rolling of the cars,
While negroes ride to freedom
Beyond the stripes and stars.

On the Southern borders
 Are the Railway stations,
Negroes get free orders
 While on the plantations;
For all, of ev'ry color,
 First-class cars are found,
While they ride to freedom
 By Railway under-ground.

Chorus.—No one hears the whistle, &c.

Masters in the morning
 Furiously rage,
Cursing the inventions
 Of this knowing age;
Order out the bloodhounds,
 Swear they'll bring them back,
Dogs return exhausted,
 Cannot find the track.

Chorus.—No one hears the whistle, &c.

Travel is increasing,
 Build a double track,
Cars and engines wanted,
 They'll come, we have no lack.
Clear the track of loafers,
 See that crowded car!
Thousands passing yearly,
 Stock is more than par.

Chorus.—No one hears the whistle, &c.

JONES: Well done! That's a good song. I'd like to have a copy of them verses. [*Knock at the door. Charlotte goes to the door, and returns.*]

Enter CATO, L., *still in disguise.*

MR. NEAL: Who is this we have? Another of the outcasts, I presume?

CATO: Yes, seer; I is gwine to Canada, an' I met a man, an' he tole me dat you would give me some wittals an' help me on de way. By golly! ef dar ain't Glen an' Melinda. Dey don't know me in dese fine clothes. [*Goes up to them.*] Ah, chillen! I is one wid you. I golly, I is here too! [*They shake hands.*]

GLEN: Why, it is Cato, as I live!

MELINDA: Oh, Cato, I am so glad to see you! But how did you get here?

CATO: Ah, chile, I come wid ole massa to hunt you; an' you see I get tired huntin' you, an' I am now huntin' for Canada. I leff de ole boss in de bed at de hotel; an' you see I thought, afore I left massa, I'd jess change clothes wid him; so, you see, I is fixed up,—ha, ha, ha. Ah, chillen! I is gwine wid you.

MRS. NEAL: Come, sit thee down, and have some breakfast.

CATO: Tank you, madam, I'll do dat. [*Sits down and eats.*]

MR. NEAL: This is pleasant for thee to meet one of thy friends.

GLEN: Yes, sir, it is; I would be glad if we could meet more of them. I have a mother and sister still in slavery, and I would give worlds, if I possessed them, if by so doing I could release them from their bondage.

THOMAS: We are all ready, sir, and the wagon is waiting.

MRS. NEAL: Yes, thee had better start.

CATO: Ef any body tries to take me back to ole massa, I'll pull ebry toof out of dar heads, dat I will! As soon as I get to Canada, I'll set up a doctor shop, an' won't I be poplar? Den I rec'on I will. I'll pull teef fer all de people in Canada. Oh, how I wish I had Hannah wid me! It makes me feel bad when I tink I ain't a-gwine to see my wife no more. But, come, chillen, let's be makin' tracks. Dey say we is most to de British side.

MR. NEAL: Yes, a few miles further, and you'll be safe beyond the reach of the Fugitive-Slave Law.

CATO: Ah, dat's de talk fer dis chile. [*Exit,* M. D.]

Scene V

The Niagara River—A Ferry

FERRYMAN, *fastening his small boat.*

FERRYMAN, [*advancing, takes out his watch:*] I swan, if it ain't one o'clock. I thought it was dinner time. Now there's no one here, I'll go to dinner, and if any body comes, they can wait until I return. I'll go at once. [*Exit,* L.]

Enter MR. WHITE, R., *with an umbrella.*

MR. WHITE: I wonder where that ferryman is? I want to cross to Canada. It seems a little showery, or else the mist from the Falls is growing thicker. [*Takes out his sketch-book and pencils,—sketches.*]

Enter CANE PEDLAR, R.

PEDLAR: Want a good cane to-day, sir? Here's one from Goat Island,—very good, sir,—straight and neat,—only one dollar. I've a wife and nine small children,—youngest is nursing, and the oldest only three years old. Here's a cane from Table Rock, sir. Please buy one! I've had no breakfast to-day. My wife's got the rheumatics, and the children's got the measles. Come, sir, do buy a cane! I've a lame shoulder, and can't work.

MR. WHITE: Will you stop your confounded talk, and let me alone? Don't you see that I am sketching? You've spoiled a beautiful scene for me, with your nonsense.

Enter 2d PEDLAR, R.

2d PEDLAR: Want any bead bags, or money purses? These are all real Ingen bags, made by the Black Hawk Ingens. Here's a pretty bag, sir, only 75 cents. Here's a money purse, 50 cents. Please, sir, buy something! My wife's got the fever and ague, and the house is full of children, and they're all sick. Come, sir, do help a worthy man!

MR. WHITE: Will you hold your tongue? You've spoiled some of the finest pictures in the world. Don't you see that I am sketching? [*Exit* PEDLARS, R., *grumbling.*]
I am glad those fellows have gone; now I'll go a little further up the shore, and see if I can find another boat. I want to get over. [*Exit,* L.]

Enter DR. GAINES, SCRAGG, *and an* OFFICER

OFFICER: I don't think that your slaves have crossed yet, and my officers will watch the shore below here, while we stroll up the river. If I once get my hands on them, all the Abolitionists in the State shall not take them from me.

DR. G.: I hope they have not got over, for I would not lose them for two thousand dollars, especially the gal.

Enter 1st PEDLAR

PEDLAR: Wish to get a good cane, sir? This stick was cut on the very spot where Sam Patch jumped over the falls. Only fifty cents. I have a sick wife and thirteen children. Please buy a cane; I ain't had no dinner.

OFFICER: Get out of the way! Gentlemen, we'll go up the shore. [*Exit,* L.]

Enter CATO, R.

CATO: I is loss fum de cumpny, but dis is de ferry, and I spec dey'll soon come. But didn't we have a good time las' night in Buffalo? Dem dar Buffalo gals make my heart flutter, dat dey did. But, tanks be to de Lord, I is got religion. I got it las' night in de meetin.' Before I got religion, I was a great sinner; I got drunk, an' took de name of de Lord in vain. But now I is a conwerted man; I is bound for hebben; I toats de witness in my bosom; I feel dat my name is rote in de book of life. But dem niggers in de Vine Street Church las' night shout an' make sich a fuss, dey give me de headache. But, tank de Lord, I is got religion, an' now I'll be a preacher, and den dey'll call me de Rev. Alexander Washington Napoleon Pompey Caesar. Now I'll preach and pull teef, bofe at de same time. Oh, how I wish I had Hannah wid me!

Cuss ole massa, fer ef it warn't for him, I could have my wife wid me. Ef I hadn't religion, I'd say "Damn ole massa!" but as I is a religious man, an' belongs to de church, I won't say no sich a thing. But who is dat I see comin'? Oh, it's a whole heap of people. Good Lord! what is de matter?

Enter GLEN *and* MELINDA, L., *followed by* OFFICERS

GLEN: Let them come; I am ready for them. He that lays hands on me or my wife shall feel the weight of this club.

MELINDA: Oh, Glen, let's die here, rather than again go into slavery.

OFFICER: I am the United States Marshal. I have a warrant from the Commissioner to take you, and bring you before him. I command assistance.

Enter DR. GAINES, SCRAGG, *and* OFFICER, R.

DR. GAINES: Here they are. Down with the villain! down with him! but don't hurt the gal!

Enter MR. WHITE, R.

MR. WHITE: Why, bless me! these are the slaveholding fellows. I'll fight for freedom! [*Takes hold of his umbrella with both hands.—The fight commences, in which* GLEN, CATO, DR. GAINES, SCRAGG, WHITE, *and the* OFFICERS, *take part.—* FERRYMAN *enters, and runs to his boat.—*DR. GAINES, SCRAGG *and the* OFFICERS *are knocked down,* GLEN, MELINDA *and* CATO *jump into the boat, and as it leaves the shore and floats away,* GLEN *and* CATO *wave their hats, and shout loudly for freedom.—Curtain falls.*

THE END

Mormon and Chinese

Joaquin Miller

(1841—1913)

"Born, in a covered wagon pointed West" (so he said), Cincinnatus Hiner (Joaquin) Miller, during an adventurous lifetime, traveled the American frontier as roustabout and writer. He worked as an Indian fighter, pony express rider, editor, and judge, in addition to writing fiction, poetry, and plays. Afflicted with an incurable wanderlust, Miller journeyed to Europe and was hailed in London literary society not merely as an accomplished frontier troubadour, but as "the Byron of Oregon"—no tepid praise from the English. Later, Miller followed the Gold Rush to Alaska; he even turned up in China at the time of the Boxer Rebellion. The spirit of the outdoors—later made popular by "Teddy" Roosevelt and Owen Wister—along with the boisterous, physical humor of the prairie and the haphazard, often savage, collision of men in the West were special interests of this colorful figure.

A pioneer scholar of our national literary experience, Fred Lewis Pattee, in *A History of American Literature Since 1870* (1915) noted that Joaquin Miller occupies a rather significant promontory overlooking the scene of our cultural evolution: "No American writer, not even Thoreau or Whitman, has ever been more uniquely individual, and none, not even Mark Twain, has woven into his writings more things that are peculiarly American, or has worked with a more thorough firsthand knowledge of the picturesque elements that went into the making of the new West." Such is the case, certainly, with his lyrical works like *Songs of the Sierras* (1871), his poems of the Far West, and *Life Among the Modocs* (1873), his sometimes fictionalized autobiography. It is, however, from his realistic sketches of the American frontier that Miller in 1877 adapted and published his most successful play, *The Danites of the Sierras.* Some years after it had been produced, he said: "I have always been sorry I printed it, as it is unfair to the Mormons and Chinese"; but this "unfair" portrait of Danite and Chinee had accurately reflected the temper of the times.

Bret Harte, Miller's famous compatriot in the literary regionalist movement of the Far West, established the popularly accepted Oriental stereotype in his comic ballad "Plain Language from Truthful James." First published in the *Overland Monthly,* September, 1870, but subsequently pirated in broadsides and newspapers, Ah Sin's machinations were quoted throughout the country. The wily Chinese immigrant met his match at the hands of a native American card-shark:

Which I wish to remark,
And my language is plain,
That for ways that are dark
And for tricks that are vain,
The heathen Chinee is peculiar,
Which the same I would rise to explain.

Ah Sin was his name;
And I shall not deny,
In regard to the same,

What that name might imply;
But his smile it was pensive and childlike,
As I frequent remarked to Bill Nye.

It was August the third,
And quite soft was the skies;
Which it might be inferred
That Ah Sin was likewise;
Yet he played it that day upon William
And me in a way I despise.

Which we had a small game,
And Ah Sin took a hand:
It was Euchre. The same
He did not understand;
But he smiled as he sat by the table,
With the smile that was childlike and bland.

Yet the cards they were stocked
In a way that I grieve,
And my feelings were shocked
At the state of Nye's sleeve,
Which was stuffed full of aces and bowers, *
And the same with intent to deceive.

But the hands that were played
By that heathen Chinee,
And the points that he made,
Were quite frightful to see,—
Till at last he put down a right bower,
Which the same Nye had dealt unto me.

Then I looked up at Nye,
And he gazed upon me;
And he rose with a sigh,
And said, "Can this be?
We are ruined by Chinese cheap labor,"—
And he went for that heathen Chinee.

In the scene that ensued
I did not take a hand,
But the floor it was strewed
Like the leaves on the strand
With the cards that Ah Sin had been hiding,
In the game "he did not understand."

In his sleeves, which were long,
He had twenty-four packs,—
Which was coming it strong,
Yet I state but the facts;
And we found on his nails, which were taper,
What is frequent in tapers,—that's wax.

Which is why I remark,
And my language is plain,

---

*In the game of euchre, the name of the two highest cards—the jack of trumps and the jack of the same color—are called right and left bower respectively.

That for ways that are dark
and for tricks that are vain,
The heathen Chinee is peculiar,—
Which the same I am free to maintain.

Ironically, Bill Nye's "good American" sleeve was similarly equipped for the euchre board; *his* cheating, perhaps, was regarded as a shrewd, thoughtful, maneuver. At any rate, along with Harte's humorous song, hailed nationally for its essential truth, Joaquin Miller's play further exaggerated the heathen chicanery of Orientals and accurately described the existing social gulf between native Americans and impious coolies: "He's drawed a pistol," cries the Parson of Washee Washee; "A Chinaman dares to draw a pistol! Has it come to this in California? A Chinaman draws a pistol on a white man in California! Bring on the rope."

There was also a general distrust of Mormons, most vividly realized in blood-curdling tales of the Danites, allegedly a secret organization of "Avenging Angel" cutthroats who held a commission for murder from Brigham Young himself. The fierce Danites were pictured by Joaquin Miller with secret signs, Biblical passwords, and atrocity-minded cultism as symptomatic of the entire Church of Jesus Christ of Latter-Day Saints: Bill Hickman, a Danite chief, gives a solemn warning to a potential apostate: "Fool! Defend yourself against the destroying angels? Whistle against the winds of the Sierras, but defy not the Danites of the Church. Hush!"

Persecuted and derided, beaten and burned out, the Mormons and the Chinese can sadly claim to be part of the American disinherited of our past. The text of Miller's frontier drama imaginatively explores the "Mormon menace" and the "yellow peril" painted against the brutal, wasteful, insensitive parochialism of the nineteenth century American West.

In Miller's mining town one finds at least one striking similarity with the old plantation drawn in *The Escape;* the emphasis on class and caste carries over into frontier settlements and produces a "first family" even in such primitive surroundings as these outer borders of civilization. While Brown's drama was written from the viewpoint of the "Disinherited," the Miller play is sympathetic to the "inherited" of the land, men who prove to be an assemblage of misfits bound together by a network of blind, primeval allegiances spawned by the survival psychology of the prairie. Intent on creating their own "new" society, the frontiersmen reveal their mistrust of those who differ in any way from the established norm. The treatment of Billy, for example, illustrates a superstitious hatred of homosexuals, another disinherited group. Despite stereotyping, Miller has portrayed conflict and alienation in the generally eulogized American Frontier.

The Danites in the Sierras

Dedicated to My Fellow Pioneers of the Sierras

Yea, I, the rhymer of wild rhymes,
Indifferent to blame or praise,
Still sing of ye as one who plays
The same old air in all strange climes;
The same wild, piercing Highland air,
Because, because his heart is there.

JOAQUIN MILLER

"Dan shall be a serpent by the way, an adder in the path, that biteth the horse's heels, so that his rider shall fall backward."—Genesis xlix:17.

Characters

SANDY, *A king, this man Sandy; a poet, a painter, a mighty moralist; a man who could not write his own name.*

THE PARSON, *So-called because he could "outswear any man in the Camp."*

THE JUDGE, *Chosen, because he was fit for nothing else in this "Glorious climate of California."*

BILL HICKMAN, *A Danite Chief.*

CARTER, *Companion to Hickman.*

LIMBER TIM, *Sandy's "Limber Pardner."*

WASHEE WASHEE, *"A Helpless little Heathen."*

BILLY PIPER, *"That Cussed Boy."*

THE WIDOW, *A Missionary to the Mines.*

CAPT. TOMMY, *A woman with a bad name but a good heart.*

BUNKERHILL, *Companion to Capt. Tommy.*

ACT I

SCENE: *"The Howlin' Wilderness" Saloon. Bar. Water bucket on table. Mining tools, rocker, etc. Miners discovered lounging about. The* JUDGE *and* LIMBER TIM *at bar, drinking.*

JUDGE: Well, well, well. And so that boy, Billy Piper, is livin' in that old cabin up the Middle Fork where them three miners handed in their checks to the Danites?

LIMBER TIM: Livin' there all alone by hisself, Judge!

JUDGE: Why, I wouldn't live in that 'ere cabin all alone by myself, Tim, for that cradle full of gold.

TIM: It's been empty, that cabin, 'bout a year, Judge.

JUDGE: Empty as a bran new coffin, Tim.

TIM: And folks just about as willin' to get into it, as into a bran new coffin, I guess.

JUDGE: Tim, me and Sandy had gone out to help the emigrants, where we seed that poor gal, Nancy Williams, killed, and we warn't here. But you was. Tell me how it was the Danites killed 'em all three in that cabin, and you fellows didn't smell a mouse till it was all over. [*Miners gather around.*]

TIM: Well, them three miners was kind o' exclusive like, just as if they war a bit afraid of suthin'. They come from Hannibal, Missouri. But they was good miners and good neighbors, too, and was a makin' money like mud.

JUDGE: Yes, hard workers. Struck it, too, in the channel afore Sandy and me went out to meet the emigrants that time.

TIM: Yes, you remember 'em, Judge. All strong, healthy, handsome fellows. But you see—shoo! Be careful, boys, when you speak of it—but they was of that hundred masked men that killed the Mormon Prophet, Joe Smith.

JUDGE: And the Danites hunted 'em down, every one, even away out here in the heart of the Sierras.

TIM: Yes. Three as fine, hearty fellows as ever you see, and a makin' money like dirt, when along comes a chap, gets in with 'em, and the first thing you know, a rope breaks in the shaft, and one of 'em is killed. Then the water breaks in one night, and one is drowned. And then the last one of the three is found dead at the foot of the crag yonder.

JUDGE: And nobody suspectin' nothin' all this time?

TIM: No. But they did, at last, and when me and the boys went there and found that long-haired stranger chap gone, and all their clothes, and all the gold scattered over the floor, why we knew it was—Shoo! Danites!

JUDGE: Left all their clothes, and just lots of gold scattered all over the cabin floor! When I got back, and heard about the gold, I went right up—

TIM: But too late, Judge. The old clothes was there, but the gold—well, that had evaporated.

JUDGE: Yes, you had been there, Tim. I don't want any more old clothes, and come to think, I don't want any gold that comes to fellow's hand like that. Why, boys, that little old cabin is haunted, and that boy a livin' in it.

TIM: And all alone, boys.

JUDGE: Well, if that boy don't see ghosts in that cabin, livin' all alone by hisself like that—there ain't any, that's all. How long's he been there, Tim?

TIM: I don't know. Month or two, maybe. You see, after the men was all dead, and that stranger chap skipped out, nobody liked to go near the cabin; kinder fraid of the Danites.

Enter BILL HICKMAN *and* CARTER

JUDGE: Shoo, Tim! See! [*Miners fall back.*]

HICKMAN: [*making sign to Barkeeper*]. Dan shall be a serpent by the way, an adder in the path, that biteth the horse's heels so that his rider shall fall backward. [*They grasp hands, drink and exit.*]

TIM: Them's Danites.

JUDGE: [*grasping pickhandle*]. Well, as Judge of this ar camp, I'd just like to purify this glorious climate of California with—

TIM: Judge! Judge! The Bar keep too? a Danite; didn't you see the grip he gave? You don't know who is and who ain't. Now just you remember them three poor fellows up the Canyon and keep still. Hello! My Pard. [*Enter* SANDY *and the* PARSON *and cross to bar.*]

SANDY: Come, boys. [*All make rush to bar.*] Well, you are all alive here, I see.

PARSON: None of these 'uns dead, Sandy, eh? [*All laugh.*] But poor Dolores. Just been a helpin' Capt. Tommy and Bunkerhill put her in the coffin.

SANDY: Was starved to death. Yes, she was, boys, and right here. Yes, and Tim, when you went to get a subscription for the Dutchman that broke his leg—

TIM: Why, she sot up in bed and took off a ring, and—

SANDY: Took off a ring—her marriage ring—the last one she had, and you didn't have sense enough to see it. Oh, I don't blame you, Tim, that was her way, you know. She was starvin' then. But, boys, look here; the Parson he wrote "Small Pox," on that butcher's door, that refused her meat, and now—well, he'll go into bankruptcy.

ALL: Good! Good! Served him right!

JUDGE: But, I say, Sandy, did you see them strangers?

SANDY: The tall, religious sort of chaps?

JUDGE: Talkin' about Dan bein' a serpent in the path.

SANDY: Yes. Seed 'em lookin' at the dead body of Dolores, down there. What of it? You seem skeered.

JUDGE: Danites!

TIM: Danites in the Sierras!

SANDY: What!

JUDGE: Yes, Danites. And the very fellows too, I think, that you and me run across when we went out to meet the emigrants, after we found this 'ere minin' camp.

SANDY: That shot—that hunted down the last of the Williams and shot, shot her—that pretty, that sweetly pretty girl that, that we found, Judge, and tried to save and bring back to camp to the boys?

JUDGE: The same hungry, Bible-howlin' varmints, I do believe.

SANDY: Judge, I'll be revenged for that poor girl's death if it takes me ten years. Why, there she came to us just at the gray of dawn, just as we seed the gold of the mornin' star croppin' out of the heavens; came to us, weary, torn, half-dead with hunger and fright, flyin' into camp like a wounded dove, there on the bank of the deep, foamin' Truckee river. "Why, poor little bird," I said, and I put my arms about her and took her up when she fell at our feet, boys, and laid her away to rest under the tree, by the bank, Judge, you know, and watched over her, we two did, Judge, as if she'd been our own kid. And then, Judge, when she waked up, you remember, and we fed her, and she talked and told us all. And how we promised and swore to save her, Judge. And then, just as we got all packed up and ready to come back, the Danites came burstin' in upon us, leadin' the Ingins, and all of 'em a shootin' at that poor, helpless baby, that never did anybody any harm.

JUDGE: [*crying and wiping eyes.*] That alkali dust out there hurts my eyes yet. [*Rushes to bar and drinks.*] That strengthens the eyes.

SANDY: And then, boys, after the battle was over and I turned to look for her—Gone! Gone! Only the deep, dark river rollin' between its willow walls. Gone! Gone! Only the dark and ugly river gurglin' sweepin' and rollin' by, and the willows leanin' over it and drippin' and drippin' and bendin' to the ugly waters. Leanin' and weepin' as if in tears for her. Only the dark river rollin' there under the bendin' willows and—and—and my heart as cold and empty as a dead man's hand.

TIM: Why, Sandy, my poor old pard, we'll all stand by you and help you git even on 'em.

PARSON: Stand by you agin the Danites, Sandy, till the cows come home; and thar's my hand.

SANDY: [*wiping his eyes and going*]. If them's them, Judge, I'll find 'em and raise 'em out of their boots. No, you needn't come, boys. If I can find 'em, that's all I ask. Let me have 'em all to myself, boys.[*Exit.*]

JUDGE: Poor Sandy. He loved her, boys. And she was pretty, *so* sweetly pretty. And to go and get shot and drowned like that, when we was fightin' for her.

TIM: Why, he talks about her yet in his sleep, Parson. But he wouldn't know her if he seed her.

JUDGE: Only seed her by the camp-fire, boys. But he hain't been the same man since.

PARSON: Always was a little soft here. [*Taps heart.*] But he's good, Tim. I ain't sayin' nothin' agin' your pard. Only he's tender hearted.

Enter WASHEE WASHEE

WASHEE WASHEE: [*down stage*]. I say, Plosson, plack tlain comee.

JUDGE: [*aside*]. The pack train! Then there will be some news. And maybe some strangers; and maybe some business. Must brush up a bit.

WASHEE: Yes, plack tlain comee down way uppee mountain, an' a somebodee alle samee a Captin' Tommy; Blunkel hillee.

TIM: All the same Capt. Tommy?

PARSON: All the same Bunkerhill? Now you git out of here. You've been lyin' enough. Git, I tell you. [*Kicks at him and* WASHEE *exits.*] Lie! Why, that Chinaman can lie the bark off of a tree. [*All laugh.*]

JUDGE: Guess he can steal some, too, Parson.

PARSON: Steal? He even steals from himself, just to keep his hand in.

Enter SANDY

SANDY: Couldn't find 'em. And that's what makes me think it *was* Danites. Judge, they come and go as if they came up out of, or sink into the ground, like that.

TIM: Maybe they're gone up to the haunted cabin to see Billy Piper?

JUDGE: Oh, do you know, Parson, Stubbs here, says he's a wearin' of them dead men's old clothes?

PARSON: Hold on, I've got an idea! That boy Billy Piper's a Danite!

SANDY: Now look here, Parson, you don't like that boy, I know.

PARSON: No. I don't like nobody that lives all alone by hisself and in a place like that. Why, the blood ain't hardly dry yet, where them three men died, and he a livin' there.

SANDY: Well, now, maybe he ain't got no other place to stay. And he ain't strong, you know. Why, the first time I ever seed him, I met him in the trail, and he got out of it as I come by, and held down his head, all for the world like a timid bit of a girl, Judge. And when I said, "Boy, what's your name?" he stammered, as if he wanted to get away, Judge, and at last, with his head still held down, he told me his name —Billy Piper—then smiled so sadly, like *her,* Judge, and went on.

JUDGE: Well, Sandy, ain't nothin' wonderful 'bout it, is there?

SANDY: No, Judge, not that. It's only Billy Piper, that's all. That's his name, boys. And don't you go for to nick-name him. But, Judge, that smile was like her—like her smile, *hers.*

TIM: Oh, now, Sandy, don't; that's a good fellow. Forget all about that.

JUDGE: Yes. Talk about—'bout suthin' new. Talk about the weather—this glorious climate of California, and—and—and—take a drink?

SANDY: Why, of course, boys. That's all right. But you, Parson, don't be too hard on little Billy Piper. I know it does make one feel kind o' skeery to think where he lives, and how he lives. But he's squar', squar', Parson.

TIM: And a poet. Yes. Says pretty things as he stands lookin' up at the moon, a wheelin' through the pine tops; prettier things than you can find in a book.

SANDY: And says things as sets you a thinkin', too. Why, he says to hisself today, kind o' quiet like, when some of the boys was tauntin' Bunker about the hump on her back, says he, takin' Bunkerhill's hand, says he, "God has made some women a little bit plain, in order that He might have some women that is perfectly good."

TIM: Just like a book, ain't it?

JUDGE: A little shaky here. [*Taps head.*] Maybe he's had trouble.

SANDY: Jest so, Judge, jest so. O, but I say, boys. Forgot to tell you. Seed Soapy Dan the storekeeper just now, when I went out to look for them fellows and what do you think? Why, his pack train is comin' in, and a missionary is a comin' in on it, too.

ALL: A missionary!

PARSON: A—a—now look here! Not a missionary? Of all things under the heavens, or on the earth, what use have we for a missionary here?

ALL: No use, no use at all.

JUDGE: No! We're too good *now*.

PARSON: A derned sight too good!

JUDGE: Why, it's insinervatious, that's what it is.

TIM: Better send him to the Cannibal Islands, eh, Parson?

PARSON: Do they take us for Cannibals out here, in this 'ere camp?

JUDGE: He'll want to be Judge and everything else.

PARSON: It is an insult. A roarin', howlin' insult, for that 'ere storekeeper to let 'em come in here on his mules. And if he sets foot in here, boys, and he will set foot in here, he'll come in here to take up a collection right off—O, yes, I know 'em. I seed 'em in Missouri and on the Mississippi, and seed 'em when I went down the river and took ship. Oh, I know the white choker gentry. They will have the best in the land and pay nothing. They never miss a meal and never pay a cent. A Boston missionary, bah!

JUDGE: [*shakes pickhandle*]. Well, then, gentlemen, it's my official opinion, as judge of this 'ere camp, that we'd best find him guilty on the spot, and execute him when he arrives.

PARSON: Tried, and found guilty.

ALL: Yes; let's all go for him.

TIM: O, but he won't come in here.

PARSON: Won't he, though? This is the sittin' room of the hotel. He'll come to the hotel to get his fodder, won't he? O, they always have the best in the land, the broadbrimmed, long-legged, lean, lantern-jawed, hymn-howlin', white-chokered sons of guns. I'm down on 'em, I am.

SANDY: Well, guess we'd better all go for him, eh, boys?

PARSON: O, no. Don't let's go for him. Let's pass around the hat for brother Tomkinsonsonson; let's take up a collection; do suthin' religious.

TIM: [*taking drink from bucket*]. Let's all be baptized. [*All laugh.*]

PARSON: Bully for Tim! Let's baptize the missionary!

SANDY: That's the idea, boys. Say, boys. Look here. When he comes in at that door—

PARSON: Baptize him, then and thar. Yes! Let's baptize him and give him his new name, like all the rest of us.

SANDY: [*all sitting; pans; water*]. We'll do it, and I'll be chief mourner.

TIM: Wonder if he's a sprinkler or a dipper?

SANDY: Well, we'll make him think he's a dipper.

PARSON: Won't he look funny though, with his broad-brimmed Quaker hat all wilted down like a cabbage leaf?

TIM: An' his long-tailed coat all a streamin'.

SANDY: And his umbrella won't do him no good, for the water will rain from below. [*All roar.*]

Enter WASHEE WASHEE

WASHEE: Missonalie—longee cloatee—comee.

PARSON: He's a comin' right in. Told you so, boys. Washee, take that, and give him one for his mother. [*Hands water.*] Comin' in. Told you so.

SANDY: There, boys! Pullin' at the latchstring. Give it to him.

Enter WIDOW, *bag in hand; scar on cheek.*

Miners fall back

ALL: Calico!

WIDOW: I am the missionary.

PARSON: The missionary!

SANDY: [*to miners; down water*]. Yes, and the very kind of missionary the camp wanted.

WIDOW: [*aside*]. Why, they all had goldpans in their hands. How industrious these honest miners are.

PARSON: Say, Sandy, let's send to the Board of Missons for a thousand missionaries.

WIDOW: I sent word by the storekeeper that I was coming. I hope you were ready to receive the missionary?

JUDGE: Hem! We—we was ready to receive the missionary, mum, but—but not that kind of a missionary, mum.

SANDY: But we're glad, we're glad it *is* this kind of one, all the same.

PARSON: [*brushing up and coming close to the* WIDOW]. Yes, we are, mum, by the—[*Hand over mouth.*]

SANDY: The biggest strike, Judge, since we found the Forks. Now go in. Make a speech. Speak for me. Don't let the Parson have it all to say.

JUDGE: This glorious climate, California, mum. Mum, mum, welcome. Welcome, mum, to the —the—to—Married, mum? [WIDOW *shakes head. Miners wild with delight.*] California widow, perhaps? [*She modestly turns away.*] A widder, boys. A real, squar', modest mite of a widder.

PARSON: Yes, she's a widder. And pretty. God bless the pretty widder.

SANDY: A widder! A California widder?

JUDGE: Yes, yes, Sandy. That's all right. You see, the other kind never gets this far. They seem to spile first.

PARSON: Have suthin' to drink, widder?

WIDOW: O, no, thank you. But if you could show me a room—

PARSON: The best room in the Forks is yourn till you can get a cabin of your own. This way. [*Showing her off.*]

SANDY: Yes; but we all must be allowed to pay for it together, Parson.

WIDOW: Parson?

SANDY: This is the Parson, mum.

WIDOW: O, I'm so glad. I shall have you preach at every service. [*Exit.*]

ALL: Have you preach? [*All laugh.*]

PARSON: Have me preach?

SANDY: Why, she don't know we call you the Parson because you can out cuss any man in the camp. Come! My treat! [*All rush to bar.*]

JUDGE: Who's goin' to be baptized now, Parson?

PARSON: I am. Yes, I am, boys. I'm converted; and I'm willin' to be baptized.

SANDY: Leastwise, we don't baptize the widder, no way. [*Sadly.*] But what strange wind or storm blew her away in here among the crags and pines, boys? And so pretty, too; pretty as poor little Nancy Williams. And the scar? But pshaw, no. This cannot be her.

PARSON: Pretty, pretty, and good as gold. But she's had trouble, old pard. That's been a bullet made that scar.

SANDY: That's just what set me to thinkin' just now. And I want to look at her pretty face agin, boys. For you see them Danites came just as she came. Now we couldn't find the body of Nancy Williams, Judge, you know, and with that scar and them Danites, I tell you this might be Nancy Williams, and if—

JUDGE: Sandy! Sandy! You—That's not possible. You're always thinkin' of poor Nancy Williams. Why, that river rolls over her, Sandy. Forget her, do. Now, here's this 'ar widder—

TIM: O, that pretty widder. [*Straightening up collar.*] I'm goin' to fix myself up.

PARSON: And me, too. [*Miners repeat this and all exit, leaving* SANDY.]

WIDOW: [*entering*]. All alone? And so thoughtful and still.

SANDY: [*starts*]. Why, I—I was a thinkin' a bit, widder. I—the boys have gone to fix up, I guess. You see you're the first woman in the Forks, mum.

WIDOW: And are there no ladies here, then?

SANDY: Ladies? No, no ladies, mum. No children. No young folks at all. Only one. Billy Piper. A pale-faced, lonesome little fellow that lives all alone by hisself.

WIDOW: Why, how sad for him. I shall seek him out and console him.

SANDY: You mind me, mum, of a face that I saw once in the dusk and in trouble; a sweet, sad face, that vanished away like a dear, tender dream. But no, no, you are taller than she.

WIDOW: Why, how strange. I must have you tell me all about it. But here are your friends.

Miners entering dressed loudly, drink, and edge up to WIDOW

PARSON: Now Sandy's had her five minutes all by hisself. She's talked to him five whole minutes. I'd a been converted and baptized by this time.

Enter BILLY PIPER; *pick and pan*

SANDY: This is the boy Billy Piper, mum, that lives all alone by hisself.

WIDOW: I'm very glad to know you. We shall be the best of friends.

BILLY: O, I thank you so much. [*Aside.*] A woman. And a kind, true woman too. Life will not be so hard now. No, not so utterly desolate. But Sandy! How he looks at her. Looks at her tenderly as he once looked at me.

WIDOW: And you are a little miner. I should so like to dig the pure gold from the earth, too.

BILLY: Then come, and I will show you how it is done. [*Exit.*]

PARSON: Curse that Danite boy! His smooth tongue and face will win that widder's heart in five minutes. Well, if she don't baptize him, I will, and in deeper water than he thinks. [*Goes to door. Shouts outside.*] Hello! Boys after that Chinaman again. Come. Let's go to work. It's dull here now, with the widder gone. [*All exit.*]

Enter WASHEE WASHEE, *blouse stuffed with clothes. Takes bottle, drinks*

WASHEE: Blandee! Blandee! Me likee blandee. [*Drinks again.*] Blandee makee Chinaman feel allee same likee fighten clock. [*Going to door.*] Melican man no comee. No catchee Chinaman. [*Drinks.*] Melican man he no comee. Chinaman he no go. [*Shouts outside.*]

Enter miners, excited

SANDY: There he is, boys. [*Rush at* WASHEE.]

TIM: Well, he's got 'em. You bet he has. Let's search him for the shirts.

JUDGE: Yes, search him. And if you find your shirts, I'll find him guilty.

PARSON: Yes, and if you find him guilty, Judge, he's got to swing. Look here. [*Miners seize Chinaman and pull shirts from blouse.*] And here, and here, and there! A hull cargo! You heathen! Got anything more?

JUDGE: Got anything more, Washee? If you got anything more the law will make you give it up. You can't go on breakin' the seventh commandment like that, in this glorious climate of California, I can tell you. No, not while I'm Judge, you can't. Got anything else about you? [*Seizes queue, and pulls about.*] Got anything else about you, I say?

WASHEE: Yesee. My gotee that! [*Draws pistol,* JUDGE *back.*]

PARSON: He's drawed a pistol! A Chinaman dares to draw a pistol! Has it come to this in California? A Chinaman draws a pistol on a white man in California! Bring that rope. [*Miners hand rope.*]

JUDGE: [*hiding behind* SANDY]. Hang him! Hang him! And I'll pronounce sentence of death on him afterwards.

SANDY: [*takes pistol*]. Hand in your checks, Washee Washee.

PARSON: Here, boys! Out to the nearest tree.

Throws noose over WASHEE'S *head; other end to miners. Dragging to door. Shouting wildly:* "Hang him!" *Enter* WIDOW, *with* BILLY. *She lifts hand; all let go.* WASHEE *at her feet. She throws off rope. Miners down stage in shame.*

CURTAIN

ACT II

SCENE: *Moonlight on the Sierras. Rocky Run crossing stage; ledge overhanging; set cabin, practical door, foot of run; background of distant snow-capped peaks.*

Enter HICKMAN *and* CARTER

HICKMAN: That's her cabin. The missionary. Humph! As if we could not find her out, though she professed herself a saint. Her time has come.

CARTER: Yes. But it seems to me, after she has escaped the bullet and the flood, and hid away here, toiling too as she does, it is hard to kill her. Maybe the Lord has willed to spare her.

HICKMAN: [*close and solemn*]. And Dan shall be a serpent in the path, that biteth the horse's heel till his rider falleth backward. Have we not our orders from the Church? Is she not sentenced to death? Do we not hold our commission from Brigham Young for her execution?

CARTER: But I—I'm tired of this hunting down helpless women. As long as it was men I did my part, but now—well, she had no hand in the Prophet's death.

HICKMAN: But her father had. And are *you* to sit in judgment now on this? You are not the judge. You are only the executioner. No! She and all her kindred shall perish from the earth. For I will be revenged, saith the Lord, unto the third and fourth generation.

CARTER: And I am to kill her? Enter that cabin like a thief and kill her with this knife? This hand? I will not! I—

HICKMAN: And be an apostate? And die by *this* knife? And *this* hand?

CARTER: I will defend myself.

HICKMAN: Fool! Defend yourself against the destroying angels? Whistle against the winds of the Sierras, but defy not the Danites of the Church. Hush! [*Exit.*]

Enter WIDOW *and* BILLY *from cabin*

BILLY: How beautiful! The whole moon's heart is poured out into the mighty Sierras. O, what a miracle; the moon and golden stars; and all the majesty and mystery of this calm, still world to love. O, life is not so hard now.

WIDOW: And you love the world, with all your sad, hard life?

BILLY: And why not? Is it less beautiful because *I* have had troubles? My sweet friend, it seems to me the highest, the holiest religion that we can have, is to love this world, and the beauty, the mystery, the majesty that environ us.

WIDOW: How strange all this from one so young. I came here, a missionary, to teach; I am being taught. But stay awhile yet. You see by the moonlight on the mountain, it is not so late as you thought. We may still read another chapter of your little Testament.

BILLY: No, I must go now. Besides, I know Sandy is coming this evening. Oh, I know you expect him. And he, he would not like to see me here.

WIDOW: And why not? His is a high, loyal nature, above the petty quarrels and jealousies of the camp. Come, come in and wait till he calls. Then, you see, you will not leave me alone.

BILLY: Alone? And do you fear to be alone? Oh! do you, too, shudder and start at strange sounds and signs as I do? Last night, up yonder on the banks of the stream, in my cabin in the thick wood, as I lay there I heard footsteps about my cabin. I heard the chapparal and the manzanitti crackle, as if monsters prowled about; wild beasts, waiting to devour me.

WIDOW: Then come in. You shall not go till you are at least in better heart. [*Into cabin.*]

Enter PARSON *up canyon at back, breathless, pick on shoulder*

PARSON: Well! That is a climb for you. If I'd a lost my footin' comin' up that precipice, good-bye Parson. But it was a mile around by the trail, and I wanted to get to the widder's cabin afore Sandy. She's in thar'. Lord love her! The sweetest thing in these 'ere Sierras. These 'ere Sierras? The sweetest and the prettiest in this universal world. Yes, and the boys all know it. They all knowed it when she came. But when she took this 'ere cabin, and took in that cussed, thievin' little heathen, kind o' absorbed him like, and set up to washin' the boys' clothes; workin' like the rest of us—when I seed that 'ere little widder a bendin' over a wash-tub, earnin' her bread by the sweat of her brow; wearin' a diadem of diamonds on her forehead; well, I thought of my mother and my sister, an' it made me better—better—and I loved her so, I loved her so. [*Has been coming down Run; is at door. Stops and listens.*] The widder readin'? And—and to him—that boy Piper. That brat that's either Danite, Devil or imp? I'll—I'll strangle him. I'll take him by the throat and choke the life out of him with these two hands and chuckle with delight while doin' it. He's comin' out. I'll wait till I catch him alone and then I'll throttle him. [*Exit.*]

Enter BILLY *and* WIDOW

BILLY: O, yes. I am quite strong now. It was only a passing shadow; as the clouds will sometimes shut out the light of the sun or the beauty of yon moon. I suppose such moments come to us all. Good-night. My cabin is not far.

WIDOW: And if anything happens, or you feel at all sad or lonely, come back, and Sandy, if he comes, I am sure will be glad to take you to his own cabin and cheer you up.

BILLY: Sandy! You know not what you say. But no. It is *I* rather, that know not what *I* say. Good-night.

WIDOW: Good-night. And come again soon to read the other chapters.

BILLY: I will come. Good-night. [WIDOW *closes door.* BILLY *looks off.*] How full of rest and peace the whole world seems. But I? I am as the dove that was sent forth from out the ark and found not where to set its foot. The olive branch? It is not for me.

Enter JUDGE *and* TIM

TIM: Yes, Judge, my pard's cut the sand clean from under the Parson's feet, I guess. He's goin' to pop tonight, he tells me, if he can only pump up the spunk to do it. [*Takes bottle from boot leg; they drink; he returns it.*]

JUDGE: Goin' to get married? Well, Tim, in this glorious climate of California, I tell you one feels like—like—well, as if he must do suthin', Tim.

TIM: If there was only more women, Judge.

JUDGE: That's it, Tim. I tell you, it makes me feel sort of, of warlike to think about what Sandy's goin' to do. I tell you, in this glorious climate of California—[BILLY *down stage and they meet.*]

TIM: Billy Piper at the widder's agin? Judge, you're the Judge of this 'ere camp. Set him up.

JUDGE: Billy, as Judge of this 'ere camp I must say that you ain't doin' the squar'. The boys talk powerful rough about you and her. You're a cryin' shame to the—the—the—this glorious climate of California. And Billy, for the reputation of this 'ere camp, I think I'll punch your head. [*About to strike.*]

Enter CAPT. TOMMY *and* BUNKERHILL

CAPT. TOMMY: [*fist in* JUDGE'S *face*]. Touch that boy and I'll knock the corn juice out of you. Yes, I will, and you, too. Light out, Billy. [*Exit* BILLY.] You bald-headed, gum suckin' old idiot.

BUNKERHILL: Tackle a boy, eh? 'Bout the only thing in the camp you could lick anyhow; both of you.

JUDGE: Well, Capt. Tommy, I'm a magistrate

and must not fight. But Tim—speak to her, Tim.

TIM: Yes, he's a magistrate; and you've got to keep the peace, too, or he'll—

CAPT. TOMMY: Well, do *you* want to take it up? You long-legged, jackass rabbit you. Come on, both of you. I'm your match.

BUNKERHILL: Take both of 'em to make one man.

Enter WIDOW *from cabin*

JUDGE: Ahem! The widder! Good evenin', marm. I'll put 'em under arrest for bein' drunk and disorderly, if they disturb you, marm.

CAPT. TOMMY: Widder, sorry to disturb you. Bunker and me is allers in trouble. Allers, allers. And not allers for faults of our own, mum; it's the bad name, mum.

BUNKERHILL: It's the bad name, mum. And we must bear it. Good-night, Widder, good-night. [*Going.*]

CAPT. TOMMY: Don't think too hard of us. We hain't had no bringin' up, like better women has. But we won't never make no rows any more, mum, if you'll forgive us.

WIDOW: Forgive you? You have done me no harm, and if you have trouble, young ladies, remember it is yourselves you harm. You do yourselves harm, young ladies.

CAPT. TOMMY: [*to* BUNKERHILL]. Young ladies! She called us young ladies.

BUNKERHILL: She's a good 'un. Tommy. A good, squar' woman. [*Both returning.*]

CAPT. TOMMY: [*weeping*]. Widder, between us rolls a wide river that has born Bunker and me from the high, sunny shore where you stand to the dark, muddy t'other side: and I'll not try to cross it, Widder. But God bless you for callin' us young ladies. We was good once, and we had mothers once. Yes, we had, mothers, and fathers, and little baby brothers and sisters, and—[TIM *affected.* JUDGE *takes out handkerchief.*]

BUNKERHILL: Yes, fathers and mothers and little brothers and sisters that loved us, before we fell into the dark river that bore us far from the high, white shores where you stand, Widder.

WIDOW: [*offering hands.*] The river is not so wide that my hands will not reach across it. If my feet are on the solid bank, take my hand, hold strong and come up and stand by my side. [*They hesitate, grasp her hands and kiss them.*]

JUDGE: Tim, I feel as if I'd been to meetin' in Missouri and, and, got religion.

TIM: You old fool, you're a cryin'; Capt. Tommy, she's a cryin'; and Bunker—she's a— [*Breaks down.*]

JUDGE: Capt. Tommy, I'm an old, busted, bald-headed old—well, I guess I am an old fool. But you've made me better. And if you'll take me for better or for worse—

TIM: And me, too, Bunker. I'm hot lead in a bullet-ladle. All melted up. Take me? [*Both greatly amazed. Confer aside, then frankly forward.*]

BUNKERHILL: Well, if you'll be good to Billy, and to everybody.

TIM: Good to Billy? You will make us good to all. Good! But come. Now let us go tell Sandy. [*Both embrace; ladies take arms and going.*]

JUDGE: O, this glorious climate of California!

WIDOW: You will all come to see me?

JUDGE: We will come. Good-night. [*Exit;* WIDOW *looking after.*]

Enter SANDY

SANDY: Why, Widder, you—you out here? You —you waitin' here for me, Widder? Say yes, Widder. Say you were waitin' for me, and it will be as if the sun, and the moon, and the stars all together shone out over the Sierras, and made this another Eden, with its one sweet woman in the centre of God's own garden of fruit and flowers, and—and—

WIDOW: Why, Sandy! You used to sit for hours in my cabin and not say one word, and now, you talk like a running brook.

SANDY: No, no, Widder. I can't talk. I never could. I never can, Widder. But Widder, it's not them that can talk that feel. You hear the waters thunderin' down that ar canyon over thar'? They are shallow, and foamy, and wild. But where they meet the river away down below, they are calm and still. But, they are deep and strong, and clear. So, widder, it seems to me with the hearts of men and women. And Widder, when I stood thinkin' of you, today—

WIDOW: You thought of me today?

SANDY: Today? Yesterday! Tomorrow! Forever! O, Widder, as I bent to my work in the runnin' water, the white clouds far up above me tangled in the high, dark tops of the pines, the gold shinin' there in the dark loam and muck, as the pure waters poured over it; the gold as pure and true, and as beautiful as your noble life, my lady, I thought of you, how that you was like that gold in the loam and in the muck, among us all. And—and—

WIDOW: Us all? [*Aside.*] Why can't he speak up for himself, now that he has learned to speak?

[*Aloud.*] And you think I have done good here —for *us* all?

SANDY: Good! You have been the seasons of the year. The spring and summer, and the fruit and flower of the year, to every one of us. Why, we'd a hung that cussed Chinaman. We would. Yes, and never a thought about it after he was buried. And, why, we hain't hardly had a funeral since you came, and we used to have 'em every Sunday, when only Bunker and Capt. Tommy and poor dead Dolores was here. O, yes, you've helped us, Widder.

WIDOW: Helped *us.* Has the little missionary done *you* no good, Sandy?

SANDY: O, yes, you—yes, you—you—you— washed my shirt.

WIDOW: Oh, Sandy!

SANDY: Yes, that was good in you, widder. But you see that's considerable trouble to a feller, too, as well as help. For when a feller has to send his pard with his shirt and go to bed till it gets back—

WIDOW: Why, Sandy, haven't you but one shirt?

SANDY: But one shirt? Do you think a man wants a thousand shirts in the Sierras?

WIDOW: O, Sandy, you do need a missionary, indeed you do, Sandy. You want a missionary badly. [SANDY *starts, and for the first time seems to understand.*]

SANDY: I—I—yes, Widder, I do want a missionary; I need a missionary. *I—I*—the great, rough heathen of this 'ere camp. Never did a cannibal hunger for a missionary as my heart hungers for—for—Widder, will you—can you—can you— will you be my missionary?—my wife?

WIDOW: Sandy, here is my hand; my heart, you ought to have known, has long been yours. [*Offering hand.*]

SANDY: You—you—you don't mean it? Is it me that's to have you? Rough, bluff, bearded old Sandy. Not the Parson; not slim Limber Tim, not that gentle, sweet boy, Billy Piper, but Sandy? Sandy, strong as a pine in Winter, and rough as the bark of a tree. And this—this soft, lily-like hand to be laid in his! O, Widder, you don't mean to give me this dear, tremblin' little hand, do you? Soft and white, and flutterin' like a dove that has just been caught. Is this little hand to be mine for storms or sunny weather, Widder?

WIDOW: Yes, Sandy.

SANDY: [*taking her in his arms.*] Jerusalem! Mine! Mine! My wife! Mine, to work for, to plan for, to love and to live for! Mine! Mine! Mine! My beauty! Mine! Mine, at last! [*Reflecting.*] But, Widder, my cabin is a rough place. Only a little log hut.

WIDOW: Sandy, true love is content to live in a very small house.

SANDY: True, Widder, true. Love, real unselfish love, it seems to me, could be content under the trees; in the boughs of the trees, like the birds; in the mountains; everywhere that love —that love—finds love—to—love, love.

WIDOW: Yes, Sandy. Anywhere that love finds love.

SANDY: Yes, yes. You see, I know about what it is I want to say, but I can't say it as well as you can.

WIDOW: Nonsense, Sandy. But the moon is low, and—

SANDY: And I must go. Well, you're right. But before I go, Widder, if you love me—[*Embraces and kisses her.*] Moses in the bulrushes! The world is a bigger world now. I seem to stand on the summit of the Sierras, six feet two inches taller than the tallest mountain. Oh, Widder, this is Paradise with its one little woman, and now you're goin' to drive me out of it.

WIDOW: Yes, you must go now. You see we are here in the open trail, and the miners on the night-watch, passing to and from their tunnels, will think it strange on seeing us together so late.

SANDY: Right, Widder. It's a man's place to brighten a woman's name, not to tarnish it. Good-night.

WIDOW: Tomorrow, Sandy. Good-night. [*Exits into cabin.*]

SANDY: Tomorrow! O, moon, go down! And sun rise up and set, for I can never wait. Tomorrow! And I kissed her! And her soul overflowed and filled mine full as a river flooding its willow banks. I must tell Tim, and Tim will tell the Judge, and the Judge will tell the boys and the boys will bust. For it's too much happiness for one little camp to hold. Tomorrow! Mine! My wife! [*Starting to go.*] And I kissed her, and kissed her, and—[*Turns to go up stage, and meets* PARSON *face to face.*]

PARSON: Talkin' in your sleep, Sandy? 'Pears to me you're actin' mighty queer, eh? Been seein' the widder agin? Mustn' get excited where woman is concerned. Sort of like buck ager. Miss your game, sure, if you get excited, Sandy.

SANDY: O, yes, I know all about that, you

know. Oh, I'm not—not afraid of a little woman like that.

PARSON: Well, say, old pard, Sandy, you—you didn't really have a serious talk with her? Squar', now, Sandy. Squar' as a coffin lid, Sandy. We were old pards once, you and me, Sandy. We don't want to send each other up on the hill thar, Sandy. So you'll be squar' with me, an' I'll be squar' with you. I love that 'ere woman thar, and—

SANDY: Well—well. The fact is, Parson—you can't help it, I guess. Now, I'll tell you. That 'ere little woman, she's—come and take a drink.

PARSON: No, thank you, Sandy. Got to set my night-watch in the tunnel, and change my drifters. But it's to be a squar' fight, Sandy, and there's my hand. And if you git her, Sandy—git her squar'!

SANDY: Squar', Parson. Squar'! [*Exit.*]

PARSON: Good-night. Got him out of the way, and I'll see her right off, and tell her—tell her like a man I love her. [*About to enter cabin.*] LIMBER TIM *and* BILLY *enter.*] Pshaw! Here comes Tim and that cussed boy. [*Exit, behind cabin.*]

BILLY: There is somebody prowling about my cabin, Tim. I can't; I won't stay there tonight.

TIM: Well, you do look skeered. [*Aside.*] Ghosts, I'll bet a gold mine! [*Aloud.*] Three men, wasn't there? Your face is white as snow, Billy.

BILLY: And my hair will be as white. O, Tim, I tell you there are two men, and—

TIM: Three! [*Aside.*] There was three of 'em killed, and they've come back. [*To* BILLY.] Pull up, Billy. I'll tell my pard, Sandy. But you see his mind is awful full now. O, he's got a powerful mind. But it takes it all, and more too, to tend to her. [*Pointing to cabin.*]

BILLY: And he really loves, and will marry her?

TIM: That's the little game he's tryin' to play, Billy. Guess he's got the keerds to do it, too, I tell you the moon shines mighty bright for my pard tonight, Billy. Oh, he's a happy man, I can tell you.

BILLY: Tim, tell me this. Why is it that the grave yards are always on a hill? Is it because it is a little nearer heaven?

TIM [*turning away.*] Well, I—I—well, Billy, I don't take to grave yards and sich like. May be it's a prettier view up thar. But then they can't see, with thar eyes full of dust.

BILLY: No. Nor feel, nor understand, nor suffer. Love and be unloved, know and be unknown through all the weary years of this weary, loveless life. Oh, Tim, Tim! [TIM *knocks at door.*]

Enter WIDOW

TIM: Widder! Billy's took sick. Poetry; pretty; stars; grave yards and sich. Mustard plaster, physic and peppermint tea. Take care of him, Widder, till I tell Sandy. [*Exit.*]

WIDOW: What is the matter, Billy?

BILLY: Sandy, Has he been here, as you expected, and told you all?

WIDOW: All, all. And I am so happy.

BILLY: And *I* am so miserable.

WIDOW: O, Billy, why is this? Why are you so miserable when your friends are to be so happy? Can you not tell me? Can you not trust me? And can you not trust Sandy, too?

BILLY: No, no, no. Down to the door of the tomb, even over the dark river, alone I must bear my secret, my sufferings and my cross. O, you cannot guess. You will never know the dark and dreadful truth, the mystery, the awful crimes—

WIDOW: Crimes! Crimes! Then you are—you are a Danite?

BILLY: I, a Danite? I?

WIDOW: Yes, I see it all now. Men have been seen prowling about your cabin at night. They have been seen to enter it in your absence.

BILLY: Merciful heavens, what do you say? Then I am doomed. Oh, if it would come. If it would come now! Now! Sudden, and swift, and certain. Now! Oh, this suspense is more than death. This waiting day and night, night and day, for the executioner to strike. Come! Come! O, I cannot bear this any longer. Come, death! Father in heaven take—take me! Pity and take me now. Oh! Oh! This is death! [*Falls.*]

WIDOW: What terrible thing is this? Will no one come? He is dying, and no one to help. Dying, choking to death. [*Opens collar.*] A woman!

BILLY: Hush. A whisper would be my death warrant. [*Danites appear on cliff watching.*] You hold the secret of my life. You hold my *life* itself.

WIDOW: You are—

BILLY: Nancy Williams. [*Danites disappear.*] But you will keep my secret?

WIDOW: As these Sierras keep the secrets of their Creator.

BILLY: Thank you! thank you! My sister, my

friend. And when all is over; when dying from this constant strain and terror; when dead in my cabin yonder; then bring him, with some wild flowers, and once let him, whom you so love, stoop and kiss the cold, cold face of her who loved him, oh, so tenderly.

WIDOW: And you love him as he loved you?

BILLY: As *you* love him, and as I shall love him while life lasts, my sister and my friend. But from him, even until death, this secret is sacred as the secrets of the grave.

WIDOW: As you will; sacred as the grave.

BILLY: And now good-night. Tim will be back soon. No, I dare not enter your cabin now. Let them still believe me of the Danites. I hear footsteps, go! Good-night.

[*Exit* WIDOW *into cabin.*]

Enter Danites

BILLY: The Danites!

[*Exits.*]

BILLY: Keep watch down the trail. Men will be passing soon to and from the tunnels on the night-watch. We must not be seen. Look sharp. This is the woman. I heard the boy call her name—Nancy Williams—as I leaned from the cliff there. The work must be done, and done now. [*Tests knife, and cautiously opens door.*]

CARTER: Shoo! Some one is coming down the trail. Out! Back!

Enter WIDOW

WIDOW: Some one opening my door. Well, what is it you want, sir?

HICKMAN: You. Your time has come. [*Throws light of lantern in her face, and grasping knife.*]

Enter PARSON

PARSON: Hello! Hello! Now what are you doin' around the widder's cabin, eh? 'Pears to me everybody in camp, night and day's a hoverin' round this 'ere cabin of yourn, Widder. Who are they? Say, who are you fellows, anyhow? [HICKMAN *and* CARTER *retreat.* PARSON *following them, seizes* HICKMAN, *holds him, and looks long and hard in his face.*]

HICKMAN: Well, friend, you'll know me when you see me again, won't you?

PARSON: Yes, I will. Yes, I will know you, and know you in a way that you will remember, if ever I see you hangin' 'round this little woman's cabin agin. Know you when I see you? Now, you just set a peg thar, and remember that the longest day you live I'll know you, you bet.

HICKMAN: Be patient, my friend, I meant no offence.

PARSON: Didn't you, though? Well, I'll remember you, and know you all the same when I see you. Who are you, anyhow?

HICKMAN: Only prospectors. Good-night, Sir. [*Exit both.*]

PARSON: Prospectors, eh? Well, prospectors don't prospect at midnight. They're ground-sluice robbers, I'll bet. You look out for them fellers, Widder, they're on the steal. [*Aside.*] All by herself; and Sandy sound asleep. Bet I'll never get another such a chance. [*To* WIDOW.] Pretty late, ain't it, Widder? Pretty fine night, but pretty late.

WIDOW: Yes! late. But it seems to me nights like this were not made for sleep.

PARSON: [*aside*]. Not made for sleep; but made for love. O, what a hint. That's what she means. Oh, was there ever anything so smart as a smart woman in such things? [*Aloud.*] Ahem! No, not made for sleep. You're right there, Widder. [*Aside.*] Ain't she pretty and smart? Ain't she smart? I'll just press her here on that point. [*Aloud.*] No, these moonlight nights were not made for sleep, but for—for—Now what were these moonlight nights in the Sierras made for, Widder?

WIDOW: For meditation and prayer.

PARSON: [*aside*]. Won't somebody please set down on my head? This is the end of the Parson. [*To* WIDOW.] Why, Widder, you—you—I understand now. And it's Billy—but to have you love a thing like Billy, Widder, that there's been so much talk and secrets about. I tell you to beware of Billy. Beware of Billy. He's a sneak; a sneak. A Danite! And I'll throttle him yet. Yes, he is a Danite; and I will kill him.

WIDOW: Parson, for shame! You asked me if you could do me a favor just now; you can.

PARSON: Name it! And if it's to throw him over that cliff, I'll do it. I'll do it.

WIDOW: No. You will befriend and defend poor little Billy Piper. Do it with your life!

PARSON: Oh, Widder, anything but that. Why, he's a snake. A snake in the grass. He has put you to shame before all the camp. All the camp is talkin' about his sneakin' in and out of your cabin, day and night, and—

WIDOW: You insult me! [*Going.*] And now show

me that you are the man Sandy is, by befriending that boy, or never speak to me again. [*Exit into cabin.*]

PARSON: By defending that boy! that boy who seeks to ruin her! And to have her slam the door in my face. O, I could twist his neck as if it were a wisp of straw. Slam your door in my face like that? I'll be revenged on you and on him if ever I—

Enter BILLY, *running and looking back*

BILLY: By my cabin! I dare not go home!

PARSON: [*suddenly confronts* BILLY]. So, youngster! [*Seizing him.*] Come here! [*Pulls him down.*] Come here with me! Now, look here! What have you been doin' at the widder's? Do you hear? Answer! Say—I'll just pitch you over them rocks there, and break your infernal slim neck—[*Pulls him up, run.*] Come here! Now you tell me the truth! What a' you been doin' at the widder's? Say! [*Shakes him.*] Don't you know that if you go on in this way, you will fall over this bluff some night, and break your infernal little neck? Don't you know that? Speak! you boy—you brat. [*Shaking him.*] Well, I'll save you the trouble of slippin' off of here; yes, the boys will like it. They'll all say, they knew you'd break your neck some night. Now look here, sir! You've got just one minute to live; to say what you want to say, quick. When that flyin' cloud covers that 'ere star yonder, you die, and may God help you and me. Speak now! Come! come! speak but once before I—murder you.

BILLY: [*falling on knees, hands clasped*]. Please, Parson, may I pray? [PARSON *lets go; staggers back;* WIDOW appears at door of cabin with candle, shading eyes.]

CURTAIN

ACT III

SCENE: SANDY'S *cabin. Flowers on table, curtains on walls and at window; practical door; fire; gun; door; cradle;* WIDOW *discovered rocking cradle;* CAPT. TOMMY *and* BUNKERHILL *sewing; both greatly improved.*

BUNKERHILL: Well, if I was Billy, I'd take the hint, I would, and leave camp. He won't fight; he can't work. He's got no spirit for nothin'.

CAPT. TOMMY: Guess we'd better 'ave let Limber and Judge shake him out of his boots, that night, eh? He's no good, I guess, eh?

BUNKERHILL: Yes, but it ain't in me, and it ain't in you, Tommy, for to see two on one. The bottom dog in the fight, that captures me. But guess Limber and Judge were right when they wanted him to git.

CAPT. TOMMY: Well, what is he, anyhow? Danite or devil?

BUNKERHILL: Can't say, Capt. Tommy. Mrs. Judge. Beg Pardon, Mrs. Judge.

CAPT. TOMMY: All right, Mrs. Tim, 'pology is accepted.

BUNKERHILL: Well, as I was sayin', I don't know whether he's Danite or devil. But I do know he's no man. [WIDOW *starts.*] Why, yes, Widder, And the sooner you know it the better. Why, don't the whole camp hate and despise him? You're the only friend he's got. You and Sandy. And you're the very ones he hurts the most.

CAPT. TOMMY: Why, he's just a ruinin' of your character in this 'ere camp, Widder. Society must be respected.

BUNKERHILL: Yes Widder; we ladies can't afford to fly into the face of society.

CAPT. TOMMY: Yes Widder; only last night, the Judge he says to me, he says, says he, "Now that I'm a family man," says he, "I must have respect for society."

BUNKERHILL: O, I tell you, I wouldn't fly into the face of society for nothin' in this world. [*To* CAPT. TOMMY.] It would be the saddest day of my life when I'd have to cut the widder for the sake of society, but she must be keerful.

WIDOW: And why should all men hate poor little Billy Piper so?

BUNKERHILL [*to* CAPT. TOMMY]. Shall I tell her, Tommy?

CAPT. TOMMY: Yes, tell her. Hit's for her own good.

BUNKERHILL: Well, then, they hates him so because you loves him so.

WIDOW: Love him? Well, yes, I do, and pity him from the bottom of my heart. Oh, if we but had money, gold, plenty of gold, Sandy and me, we would leave here. We would go away silently and secretly some night, to another land, and take him away out of it all. Yes, I do love him.

CAPT. TOMMY: [*to* BUNKERHILL]. Well, that just fetches me. What will society say to that?

BUNKERHILL: The butcher's wife will cut her.

CAPT. TOMMY: The baker's wife turned all streaked and striped last night as she told me about Billy comin' here so much. I never!

BUNKERHILL: Well, *I* never.

CAPT. TOMMY: Why, the new Parson's wife won't even look this way.

BUNKERHILL: Hexcept when she goes out to take up a collection. Capt. Tommy, Mrs. Judge; beggin' pardon, Mrs. Judge.

CAPT. TOMMY: Well, if she'd a married the Parson, I tell you, ther'd been [no] hangin' round of Billy Piper at the parsonage. Why, he'd a kicked him out, and respected society, he would.

BUNKERHILL: Poor Parson. Wish he had a got her. Why, he's all broke up. He's a perfect walkin' corpse. Asks always 'bout the widder when I meets him on the trail; tender like; so tender like, Capt. Tommy, with his eyes all wet, and a lookin' to the ground.

CAPT. TOMMY: Well, now, the Parson's not a corpse, I guess. Look here, I seed him at the store, a fixin' of his irons; heelin' himself like a fightin' cock. Yes, he did look powerful pale. But the Judge says to me, last night, says he, "Mrs. Judge, I hearn the Parson's bull pup bark;" that's his pistol, you know, Bunker. And the Judge, he says to me, says he, "There's goin' to be a row." And the Judge, he says to me, says he, "I know there's goin' to be a row, because, as I came home, I heard the Dutch undertaker hammerin' away like mad." And the Judge, he says to me, says he, "Mrs. Judge, that undertaker is a good business man, and a very obligin' man; he allers looks ahead, and when he's sure there's goin' to be a row at the Forks, he takes the size of his man and makes his coffin in adwance."

Enter JUDGE *and* TIM; *dressed; polite*

JUDGE: Good mornin', madam; Mrs. Sandy, good mornin'. A very infusin' sermon last Sunday, Mrs. Sandy. Sorry you was not out. Mustn't neglect the church, Mrs. Sandy. Splendid sermon 'bout—'bout—And splendid collection. Took up a damned splendid collection. Got my handkerchief hemmed, Capt. Tommy? [*Glasses; to table, takes up baby garment;* CAPT. TOMMY *hides face.*] You don't mean to say that—that—that—God bless you, Tommy, God bless you. Oh, this glorious climate of California. Tim, let's take our wives home and go on a tear. [*Arms to ladies.*] Goodbye, Widder.

CAPT. TOMMY: Goodbye, Widder, And, say, Widder, we love you, but be careful about Billy Piper, won't you?

BUNKERHILL: Widder, that's so; we loves you. You made suthin' of us, and we'll try to don't forgit it. But there's trouble comin', Widder. Cut Billy, and tell Sandy to look out for the Parson.

JUDGE: Come, my family. Oh, this glorious climate of California. [*Exit* JUDGE, TIM, CAPT. TOMMY *and* BUNKERHILL.]

WIDOW: They are so happy. And the great baldheaded boy, the Judge, is the happiest of all. O, they have so improved the poor girls. 'Tis love that makes the world go round, my baby. And you, my little pet, smiling there, I wonder what these Sierras hold in their hearts for you? And I wonder, as I look in your rosebud face, what manner of men and women will grow here in this strong, strange land, so new from the Creator's hand? Shall there be born under the burning sun of the Sierras a race of poets? Of good and eloquent men? Or men, mighty for ill? These are your mother's thoughts, my darling, as she tries to fill her little place in life and do her duty to her baby and to her husband. [*Enter* SANDY; *gold pan, pick, shovel; pan on table; pick and shovel by door.*] Oh, Sandy, I was just thinking of you, just saying, *my husband.*

SANDY: My wife! And the baby is well?

WIDOW: Smiling, Sandy.

SANDY: So it is; smilin' like a new Spring mornin', when the sun leaps up a laughin' from its bed. Now this is happiness. This 'ere is the edge of God-land, my pretty. I think if I should go on and on a thousand years, a hundred thousand miles, my darlin', I wouldn't get nearer to the Garden of Eden, that the preacher tells about, than I am now.

WIDOW: And this little home is Paradise to you, as it is to me, Sandy?

SANDY: Paradise! It is the best part of Paradise. It is the warm south side of Paradise, my darlin'. But there, I must put up the gold in the bag, and put it under the hearthstone for baby. [*Cleaning gold.*]

WIDOW: If we only had plenty of it, Sandy.

SANDY: My pretty, is there anything you want?

WIDOW: No, Sandy. Not that I really want.

SANDY: But what is it, my pretty? Now, come, there's a cloud over your face. Don't, my darlin', don't. This is Paradise; and the new preacher tells us that never a cloud or a rude wind crossed the Garden of Eden. Yonder are our walls; the white watch towers of the Sierras, keeping eternal guard over *our* Garden of Eden here in the heart of the Sierras. Now, what is it?

WIDOW: Why, nothing at all, Sandy. Only I was thinking this morning that if we had plenty of gold, a great, great plenty, Sandy; so that you had so much, you might never have to work so hard any more, that,—that—

SANDY: Well, my pretty? O, I see. You would give it to my old pard, the Parson. That's right; that's good. He's goin' away and will need it. I'll make him take this—

WIDOW: No, no, Sandy. He is not going. He is mad, desperate; and will do you harm if you go near him. Do not speak to him. Do not go near him.

SANDY: Well, I won't then, if he's mad with me, my pretty. No sir'ee. And I'll buckle on a bull-dog, too. [*Buckles on and tapping pistol.*] Bark at him, boy. Bark at him. Bite him if he bothers us. But I say, what is this you want with gold? Take all there is. Take it, my pretty, and do as you please with it. Is it Washee Washee that wants to bring out some more of his seventy cousins? Or is it the old man that got washed through the ground sluice? No; I won't ask you; take it. For what do I want with it but to please you? What good is all the gold in the Sierras if you are not satisfied and happy?

WIDOW: No! Take it back, Sandy; you have worked too hard for this, for me to give it away to poor little—[*Shouts,* WIDOW *to window.*] Why, what can that be, Sandy?

SANDY: Is it the Parson, my pretty?

WIDOW: Why, no, it's Billy Piper! And the boys howling and running after him! Oh, Sandy!

Enter BILLY, *breathless*

BILLY: [*behind* SANDY; *enter mob*]. Sandy! Sandy! They have run me out of my cabin. They threaten to kill me.

SANDY: Run him out of his cabin?

TIM: Yes, and we'll hang him to the nearest tree!

SANDY: Now hold up, Tim! And tell me what's he done? And what all you men are runnin' after a boy like that for?

ALL: Bah!

JUDGE: A boy like that! And you a family man?

TIM: Them Danites was seen a sneakin' about his cabin only ten minutes ago. And that's why I say run him out.

JUDGE: Yes, I say git.

ALL: Yes, run him out!

CAPT. TOMMY: Too many on one, Bunker. I'm goin' in for the bottom dog, and society can just go to the devil. [*Throws off bonnet and rolls up sleeves.*]

JUDGE: Now, my Capt. Tommy, just think what society—

CAPT. TOMMY: Shut up! You bald-headed old jackass! I'm just goin' in on this fight, bet your life.

BUNKERHILL: Yes; we're all gettin' too dern'd respectable, anyhow. [*Throws hat.*]

WIDOW: Sandy, Sandy, stand by Billy.

ALL: He's a Danite!

SANDY: Stand back! I don't care what he is, or what he has done. He has come to me for protection. Why, if the meanest Digger Injin runs to another Injin for protection, won't he protect him? Well, now, this boy is as safe here as if he were my own kid.

BILLY: O, thank you, Sandy! Thank you with all my poor broken heart. But it won't be for long, Sandy. It won't be for long, and then you shall know all. She will tell you all. [*Exit.*]

SANDY: She! She will tell me all? Why this mystery? Why this—

WIDOW: Sandy, what do you mean? Can you not trust your wife?

SANDY: I *can* trust you. I *do* and I *will* to the end of my life and of yours.

JUDGE: That's right. Family man myself; trust your wife. Now you see, Sandy, the boys been askin' me to make a sort of explanation of this 'ere intrudin' into your house like this 'ere. You see, Sandy, we was makin' up a purse for —for your family. And as the boys had never seed a baby, and—and as I—as we wanted to see how they look, we had concluded to call *en masse.* But just as we was a comin' down the trail we seed two Danites skulkin' about Billy Piper's cabin. And on the spur the boys went for him. But we brought the purse all the same, and here it is. [*Purse to* TIM.]

TIM: As the pardner of—of my pardner. I—I have been appointed a committee of this 'ere delegation to deliver this 'ere dust and make the speech for the occasion. Widder—[*Breaks down.*]

JUDGE: [*pushing himself forward*]. Widder, in—in this—glorious climate of California—[*Breaks down.*]

TIM: Widder, this 'ere bag of gold what you now behold; this purse of pure bright gold, dug from out the—the Sierras. This purse of gold, Widder, is—is—is—yourn.

WIDOW: Mine, mine? All mine to do what I will with it?

TIM: Yourn, Widder, all yourn. Yourn to git up and git, out of this hole in the ground, to go back to the States and live like a Christian, as you are, and git away from all that's bad here in this hole in the ground, like a wild beast in a carawan.

ALL: Bully for Tim!

JUDGE: And now let the boys see your family, Sandy.

SANDY: Here, Washee Washee, give *it* to Mrs. Sandy and set up the bottles for the boys. [WASHEE, *who has been feeding baby by fire, with bottle and spoon, gives baby, bottles, etc.* WIDOW *sits.*]

ALL: Oh! Oh! what is that? The little cuss!

TIM: Little thing to make sich a big row, eh, Sandy?

WASHEE: He judgee babee, baldee headee. He no Sandee.

TIM: You speak to the boys, Judge; that effort of mine exhausted me.

[JUDGE, *attitude for speech; to table, drinks, and again striking attitude; drinks again.*]

JUDGE: Gentlemen of—of the committee! Fellow citizens, this, what you now behold is—is —[*Stops and* WIDOW *whispers in ear.*] This which you now behold before you is—is an—an infant. The first white born baby citizen ever born in these Sierras. The first, but not the —the—[CAPT. TOMMY *stops him.*] Feller citizens, this little infant sleeping here in its mother's arms, with the mighty snow-peaks of the Sierras about us; this innocent little sleepin' infant, which has been born to us here, gentlemen, shows us that—well, in fact, shows us—shows us what can be done in this glorious climate of California. [*All shout and file past, and look at baby.*]

TIM: [*going*]. Well, come, boys, I've got a family myself and must be lookin' after my mine. [*Exit. Re-enter.*] Sandy! Sandy! Heel yourself! The Parson! The Parson with his bull pups—shootin' irons.

WIDOW: Oh, Sandy! Sandy!

SANDY [*hand on pistol*]. Stand back, boys, and let him come. Quiet, quiet, my girl.

PARSON *enters, hand behind; down, and walks quickly towards* SANDY; SANDY *raises pistol;* PARSON, *after emotion:*

PARSON: I've been a waitin' to see you, Sandy, a waitin' a long time.

SANDY: Stop!

PARSON: Sandy, I'm goin' away from here. I can't stand it any longer. Your cabin here will be too small now, so I want you to promise me to take care of the parsonage till I come back.

SANDY: The parsonage?

PARSON: Yes, that's what the boys call my cabin. The parsonage. You'll move in there, at once. It's full of good things for winter. You'll take my cabin, and all that's there in it, I say you'll take it at once. Promise me that. [*Handing key.*] There's the key. Now say you will.

SANDY: Yes, I will.

PARSON: It was your luck, Sandy, to git her. Good-bye, old pard. Widder—I—what! You shake hands with me, the poor, old, played out Parson, after I broke my word with you! God bless you! Widder! Yes, Yes! God bless you both! [*Exit.*]

SANDY: Poor, honest old Parson. Thar's many a worse man than he in mighty high places, boys.

TIM [*at door looking up*]. Yes, Sandy, and he is climbing for a high place now.

SANDY: What! Gone already! And it's dark and snowin'.

TIM: Started up the steep mountain right here. A climbin' and climbin' right straight up the mountain; as if he was a climbin' for the mornin' star.

SANDY: And may he reach it, and find rest at last, Tim.

ALL: And find rest at last.

TIM: But Sandy, you must move into the parsonage. Yes, you must. You see, you promised it. And then it takes a pretty big cabin to hold a pretty small baby. [*All laugh and gather around table and drink.*]

JUDGE: Well, one more boys, to—to—

TIM: To *it*. But come, boys, it's gettin' dark. [*All drink and exit.*]

WIDOW: My baby! What a name, Sandy. It!

SANDY: Poor, poor old Parson. It's a hard world on some of us, Widder.

WIDOW: It *is* hard on some, those who cannot work and are all the time persecuted and misunderstood. Now, Sandy, dear, do you know who I am going to give that gold to which the miners gave me just now? Come, guess. Can't you guess, Sandy, dear?

SANDY: Why no, Widder. I can't guess. To who?

WIDOW: Why, to Billy Piper.

SANDY [*starting*]. To Billy Piper! No, no, not to him. You know not what you say. You know not what you ask of me to bear. You know not what you are asking me to bear, my wife. That boy? Why, now that he is once out of my cabin I will kill him as I would a rattlesnake wherever I can find him.

Enter TIM, *running and breathless*

TIM: Sandy! Sandy! The Danites! Your gun, Sandy! The two Danites have just left Billy

Piper's cabin, their dark lanterns in their hands and are coming this way through the chapparal. Quick, your gun! Billy's in with them.

SANDY [*reaching gun*]. Billy Piper in with them! Danite or devil, this shall be the end of him.

WIDOW: Sandy, you will not, you *shall* not harm him. You shall not leave this cabin till you promise you will not harm him. See, Sandy, see, on my knees I beg of you. Never before on my knees to aught but my maker, Sandy, yet you see me here now on my knees to you.

SANDY: You take from me my life and my honor.

WIDOW: Sandy, Sandy! Do not be so blind. It is to save your soul.

SANDY: What!

WIDOW: It is to save your soul from the stain of innocent blood. Will you not believe her whom you promised to trust to the end of your life, and of hers?

SANDY: Yes, Yes! I *can,* and I *do* trust you. I will not harm him.

WIDOW: O brave, generous Sandy. But I ask more still. Promise me that you will protect him. Yes, protect him as you would protect me with this strong right arm, Sandy.

SANDY: Why, Widder, I—

WIDOW: O Sandy, promise me, promise me. I feel that something dark and dreadful is about to happen. I see him lying dead in his innocent blood with no one to pity, to pray for, or to understand. Oh, promise me, Sandy, that whatever happens, you will be his friend and defender to the end.

SANDY: I promise.

WIDOW: Swear it.

SANDY: I swear it. [*Exit with* TIM.]

WIDOW: The Danites here, and on his track! Oh, this is too dreadful to believe. [*noises.*] What is that? It may be poor Billy now trying to find his way to my door, in the dark and cold. I will go find him, help him, save him. [*Snatches up candle.*] Lie still, my baby. [*Exit hastily.*]

Enter BILLY, *cold and snow*

BILLY: It is a fit night for the bloody deeds of the Danites. But I must not stay here. Where can she be! I must see her, and then fly, fly, fly! [*Sees cradle.*] Oh she's not far off. [*Kneels by cradle.*]

Enter WIDOW. *Very dark stage*

WIDOW: Why, how dark it has grown! The wind has blown out my candle, too. I left some matches here somewhere. [*Feels about, comes to cradle and finds* BILLY.] Billy! You here! But Sandy must not see you here now. Quick! hide here; I hear some one. [*Hides* BILLY *behind curtain, and down stage. Door opens softly.*]

Danites enter and come stealthily down stage

HICKMAN: I saw her enter at that door, not a minute since. She *must* be here. [*Sees* WIDOW.] Ah, there! [HICKMAN *conceals lantern; advances on* WIDOW *from behind with knife and strikes her; then child.* WIDOW *screams and dies as crowd rushes in. Danites exit unseen.* SANDY *and* CAPT. TOMMY *bend over* WIDOW.]

CAPT. TOMMY: She is dead! Murdered in cold blood!

SANDY: Dead! My wife dead! Oh, has the sun gone down forever? Dead? Dead?

TIM: Yes! [*Pointing to* BILLY.] And there is her murderer.

JUDGE: Hang him to the cabin loft.

ALL: Hang him! Hang him! Hang him!

SANDY: No, you *shall not* hang him. [*Springs between as they attempt to seize* BILLY.] I promised that poor, poor, dead woman there to defend this boy, and I'll *do* it, or die right here.

CURTAIN

ACT IV

SCENE: *Old mining camp. Moss-grown cabin. Set tree. Sunrise on the Sierras. Lapse of three years.*

Enter LIMBER TIM, *with* JUDGE, *older and better dressed*

TIM: Warn't down to the saloon last night and don't know the news, eh?

JUDGE: No, no. Since I've come to be a family man, I'm sort of exclusive; got to set an example for my family. But what's this news?

TIM: The Parson's back.

JUDGE: What! Him that loved the widder so? No! Impossible! Why, he went away North to Frazer River; got smashed up in a mine there, I hear; washed through a flume and his limbs all broke up till he had as many joints as a sea crab. O, no, he can't never get back here.

TIM: But he *is* back. And the sorriest wreck, too, that ever you seed, I reckon. Ought to have seed him and Sandy meet. Cried like babies, both on 'em. Come back here to be buried up on the hill there, he says.

JUDGE: Well, well, well! The Parson wasn't bad, Tim; he was about the best of the old boys of forty-nine, 'ceptin' always Sandy. And Sandy, after the murder of the widder and his kid—well, he's all broke up, body and mind. Spec' he's 'bout as near gone up the flume as the Parson is. But I must get round and see how Billy Piper is this mornin'. The school master, what's boardin' 'round, came home by his cabin here, and didn't see him at all last night; but Tim, he seed a black cat a sittin' in the door a washin' of its face. It's a bad sign when you see a black cat, Capt. Tommy, my wife, Missus Judge, says. Guess that boy's pretty sick. [*Going.*]

TIM [*aside*]. That *boy.* 'Pears to me that varmint won't never grow to be a man. And he twists *his* wife and my wife right around his cussed little fingers, and makes 'em look after him. Well, Judge can look after him, cussed if I will. [*To* JUDGE.] O, I say, Judge; there was two others came to camp last night, too.

JUDGE: Two others? Who?

TIM: Don't know 'zactly. Quartz speculators, they say: Mormon elders, I say.

JUDGE: Mormon elders! Bet a dog skin they're Danites. But so long; must look after Billy and get back to my family. [*Going, meets* HICKMAN *and* CARTER *disguised. They shake hands and converse.*]

TIM [*Solus*]. Hello! Here's them quartz speculators now, and Judge shakin' hands and jist a talkin'. 'Spec he's tryin' to impress them with the glorious climate of California. Guess I'll go back down to the "howlin' wilderness." Judge will be powerful dry time *he* gets there, if he keeps on talkin' like that. [*Exit.*]

HICKMAN [*coming down stage*]. And so you are a family man and your wife was one of the first families of the Sierras?

JUDGE: Family man; yes, sir; and my wife is one of the very first families. The very first. That is, she and Mrs. Limber Tim. Mr. Limber Tim's member of the Legislature now, wife, family name Bunkerhill, of the Bunkerhills of Boston. Yes, my wife and his wife, too, trace family clean back to Boston, sir. Yes, proud to say I'm a family man, sir.

HICKMAN: But this widow the miners spoke of as one of the first settlers? She who came as a sort of missionary. She here yet?

JUDGE: Dead. Buried up yonder, sir, with her baby. First baby born in the Sierras, sir.

HICKMAN: Dead, eh? Fever? Natural death, or accident?

JUDGE: No, sir! Neither natural death nor accident. No, sir! But murder! Why, that was the pitifullest thing; and it was the meanest murder that ever happened, I reckon. The boys at first thought it might be Sandy; for he was angry because of Billy Piper, that night. And then the boys thought it might be Billy, because;—well, because they didn't like him, never did, and never will, I guess. But when they came to examine Sandy, there was no blood on the knife he had in his belt. And, as to Billy, well, he had no knife at all.

CARTER: Why, we heard about this last night.

JUDGE: Dare say; dare say; may be the miners talked about it last night. They don't forget it. You bet.

CARTER: Mother and child found murdered?

HICKMAN: And no trace of the murderers was ever found?

JUDGE: None, It's the queerest case that ever was, I reckon. For whatever beast or devil could murder a little baby like that, asleep and helpless? Why! Well, sir, since I've come to be a family man, sir—if I should ever find a man that murdered a baby—sir—as judge of this 'ere camp, I'd hang him first and try him afterwards.

HICKMAN: Yes, yes. That's all right. But this boy Billy; he here still?

JUDGE: There's his cabin. Same old cabin been in for years; the same one the Danites killed three fellers in. Pretty sick, too, I guess. Wife told me to drop in, see how he is. You'll excuse me. Must go in and see the boy and get back to my family. [*Exit into cabin.*]

HICKMAN [*to* CARTER]. That *boy* is Nancy Williams!

CARTER: Well, and if it is, she's dying, they say. Can't you wait till nature does the work for you?

HICKMAN: Though that boy should, by nature, die tomorrow, our duty is to slay today.

CARTER: You seem to thirst for blood. A wife and babe dead at our hands will cry for revenge yet. Make no more mistakes like that. If this should not be she—

HICKMAN: It *is* she! There shall be no second mistake. Look here. [*Takes out small Testament.*] Yesterday, I saw this boy's face, as he sat reading up yonder, by his mine; our eyes met as I stood over him. His lips trembled with fear, and his eyes fell. He remembered the time, on the Plains, years ago, when we were commissioned by the church to slay the last of the Williams'. I say that boy is the last of the family. I know it.

CARTER: Then, I say, you must do the murder yourself, if it is to be done on such slender evidence as your word.

HICKMAN: It is not to be done on slender evidence. Look here! Frightened, he let this fall and slunk away.

CARTER: A little, old Testament. Well?

HICKMAN: The boy was reading this as I appeared and spoke to him.

CARTER: Well, he might read something worse than a Testament.

HICKMAN: But, look here! On the fly leaf. Read this dim and faded dedication. "To NANCY WILLIAMS, FROM HER AFFECTIONATE MOTHER, NANCY WILLIAMS, CARTHAGE, MISSOURI, 1850."

CARTER: Too true! Too true! He *must* die. But not here. Give him a chance to fly. It is not as safe as it was when we were here before. The Vigilantes!

HICKMAN: Ha! ha! I have thought of all that. The Vigilantes shall be for us. They will be made to accuse him of the widow's death. Did the Judge not say he is suspected?

CARTER: Yes, yes. Let them then accuse and hang him. But see, the door opens. He is coming from the cabin.

HICKMAN: I'll back till that man is gone, and you go stir up the Vigilantes. Tell them he murdered the widow and her child. I'll console him with this. [*Lifts Testament. Exit* CARTER. *Enter* BILLY *from cabin, supported by* JUDGE, *who seats him by the door.* HICKMAN *up stage, behind tree.*]

JUDGE: Now don't break up here, just as the birds begin to sing, and the leaves come out. I'll send my family 'round to cheer you.

BILLY: You are so kind. Do send her; and the children, too. And please, won't you let them stay? Let them stay all day. Yes, and all night. O, all the time, always.

JUDGE: Why, now, don't tremble like that. I'll—I'll send my family 'round. Why, it's the sweetest day that ever was in this glorious climate of California. [*Aside.*] O, I can't bear to see a body cry. I'll go and send 'round my family. [*Going.*]

BILLY: And you won't be long? You won't leave me long? You will not?

JUDGE: Why, no, Billy. I'll send my family right 'round.

BILLY: And Sandy. You will tell Sandy to come, will you not? I have kept away from him, and he from me, all this time; ever since she, and—and the baby died. But, now you will bring him. For I feel that the sands of my life are almost run. My feet touch the dark waters of death. I hear the ocean of Eternity before me.

JUDGE [*takes out handkerchief and going*]. Confound it! This bright sun on the snow hurts my eyes.

HICKMAN: [*coming from behind tree, and speaking to* JUDGE *aside*]. Ah, going? I've been thinking, Judge, about that murder of the widow. A very remarkable case. And do you know, I have a theory? Yes, It's that boy. No, don't start. What's the matter with him now? Conscience! Conscience stricken! Of course it's very sad. The idea is not mine. I got it from the miners last night. If the boy wasn't sick, they'd *hang* him now. As for Sandy, poor man, he is certain the boy did it. My friend has gone down to lay his opinion before the camp. For my part, I am very sorry for the boy.

JUDGE: Well, now, 'tween you and me, I think—[*Aside.*] But if my family, Capt. Tommy, was to hear me—O Lord! [*To* HICKMAN.] But I'll go and send 'round my family.

HICKMAN: Yes. Meantime, while you are gone, I will offer him consolation. [*Exit* JUDGE. HICKMAN *approaches* BILLY *from behind, and taps shoulder.*] Beg pardon, but is this yours? A little Testament I picked up where you sat reading yesterday. Is it yours?

BILLY: Yes, yes. Oh, thank you. It is mine; given me by my mother—

HICKMAN: Yes. I thought it was yours; I saw your name on the fly leaf. No mistake about it, I suppose? That is your name!

BILLY [*looks up and sees face; starts*]. No, no, no! Not my name. No, no, no!

HICKMAN: Well, I think it is yours, and you had better keep it; and read it, too. You will not live long. [*Aside and going.*] Condemned out of your own mouth! Now to make them believe that this is the murderer, and the last seed of this cursed tree is uprooted. [*Exit.*]

BILLY: [*rising, and wildly*]. At last! My time has come at last! Over her grave they have reached me at last; and it no longer lifts between me and a dreadful death at these men's hands. Fly! Fly! But where? And how? [*Staggers and leans against cabin for support.*] I have no strength to fly! I have no heart or will. All, all, ends here! I must die here! Now! That knife! That knife that entered her heart, that pierced the baby's breast, dripping with its mother's blood! Oh! [*Falls at cabin door.*]

Enter PARSON, *dragging a leg, old and broken up.* BILLY *starts up and about to enter cabin.*

BILLY: They come! They come! O, will not Sandy help me now?

PARSON: Billy Piper, no. Don't—don't go.

BILLY: Why, who are you? And what do you want here?

PARSON: Have a few years then made such a change in me?

BILLY: The Parson!

PARSON: Yes, the Parson. Come back to the Forks to die.

BILLY: To die?

PARSON: Yes. To die, and lay my bones by the side of hers, up yonder on the hill.

BILLY: And you loved her so?

PARSON [*half falls to seat on log*]. Loved her so? Can't you understand, that when a man like me loves, he loves but once, and but one thing in all this world?

BILLY: O, yes, I understand. For I, too, loved her, Parson.

PARSON: [*Starting up, and crosses*]. Yes, you loved her, too. But how? To put her to shame; to make her the mockery and shame of the camp; to hide away in her cabin like a spotted house-snake; to creep there like a reptile warmed to life by her hearth-stone in winter, and then sting her to death after she warmed you into life.

BILLY: And do you think I ever harmed her?

PARSON: Ever harmed her? Ever harmed her? She is dead and beyond the reach of word or deed. A few more days and I shall meet her. But here, standing here on the edge of the dark river, I tell you, you murdered her.

BILLY: I? Great heavens! What do you mean!

PARSON: I mean what they say down there, now, this morning. Yes, they are saying it now. No, don't start, or run away. I am powerless to harm or to help now. But I, when I heard that, that you murdered her that night, I hobbled up here; I wanted this revenge before they came. I wanted to see you, to tell you that while I gave her all I had, and climbed that mountain in the storm, and went forth to begin life over, a broken man, you stayed here, a Danite, to take, first, her good name, and then her life, her baby's life, and Sandy's life, and now my life, too.

BILLY [*starts, staggers forward, lifts hand with Testament*]. Parson, hear me! And look in my face! Do you not see the dark shadow of the Angel's wings that are to waft my soul away? Oh, I, too, am sadly broken. And today, tonight, maybe this very hour, from somewhere, a hand will strike to lay me low in death. We stand beside the dark river together.

PARSON: Why, boy, you tremble. Your hand is cold and helpless. And you are not guilty?

BILLY: Guilty? Do you see this? The last, the only gift of my poor murdered mother, who died by the Danites' hands.

PARSON: Why, you! You not a Danite? Then swear by the book; swear by the book that you never did her harm by word or deed.

BILLY [*falling on knees and lifting book*]. By the holy book and by my mother's memory, I swear!

PARSON: Why, what is this? The boy tells the truth! The boy is honest and true. Some devilish work is against him, and I will stand by him. I'll stand by you, boy. You are true as the stars in heaven. I know it—I know it. I'll meet them. I'll face and fight them all, all as I did—[*Half falls.*] no, no, not as I did. I'm on the down grade and can't reach the brake. But stand up, boy, and be strong. You are young yet, and the world is all before you. And while I live, you'll find a friend in me. Yes, in the old Parson, to the last drop of blood. Yes, yes. I'll die right here by your side when they come. Don't you be skeered, Billy. When they come, I'll come, too, and be your friend to the last bone and muscle in the old Parson's body. [*Leads* BILLY *to seat on log by cabin, and exit.*]

BILLY: A friend at last! O, then there *is* hope. I may at last escape from this and again be strong and well. O, thank Heaven for one friend at least. But I am so afraid!

Enter HICKMAN *and* CARTER

HICKMAN: You shall see and be satisfied. The Vigilantes are gathering and will be here. We have only to say that he has confessed the murder to us, and the work is done. [*Crosses, taps* BILLY *on shoulder.*] I have come back to console you. We will talk over the holy little book, which your mother gave you before she died. You see you will not live long. [*Half exposes knife.*]

BILLY: No, no, no! Not with the knife! No! Oh, no, no. See! I am but a woman, a poor weak girl.

HICKMAN: [*to* CARTER]. *You* see. [*To* BILLY.] Yes, we have come to offer you the consolation of religion.

BILLY: My God! My God! Why is this cup given me to drink?

CARTER: Here! Some one comes! [*Pulls* HICKMAN *aside.*] Quick. [*Both exit.*]

Enter SANDY

SANDY: Why, Billy? Don't you know me? It's been a long time, Billy; but there's my hand. What! Got the fever, Billy?

BILLY: O, Sandy, Sandy! I'm so glad you have come at last, for my time to die has come.

SANDY: No, no. Now you look here. I'm goin' to

take care of you after this, whether the camp likes it or not. Yes, I will; and just 'cause they make it too hard on you. I'll come to your cabin and stay right here.

BILLY: No, Sandy. But let the school children come, and not be frightened and run away. Let some one stay with me all the time. O, please, all the time, Sandy.

SANDY: I will stay with you all the time. Yes, I will. Why not? What else am I fit for now?

BILLY: No, Sandy, no. But when it's all, all over, Sandy, I want to be laid by her side, Sandy. She was so good to me; so unselfish; pure as the lily's inmost leaf; white and high as yonder snowy mountains in their crown of clouds. Yes, by her side. Promise me that, Sandy; by her side.

SANDY [*aside*]. By her side! [*Aloud.*] Well, yes. Yes, Billy, by her side.

BILLY: And, Sandy, you will set up a little granite stone, and you will place on that stone the name that you find in this book.

SANDY: The name I find in that book?

BILLY: Promise me. Trust me and promise me. It is a little thing I ask and the last, the last I shall ever ask of any one. A little stone by your own hand, and the name you find here, Sandy. Promise! O, promise me this last, last request. No, don't open the book now; don't look at the book now; but promise me.

SANDY: I promise.

BILLY: O, thank you; thank you. Why, what is that! O, Sandy, I tremble at every sound. It may be that it is death calling me now. Help me! Help!

Enter CAPT. TOMMY *and* BUNKERHILL, *running, and out of breath*

CAPT. TOMMY: Sandy! Sandy! [*Twisting up hair.*] Now, where's that bald-headed old mule of mine?

SANDY: Why, what's up in the Forks, now?

BUNKERHILL: What's up? Why, them strangers have called out the Vigilantes. They say that this boy, Billy Piper, has confessed he killed her; yes, her and the baby.

SANDY: Then *I'll* kill him. [*About to strike.*]

CAPT. TOMMY: [*catching him*]. You're a fool! Come here! That boy is—well, that boy is—is —well, if you don't stand up and fight for him —O, a man never has no sense, nohow. [BUNKERHILL *and she roll up sleeves.*]

BUNKERHILL [*talking off*]. If you want to pitch in, just pitch into us.

SANDY: Well, if he's squar'.

CAPT. TOMMY: Squar'! In there, Billy. [*Pushes him into cabin and closes door.*] You just win this fight and swing them Danites! Yes, Danites! Nobody dares say it but me and Bunkerhill. I tell you they are Danites. Shoo, here they come!

Enter JUDGE, *puffing and blowing, and moping face. Shouts heard.* CAPT. TOMMY *catches him and spins him round.*

JUDGE: A hot mornin' for the glorious climate of—

CAPT. TOMMY: Now you fight on the right side, you old simpleton, or it'll be hotter. And I'll teach you suthin' about the glorious climate of California you never heard of before.

BUNKERHILL: And there's Tim a leadin' of the Vigilantes! [*Enter* TIM.] Here! [*Wheels him in place by* SANDY *and* JUDGE.] There's your place.

Enter mob of miners, led by HICKMAN *and* CARTER

TIM: But Billy's got to go, Bunker.

MINERS: Yes, run him out!

PARSON [*entering and drawing pistol*]. What's that? You run out Billy Piper? Poor, sickly little Billy, that never gets any bigger and never has a beard? Look here! When you run him out, you do it right here over my bones. [*Pistol at face of* HICKMAN.]

HICKMAN: But he is a murderer. He has confessed to us both that it was he who murdered that poor wife and babe. He is a murderer and must die.

PARSON: That voice! That face! Here! Didn't I tell you we should meet again? And didn't I tell you I should know you when we met? [*Tears off beard disguise from* HICKMAN'S *face.*] These are the men I saw at her cabin. These are the men that murdered her. Danites! Danites! Danites! Boys, what shall be their sentence?

Enter WASHEE WASHEE, *brandishing razor*

JUDGE: [*draws long pistol*]. Well, as I am the only Judge in this part of this glorious climate of California, I pronounce them guilty and sentence them to die with their boots on.

ALL: Hang them! Hang them! [HICKMAN *and* CARTER *are seized and hurried off.*]

CAPT. TOMMY: Well, I guess the Judge will look after them. And Bunker, we better look after Billy. Sandy, you stay here; we may need you. Billy's pretty sick. But he won't be half so sick, when they're dancin' in the air.

SANDY: I'll stop right here, and if I can help poor Billy, say so.

BUNKERHILL: You're right. Billy's the best friend

you ever had. [*Exit with* CAPT. TOMMY *into cabin. Enter* TIM *and* JUDGE, *followed by miners.*]

TIM: Well, they're on their way, Sandy.

SANDY: To San Francisco?

JUDGE: To Kingdom Come!

SANDY: Good, good! Served 'em right. True, it don't bring her and the baby back to us boys: but we can be kind to Billy now. Poor little Billy. We've been mighty hard on him.

TIM: Well, I feel kind o'cheap about it, too. Let's go in and cheer him up.

JUDGE: And get him out in this glorious—[*About to lead into cabin. Is met by* CAPT. TOMMY.]

CAPT. TOMMY: Stop! Only women must enter that cabin now. For it is a woman who has lived there all these years. Billy Piper is no more.

ALL: What, dead?

BUNKERHILL [*leading out* BILLY *in woman's dress*]. Yes, Billy Piper is dead. But Nancy Williams lives!

ALL: Nancy Williams!

PARSON: Shake hands! Shake hands with the old Parson. [*Takes hand, shakes and kisses it.*] And Sandy, old pard, I know where this little hand, like a fluttered bird, wants to fly to. [*Gives hand to* SANDY.]

SANDY: And you give me your hand, to—to—to —keep always?

BILLY: To keep as the stars keep place in heaven, Sandy.

MINERS [*forward; hats in hand*]. We all begs your pardon, Miss.

SANDY: Yes, we all do. We don't mean bad; but it's a rough country, and we're rough, and we've not been good to you. But there is an old and beautiful story in the Bible—[*To audience.*] —You've all heard it before you learned to read, I reckon. It is of that other Eden. There the living God met man face to face, communed with him every day in his own form. And yet that man fell. Well, now, we don't claim to be better than they were in Eden, even in the heart of the Sierras.

CURTAIN

American Immigrants and Vaudeville

Developing from variety shows staged in town halls and honky-tonks, vaudeville (*voix de ville,* songs of city streets) evolved into America's standard playhouse diversion. The first theater solely for this purpose was opened in New York during the late 1840's. By the twentieth century, traveling circuits were well established, successfully challenging the popular minstrel shows, those stage and showboat entertainments put on by musicians and comics in blackface —Bones, Interlocutor, and all.

Until the late 1930's vaudeville was, as theater historian Douglas Gilbert says, "America in motley, the national relaxation." Dedicated troupers followed "The Death Trail" and "The Aching Heart" (small-time theaters in towns with substandard accommodations) in the hope that their act, musical, comic, or acrobatic, would eventually bring them to their Mecca, the Palace Theater in New York. But by the early 1940's, variety stage shows linked to the vaudeville circuit had virtually disappeared. First the radio and then the TV variety hours became the closest approximations of the style embodied in vaudeville.

Vaudeville humor relied on the slapstick, sledge-hammer approach to laughter. Crude comedy, ethnic caricature, and racial slurs, taboo in our own time, delighted audiences who were convulsed by mirth as stereotype after stereotype somersaulted onto the stage. From the vantage point of the inherited, vaudeville dramatized the attitudes and prejudices of the American man-in-the-street of our recent past. Insensitive, thoughtless, cruel, the humor was reminiscent of the barbaric "fun" that had characterized life on the frontier.

While America's reputation as the Melting Pot increased, comedians who made fun of immigrants increased too. Minority humor aimed at the Irishman ("Mick"), German ("Dutch"), Jew ("Sheeny") and Italian ("Dago") was exceeded only by the slanderous caricatures of the Negro ("Coon"). Know-nothing audiences who were absolutely convinced that an iota of foreign or black blood signified intellectual, spiritual, and moral disinheritance were enchanted by cartoon types from the "funny papers" and distorted grotesques of the street, as well as by language barbarisms, vulgarisms, and malapropisms, but especially by mental stupidity or deviousness on the part of stage stereotypes.

The Irishman: *Now if they'd let me be, I'd set Ireland free;*
On the railroad you'd never pay fare.
I'd have the United States under my thumb,
And sleep in the President's chair. *

The German: *Ve go around de sdreeds almosd every day,*
Und set de beoble vild mit de music dot ve blay;
"Good-by, Sourheart," und "Hime Sweed Hime" ve blay so fine,
But ve always do our best ven ve blay "Die Wacht am Rhein."†

The Jew: *Oh, my name is Solomon Moses I'm a bully Sheeny man,*
I always treat my customers the very best what I can.
I keep a clothing store 'way down on Baxter Street,
Where you can get your clothing now I sell so awful cheap.‡

The Negro: *O, de ham bone am good, de bacon am sweet,*
'Possum meat am very, very fine;
But gib me, Oh, gib me, oh how I wish you would,
Dat watermillion hangin' on de vine.§

---

*Douglas Gilbert, *American Vaudeville, Its Life & Times* (New York, 1940), p. 68.
†Mark Sullivan, Our Times: The United States, 1900–1925, III (New York, 1931), p. 388.
‡Gilbert, p. 288.
§Sullivan, p. 375.

The ultimate blinding of perspective came with the clownish makeup on these "types"; it accentuated the shabby, the decadent, and the tawdry.

The following typical vaudeville skits demonstrate some of the false basic assumptions which, during the golden era of these variety shows, masqueraded happily as humor. The Jew admires the man who "invented" interest; the Italian is a menial laborer; the Irishman is quick-tempered and dull, always spoiling for a fight; the Negro schoolboy entertains the class with a buck-and-wing. Much of the humor, too, grows out of the heavy dialect. Audiences, satisfied that they knew the proper pronunciations of all mispronounced words and that they knew the correct usage of misused words, easily could distinguish between their own inheritance and the "disinheritance" of those ignoramuses cavorting over the stage.

The School Act

SCENE: *Schoolroom with desks and seats. Teacher's desk stage Left. Blackboard on walls with funny pictures of teacher on it, tick-tack-toe, etc. etc.*

Cast:

PERCY HAROLD, *Sissy*
JESSE JAMES, *Tough*
TONY, *Italian*
GLADYS UMPAH, *Lisping Girl*
SKINNY JONES, *Fat Boy*
ABEY MALONEY GOLDSTEIN, *Jewish Boy*
RASTUS JOHNSON, *Colored Boy*

AT RISE: TEACHER, *who is a Dutchman with chin piece, Prince Albert coat, small brown derby hat, enters with books under his arm. Music plays "Schooldays" until he picks up large bell on his desk and rings it. Then music fades out as* PERCY HAROLD *enters.*

PERCY: [*Singing*] La La La La . . .

TEACHER: That must be one of the girls.

PERCY: Oh, you go on.

TEACHER: I'm the new teacher. Vot's the meaning of dis la la la la business?

PERCY: It's none of your business.

TEACHER: Oh, ist dot so? I am going to make it some of my business. Where ist the rest of my pimples?

PERCY: Downstairs playing a game of pinochle, teacher.

TEACHER: Pigsnuckles, eh? What a fine bunch dis must be. I'll bring the rest of 'em here. [*Rings bell. Pupils rush in like a football team, grab teacher's hat, and throw it around as if it was a football.* TEACHER *gets all excited chasing them etc.*] Say, what do you think dis ist, a feetball game?

TOUGH: Hey mug, I'm in.

TEACHER: I'm glad oft dot. Where voss you?

TOUGH: Downstairs playin a game of ping-pong.

TEACHER: Stick out your hand. [TOUGH *does so and* TEACHER *hits him over the head with umbrella*] Zit down. The pimples will please be seated. We will open up the class wit singing the national antem. [*Everybody sings "How Dry I Am"*] Dot voss nice. Now I will open the school by calling the roll.

PERCY: Oh, teacher.

TEACHER: Vos ist the madder wit you, you sick?

PERCY: We had them this morning for breakfast.

TEACHER: Vot did you have for breakfast?

PERCY: Nice Vienna Rolls.

TEACHER: Who said anything about Vienna Rolls? I mean rolls the names of the pimples, vot ist here in school. The first name ist Percy Harold.

PERCY: Here teacher.

TEACHER: Tony Baccicolupe.

TONY: Here I am, boss.

TEACHER: Gladys Umpah.

GLADYS: [*Lisping*] I'm here, teacher.

TEACHER: Skinny Jones.

SKINNY: Can't you see I'm here?

TEACHER: Rastus Johnson.

RASTUS: Here too. Here too, teacher.

TEACHER: Abey Maloney Goldstein.

ABEY: I'm in the place.

TEACHER: What's the idea of Maloney in the middle of your name?

ABEY: I use it for protection.

TEACHER: Jesse James.

TOUGH: Couldn't come today.

TEACHER: Don't say you couldn't come when you are sitting here. And face about; vot you think, I can talk to the front of your face behind your back? Vell, I am glad all the pimples are present. Ve vill start with the first lesson this morning in geography.

EVERYBODY: Oh.

TEACHER: Cut it oud. Oh, ist not in the lessons. Vot ist an island?

TONY: An island is a pimple on the ocean.

TEACHER: No, it's no pimple on the ocean. Stick out your hand. [*Hits* TONY *over head with umbrella*]

PERCY: I know, teacher.

TEACHER: You're so smart, what ist an island?

PERCY: An island is a keg of beer surrounded by [*local*] policemen.

TEACHER: Hold out your hand. [*Hits him on head with umbrella*] Say, tough mug, name me some of the principal oceans.

TOUGH: Atlantic and Pacific.

TEACHER: Dem's not oceans, dem's a tea company.

TOUGH: Oh, you mean oceans. Alright, Montreal, New Hampshire, and Sigel and Coopers.[1]

TEACHER: Dem's not oceans, dem's mountains.

TONY: You mean oceans? I got a notion in my head.

TEACHER: [*Hitting* TONY *on head with umbrella*] Now you got water on the brain. Just for dot, Tony, you gotta sing a song. [TONY *sings a song. After song by* TONY] Dot vos very nice, Tony. Now Skinny, vot ist a cow?

SKINNY: My mother.

TEACHER: Vot its dot foolishness? Vot makes you say your mama's a cow?

SKINNY: I heard my daddy say to her this morning, "You're as big as a cow."

TEACHER: A cow ist an animal with four legs, one on each corner. Now Gladys, can you tell me the use of cowhide?

GLADYS: Sure I can. It keeps the cow together.

TEACHER: Now pimples, can anyone tell me the greatest invention in the world?

SKINNY: The telephone.

GLADYS: The automobile.

TONY: The radio.

PERCY: The airplane.

TEACHER: You are right, poys and girls. They were great inventions.

ABEY: Say teacher, the fellow dot invented interest was no slouch.

TEACHER: Just for that ve will have a dance by Rastus Johnson. [JOHNSON *does a dance. After dance*] Dot voss very goot. Now for the spellink lesson.

EVERYBODY: I-N-K.

TEACHER: I didn't say ink. I don't mean ink vots here in the ink well, I mean spell-ink vot ist here in the book. Jesse James, how do you spell giraffe?

TOUGH: G-I-R-A-F-E.

TEACHER: In the dictionary they spell it with two *fs*.

TOUGH: Well, you ast me how did *I* spell it.

TEACHER: Put your hand out. [*Hits him on head with umbrella*] Tony, make for the teacher a sentence mit the word delight on the inside.

TONY: The wind blew so hard it blew out de light.

TEACHER: Yes, and I'll blow out your light. Cut out dese nonesense. Ah, dere's a goot vord—nonsense. Skinny, give me an example of nonsense.

SKINNY: An elephant hanging over a cliff with his tail tied to a daisy.

TEACHER: Just for that you will haf to sing a song. [SKINNY *sings. After song*] Dot voss very goot. Vot ist the great American desert?

EVERYBODY: Prunes.

TEACHER: Abey, can you tell me where Pittsburgh ist?

ABEY: They are playing in Chicago.

TEACHER: Percy, when was Rome built?

PERCY: At night.

TEACHER: Who told you dot?

PERCY: You said Rome wasn't built in a day.

TEACHER: Put out your hand. [*Hits him on head with umbrella. Sees* RASTUS *raising his hand*] Vot do you want, Rastus?

RASTUS: I want to leave de room.

TEACHER: No. You stay here and fill up the ink wells. Gladys, vot ist the opposite of misery?

GLADYS: Happiness.

---

[1]Sigel and Cooper's was a well-known New York City department store of the early 1900's. The imagined joke is that the ignorance of the teacher is reflected in his not recognizing the obvious stupidity of the answer.

TEACHER: Dot's right. Now Abey, tell me vot ist the opposite of woe?

ABEY: Giddap. [*Puts head out to get hit with umbrella*]

TEACHER: Has anybody else got any questions?

TOUGH: Yeh, what time is it?

TEACHER: I'll show you vot is it. [*Goes after him; pupils all go after teacher—free-for-all fight*] Vell, if you don't let me be the teacher I may as vell be one of the gang. School ist over, boys and girls . . . Now let's sing and dance. [*Finish with everybody singing and dancing as Curtain descends.*]

The Double Dutch Act

The Team consists of a STRAIGHT MAN *and a* COMEDIAN. *The* STRAIGHT MAN *should be tall and wear a large-checkered suit, with the coat short and with large pearl buttons. He wears a small brown derby hat, large collar, loud tie, big squeaky tan shoes. The* COMEDIAN *has a "belly pad" which makes him look short and real fat. He wears a wide-striped suit, flat-brown derby, large shoes. They both wear chin pieces.*

Open with a popular song, of which they only sing the Chorus; on last few notes they strike bum harmony as the orchestra plays a discord.

BOTH: [*Shaking hands*] By golly, dot vos alright.

S.M.: Hey Miller, I hear your uncle vot ain't dead yet left you a lot of money.

COMIC: [*Showing big roll of bills*] Sure, here 'tis.

S.M.: Vot are you going to do mit it?

COMIC: I don't know. I dink I'll sell it to somebody.

S.M.: Don't do dot. I got a idea. Let's open a restaurant mit it.

COMIC: Vot? I put in all dot money and vot do you did?

S.M.: Vy, don't you sees it? I vill let you be the vaiter and I vill be the boss. Dot vay you get all the money and the tips, vot comes in first, den all you have to do ist to hand it to me.

COMIC: Py Gollies, dot listens easy. How much costs it to open this dump?

S.M.: Vell, how much have you got?

COMIC: All I got ist $60,000.

S.M.: Dot's hardly enough but I think it will do to staht mit.

COMIC: Oh. Ve could staht someding mit it, by golly.

S.M.: Now, do you dink you can be a schvell vaiter?

COMIC: They couldn't make 'em any schveller.

S.M.: Goot. Ve vill now open the restaurant.

COMIC: Goot. Here ist where ve eat. I luv to eat. Excuse Phillip till he moves in. [*Pushes* S.M. *aside*]

S.M.: Don't push. Now dis ist a schvell café und you are a handsome vaiter. Now, ven a schvell lady comes in, vot do you do?

COMIC: Vy, I rush oud and get a schvell vaiter.

S.M.: No, no. *You* are a schvell vaiter. Now I vill be a schvell lady. I am coming to eat somedings. Get ready.

COMIC: Business ist now open. [STRAIGHT *enters like a woman would*] Oh, vot a rotten shape.

S.M.: [*As if talking to porter outside the door*] John, gif my horse a bucket of champagne und some strawberry shortcake.

COMIC: Oh, vot a schvell jackass dot ist. [*Use "horse" if they don't allow you to use "jackass"*]

S.M.: Und John, take the carriage to the insane asylum.

COMIC: Insane asylum?

S.M.: Yes, von of the wheels ist off its nut.

COMIC: Oh, he ist getting loose house.

S.M.: Vaiter, Vaiter.

COMIC: Yes sir, yes sir.

S.M.: Not yes sir to me, I'm a lady.

COMIC: Oh, git oud, you ain't no lady, you're de boss.

S.M.: No, no, I ain't the boss no more.

COMIC: Oh, you quits.

S.M.: No, I didn't quits. I am de boss.

COMIC: Yes sir.

S.M.: I vos de boss, but now de boss ain't und de boss vot ist not, ist now, vot am I?

COMIC: I dink you're a cockeyed liar. [*Use "piece of cheese" if they don't allow "cockeyed."*] Vell, vot do you vont to eat?

S.M.: I don't know. Give me the menu.

COMIC: De vot?

S.M.: De menu.
COMIC: I know you mean me. Vot do you vont?
S.M.: Menu.
COMIC: Mean me?
S.M.: Ven I say menu I don't mean you.
COMIC: Ach, vot do you mean?
S.M.: Menu. [*Pointing to menu*]
COMIC: Ach, de book.
S.M.: [*Looking over menu*] Hav you got any brains?
COMIC: Yes mam.
S.M.: Stop dot. Vot do you think I am, a fool?
COMIC: Yes mam.
S.M.: I am not a yes mam.
COMIC: Ain't you a lady?
S.M.: Yes mam. My Gott, you got me saying it. Now listen. I am going to let you be the schvell lady und I vill be the vaiter und I vill show you how to vait. Can you be a schvell lady?
COMIC: Yes mam.
S.M.: Can't you say anyding but yes mam?
COMIC: Yes mam.
S.M.: Den say it.
COMIC: No mam.
S.M.: [*All excited*] I vill choke all de yes mams and no mams out of you. Now come into the cafe and act like a lady.
COMIC: I'll order some liver and milk.
S.M.: Goot evening, madame.
COMIC: Ist dis a restaurant?
S.M.: [*Disgusted*] Ist dis a restaurant? No, ist a sawmill. Vot did you come in for, a haircut? Vy certainly it ist a restaurant. Go oud und come in like a lady.
COMIC: Oh, like a lady?
S.M.: Goot evening, madame.
COMIC: Vy hello, boss.
S.M.: No. No. You are a schvell lady. I am not your boss, don't you understand?
COMIC: Yes mam.
S.M.: You musn't say yes mam to a vaiter. You must treat me like a dog.
COMIC: Oh I knock his eyes in.
S.M.: Goot evening, madame.
COMIC: Shut up, dog.
S.M.: Vot do you vont?
COMIC: None of your business.
S.M.: Vot are you going to have?
COMIC: I would like some fishes' eyebrows. How ist your eyebrows today?
S.M.: Pretty goot, how's yours?
COMIC: Fine. Ist your kidneys alright too. Giv me one of your kidneys and a couple of pigs' feets.
S.M.: Vill you have them enfinanceree or encasserole?
COMIC: In castor oil?
S.M.: No. Not in castor oil. I said encasserole.
COMIC: [*Bewildered*] Hey, Phillip, vot should I say?
S.M.: Say it's immaterial.
COMIC: Vot kind of material?
S.M.: Don't you know vot immaterial means? Den I vill expire to you. Now, for inkstands, you pick up a handful of mud mit de juice oozing out.
COMIC: Juicy mud?
S.M.: Yeh.
COMIC: I couldn't do dot—I'm a lady.
S.M.: You do dot only for inkstands. You pick up the mud mit your left hand, now ven you got dot handful of mud, close up your hand like dis [*Demonstrates*] und you squeeze it. Now, whether de mud comes oud of dese fingers or dose fingers it ist immaterial.
COMIC: Now I sees it.
S.M.: Now you know vot immaterial ist?
COMIC: Sure.
S.M.: Vot is it, immaterial?
COMIC: A lady mit a handful of mud.
S.M.: [*Chokes little fellow*] Ach, you're too dumb to be a vaiter. I'll make an opera singer oud of you.

[*Cue for music. Both sing parody on opera—and exit*]

The Double Wop Act

Both enter as music plays "My Mariutch She Take a Steamboat." STRAIGHT MAN *walks a bit ahead of the* COMEDIAN. *They are both dressed in misfit suits. Comedian has long mustache and bandanna handkerchief around neck. Straight man wears celluloid collar, red tie, big watch chain, yellow shoes that squeak, and is sort of sporty in an Italian way.*

STRAIGHT: Come ona—wassa madder—come ona. . . .

COMIC: Waita one minoots. I no can walka fast. My uncle isa sick.

STRAIGHT: Whatsa your uncle gotta to do wit you no walka fast?

COMIC: I tella you my uncle isa sick.

STRAIGHT: Your uncle isa sick?

COMIC: [*A little angrily*] Yeh, my uncle. [*Points to ankle*]

STRAIGHT: Oh, you meana ankles. Say, whatsa your name?

COMIC: My namesa Tom Giariba Idi Columbo Scabootcha Castella Mascrici, but day calla me Tom for short.

STRAIGHT: Well, Tom is no high classa. I will calla you Tommas.

COMIC: Say, my namesa Tom and you calls me Tommas?

STRAIGHT: Sure. Dots ahigh classa for Tom.

COMIC: I gotta brudder his names Jack. What you calla him, Jackass.

STRAIGHT: Say, howsa your big brud Sylvest?

COMIC: Hesa nunga fella so good.

STRAIGHT: Wassa matter wid him?

COMIC: You know Sylvest hesa gotta big ship tattoed on hisa chest.

STRAIGHT: Yeh, I know.

COMIC: Well, de odera days a bigga man comes up to my brudda Sylvest and givea him onea punch on his chest and sank the ship.

STRAIGHT: Say, how manna kids you gotta 'em now?

COMIC: I gotta twelve bambinos.

STRAIGHT: All together?

COMIC: No, one at a time.

STRAIGHT: How many girls?

COMIC: Fivea girls.

STRAIGHT: And how many boys?

COMIC: Fivea boys.

STRAIGHT: Dats only ten kids.

COMIC: Fivea boys and fivea girls and two other kids. Mixem up.

STRAIGHT: You workin now?

COMIC: Sure Mike. I'm a politich in an auto factory.

STRAIGHT: What, you mean you're a politician in an auto factory?

COMIC: Sure, I'ma assembly man.

STRAIGHT: I gotta a good job for you.

COMIC: What doin?

STRAIGHT: Manicurin boulevards.

COMIC: How mucha you pay?

STRAIGHT: Twenty-two dollars a week.

COMIC: Twenty-two dollars a week?

STRAIGHT: Yeh—two twos.

COMIC: Datsa nice. Whatsa the hours?

STRAIGHT: You start at eight in the morning and stop at six ata night.

COMIC: Datsa too mucha work.

STRAIGHT: Okay. I makea it easier for you. You start at six anda finish at eight.

COMIC: Datsa nice man. I go now and tella my friend at the city hole.

STRAIGHT: Whatsa your friendsa name?

COMIC: He livesa at the city hole, I nunga remember hisa name. Hisa gotta name somethin like a horse.

STRAIGHT: You don't mean the mayor?

COMIC: Sure, datsa him, the Mare. He's a fine fellow. He invite me to a polar bear.

STRAIGHT: You got invitaish to be a polar bear? You nunga can be a polar bear.

COMIC: Sure, I gotta be a polar bear.

STRAIGHT: You know whata polar bear is?

COMIC: No, but I gotta be one.

STRAIGHT: Listen—polar bear sits on ice and eatsa fish.

COMIC: Nunga folla me now.

STRAIGHT: I'ma no foolin you. Wasa matter?

COMIC: You know my frienda Guiseppi? He died and hisa family wanna me to be a polar bear. I no sit on ice and eat fish for nobody.

STRAIGHT: [*Laughingly*] You mean the pallbearer.

COMIC: Sure.

STRAIGHT: You are astronga man. You can be pallbearer.

COMIC: I'ma strong but my fadder he'sa bigga strong man.

STRAIGHT: Yeh?

COMIC: My fadder he takes two billiard balls, squeeza 'em together and makes *talcum powder.*

STRAIGHT: Youa stronga man, you wannt be a fighter?

COMIC: Sure Mike. Makea lotta money fighting.
STRAIGHT: First you gotta loin how to block a punch.
COMIC: Whata you mean block de punch?
STRAIGHT: I mean you gotta learn how to stop a blow.
COMIC: Datsa ease. When he hit me it stop himself.
STRAIGHT: Say, howsa your wife?
COMIC: My wifea and me fight alla the time like United States and Mexico.
STRAIGHT: What do you mean you and your wife fight like United States and Mexico?
COMIC: We fight on account de boarder.
STRAIGHT: Where isa your wife now?
COMIC: My wifesa in the country with pendicitus.
STRAIGHT: I tolda you she likes Greeks.
COMIC: And I nunga feel so good either, on account of my kid niece.
STRAIGHT: You mean your sister's gal?
COMIC: Whosa talk about my sister's gal? I say my kid niece, my kid niece. [*Points to kidneys*]
STRAIGHT: Oh, you mean your kidneys.
COMIC: Sure. I say kid niece.
STRAIGHT: Where you liva now?
COMIC: I live on not-feeling-good street.
STRAIGHT: What you mean not-feeling-good street?
COMIC: I liva on sick street.
STRAIGHT: Your littlea girl Maria—how's she?
COMIC: She'sa bigga gal now. She'sa gonna geta de pluma.
STRAIGHT: She'sa gonna for de pluma? Wasa matter, your pipes broke?
COMIC: Whatta you talka bout my pipes? I say my gal Maria she'sa gonna getta de pluma.
STRAIGHT: Well if she's gonna getta de pluma somethin musta be wrong witha de pipes.
COMIC: [*Angrily*] Listen. My little girl Maria goesa to school and she's agonna getta de pluma.
STRAIGHT: Oh, you mean a diploma.
COMIC: Sure. Can't I understanda what I speak? Well, so long, I'ma gonna get a drink.
STRAIGHT: Ain't you gonna treat me?
COMIC: No, I'ma gonna drinka myself.
STRAIGHT: You selfish.
COMIC: What?
STRAIGHT: I say you selfish.
COMIC: You crazy in the head. I no sell fish, I buy junk.
STRAIGHT: You drive me coconuts. What happened on the boat the other day?
COMIC: Nunga hear? I was on de bigga boat and somethin hit it and madea bigga hole in de front of de boat on the bottom, an the water she com arushin in.
STRAIGHT: What did you do?
COMIC: I'ma smarta guy. I go down to the bottom of de boat and makea another big hole in de backa of de boat.
STRAIGHT: Whata you do that for?
COMIC: When de water comea in from the front, it *goes out in de back.*

Finish with parody of "Dorando."[1]

The Straight and the Jew

STRAIGHT MAN *enters and sings a song. After the song, Shots are heard off stage and* JEW COMIC [*with hat over ears, short beard, and misfit suit*] *comes running out.*

S.M.: Mr. Cohen, what are you running for?
COHEN: I'm trying to keep two fellows from fighting.
S.M.: Who are the fellows?
COHEN: An Irishman and me. [*After laugh is over*] Say, why don't you pay me for that suit you got on?
S.M.: Well really, Mr. Cohen, I would pay you, only I haven't the money.
COHEN: [*Mocking* STRAIGHT MAN] Yeh, I'd be a rich man, only I ain't got the money. Can't you pay me something on the bill?
S.M.: How much do you want?
COHEN: I'd like enough to hire a lawyer to sue you for the balance.

---

[1]*dorare* (Ital.): lively; hence, a lively "Italian exit" song.

S.M.: You're a pretty smart fellow. Are you good at spelling?

COHEN: You betcha my life I'm a good speller.

S.M.: I'll bet you that you can't spell needle.

COHEN: I'll bet you my life I can spell it.

S.M.: I won't bet you that.

COHEN: I'll bet you my whole family's life.

S.M.: No, I won't bet you that, but I'll tell you what I will do, I'll bet you ten dollars that you can't spell needle.

COHEN: No siree. When it comes to betting money, that's another matter.

S.M.: I'll try you anyway. How do you spell needle?

COHEN: N-I-E-D-L-E.

S.M.: You're wrong.

COHEN: I'm right.

S.M.: We will leave that to the leader. He looks like an intelligent person. [*Goes over to* LEADER *of the orchestra*] You heard the argument, George. Who is right?

LEADER: Why, you are, of course.

S.M.: [*To* COHEN] You see? [*To* LEADER] Do you smoke?

LEADER: Why, of course.

S.M.: [*Takes cigar out of pocket*] Well, here's a cigar. Try spelling it again, Mr. Cohen.

COHEN: [*Looks at* LEADER *through the business of* S.M. *giving* LEADER *cigar, etc. Is disgusted with* LEADER *when he says that* S.M. *is right, after tries in vain with motions behind* S.M.'S *back to make the* LEADER *say that he is right*] Alright, here I go again. N-E-E-D-D-L. [*Triumphantly*] Now *that's* right.

S.M.: [*Laughing heartily*] Why no, that's worse than your first attempt.

COHEN: No, that's spelt right.

S.M.: We'll ask George. [*Goes to* LEADER *again*] Who was right that time, George?

GEORGE: [*Paying no attention to* COHEN, *who is again trying to make motions behind* S.M.'S *back to make* GEORGE *say he is right*] Why, you are right.

S.M.: Have another cigar. [*Gives* LEADER *cigar*] Well, Cohen, I will give you one more chance.

COHEN: Needle. Is that the word?

S.M.: Yes.

COHEN: Why didn't you say so? N-I-D-L-E.

S.M.: Wrong again.

COHEN: I'm right.

S.M.: We will ask . . .

COHEN: I will ask him this time. Mr. Musiker, who is right this time?

LEADER: Why, you are, Mr. Cohen.

COHEN: [*Very happy, making faces at* S.M.] See? [*To* LEADER] Do you smoke?

LEADER: Why, yes.

COHEN: [*Hand in pocket as if to take out cigar*] Here's a match.

S.M.: [*Laughs*] Mr. Cohen, you are a card. Say, Cohen, I was reading the papers this morning and I see that [*local town*] has three saloons to one policeman.

COHEN: That gives you three guesses as to where the policeman is.

S.M.: By the way, where is your boy?

COHEN: You mean my boy Abie? He is an eye doctor.

S.M.: [*Surprised*] Why I thought he was a chiropodist.

COHEN: He *was* a chiropodist. You see, he began at the foot and worked himself up.

S.M.: Are you still happily married?

COHEN: Yeh, I don't live with my wife.

S.M.: You know, I've been married since I saw you last. I married a sharpshooter from the Buffalo Bill Show.

COHEN: A shipshopper, eh?

S.M.: Yes, sir. My wife's a very good shot. Why, she can hit a silver dollar at a hundred yards.

COHEN: Dot's nothing. My wife goes through my pockets and never misses a dime. You know, I got a great idea how to get along with my wife.

S.M.: I'd like to hear it; it may come in handy sometime.

COHEN: When I come home I throw things around the house, I put cigar ashes on the floor.

S.M.: Why, what's the idea of that?

COHEN: I get my wife so mad she won't speak to me. Then we get along fine.

S.M.: A woman that doesn't speak, why that's a miracle. Of course, you know what a miracle is?

COHEN: Sure I know what a miracle is.

S.M.: Well, tell, me what is a miracle?

COHEN: Well, if you see a bull in the field . . ..

S.M.: Yes, if you see a bull in the field?

COHEN: Dot ain't no miracle.

S.M.: Of course not.

COHEN: If you see a thistle in a field, dot ain't no miracle.

S.M.: Of course a thistle in a field is no miracle.

COHEN: And if you hear a lark singing, dot ain't no miracle.

S.M.: Of course hearing a lark sing is no miracle.

COHEN: But if you see a bull sitting on a thistle singing like a lark, dot's *a miracle.*

S.M.: [*Laughs*] You're a card, Cohen. Will you have dinner at my house tonight?

COHEN: Say, that was a nice dinner we had at your house last week. The salmon was wonderful.

S.M.: Why, that wasn't salmon, that was *ham.*

COHEN: [*Makes funny face*] Who asked you?

S.M.: Say, are you still playing the horses?

COHEN: I played a horse yesterday twenty to one.

S.M.: And did he win?

COHEN: He didn't come in until a quarter past six.

S.M.: By the way, how is your uncle, the one that was so sick?

COHEN: My sick uncle? You know, the Board of Health wouldn't let me bury him?

S.M.: [*Indignantly*] Why I never heard of such a thing. Why wouldn't they let you bury him?

COHEN: Because he ain't dead yet.

S.M.: [*Laughs*] You're a card, Cohen.

COHEN: I'm a whole deck. I'm going to get a drink.

S.M.: What's the idea?

COHEN: Then I'll be a *full* deck.

S.M.: You're incorrigible.

COHEN: Why bring religion into this? I'm going now.

S.M.: Where are you going?

COHEN: I'm going to get my wife a nice dog. He must be able to swim.

S.M.: Why must he be able to swim?

COHEN: You see, my wife holds him on her lap and she has water on the knee.

S.M.: [*Laughs*] I think we better sing.

STRAIGHT MAN *sings a popular song. Then* COHEN *sings a parody on it. Then they both exit.*

Appalachia

"Appalachia" denotes in our time a socioeconomic segment of the American disinherited whose political "invisibility" has never, unfortunately, protected its people from prejudicial caricature antagonistic to an understanding of their plight. The "Dogpatch syndrome" of Li'l Abner cartooning, the popularly styled barefoot grotesqueries of Tobacco Road, and tawdry television stereotypes imported "down from the hills" tend to hide the actual lives of sharecropper and ridgerunner quietly passing their repetitious days along the rural backroads of America. The humor and exoticism of feuding moonshiners in slanted gray shacks exist only in the minds of the thoughtless. In reality, the Appalachian disinherited are victims of poverty from the moment of birth, cut off from the material goods and status symbols that we associate with the American standard of living. Existing in chronically depressed areas, these simple folk are virtually imprisoned by their poverty and isolation.

In 1960 at the Appalachian Governors Conference on Unemployment, the term "Appalachia" was officially applied to the impoverished mountain and backwoods areas of Alabama, Georgia, Kentucky, Maryland, North Carolina, Pennsylvania, South Carolina, Tennessee, Virginia, and West Virginia. Health, housing, and education in these geographical pockets were evaluated as grossly substandard. Roads linking communities with the outside world were poor. Unemployment was high and the land, for either farming or mining, was pretty thoroughly worked out. Isolated in poverty, barely existing, their water frequently contaminated by sewage as well as by sulfuric acid draining from abandoned mines, the "hillbillies" have lived under this yoke for years. Unseen, except on an occasional TV special, their life continues in this sad tempo.

Paul and Erma Green

(1894–) (1897–)

From the Carolina Playmakers, a pioneer theatrical group founded by Frederick Henry Koch in 1918, emerged a significant American dramatist, Paul Green, who in collaboration with his sister Erma wrote *Fixin's.* The purpose of the Playmakers, whose headquarters were at the University of North Carolina, was to encourage the writing and staging of plays based on the common experiences and interests of life in Appalachia. They went on tour to present their folk dramas to the culturally and economically deprived of the area. Erma and Paul Green were born on a farm near Lillington, North Carolina, and knew firsthand the rural people they represented so faithfully in their drama. Erma became prominent actress with the troup, and Paul, a playwright.

In 1927 Paul Green was awarded the Pulitzer Prize for *In Abraham's Bosom,* a play representing the tragic frustration of the aspirations of a black man. During the 1930's when the proletarian* stage thrived on dramas of controversy and rebellion, Green contributed *Hymn to the Rising Sun,* a portrayal of Southern chain gang brutality delivered with a shocking, ironic twist. (It is the Fourth of July. According to the daily custom, prisoners, black and white, are beaten. While one man is whipped viciously, another, less fortunate, is tortured until he dies "of natural causes." To celebrate the national holiday, the Captain delivers a patriotic oration. The prisoners must then sing *America,* "sweet land of liberty." Curtain.) Indignation and outrage are passions Green knew how to inflame. It was he who, with Richard Wright, made the stage adaptation of Wright's novel *Native Son.*

Fixin's is a poignant examination of the oppressive poverty of tenant farmer life, contrasting its dull, lethargic quality with the hopes of a young woman who vaguely and restlessly feels that something available in the large outside world is eluding her. Her dreams, the "purty fixin's" she delights in, bring no response from a husband who has been beaten down by Nature and made a slave to the soil. The earth, cheating him of youth and strength, and depriving his wife of even the simplest pleasures of life, relentlessly grinds them into mute submission. Appalachia dwellers viewing *Fixin's* were thunderstruck, so Frederick Koch observed, at the tragic delineation of their lives.

Even in 1924 when the Green and Green collaboration was first presented, Appalachia had come to symbolize defeat and resignation. America's attitude toward the farmer had drastically changed from her beginnings, when Thomas Jefferson had characterized the American farmer as "the most independent [and] the most virtuous" of citizens. In 1924, though, Henry Louis Mencken, viciously attacking "Bible Belt" fundamentalist religion, had arrogantly described the farmer as a "prehensile moron," addicted to inescapable rural ignorance.

Fundamentalism (staunchly championed by William Jennings Bryan) was still ably withstanding the challenges of modernism. The notorious Scopes Trial in

*The radical stage, "Agitprop" (agitation + propaganda), was interested in portraying the "Class Struggle," a frequent theme being the oppression of the proletariat by the "iron heel" of Capitalism. See Morgan Y. Himelstein, *Drama Was a Weapon* (Rutgers University Press, 1963).

Dayton, Tennessee, to determine whether man was descended from the monkey, as Evolutionists ("evil-lutionists") now asserted, was one year off. Tenant farmers' preoccupation with old-time religion, the past, family roots, and geographic loyalty helped them erect a barrier against what many sharecroppers regarded as the blandishments of Satan. This barrier worked effectively at keeping the modern world beyond the horizon. As research by contemporary rural sociologists has shown, Appalachia still remains a static pocket of resistance to change.

Every once in a while, though, a restless spirit tries to rise above the ploughshare and cabin: thus, the vital materials of *Fixin's,* a drama of poor-white disinherited.

Fixin's

The Tragedy of a Tenant Farm Woman

Characters

ED ROBINSON, *a young tenant farmer.*
LILLY ROBINSON, *his wife.*
JIM COOPER, *his landlord.*

SCENE: *The kitchen of the Robinson farmhouse in Eastern North Carolina.*

TIME: *The present. An Autumn evening, about half-past six o'clock.*

Scene: *The kitchen of the Robinson home, the bare cold room of a tenant farmer. In the rear wall is a door leading to the outside, a small window to the right of it. A door on the left leads into the only other room of the house, both a bedroom and sitting room. At the right is a cooking stove, and in the center of the room is an eating-table made of rough timbers and covered with a checkered oil-cloth. Between the table and the wall is an old-fashioned bench. There is a chair near the table and another near the stove.*

The scene opens with ED ROBINSON *preparing supper at the stove. He is a stockily-built man of twenty-five or thirty, with a plain, honest face, but a face that shows strength and will and maybe a violent passion when aroused. His movements with the supper are awkward and detached, showing that he is unused to the job of cooking and, too, that he is thinking of something besides his present task. He is dressed in overalls, a rough jacket, and heavy shoes. As he is cutting the meat, steps are heard on the porch. He stops and listens. The door is pushed slowly open, and* JIM COOPER, *a broad-shouldered pushing, genial man, past middle-age, comes in. He is blunt and outspoken.*

COOPER: Heigho, Ed, havin' it all by yerself, uh?

ED [*Turning from the stove*]: Why, how you, Mr. Cooper? Come in and have a che'r. [*He pushes a chair towards* COOPER *who sits at the left of the table.*]

COOPER [*Looking around the room*]: Thanks. Sort o' lonesome here by yerself, you know, ain't it, Ed? [*Hurriedly.*] Course some folks likes it that-a-way . . . but . . .

ED: Yeh, 'tain't no picnic mebbe. . . . [*He lapses into gloomy silence, stares at his knife-handle a moment, then begins putting the meat quickly into the pan, stirring around as if anxious to forget something that is worrying the life out of him.*]

COOPER: Well, I thought I'd come over and have a settlement about the cotton before you got off some'r's or went to sleep. [*Watching him closely.*] But you ain't no night-hawk fer traveling, are you?—Not lately anyhow.

ED: Nope, I stick clost about. [*He taps on the pan with the knife-blade.*]

COOPER: You shore do, and that's the God's truth. But just because she's gone off making a fool of herself, you needn't. [ED *straightens up and stands listening, threatening.*] Never mind—'scuse me, Ed—you know I will talk. My daddy was a great hand for it. . . . [*Pulling out a pencil and paper and leaning over on the table.*] Cotton was bringing thirty cents to-day —got thirty for Lilly's bale.

ED [*With a show of interest*]: Quair it run up so —boll weevil, I reckon, 's e't it all up from Texas to I don't know where.

COOPER: That's it, I 'spect. Fine on us though,

fer it ain't hurt us none as yet. [*He lays down his pencil and pulls a roll of money from his pocket.* ED *sits on the opposite side of the table.*] Your bale weighed 505 pounds, the seed $20, all told $171.50. Your half comes to $85.75. [*He counts out the money and lays it on the table.*] There it is, Ed, a right smart pile. If you turn this money over to her, I reckon she'll cut a splu'ge.

ED: Thank y', Mr. Jim. I'll put it away soon's I finish my cooking. How much I owe you fer the hauling?

COOPER: Nothing, nothing. Glad to do it fer you; we'll strike off even fer that day you holp me pull stumps. [*He gets up, as if to leave.*]

ED: All right, sir. Suits me, if it does you.

COOPER [*Making as if to go, but plainly in no hurry*]: You got . . . got any certain thing you want to sink this money in, Ed?

ED: Not exactly. . . . I had been thinkin'—least-ways Lilly's been thinkin'—you see 'tain't my money, it's hers.

COOPER: I know what's she's been thinking. [*He sits back down decisively.*] Look-a-here, Ed, seems like a good time fer you an' me to talk business.

ED [*Uncertainly*]: Yes, sir. . . .

COOPER: I'm plumb good an' ready to sell you that land. The $400 you lent me is due about now. Course, I can pay it back. [*Edging his chair nearer.*] But I got a note over in Lillington to pay off next Sat'd'y for $500. Tell you what I'll do. Pay me $80 down now and I'll credit you with a plain five-hundred on the land.

ED [*Hurrying to turn his meat*]: I dunno just exactly. . . . That's Lilly's money. . . .

COOPER: Lilly's nothing. You use' ter talk right sharp about that trade, and last spring fer a while—But you ain't 'peared to take much stock in it lately.

ED [*Fingering the money*]: Well, this here's the first time cotton's been bringing anything since Lilly an' me got married. And I'd sorter been thinkin' . . .

COOPER [*Filling up a clay pipe and lighting it*]: Thinking what?

ED: Oh, nothin', mebbe. I had sorter begun to git out'n the notion of the land business.

COOPER [*Dropping the burning match with a smothered exclamation of pain*]: Who put you out'n the notion, Ed?

ED [*Sitting down again*]: Nobody . . . that is . . . well, I just got out'n the notion, that's all.

COOPER: I know who done it. Ed, I remember, same as yesterday, the day you and Lilly drove off to git married. What had you been talking about before that,—buying you a place of yer own, that's what. You talked the same way the year after—even went so far early this fall as to lend me the four-hundred with the land matter in mind. And now you're all changed. What's the matter?

ED: Land costs a whole sight more'n it use' ter.

COOPER: Yes, but cotton's bringin' a terrible high price and going higher. You know, Ed, I want you to have that 25 acres. Drat it, I can git rid of it to-morrow fer cash money, but—well, you've been good to wait on us all—sickness, cold, hot or whatsoever—and Mary says herself that if that piece o' ground is ever sold, she wants it sold to you two.

ED: That's shore good of her—of you too. She's tuk a sight with my Lilly.

COOPER: Well—business is business and feelin's is feelin's—but if you want that place you can—

ED: Mr. Jim, Lilly . . . she ain't—

COOPER [*Stamping the floor*]: Of course it's Lilly behind it all—knowed it from the fu'st—everybody knows it! [ED *looks at the floor, then goes to his cooking. His complete silence makes* COOPER *uneasy and he speaks in a more placating tone.*] What does Lilly say, Ed?

ED: Mr. Jim, you remember that time at Tom Atkins's saw mill when I forgot myself and nearly come to—to—scrushing in his head—

COOPER: Lord, Ed, I didn't mean to rile you.

ED [*Quietly*]: That's all right, I hadn't ought to git mad either. And they ain't no harm in my telling you that Lilly ain't tuck with farming no more. In place of land, she wants to buy fixin's and sich, and purty up the house.

COOPER: Wants to buy furniture, and graffyfoans, and lace curtains, and the like, uh?

ED: Somethin' like that, I reckon, if you say so.

COOPER: And all that there talk o' hern's caused you to change yer mind?

ED: The main reason, I 'spect, Mr. Cooper.

COOPER: Well, Ed, I'm goin' ter talk to you plain, man to man, and I don't want you to git stirred up nuther.

ED: What's . . . what you want to tell me?

COOPER: Well—Lilly ain't treating you right, and that's the p'int-blank truth.

ED [*Going to him*]: What you mean?

COOPER: Now don't git on a high horse. I'm goin' ter say out my say.

ED [*Stubbornly*]: All right, sir.

COOPER: Lilly wants to move to town, don't she?

ED: Well, she's plumb wore out with choppin'

cotton and pickin' till her fingers drip blood. [*Bursting out.*] And who can blame her?

COOPER: I can, fer one. Women ain't made jest to be dolls and kept in a show-case, and Lilly Robinson ain't never hurt herself at work, now has she?

ED: I said I'd let you tell what you wanted to.

COOPER: And I will too. She's been over in Dunn now for nigh three weeks, ain't she?

ED [*Controlling himself*]: She was needin' a change. It's been hard . . . hard on her since . . . since little Charlie died.

COOPER [*Kindly*]: Yes, yes. [*Sternly.*] But not as big a change as she's gittin' from what I hear.

ED: Do, how?

COOPER: Oh, I know you've promised to give her that money to buy flim-flams fer herself.—Yes, you have.—And what's she doing? . . . Lloyd Mangum told me today that she's over there in Dunn riding around with a traveling man, some sort o' agent, one of these guys, I reckon, that squirts cologne on hisself and wears two or three rings at a time.

ED: Lloyd Mangum is a damn liar, and I'll wring his damn neck.

COOPER: What 'n the thunder you want to git het up so sudden fer? I ain't talkin' up fer Lloyd, or fer you, or anybody. But he's never been known to have a loose tongue, now has he?

ED [*Muttering to himself*]: God a'mighty, she can't be doing that! [*He bows his head, staring at the floor.*]

COOPER: It's fer your own good I'm telling you this. You know well enough Lilly ought to be here helping you git out your cotton—right in the busiest time o' the year too—and she gallivantin' 'round! And Lloyd Mangum ain't the only one that's been talkin' and seein' the truth, with you as blind as a bat. Mary got a letter to-day from Marthy Sikes over in Dunn, and she spoke about Lilly's ridin' around and goin' to movin' pictur' shows with that fellar. It's true, Ed, true as gospel that she ain't a-doing you right.

ED [*Starting up*]: I'm going to Dunn to-night!

COOPER: Your meat's burning up, Ed. [*Going to the stove.*] And you ain't going to no Dunn to-night.

ED [*Sitting down, rolling the dish-cloth in his hands:*] It's a passel o' lies somebody's startin'. It shore God is!

COOPER: Lies or no lies, that's not the question. It's this. Ed—Are you goin' ter let her with her honey-sugar ways keep you from being a man? She studies herself.—Oh, yes she does, and you needn't deny it.—If I was you I'd put on the britches and wear 'em awhile. [*He walks angrily about the table.*] Good Lord! do you reckon I'd let a bright-haired looking glass hugger run over me like that? And, Ed Robinson, if you've got any guts in you, you'll not. [*He takes up the burning meat and sets it off the stove.*]

ED: Oh, I hear what you say about my wife, Mr. Jim Cooper. And I don't want to hear any more of it.

COOPER [*Shouting*]: Don't want to hear any more of it? Well, you will all right!

ED [*Standing up, holding the knife in his hand*]: That I won't. Stop talking about my wife like that. [*He dashes the knife on the table, and stands closing and unclosing his enormous hands.*]

COOPER [*Laughing bitterly*]: Stop talking? You order me to stop talking. Well, my boy, if I wanted to I could tell you a streak, before I finish. Why in this world you want to go around with your eyes shut and seein' nothin', never suspicionin' what everybody has talked over and over a thousand times, I can't see!

ED [*Slumping down in his chair, and sitting with bowed head*]: All right, say what you think then.

COOPER [*Coming out of his flood of anger, and speaking more kindly*]: I ain't doing you right, I reckon, Ed. But I couldn't wait no longer. I just had to say what I felt fer onct. [*They are both silent a moment. Then* COOPER *goes towards the door.*] I got to be goin' now. Mebbe I done wrong talkin' to you so, and beggin' you to buy that piece of ground. [*Turning back.*] But, Ed, think of the *bargain* I'm offerin' you. Why this evening at the gin, Joe Langdon offered me $3000 fer that piece. And . . . I tell you what I'll do—I'll let you have it fer $2500, and five years to pay fer it. Count what you lent me and the eighty, as five hundred. [ED *sits hunched over.*] Shore 'nough, Ed, don't take on so about that little piece o' news.

ED: It ain't no little piece o' news. [*Throwing his hands out before him helplessly.*] Why, Mr. Jim, she's so . . . so . . . well, it's all lies, that's what.

COOPER: Well, poke up yer chin, and don't git down—don't you now. Everything will come out fer the best. It always does. [COOPER *stands with his hands on the door-knob. They are both silent.*] Well? . . .

ED [*Turning, and pushing the money across the table:*] Here it is, Mr. Jim. Mr. Jim.

COOPER [*Coming again back into the room. He sits down at the table and picks up the money. Then he takes out his pencil and writes on a piece of paper*]: Here's a receipt for the full five-hundred, Ed. Come over in the morning and we'll fix up all the papers. [ED *mechanically takes the receipt from him.*]

ED: Much obliged to you.

COOPER [*Blustering*]: Keep your thanks, boy. I'm more tickled over it than you seem to be. I feel like a man who has done a bit of missionary work, or something. Say, come on and walk home with me now and take supper at our house. Mary'll be plumb glad to have you in. Reckon she thinks old Bloody-bones's got me, or something. Come on.

ED: I cain't. I'll git my supper here . . . don't mind. [COOPER *turns around awkwardly, then moves to the door.*]

COOPER: Well, good-by. Take care o' yerself.

ED: Thank y'. . . . You do the same. [COOPER *goes out.* ED *sits staring before him. The receipt drops unnoticed to the floor. He gets up, looks ruefully at the burnt meat, and punches up the fire in the stove. He leans back against the table, his hands shoved deep into his pockets, and begins whistling "Oh, Sally dear. . . ." He sees the receipt on the floor, picks it up, crams it into his pocket, sits back heavily against the table, knocking over a vase of dried flowers. After looking intently at the vase for a moment, he takes it up and, without any show of emotion, hurls it into the corner, smashing it into bits. He punches the fire up once more, and stands warming his hands. He hesitates a moment, then suddenly hurries into the room at the left. Almost immediately he returns carrying a suit of clothes on a coat-rack and a pair of shoes. He drops them on the table, takes off his overall jacket and begins to take off his shoes. Light footsteps are heard coming up the porch. He stops, an incredulous look on his face which gives way to one of joy and anger. He watches the door in a sort of stupefaction. There is a fluttering of knuckle knocks on the door, and a voice calls, "Ed!". But* ED *makes no response. The door opens, and* LILLY ROBINSON *comes in, carrying a cheap suitcase in her hand. She is a tall young woman of twenty-three or twenty-four years, dressed in plain, becoming clothes—white waist, dark shirt and lacy collar. She has a fresh sweet face and youthful manner; yet behind her apparent gayety and childlikeness there hides a strong will and a hint of recklessness, now hidden in weariness. As she enters,* ED *begins lacing up his shoes and putting his overall jacket on again. He does not look at her after the first glance of recognition.* LILLY *stands, undecided, in the doorway, waits an instant, then moves into the room, closing the door behind her.*

LILLY: Ed, I was sorter expecting you to meet me. [ED *makes no reply, but picks up his clothes and carries them back to the room at the left.* LILLY *watches him uncertainly.*] Was you going somewheres, Ed?

ED: [*Reappearing*] No, not now.

LILLY: [*Dropping her suitcase on the floor and standing, undecided*] Ed. . . . I didn't mean to stay an extry week . . . but I wrote you why I wanted to. You got my letter; didn't you?

ED: [*Glumly*] No, I hain't heard a word from you. [*Picking up the dishcloth and moving to the stove.*] But I've heerd about you.

LILLY: What, what have you heard?

ED: [*Dully*] Have off yer things, and make yerself at home.

LILLY: [*Mechanically pulling off her coat and hat and laying them on the table*] What'n the world ails you, Ed? You ain't mad about something, are you?

ED: I reckon I'm not.

LILLY: I wrote to you, Ed, and told you to meet me in Angier this evenin'. If it hadn't been for Mr. Jake Turlington coming this way, I don't know how I'd 'a' got home.

ED: [*After a pause*] I ain't had no letter from you.

LILLY: I give it to Mr. . . . Mr. . . . Ryalls to mail for me. [*Thinking.*] No, I declare, I plumb forgot to mail it. It's lying on the bureau at Aunt Margaret's.

ED: [*A hard note slipping into his voice*] Who is Mr. Ryalls?

LILLY: He was just a man who boarded there at Aunt Margaret's. I got acquainted with him over there.

ED: [*Turning to look her full in the face a moment*] How well did you git acquainted?

LILLY: [*In surprise*] I . . . I don't know must what you mean.

ED: He don't happen to be a fellow you knowed last spring when you was over there, does he?

LILLY: Why, no, I never saw him before this time. And . . . he . . . he was purty nice to May Belle—

ED: And how about you?

LILLY: Well . . . why he treated me all right.

ED: [*Suddenly flaring out*] By God, I reckon he did! [*And he goes on with his cooking.*]

LILLY: [*Startled*] Ed, what you so upset about? You said you'd heard about me. What . . . what have you heard?

ED: I reckon you been enjoying yerself all right.

LILLY: [*Dubiously*] Yes, I sure have. [*Turning quickly to him.*] What's all this you're driving at?

ED: Nothing. [*After a moment.*] Looks like you could help me git a little supper—if you ain't above it. [*She leans against the table a moment, looking at her hands. Her brow is wrinkled in thought. Suddenly she looks up at his broad back with a touch of fear in her face.*]

LILLY: Oh, what am I thinking about.—Here, you set down and let me fix for you. My goodness, you've burnt your meat slam to pieces! [*She bustles around the stove, putting in wood, cutting meat, and straightening the table, laying out dishes, etc.* ED *sticks the dish-cloth towards her, sits down in a chair and begins drumming on the table.*] How you been getting along?

ED: Oh, purty good. How's Aunt Margaret and all of 'em over there?

LILLY: All right. [*Fumbling in the cupboard.*] Cain't we have some eggs? [ED *makes no reply.*] Oh, here they are. My, my, the hens must have been a-laying! Must 'a' tuk a notion and started in all of a sudden. Ain't been eating many of 'm, have you?

ED: [*Beginning to whistle a low meaningless tune and tapping with his fingertips on the table*] No, not many. [*He goes on whistling.* LILLY *turns from her work now and then to glance to him. Her quickening movements show her nervous perturbation. She goes on talking.*]

LILLY: Has the little white pullet we set come off yet? She was to come off sometime this week.

ED: [*Mechanically*] Uh huh. [*He continues whistling and tapping.*]

LILLY: [*Begins breaking the eggs into a dish*] How many eggs did she hatch? You know we put twelve under her. [ED *makes no reply, his eyes narrowing to slits and his jaw taking on a more and more firm look. His whistle is more pronounced and the tapping on the table sharper and more staccato. As* LILLY *moves around the table, she crunches a piece of the broken vase underfoot. Suddenly she stoops, finds the remains of the vase and flowers, and with an exclamation of pain and hurt, she gathers them up. She turns sharply towards* ED *with a defiant and bitter word on her lips, but his inner absorption deters her for the moment. Tears of anger glisten in her eyes. She stirs the eggs more and more rapidly. At last with a stifled sob she whirls upon him.*] Who . . . who broke my purty blue vase? [*He makes no answer. She bursts out more shrilly.*] Ed Robinson, I want to know who broke my vase?

ED: [*Suddenly bringing his fist down on the table in a shattering blow and roaring out his words in a rage*] Damn it to hell, I want to know what you been doin' with that Ryalls fellow over there at Dunn?

LILLY: [*Laying the remnants of the vase on the table and backing away from him*] I . . . I ain't been doing nothing. What . . . you . . . mean?

ED: Yes, you have been doing something, or else. . . . [*She looks miserably into his face, his words dying away into a mutter. They both are silent a moment.* LILLY *twists the dried flowers in her hands.*]

LILLY: What in the world's got into you? Somebody's been telling lies, that's what. Well—[*Defiantly.*] If you want to think *that* about your wife, go ahead and think what you please. I ain't done nothing I'm ashamed of, and that's the truth if I ever spoke it.

ED: Well, what you doing ridin' 'round with that Ryalls fellow—or whatever his name was?

LILLY: They wa'n't no harm in that. And, besides, he took May Belle around a sight more'n he did me.

ED: You went around enough to set everybody talkin' about you.

LILLY: 'Tain't the first time they've talked about me, and—[*recklessly*] it may not be the last, if you cain't treat me any better than you have to-night.

ED: What . . . you . . . mean?

LILLY: I mean that I ain't goin' to be stormed at and driv 'round like a dumb brute by a slave-drivin' husband—that's what!

ED: You needn't to r'ar so. Why'd you stay away another week, and me here with the cotton all fallin' out and nobody to pick it? Ain't no other woman in the neighborhood'd treat her man so.

LILLY: No, they ain't. They're all plumb fools! [*She turns to the stove, her lips trembling in anger, and begins putting the supper on the table.*]

ED: [*Presently*] Lilly, I've tried to treat you right, but a man cain't stand everything.

LILLY: [*Now and then wiping the tears from her eyes*] Come on and eat yer supper. [*She waits for him.*]

ED: I don't want nothin'.

LILLY: Ed, come on and eat. [*After a moment*] Cain't we have a little peace? Seems lak . . . seems lak . . . [*Stifling a sob.*]

ED: [*Moving to the table and slouching his heavy arms down on it. He begins eating in huge mouthfuls as if he would drown his wrath with food. He *lays down his knife and looks at her, sitting in her chair near the stove*] Ain't you goin' ter take a bite yourself?

LILLY: I ain't hongry nuther.

ED: Oh . . . well . . . [*He goes on eating. Presently he shoves his plate from him and leans his head on his hands.*] You . . . don't seem glad much to be back home.

LILLY: [*Cleaning the dough from her fingers with a hairpin*] You shore don't seem glad to see me back either.

ED: Well . . . I reckon I am, too . . . but—[*He lapses into silence. Suddenly he flares out.*] I want to know what in the devil is up 'tween you and that man?

LILLY: [*Laughing nervously*] Well you won't know, 'cause they ain't nothin' betwixt us. But I can tell you this, if it'll do you any good, he knows a heap sight better how to treat a woman than you do.

ED: I reckon he does—if she's the kind of a woman he wants to treat.

LILLY: Watch out what you're sayin', Ed Robinson.

ED: I am watchin'. They ain't no woman with a grain o' sense in her head 'd be flying around with a fellow lak that, and her husband at home workin' his head off. And you orter know that.

LILLY: He took me to a pictur' show onct or twice, and give me a good time, and that's more than you've ever thought of doing the five long years I've been married to you. [*A pause.*] There you set in that there chair, laying down the gospel to me. Well, I'm goin' ter tell you a thing or two right now. You'd *kill* any woman God ever made, with your hard, stingy ways. [*She rises from her chair and stands before him.*] Oh, yes you would. You don't care for nothin' but a mule to plow in the day time and a shuck mattress to sleep on at night—that you don't; and a-always laying up for land, always a-talking about it, and lettin' me and everything I want go with never a thought.

ED: [*Weakening*] Well, Lilly, you hadn't ort to—

LILLY: Hadn't ort to what, I'd like to know. I've worked for you, washed your clothes, hoed your grassy corn, and you off fishing, stayed here at night, with you and Jeems Atkins 'possum huntin' in the swamp, and me so lonesome I jest lay there listenin' to the wind whistlin' through the trees. And I've set out your rations over this here table three-hundred and sixty-five days in the year for five long winters and summers, and I ain't never heard a dozen sweet words out'n you the whole time. God *help* me! Who wouldn't go crazy for a sight of a town and purty things onct in a while?

ED: [*Mumbling*] I cain't see why you always got to be thinkin' o' somethin' better'n you got—that I cain't.

LILLY: [*Swallowing her sobs*] That you cain't. You're blind as a bat. All you study is yourself. —Look at Jim Cooper—worked his head off—after you to do the same, though the Lord knows you don't need no coaxing about saving money. Look at him. And then, look at his wife. She's nothing but a ghost of a woman. She won't cast a shadow in the sun she's so thin. He's run her to death, the dirty devil!

ED: [*With a show of anger*] She's been a good wife to him, that's what. She ain't never had no crazy notions about gettin' fixin's, and movin' to town and dressing up in finery, and smearing herself in paint—like them hussies in Dunn. And you might ca'm yerself and not fly complete off'n the handle.

LILLY: How you know she ain't? What do you men know about a woman's wants anyway?—Nothin', not nothin'. She ain't never had the heart to go ag'in his wishes, poor thing. But Ed Robinson, here's one ain't goin' ter be druv' lak that. I come back home to tell you that. Leonard Ryalls showed me that they's things in this world you ain't never dreamt of. And I've made up my mind from now on to have my way about a few things, I will that!

ED: [*With a hurt in his voice*] God a'mighty, ain't you had your way! They ain't another man in the country would let his wife go off and stay three weeks and him pickin' out her own cotton.

LILLY: How much o' yourn have I picked, I'd lak to know? Don't you say nothin' to me about work, don't you! [*She drops down in her chair and begins sobbing.*]

ED: Now you needn't think crying' git you anything. [*He moves around the room, kicks at the table, seats himself again.*] Shet up yer crying, Lilly. [*She rocks in her grief. He watches her a moment.*] Shet up, I tell you! They'll hear you slam over to Mr. Jim's. [*He picks up a biscuit and begins chewing on it.* LILLY *bursts out into another tirade.*]

LILLY: [*In shrill anger*] Let them hear me! I don't care if the whole world was a-watching me. I got reason to cry, I have. [*Then she grows more calm, and speaks with more control but with more bitterness.*] I'm goin' ter say something to you now, Ed Robinson, I ain't never said to nobody before. [*She pauses a moment, swallowing hard.*]

ED: Say it if you want to—but it seems you've said enough fer one night.

LILLY: [*Getting up and going to the door, she opens it and stands looking out into the darkness. Quietly*] I can see why yonder that clump o' pines black against the sky.

ED: [*Uneasily*] Come on back, Lilly, and eat a bite o' supper.

LILLY: I can see them trees there looking all thick and dark and . . . [*Turning back vehemently into the room*] you know what I'm thinking of—you know well enough.

ED: [*Getting up quickly and closing the door, pushing her gently away*] You quit that lookin' out thar. [*Kindly.*] Come on, gal, drink some coffee . . . or somethin'. [*He stands at the stove stirring a pan idly.*]

LILLY: I'm goin' ter tell you. [*A pause, twisting her dress in her hand.*] Who was too stingy to have a doctor? Who said they wa'n't no use putting up screens in the house? Who said all them new-fangled idees 'bout baby food and taking care was foolishness? You did, you did! And that's the reason he's out there dead and buried under them pines, with his little white dress all wet and rotten. You killed him, that's what you did, you *killed* him! [*She sits down in her chair with the tears rolling down her face.*]

ED: [*In a stifled voice*] Lilly . . . Lilly, don't——

LILLY: I jest wanted you to know that you are just as much a murderer as if you shot a man down in the road—yes, and a sight worse!

ED: I didn't . . . I didn't know . . . Lilly . . . [*He looks at her in pain.*]

LILLY: Thank God, it hurts you a little bit. [ED *sits down at the table, staring before him with set face.* LILLY *speaks very quietly.*] Now that I've told you how I feel about it maybe you won't think it so quair that I want to git away from you onct in a while.

ED: [*Uncomprehendingly*] You don't mean . . . you don't believe all that, do you, Lilly? Do you feel that way about it? Shore enough? . . . [*He turns away, choking.*]

LILLY: So you did like him some yourself, didn't you? But you see it's too late now. You see, Ed, you can tap on the table and make a funny gooin' sound, and he won't answer you from over there in the corner on his pallet. [ED *looks up perplexed.*] Try it and see. He can't, you know, for he's dead . . . dead . . . dead . . . dead.

ED: What . . . what you mean? [*He stares at her blankly.*]

LILLY: You watch me now. [*She goes to the door, opens it, and calls.*] Charlie! Charlie, come here! [*Her voice goes out across the dark.* ED'S *amazement increases. She closes the door softly and turns back to him.*] You didn't hear him answer, did you, Ed? No, I could call, and call, and call, and he wouldn't make a sound. Oh, yes, I used to call when you was out in the fields workin'—oh yes, I did. But you didn't hear me then. But you hear me now, don't you?

ED: What'n the name o' God ails you?

LILLY: You couldn't understand if I told you. [*She looks around the room.*] Ed, did you bring in my flowers off the porch at night the way I told you to? [ED *makes no reply. She goes out and brings in a pot.*] No you didn't. Here's my purtiest geranium all forst-bitten. [*She crumples up the leaves in her hand.*] All the others is dead . . . dead. You see how it is, Ed. You kill things you tech.

ED: Lilly, I forgot all about them flowers.

LILLY: No, you mean you didn't never think of 'em. [*She sits down wearily, thinking. They both are silent. Presently* ED *begins watching her.*]

ED: Say something. Don't set there—so still lak.

LILLY: I was jest thinkin' that . . . it'd take a long time to git any flowers growing agin lak them you killed.

ED: I told you I forgot 'em, and I didn't kill 'em. Don't lay that to me.

LILLY: It'd take too long, wouldn't it? . . . And I guess we've about come to the end of our rope, hain't we, Ed?

ED: I don't un . . . der . . . stand. What . . . you . . . mean?

LILLY: I didn't think you would. [*She sits tapping her fingers.*]

ED: [*Unable to endure the silence any longer*] Le's don't keep on lak this. Mebbee I ain't done you . . . well—mebbe not just right. Mebbe nuther of us 's done tother'n jest right.

LILLY: Maybe not. That's mighty hard to do as I've found out . . . after a long time.

ED: Le's sorter forgit about all this mix-up, and go on. Things'll turn out better; they always do.

LILLY: I didn't expect to hear you say that.

ED: But, Lilly, that fellow—shore you didn't mean nothin' by goin' around with him, did you?

LILLY: [*Thoughtfully*] I mought 'a meant a lot,—who knows?

ED: [*Bitterly*] You talk lak that an 'spect me to be humble as a dog.

LILLY: You needn't worry about him. He and

May Belle was married to-day before I left. I helped 'em decorate all the week. That's what I wanted to stay over for.

ED: [*A joy breaking his voice*] Is that so? I knowed somehow they was talkin' out'n their heads when they said all that about you. [*Sincerely.*] I'm sorry as kin be about that vase. But I'll git you another one, that I will.

LILLY: [*With gentle irony*] There's a bed-room suite over there in Holiday's store I was looking at for seventy dollars. It's priced at a hundred; but he said I could have it for seventy, if I'd send for it in in the morning. Do you think you could go for it in the morning, Ed?

ED: [*Quickly*] I mought. [*Doubiously.*] But that's a heap o' money to put in on such fixin's.

LILLY: But they ought to be enough of my cotton money to buy that. And I was wondering if you couldn't take off my cotton then and sell it.

ED: But . . . Lilly . . . I . . .

LILLY: Well, you needn't to, if you don't want to? But I was just thinking. . . .

ED: [*Blurting out*] I sold it to-day.

LILLY: [*Still going on in her even voice*] You did?

ED: Yes, and . . . and . . . I tell you . . . I let Mr. Jim have the money.

LILLY: [*A flame in her voice for a moment*] Oh, yes, the same way you done time and time ag'in—give me a cotton patch, and then by hook or crook get me to believing you needed it worse'n I did. Women don't need money lak men, do they?

ED: But I kin git it back; I know I kin. He begged it out'n me to fix up the deal about . . . about the land. I'll go over thar right now and get him to break it off. [*He stirs in search of his hat and old overcoat..*]

LILLY: [*Pleasantly*] You needn't bother about it. [*Almost yawning.*] 'Tain't no use now.

ED: [*Again perplexed*] Lilly, what ails you anyhow? You act quair at times.——[*Hurriedly.*] But I'll go and get it right now. [*He pulls on his coat. There is a noise of stamping feet on the porch. Ed slips off his coat.*]

LILLY: There's somebody coming in. [*She picks up her coat and puts it on. There is a knock on the door.*]

ED: Come in. [JIM COOPER *enters*]

COOPER: What'n the world's all this racket over here about? We heard it clean over home. [ED *stares at the floor.*] Oh, hello, Lilly. Come back, have you?

LILLY: [*Pulling on her hat*] Yes, but I'm passing by. . . .

ED: Mr. Jim, I just started over to your house to see you. Lilly ain't satisfied about that trade. She wants her money back. Mebbe I ain't done jest right about it anyhow.

COOPER: I'll swear. Goin' ter let her run over you ag'in? Lilly, ain't you got no sense? Cain't you quit thinking about yerself long enough to help Ed git a start in the world?

LILLY: I ain't asked him to get it back. It'd be fine if Mis' Mary could ask you a question or two, wouldn't it?

COOPER: [*Blinking*] None o' yer sassy talk.

ED: Mr. Jim, I'll have to back out about that trade. That was Lilly's cotton money, and if you'll give it back, I'll fix it somehow. [LILLY *picks up her suitcase and moves towards the door.*] What you mean? [*In alarm.*] Where you goin'?

LILLY: [*Blankly*] I'm . . . jest . . . goin'. You all can fix up about the money to suit yourselves. I don't want none of it.

COOPER: What'n the thunder is all this foolishness about?

ED *stands with his hand on the knob of the door. The two men eye her in astonishment.*

LILLY: I told Ed a minute ago that we had come to the end of our rope. [*Turning to* COOPER.] You know what that means, don't you? Maybe you don't, but Mis' Mary does. Ask her when you get back home, Good-by to you, Ed. . . .

ED: [*Amazed*] Where you goin' this time o' night? What? . . .

LILLY: It don't matter. I'm a-goin' all right. And I ain't never coming back never . . . never . . . never. [*She pronounces the words with the same intonation as "dead . . . dead . . . dead."*] Good-by ag'in to you all.

She goes out, closing the door behind her—singing, as she goes.

Oh, Georgie Buck is dead, and the
last word he said, was,

"Nev - er let a wo-man have her
way."

Repeat Refrain

"Never let a woman have her
way."

COOPER: [*Puzzled*] Ed, what ails her? You ain't

goin' ter let her go off lak that, are you, traipsing out into the night?

ED: [*Blankly, dropping down into a chair*] I dunno . . . what she means.

COOPER: [*Taking the money from his pocket*] Here—here's yer money, Ed. I ain't anxious about the trade if you ain't. . . .

ED: I dunno . . . I dunno . . . exactly. . . .

SLOW CURTAIN

Note: Copies of this play, in individual paper covered acting editions, are available from Samuel French, Inc., 25 W. 45th St., New York, N.Y. or 7623 Sunset Blvd., Hollywood, Calif. or in Canada Samuel French, (Canada) Ltd., 26 Grenville St., Toronto, Canada.

Urban Robots

Elmer Rice

(1892–1967)

"I became an advocate of socialism in my teens," wrote Elmer Rice in his autobiography, "and have been one ever since." Then, defining his concept of Socialism as "the development of a society in which the implements of production are employed primarily for the satisfaction of human needs," the playwright argued that "there is no more relationship between the policies of the Kremlin and the aims of ideal socialism than there is between the practices of the Christian church and the teachings of Jesus." Rice's most important play, *The Adding Machine,* is grounded in his social and political philosophy, but it is not a purely polemic drama.

Elmer Leopold Reizenstein was born on the Lower East Side of New York City, attended public schools, and by the age of twenty was graduated *cum laude* as a lawyer. To the surprise of his family, he turned his back on both law and business ("the highest goal of American manhood") and became a playwright. He made a quick commercial success with *On Trial* (1914), a murder mystery melodrama employing both courtroom expertise and a motion picture flashback technique, then a novelty on the stage. But his reputation with intellectuals grew when he became affiliated with the Morningside Players, a little theater group. Then, while mulling over the possibilities of a drama concerning divorce, a total vision of *The Adding Machine* flashed through his mind. As quickly as possible, he put it all on paper, conglomerate symbols of maladjustment in a mechanical society.

In Rice's own words, *The Adding Machine* was "the case history of one of the slave souls who are both the raw material and the product of a mechanized society." It depicts a typical "treadmill existence," with mankind foolishly sustained by the "mirage of hope." Deliberately experimenting with what he terms "condensations" and "devices," Rice pictures the decline of individuality, the encroachments of standardization, and the dehumanimation of man by his tools all in the name of Normalcy and Progress. Mr. Zero is alternately the Everyman, Scapegoat, and Nigger of a machine-dominated economy.

Philip Moeller, who directed *The Adding Machine* when it opened March 19, 1923, at the Garrick Theater in New York under Theater Guild auspices, saw the play as a confrontation between freedom and bondage. Rice, Moeller said, "has studied the rich barrenness and the ridiculous un-beauty of these 'white collar' slaves. How many machine-forged minds are there who as the grind goes on and on are wishing to others these calamities of hate and for themselves these [expressionistic] escapes in stumbling and half-articulate dreams?"

During his distinguished theatrical career Rice portrayed various social, economic, and political dilemmas in America. His realistic drama of ghetto love and violence, *Street Scene,* won him the Pulitzer Prize in 1929. *We The People* (1933) chronicled the decline of a family wasted by the Depression. *American Landscape* (1938) examined patriotism, economic distress, and the specter of the rising Nazi-American Bund. It was, however, *The Adding Machine* (1923) that best brought into unity his young fervent radicalism and his intense dedication to dramatic art, for in this play Elmer Rice combined the reality of protest with the art of theatrical expressionism.

Clearly, *The Adding Machine* is a good deal more than an experimental surrealistic protest against the blandness of American life under Warren Gamaliel Harding. It stands as a fundamental expression of the point Emerson made in an earlier age: "Things are in the saddle/ And ride mankind." Rice shines his spotlight on America and the machine driving it; he suggests that our pastoral inheritance is disappearing, our natural compassion is being eroded, and our humanity is dying. Mr. Zero and Daisy Diana Dorothea Devore: eternal misfits, eternal martyrs.

The Adding Machine

Characters

MR. ZERO
MRS. ZERO
DAISY DIANA DOROTHEA DEVORE
THE BOSS
MR. ONE
MRS. ONE
MR. TWO
MRS. TWO
MR. THREE
MRS. THREE
MR. FOUR
MRS. FOUR
MR. FIVE
MRS. FIVE
MR. SIX
MRS. SIX
POLICEMAN
JUDY O'GRADY
YOUNG MAN
SHRDLU
A HEAD
LIEUTENANT CHARLES
JOE

Scene One: *A bedroom.*
Scene Two: *An office.*
Scene Three: *A dining room.*
Scene Four: *A court of justice.*
Scene Five: *A death cell.*
Scene Six: *A graveyard.*
Scene Seven: *A pleasant place.*
Scene Eight: *Another office.*

Scene I

Scene: *A bedroom.*

A small room containing an "installment plan" bed, dresser, and chairs. An ugly electric light fixture over the bed with a single glaring naked lamp. One small window with the shade drawn. The walls are papered with sheets of foolscap covered with columns of figures.

MR. ZERO *is lying in the bed, facing the audience, his head and shoulders visible. He is thin, sallow, under-sized, and partially bald.* MRS. ZERO *is standing before the dresser arranging her hair for the night. She is forty-five, sharp-featured, gray streaks in her hair. She is shapeless in her long-sleeved cotton nightgown. She is wearing her shoes, over which sag her ungartered stockings.*

MRS. ZERO [*as she takes down her hair*]: I'm gettin' sick o' them Westerns. All them cowboys ridin' around an' foolin' with them ropes. I don't care nothin' about that. I'm sick of 'em. I don't see why they don't have more of them stories like *For Love's Sweet Sake.* I like them sweet little love stories. They're nice an' wholesome. Mrs. Twelve was sayin' to me only yesterday, "Mrs. Zero," says she, "what I like is one of them wholesome stories, with just a sweet, simple little love story." "You're right, Mrs. Twelve," I says. "That's what I like, too." They're showin' too many Westerns at the Rosebud. I'm gettin' sick of them. I think we'll start goin' to the Peter Stuyvesant. They got a good bill there Wednesday night. There's a Chubby Delano comedy called *Sea-Sick.* Mrs. Twelve was tellin' me about it. She says it's a scream. They're havin' a picnic in the country and they sit Chubby next to an old maid with a great big mouth. So he gets sore an' when she ain't lookin' he goes and catches a frog and drops it in her clam chowder. An' when she goes to eat the chowder the frog jumps out of it an' right into her mouth. Talk about laugh! Mrs. Twelve was tellin' me she laughed so she nearly passed out. He sure can pull some funny ones. An' they got that big Grace Darling feature, *A Mother's Tears.* She's sweet. But I don't like her clothes. There's no style to them. Mrs. Nine was tellin' me she read in *Pictureland* that she ain't livin' with her husband. He's her second, too. I don't know whether they're divorced or just separated. You wouldn't think it to see her on the screen. She looks so sweet and innocent. Maybe it ain't true. You can't believe all you read. They say some Pittsburgh millionaire is crazy about her and that's why she ain't livin' with her husband. Mrs. Seven was tellin' me her brother-in-law has a friend that used to go to school with Grace Darling. He says her name ain't Grace Darling at all. Her right name is Elizabeth Dugan, he says, an' all them stories about her gettin' five thousand a week is the bunk, he says. She's sweet, though. Mrs. Eight was tellin' me that *A Mother's Tears* is the best picture she ever made. "Don't miss it, Mrs. Zero," she says. "It's sweet," she says. "Just sweet and wholesome. Cry!" she says. "I nearly cried my eyes out." There's one part in it where this big bum of an Englishman—he's a married man, too—an' she's this little simple country girl. An' she nearly falls for him, too. But she's sittin' out in the garden, one day, and she looks up and there's her mother lookin' at her, right out of the clouds. So that night she locks the door of her room. An' sure enough, when everybody's in bed, along comes this big bum of an Englishman an' when she won't let him in what does he do but go an' kick open the door. "Don't miss it, Mrs. Zero," Mrs. Eight was tellin' me. It's at the Peter Stuyvesant Wednesday night, so don't be tellin' me you want to go to the Rosebud. The Eights seen it downtown at the Strand. They go downtown all the time. Just like us—nit! I guess by the time it gets to the Peter Stuyvesant all that part about kickin' in the door will be cut out. Just like they cut out that big cabaret scene in *The Price of Virtue.* They sure are pullin' some rough stuff in the pictures nowadays. "It's no place for a young girl," I was tellin' Mrs. Eleven, only the other day. An' by the time they get uptown half of it is cut out. But you wouldn't go downtown—not if wild horses was to drag you. You can wait till they come uptown! Well, I don't want to wait, see? I want to see 'em when everybody else is seein' them an' not a month later. Now don't go tellin' me you ain't got the price. You could dig up the price all right, all right, if you wanted to. I notice you always got the price to go to the ballgame. But when it comes to me havin' a good time then it's always: "I ain't got the price, I gotta start savin'." A fat lot you'll ever save! I got all I can do now makin' both ends meet an' you talkin' about savin'. [*She seats herself on a chair and begins removing her shoes and stockings.*] An' don't go pullin' that stuff about bein' tired. "I been workin' hard all day. Twice a day in the subway's enough for me." Tired! Where do you get that tired stuff, anyhow? What about me? Where do I come in? Scrubbin' floors an' cookin' your meals an' washin' your dirty clothes. An' you sittin' on a chair all day, just addin' figgers an' waitin' for five-thirty. There's no five-thirty for me. I don't wait for no whistle. I don't get no vacations neither. And what's more I don't get no pay envelope every Saturday night neither. I'd like to know where you'd be without me. An' what have I got to show for it?—slavin' my life away to give you a home. What's in it for me, I'd like to know? But it's my own fault, I guess. I was a fool for marryin' you. If I'd 'a' had any sense, I'd 'a' known what you were from the start. I wish I had it to do over again, I hope to tell you. You wasn't goin' to be a bookkeeper long—oh, no, not you. Wait till you got started—you was goin' to show 'em. There wasn't no job in the store that was too big for you. Well, I've been waitin'—waitin' for you to get started—see? It's been a good long wait, too. Twenty-five years! An' I ain't seen nothin' happen. Twenty-five years in the same job. Twenty-five years to-morrow! You're proud of it, ain't you? Twenty-five years in the same job an' never missed a day! That's somethin' to be proud of, ain't it? Sittin' for twenty-five years on the same chair, addin' up figures. What about bein' store-manager? I guess you forgot about that, didn't you? An' me at home here lookin' at the same four walls an' workin' my fingers to the bone to make both ends meet. Seven years since you got a raise! An' if you don't get one to-morrow, I'll bet a nickel you won't have the guts to go an' ask for one. I didn't pick much when I picked you, I'll tell the world. You ain't much to be proud of. [*She rises, goes to the window, and raises the shade. A few lighted windows are visible on the other side of the closed court. Looking out for a moment.*] She ain't walkin' around to-night, you can bet your sweet life on that. An' she won't be walkin' around any more nights, neither. Not in this house, anyhow. [*She turns away from the window.*] The dirty bum! The idea of her comin' to live in a house with respectable people. They should 'a' gave her six years, not six months. If I was the judge I'd of gave her life. A bum like that. [*She approaches the bed and stands there a moment.*] I guess you're sorry she's gone. I guess you'd like to sit home every night an' watch her goin's-on. You're somethin' to be proud of, you are! [*She stands on the bed and turns out the light. . . . A Thin stream of moonlight filters in from the court. The two figures are dimly visible.* MRS. ZERO *gets into bed.*]

You'd better not start nothin' with women, if you know what's good for you. I've put up with a lot, but I won't put up with that. I've been slavin' away for twenty-five years, makin' a home for you an' nothin' to show for it. If you was any kind of a man you'd have a decent job by now an' I'd be gettin' some comfort out of life—instead of bein' just a slave, washin' pots an' standin' over the hot stove. I've stood it for twenty-five years an' I guess I'll have to stand it twenty-five more. But don't you go startin' nothin' with women— [*She goes on talking as the curtain falls.*]

Scene II

SCENE: *An office in a department store. Wood and glass partitions. In the middle of the room, two tall desks back to back. At one desk on a high stool is* ZERO. *Opposite him at the other desk, also on a high stool, is* DAISY DIANA DOROTHEA DEVORE, *a plain, middle-aged woman. Both wear green eye-shades, and paper sleeve-protectors. A pendent electric lamp throws light upon both desks.* DAISY *reads aloud figures from a pile of slips which lie before her. As she reads the figures,* ZERO *enters them upon a large square sheet of ruled paper which lies before him.*

DAISY [*reading aloud*]: Three ninety-eight. Forty-two cents. A dollar fifty. A dollar fifty. A dollar twenty-five. Two dollars. Thirty-nine cents. Twenty-seven fifty.

ZERO [*petulantly*]: Speed it up a little, cancha?

DAISY: What's the rush? To-morrer's another day.

ZERO: Aw, you make me sick.

DAISY: An' you make me sicker.

ZERO: Go on. Go on. We're losin' time.

DAISY: Then quit bein' so bossy. [*She reads.*] Three dollars. Two sixty-nine. Eighty-one fifty. Forty dollars. Eight seventy-five. Who do you think you are, anyhow?

ZERO: Never mind who I think I am. You tend to your work.

DAISY: Aw, don't be givin' me so many orders. Sixty cents. Twenty-four cents. Seventy-five cents. A dollar fifty. Two fifty. One fifty. One fifty. Two fifty. I don't have to take it from you and what's more I won't.

ZERO: Aw, quit talkin'.

DAISY: I'll talk all I want. Three dollars. Fifty cents. Fifty cents. Seven dollars. Fifty cents. Two fifty. Three fifty. Fifty cents. One fifty. Fifty cents.

She goes bending over the slips and transferring them from one pile to another. ZERO *bends over his desk, busily entering the figures.*

ZERO [*without looking up*]: You make me sick. Always shootin' off your face about somethin'. Talk, talk, talk. Just like all the other women. Women make me sick.

DAISY [*busily fingering the slips*]: Who do you think you are, anyhow? Bossin' me around. I don't have to take it from you, and what's more I won't.

They both attend closely to their work, neither looking up.

ZERO: Women make me sick. They're all alike. The judge gave her six months. I wonder what they do in the workhouse. Peel potatoes. I'll bet she's sore at me. Maybe she'll try to kill me when she gets out. I better be careful. Hello Girl Slays Betrayer, Jealous Wife Slays Rival. You can't tell what a woman's liable to do. I better be careful.

DAISY: I'm gettin' sick of it. Always pickin' on me about somethin'. Never a decent word out of you. Not even the time o' day.

ZERO: I guess she wouldn't have the nerve at that. Maybe she don't even know it's me. They didn't even put my name in the paper, the big bums. Maybe she's been in the workhouse before. A bum like that. She didn't have nothin' on that one time—nothin' but a shirt. [*He glances up quickly, then bends over again.*] You make me sick, I'm sick of lookin' at your face.

DAISY: Gee, ain't that whistle ever goin' to blow? You didn't used to be like that. Not even good mornin' or good evenin'. I ain't done nothin' to you. It's the young girls. Goin' around without corsets.

ZERO: Your face is gettin' all yeller. Why don't you put some paint on it? She was puttin' on paint that time. On her cheeks and on her lips. And that blue stuff on her eyes. Just sittin' there in a shimmy puttin' on the paint. An' walkin' around the room with her legs all bare.

DAISY: I wish I was dead.

ZERO: I was a goddam fool to let the wife get on to me. She oughta get six months at that. The dirty bum. Livin' in a house with respectable people. She'd be livin' there yet, if the wife hadn't o' got on to me. Damn her!

DAISY: I wish I was dead.

ZERO: Maybe another one'll move in. Gee, that would be great. But the wife's got her eye on me now.

DAISY: I'm scared to do it, though.

ZERO: You oughta move into that room. It's cheaper than where you're livin' now. I better tell you about it. I don't mean to be always pickin' on you.

DAISY: Gas. The smell of it makes me sick.

ZERO *looks up and clears his throat.*

DAISY [*looking up, startled*]: Whadja say?

ZERO: I didn't say nothin'.

DAISY: I thought you did.

ZERO: You thought wrong.

They bend over their work again.

DAISY: A dollar sixty. A dollar fifty. Two ninety. One sixty-two.

ZERO: Why the hell should I tell you? Fat chance of you forgettin' to pull down the shade!

DAISY: If I asked for carbolic they might get on to me.

ZERO: Your hair's gettin' gray. You don't wear them shirt waists any more with the low collars. When you'd bend down to pick somethin' up—

DAISY: I wish I knew what to ask for. Girl Takes Mercury After All-Night Party. Woman In Ten-Story Death Leap.

ZERO: I wonder where'll she go when she gets out. Gee, I'd like to make a date with her. Why didn't I go over there the night my wife went to Brooklyn? She never woulda found out.

DAISY: I seen Pauline Frederick do it once. Where could I get a pistol though?

ZERO: I guess I didn't have the nerve.

DAISY: I'll bet you'd be sorry then that you been so mean to me. How do I know, though? Maybe you wouldn't.

ZERO: Nerve! I got as much nerve as anybody. I'm on the level, that's all. I'm a married man and I'm on the level.

DAISY: Anyhow, why ain't I got a right to live? I'm as good as anybody else. I'm too refined, I guess. That's the whole trouble.

ZERO: The time the wife had pneumonia I thought she was goin' to pass out. But she didn't. The doctor's bill was eighty-seven dollars. [*Looking up*]: Hey, wait a minute! Didn't you say eighty-seven dollars?

DAISY [*looking up*]: What?

ZERO: Was the last you said eighty-seven dollars?

DAISY [*consulting the slip*]: Forty-two fifty.

ZERO: Well, I made a mistake. Wait a minute. [*He busies himself with an eraser*]: All right. Shoot.

DAISY: Six dollars. Three fifteen. Two twenty-five. Sixty-five cents. A dollar twenty. You talk to me as if I was dirt.

ZERO: I wonder if I could kill the wife without anybody findin' out. In bed some night. With a pillow.

DAISY: I used to think you was stuck on me.

ZERO: I'd get found out, though. They always have ways.

DAISY: We used to be so nice and friendly together when I first came here. You used to talk to me then.

ZERO: Maybe she'll die soon. I noticed she was coughin' this mornin'.

DAISY: You used to tell me all kinds o' things. You were goin' to show them all. Just the same, you're still sittin' here.

ZERO: Then I could do what I damn please. Oh, boy!

DAISY: Maybe it ain't all your fault neither. Maybe if you'd had the right kind o' wife—somebody with a lot of common sense, somebody refined—me!

ZERO: At that, I guess I'd get tired of bummin' around. A feller wants some place to hang his hat.

DAISY: I wish she would die.

ZERO: And when you start goin' with women

you're liable to get into trouble. And lose your job maybe.

DAISY: Maybe you'd marry me.

ZERO: Gee, I wish I'd gone over there that night.

DAISY: Then I could quit workin'.

ZERO: Lots o' women would be glad to get me.

DAISY: You could look a long time before you'd find a sensible, refined girl like me.

ZERO: Yes, sir, they could look a long time before they'd find a steady meal-ticket like me.

DAISY: I guess I'd be too old to have any kids. They say it ain't safe after thirty-five.

ZERO: Maybe I'd marry you. You might be all right, at that.

DAISY: I wonder—if you don't want kids—whether—if there's any way—

ZERO [*looking up*]: Hey! Hey! Can't you slow up? What do you think I am—a machine?

DAISY [*looking up*]: Say, what do you want, anyhow? First it's too slow an' then it's too fast. I guess you don't know what you want.

ZERO: Well, never mind about that. Just you slow up.

DAISY: I'm gettin' sick o' this. I'm goin' to ask to be transferred.

ZERO: Go ahead. You can't make me mad.

DAISY: Aw, keep quiet. [*She reads*]: Two forty-five. A dollar twenty. A dollar fifty. Ninety cents. Sixty-three cents.

ZERO: Marry you! I guess not! You'd be as bad as the one I got.

DAISY: You wouldn't care if I did ask. I got a good mind to ask.

ZERO: I was a fool to get married.

DAISY: Then I'd never see you at all.

ZERO: What chance has a guy got with a woman tied around his neck?

DAISY: That time at the store picnic—the year your wife couldn't come—you were nice to me then.

ZERO: Twenty-five years holdin' down the same job!

DAISY: We were together all day—just sittin' around under the trees.

ZERO: I wonder if the boss remembers about it bein' twenty-five years.

DAISY: And comin' home that night—you sat next to me in the big delivery wagon.

ZERO: I got a hunch there's a big raise comin' to me.

DAISY: I wonder what it feels like to be really kissed. Men—dirty pigs! They want the bold ones.

ZERO: If he don't come across I'm goin' right up to the front office and tell him where he gets off.

DAISY: I wish I was dead.

ZERO: "Boss," I'll say, "I want to have a talk with you." "Sure," he'll say, "sit down. Have a Corona Corona." "No," I'll say, "I don't smoke." "How's that?" he'll say. "Well, boss," I'll say, "it's this way. Every time I feel like smokin' I just take a nickel and put it in the old sock. A penny saved is a penny earned, that's the way I look at it." "Damn sensible," he'll say. "You got a wise head on you, Zero."

DAISY: I can't stand the smell of gas. It makes me sick. You coulda kissed me if you wanted to.

ZERO: "Boss," I'll say, "I ain't quite satisfied. I been on the job twenty-five years now and if I'm gonna stay I gotta see a future ahead of me." "Zero," he'll say, "I'm glad you came in. I've had my eye on you, Zero. Nothin' gets by me." "Oh, I know that, boss," I'll say. That'll hand him a good laugh, that will. "You're a valuable man, Zero," he'll say, "and I want you right up here with me in the front office. You're done addin' figgers. Monday mornin' you move up here."

DAISY: Them kisses in the movies—them long ones—right on the mouth—

ZERO: I'll keep a-goin' right on up after that. I'll show some of them birds where they get off.

DAISY: That one the other night—*The Devil's Alibi*—he put his arms around her—and her head fell back and her eyes closed—like she was in a daze.

ZERO: Just give me about two years and I'll show them birds where they get off.

DAISY: I guess that's what it's like—a kinda daze—when I see them like that, I just seem to forget everything.

ZERO: Then me for a place in Jersey. And maybe a little Buick. No tin Lizzie for mine. Wait till I get started—I'll show 'em.

DAISY: I can see it now when I kinda half-close my eyes. The way her head fell back. And his mouth pressed right up against hers. Oh, Gawd! it must be grand!

There is a sudden shrill blast from a steam whistle.

DAISY AND ZERO [*together*]: The whistle!

*With great agility they get off their stools, remove their eye shades and sleeve protectors and put them on the desks. Then each produces from behind the desk a hat —*ZERO, *a dusty derby,* DAISY, *a frowsy straw. . . .*

DAISY *puts on her hat and turns toward* ZERO *as though she were about to speak to him. But he is busy cleaning his pen and pays no attention to her. She sighs and goes toward the door at the left.*

ZERO [*looking up*]: G'night, Miss Devore.

But she does not hear him and exits. ZERO *takes up his hat and goes left. The door at the right opens and the* BOSS *enters—middle-aged, stoutish, bald, well-dressed.*

THE BOSS [*calling*]: Oh—er—Mister—er—

ZERO *turns in surprise, sees who it is, and trembles nervously.*

ZERO [*obsequiously*]: Yes, sir. Do you want me, sir?

BOSS: Yes. Just come here a moment, will you?

ZERO: Yes, sir. Right away, sir. [*He fumbles his hat, picks it up, stumbles, recovers himself, and approaches the* BOSS, *every fibre quivering.*]

BOSS: Mister—er—er—

ZERO: Zero.

BOSS: Yes, Mr. Zero. I wanted to have a little talk with you.

ZERO [*with a nervous grin*]: Yes sir, I been kinda expectin' it.

BOSS [*staring at him*]: Oh, have you?

ZERO: Yes sir.

BOSS: How long have you been with us, Mister —er—Mister—

ZERO: Zero.

BOSS: Yes, Mister Zero.

ZERO: Twenty-five years today.

BOSS: Twenty-five years! That's a long time.

ZERO: Never missed a day.

BOSS: And you've been doing the same work all the time?

ZERO: Yes, sir. Right here at this desk.

BOSS: Then, in that case, a change probably won't be unwelcome to you.

ZERO: No, sir, it won't. And that's the truth.

BOSS: We've been planning a change in this department for some time.

ZERO: I kinda thought you had your eye on me.

BOSS: You were right. The fact is that my efficiency experts have recommended the installation of adding machines.

ZERO [*staring at him*]: Addin' machines?

BOSS: Yes, you've probably seen them. A mechanical device that adds automatically.

ZERO: Sure. I've seen them. Keys—and a handle that you pull. [*He goes through the motions in the air.*]

BOSS: That's it. They do the work in half the time and a high-school girl can operate them. Now, of course, I'm sorry to lose an old and faithful employee—

ZERO: Excuse me, but would you mind sayin' that again?

BOSS: I say I'm sorry to lose an employee who's been with me for so many years—

Soft music is heard—the sound of the mechanical player of a distant merry-go-round. The part of the floor upon which the desk and stools are standing begins to revolve very slowly.

BOSS: But, of course, in an organization like this, efficiency must be the first consideration —

The music becomes gradually louder and the revolutions more rapid.

BOSS: You will draw your salary for the full month. And I'll direct my secretary to give you a letter of recommendation—

ZERO: Wait a minute, boss. Let me get this right. You mean I'm canned?

BOSS [*barely making himself heard above the increasing volume of sound*]: I'm sorry—no other alternative—greatly regret—old employee—efficiency—economy—business—*business*— BUSINESS—

His voice is drowned by the music. The platform is revolving rapidly now. ZERO *and the* BOSS *face each other. They are entirely motionless save for the* BOSS'S *jaws, which open and close incessantly. But the words are inaudible. The music swells and swells. To it is added every offstage effect of the theatre: the wind, the waves, the galloping horses, the locomotive whistle, the sleigh bells, the automobile siren, the glass-crash. New Year's Eve, Election Night, Armistice Day, and the Mardi-Gras. The noise is deafening, maddening, unendurable. Suddenly it culminates in a terrific peal of thunder. For an instant there is a flash of red and then everything is plunged into blackness.*

CURTAIN

Scene III

SCENE: *The* ZERO *dining room. Entrance door at right. Doors to kitchen and bedroom at left. The walls, as in the first scene, are papered with foolscap sheets covered with columns of figures. In the middle of the room, upstage, a table set for two. Along each side wall, seven chairs are ranged in symmetrical rows.*

At the rise of the curtain MRS. ZERO *is seen seated at the table looking alternately at the entrance door and a clock on the wall. She wears a bungalow apron over her best dress.*

After a few moments, the entrance door opens and ZERO *enters. He hangs his hat on a rack behind the door and coming over to the table seats himself at the vacant place. His movements throughout are quiet and abstracted.*

MRS. ZERO [*breaking the silence*]: Well, it was nice of you to come home. You're only an hour late and that ain't very much. The supper don't get very cold in an hour. An' of course the part about our havin' a lot of company to-night don't matter. [*They begin to eat.*] Ain't you even got sense enough to come home on time? Didn't I tell you we're goin' to have a lot o' company to-night? Didn't you know the Ones are comin'? An' the Twos? An' the Threes? An' the Fours? An' the Fives? And the Sixes? Didn't I tell you to be home on time? I might as well talk to a stone wall.

[*They eat for a few moments in silence.*] I guess you musta had some important business to attend to. Like watchin' the scoreboard. Or was two kids havin' a fight an' you was the referee? You sure do have a lot of business to attend to. It's a wonder you have time to come home at all. You gotta tough life, you have. Walk in, hang up your hat, an' put on the nose-bag. An' me in the hot kitchen all day, cookin' your supper an' waitin' for you to get good an' ready to come home!

[*Again they eat in silence.*] Maybe the boss kept you late to-night. Tellin' you what a big noise you are and how the store couldn't 'a' got along if you hadn't been pushin' a pen for twenty-five years. Where's the gold medal he pinned on you? Did some blind old lady take it away from you or did you leave it on the seat of the boss's limousine when he brought you home?

[*Again a few moments of silence.*] I'll bet he gave you a big raise, didn't he? Promoted you from the third floor to the fourth, maybe. Raise? A fat chance you got o' gettin' a raise. All they gotta do is put an ad in the paper. There's ten thousand like you layin' around the streets. You'll be holdin' down the same job at the end of another twenty-five years—if you ain't forgot how to add by that time.

A noise is heard offstage, a sharp clicking such as is made by the operation of the keys and levers of an adding machine. ZERO *raises his head for a moment, but lowers it almost instantly.*

MRS. ZERO: There's the doorbell. The company's here already. And we ain't hardly finished supper. [*She rises.*] But I'm goin' to clear off the table whether you're finished or not. If you want your supper, you got a right to be home on time. Not standin' around lookin' at scoreboards.

[*As she piles up the dishes,*] ZERO *rises and goes toward the entrance door.* Wait a minute! Don't open the door yet. Do you want the company to see all the mess? An' go an' put on a clean collar. You got red ink all over it.

[ZERO *goes toward bedroom door.*] I should think after pushin' a pen for twenty-five years, you'd learn how to do it without gettin' ink on your collar.

[ZERO *exits to bedroom.* MRS. ZERO *takes dishes to kitchen, talking as she goes.*] I guess I can stay up all night now washin' dishes. You should worry! That's what a man's got a wife for, ain't it? Don't he buy her her clothes an' let her eat with him at the same table? An' all she's gotta do is cook the meals an' do the washin' an' scrub the floor, an' wash the dishes, when the company goes. But, believe me, you're goin' to sling a mean dish-towel when the company goes to-night!

While she is talking ZERO *enters from bedroom. He wears a clean collar and is cramming the soiled one furtively into his pocket.* MRS. ZERO *enters from kitchen. She has removed her apron and carries a table cover, which she spreads hastily over the table. The clicking noise is heard again.*

MRS. ZERO: There's the bell again. Open the door, cancha?

ZERO *goes to the entrance door and opens it. Six men and six women file into the room in a double column. The men are all shapes and sizes, but their dress is identical with that of* ZERO *in every detail. Each, however, wears a wig of a different color. The women are all dressed alike, too, except that the dress of each is of a different color.*

MRS. ZERO [*taking the first woman's hand*]: How de do, Mrs. One.

MRS. ONE: How de do, Mrs. Zero.

Mrs. ZERO *repeats this formula with each woman in turn.* ZERO *does the same with the men, except that he is silent throughout. The files now separate, each man taking a chair from the right wall and each woman one from the left wall. Each sex forms a circle with the chairs very close together. The men—all except* ZERO*—smoke cigars. The women munch chocolates.*

SIX: Some rain we're havin'.

FIVE: Never saw the like of it.

FOUR: Worst in fourteen years, paper says.

THRE:: Y'can't always go by the papers.

TWO: No, that's right, too.

ONE: We're liable to forget from year to year.

SIX: Yeh, come t' think, last year was pretty bad, too.

FIVE: An' how about two years ago?

FOUR: Still this year's pretty bad.

THREE: Yeh, no gettin' away from that.

TWO: Might be a whole lot worse.

ONE: Yeh, it's all the way you look at it. Some rain, though.

MRS. SIX: I like them little organdie dresses.

MRS. FIVE: Yeh, with a little lace trimmin' on the sleeves.

MRS. FOUR: Well, I like 'em plain myself.

MRS. THREE: Yeh, what I always say is the plainer the more refined.

MRS. TWO: Well, I don't think a little lace does any harm.

MRS. ONE: No, it kinda dresses it up.

MRS. ZERO: Well, I always say it's all a matter of taste.

MRS. SIX: I saw you at the Rosebud Movie Thursday night, Mr. One.

ONE: Pretty punk show, I'll say.

TWO: They're gettin' worse all the time.

MRS. SIX: But who was the charming lady, Mr. One?

ONE: Now don't you go makin' trouble for me. That was my sister.

MRS. FIVE: Oho! That's what they all say.

MRS. FOUR: Never mind! I'll bet Mrs. One knows what's what, all right.

MRS. ONE: Oh, well, he can do what he likes—'slong as he behaves himself.

THREE: You're in luck at that, One. Fat chance I got of gettin' away from the frau even with my sister.

MRS. THREE: You oughta be glad you got a good wife to look after you.

THE OTHER WOMEN [*in unison*]: That's right, Mrs. Three.

FIVE: I guess I know who wears the pants in your house, Three.

MRS. ZERO: Never mind. I saw them holdin' hands at the movie the other night.

THREE: She musta been tryin' to get some money away from me.

MRS. THREE: Swell chance anybody'd have of gettin' any money away from you. [*General laughter.*]

FOUR: They sure are a loving couple.

MRS. TWO: Well, I think we oughta change the subject.

MRS. ONE: Yes, let's change the subject.

SIX [*sotto voce*]: Did you hear the one about the travelin' salesman?

FIVE: It seems this guy was in a sleeper.

FOUR: Goin' from Albany to San Diego.

THREE: And in the next berth was an old maid.

TWO: With a wooden leg.

ONE: Well, along about midnight—

They all put their heads together and whisper.

MRS. SIX [*sotto voce*]: Did you hear about the Sevens?

MRS. FIVE: They're gettin' a divorce.

MRS. FOUR: It's the second time for him.

MRS. THREE: They're two of a kind, if you ask me.

MRS. TWO: One's as bad as the other.

MRS. ONE: Worse.

MRS. ZERO: They say that she—

They all put their heads together and whisper.

SIX: I think this woman suffrage is the bunk.

FIVE: It sure is! Politics is a man's business.

FOUR: Woman's place is in the home.

THREE: That's it! Lookin' after the kids, 'stead of hangin' around the streets.

TWO: You hit the nail on the head that time.

ONE: The trouble is they don't know what they want.

MRS. SIX: Men sure get me tired.

MRS. FIVE: They sure are a lazy lot.

MRS. FOUR: And dirty.

MRS. THREE: Always grumblin' about somethin'.

MRS. TWO: When they're not lyin'!

MRS. ONE: Or messin' up the house.

MRS. ZERO: Well, believe me, I tell mine where he gets off.

SIX: Business conditions are sure bad.

FIVE: Never been worse.

FOUR: I don't know what we're comin' to.

THREE: I look for a big smash-up in about three months.

TWO: Wouldn't surprise me a bit.

ONE: We're sure headin' for trouble.

MRS. SIX: My aunt has gall-stones.

MRS. FIVE: My husband has bunions.

MRS. FOUR: My sister expects next month.

MRS. THREE: My cousin's husband has erysipelas.
MRS. TWO: My niece has St. Vitus's dance.
MRS. ONE: My boy has fits.
MRS. ZERO: I never felt better in my life. Knock on wood!
SIX: Too damn much agitation, that's at the bottom of it.
FIVE: That's it! too damn many strikes.
FOUR: Foreign agitators, that's what it is.
THREE: They ought be run outa the country.
TWO: What the hell do they want, anyhow?
ONE: They don't know what they want, if you ask me.
SIX: America for the Americans is what I say!
ALL [*in unison*]: That's it! Damn foreigners! Damn dagoes! Damn Catholics! Damn sheenies! Damn niggers! Jail 'em! shoot 'em! hang 'em! lynch 'em! burn 'em!

They all rise

ALL [*sing in unison*]: "My country' tis of thee, Sweet land of liberty!"
MRS. FOUR: Why so pensive, Mr. Zero?
ZERO [*speaking for the first time*]: I'm thinkin'.
MRS. FOUR: Well, be careful not to sprain your mind.

Laughter.

MRS. ZERO: Look at the poor men all by themselves. We ain't very sociable.
ONE: Looks like we're neglectin' the ladies.

The women cross the room and join the men, all chattering loudly. The doorbell rings.

MRS. ZERO: Sh! The doorbell!

The volume of sound slowly diminishes. Again the doorbell.

ZERO [*quietly*]: I'll go. It's for me.

They watch curiously as ZERO *goes to the door and opens it, admitting a policeman. There is a murmur of surprise and excitement.*

POLICEMAN: I'm lookin' for Mr. Zero. [*They all point to* ZERO.]
ZERO: I've been expectin' you.
POLICEMAN: Come along!
ZERO: Just a minute. [*He puts his hand in his pocket.*]
POLICEMAN: What's he tryin' to pull? [*He draws a revolver.*] I got you covered.
ZERO: Sure, that's all right. I just want to give you somethin'. [*He takes the collar from his pocket and gives it to the policeman.*]
POLICEMAN [*suspiciously*]: What's that?
ZERO: The collar I wore.
POLICEMAN: What do I want it for?
ZERO: It's got bloodstains on it.
POLICEMAN [*pocketing it*]: All right, come along!
ZERO [*turning to* MRS. ZERO]: I gotta go with him. You'll have to dry the dishes yourself.
MRS. ZERO [*rushing forward*]: What are they takin' you for?
ZERO [*calmly*]: I killed the boss this afternoon.

Quick Curtain as the policeman takes him off.

Scene IV

SCENE: *A court of justice. Three bare white walls without door or windows except for a single door in the right wall. At the right is a jury box in which are seated* MESSRS. ONE, TWO, THREE, FOUR, FIVE, *and* SIX *and their respective wives. One either side of the jury box stands a uniformed* OFFICER. *Opposite the jury box is a long, bare oak table piled high with law books. Behind the books* ZERO *is seated, his face buried in his hands. There is no other furniture in the room. A moment after the rise of the curtain, one of the officers rises, and going around the table, taps* ZERO *on the shoulder.* ZERO *rises and accompanies the officer. The* OFFICER *escorts him to the great empty space in the middle of the courtroom, facing the jury. He motions to* ZERO *to stop, then points to the jury, and resumes his place beside the jury box.* ZERO *stands there looking at the jury, bewildered and half-afraid. The* JURORS *give no sign of having seen him. Throughout they sit with folded arms, staring stolidly before them.*

ZERO [*beginning to speak; haltingly*]: Sure I killed him. I ain't sayin' I didn't, am I? Sure I killed him. Them lawyers! They give me a good stiff pain, that's what they give me. Half the time I don't know what the hell they're talkin' about. Objection sustained. Objection overruled. What's the big idea, anyhow? You ain't heard me do any objectin', have you? Sure not! What's the big idea of objectin'? You got a right to know. What I say is if one bird kills another bird, why you got a right to call him for it. That's what I say. I know all about that. I been on the jury, too. Them lawyers! Don't let 'em fill you full of bunk. All that bull about it bein' red ink on the bill-file. Red ink nothin'! It was blood, see? I want you to get that right. I killed him, see? Right through the heart with the bill-file, see? I want you to get that right—all of you. One, two, three, four, five, six, seven, eight, nine, ten, eleven, twelve. Twelve of you. Six and six. That makes twelve. I figgered it up often enough. Six and six makes twelve. And five is seventeen. And eight is twenty-five. And three is twenty-eight. Eight and carry two. Aw, cut it out! Them damn figgers! I can't forget 'em. Twenty-five years, see? Eight hours a day, exceptin' Sundays. And July and August half day Saturday. One week's vacation with pay. And another week without pay if you want it. Who the hell wants it? Layin' around the house listenin' to the wife tellin' you where you get off. Nix! An' legal holidays. I nearly forgot them. New Year's, Washington's Birthday, Decoration Day, Fourth o' July, Labor Day, Election Day, Thanksgivin', Christmas. Good Friday, if you want it. An' if you're a Jew, Young Kipper an' the other one—I forget what they call it. The dirty sheenies—always gettin' two to the other bird's one. An' when a holiday comes on Sunday, you get Monday off. So that's fair enough. But when the Fourth o' July comes on Saturday, why you're out o' luck on account of Saturday bein' a half-day anyhow. Get me? Twenty-five years—I'll tell you somethin' funny. Decoration Day an' the Fourth o' July are always on the same day o' the week. Twenty-five years. Never missed a day, and never more'n five minutes late. Look at my time card if you don't believe me. Eight twenty-seven, eight thirty, eight twenty-nine, eight twenty-seven, eight thirty-two. Eight an' thirty-two's forty an'—Goddamn them figgers! I can't forget 'em. They're funny things, them figgers. They look like people sometimes. The eights, see? Two dots for the eyes and a dot for the nose. An' a line. That's the mouth, see? An' there's others remind you of other things—but I can't talk about them, on account of there bein' ladies here. Sure I killed him. Why didn't he shut up? If he'd only shut up! Instead o' talkin' an' talkin' about how sorry he was an' what a good guy I was an' this an' that. I felt like sayin' to him: "For Christ's sake, shut up!" But I didn't have the nerve, see? I didn't have the nerve to say that to the boss. An' he went on talkin', sayin' how sorry he was, see? He was standin' right close to me. An' his coat only had two buttons on it. Two an' two makes four an'—aw, can it! An' there was the bill-file on the desk. Right where I could touch it. It ain't right to kill a guy. I know that. When I read all about him in the paper an' about his three kids I felt like a cheapskate, I tell you. They had the kids' pictures in the paper, right next to mine. An' his wife, too. Gee, it must be swell to have a wife like that. Some guys sure is lucky. An' he left fifty thousand dollars just for a rest-room for the girls in the store. He was a good guy, at that. Fifty thousand. That's more'n twice as much as I'd have if I saved every nickel I ever made. Let's see. Twenty-five an' twenty-five an' twenty-five an'—aw, cut it out! An' the ads had a big, black border around 'em; an' all it said was that the store would be closed for three days on account of the boss bein' dead. That nearly handed me a laugh, that did. All them floor-walkers an' buyers an' high-muck-a-mucks havin' me to thank for gettin' three days off. I hadn't oughta killed him. I ain't sayin' nothin' about that. But I thought he was goin' to give me a raise, see? On account of bein' there twenty-five years. He never talked to me before, see? Except one morning. we happened to come in the store together and I held the door open for him and he said "Thanks." Just like that, see? "Thanks!" That was the only time he ever talked to me. An' when I seen him comin' up to my desk, I didn't know where I got off. A big guy like that comin' up to my desk. I felt like I was chokin' like and all of a sudden I got a kind o' bad taste in my mouth like when you get up in the mornin'. I didn't have no right to kill him. The district attorney is right about that. He read the law to you, right out o' the book. Killin' a bird —that's wrong. But there was that girl, see? Six months they gave her. It was a dirty trick tellin' the cops on her like that. I shouldn't 'a' done that. But what was I gonna do? The wife wouldn't let up on me. I hadda do it. She used to walk around the room, just in her undershirt, see? Nothin' else on. Just her undershirt. An' they gave her six months. That's the last I'll ever see of her. Them birds—how do they get away with it? Just grabbin' women, the way you see 'em do in the pictures. I've seen lots I'd like to grab like that, but I ain't got the nerve—in the subway an' on the street an' in the store buyin' things. Pretty soft for them shoe-salesmen, I'll say, lookin' at women's legs all day. Them lawyers! They give me a pain, I tell you—a pain! Sayin' the same thing over an' over again. I never said I didn't kill him. But that ain't the same as bein' a regular murderer. What good did it do me to kill him? I didn't make nothin' out of it. Answer yes or no! Yes or no, me elbow! There's some things you can't answer yes or no. Give me the once-over, you guys. Do I look like a murderer? Do I? I never did no harm to nobody. Ask the wife. She'll tell you. Ask anybody. I never got into trouble. You wouldn't count that one time at the Polo Grounds. That was just fun like. Everybody was yellin', "Kill the empire! Kill the empire!" An' before I knew what I was doin' I fired the pop bottle. It was on account of everybody yellin' like that. Just in fun like, see? The yeller dog! Callin' that one a strike—a mile away from the plate. Anyhow, the bottle didn't hit him. An' when I seen the cop comin' up the aisle, I beat it. That didn't hurt nobody. It was just in fun like, see? An' that time in the subway. I was readin' about a lynchin', see? Down in Georgia. They took the nigger an' they tied him to a tree. An' they poured kerosene on him and lit a big fire under him. The dirty nigger! Boy, I'd of liked to been there, with a gat in each hand, pumpin' him full of lead. I was readin' about it in the subway, see? Right at Times Square where the big crowd gets on. An' all of a sudden this big nigger steps right on my foot. It was lucky for him I didn't have a gun on me. I'd of killed him sure, I guess. I guess he couldn't help it all right on account of the crowd, but a nigger's got no right to step on a white man's foot. I told him where he got off all right. The dirty nigger. But that didn't hurt nobody, either. I'm a pretty steady guy, you gotta admit that. Twenty-five years in one job an' I never missed a day. Fifty-two weeks in a year. Fifty-two an' fifty-two an' fifty-two an' —They didn't have t' look for me, did they? I didn't try to run away, did I? Where was I goin' to run to! I wasn't thinkin' about it at all, see? I'll tell you what I was thinkin' about—how I was goin' to break it to the wife about bein' canned. He canned me after twenty-five years, see? Did the lawyers tell you about that? I forget. All that talk gives me a headache. Objection sustained. Objection overruled. Answer yes or no. It gives me a headache. And I can't get the figgers outta my head, neither. But that's what I was thinkin' about—how I was goin' t' break it to the wife about bein' canned. An' what Miss Devore would think when she heard about me killin' him. I bet she never thought I had the nerve to do it. I'd of married her if the wife had passed out. I'd be holdin' down my job yet, if he hadn't o' canned me. But he kept talkin' an' talkin'. An' there was the bill-file right where I could reach it. Do you get me? I'm just a regular guy like anybody else. Like you birds, now.

For the first time the JURORS *relax, looking indignantly at each other and whispering.*

Suppose you was me, now. Maybe you'd 'a' done the same thing. That's the way you oughta look at it, see? Suppose you was me—

THE JURORS [*rising as one and shouting in unison*]: GUILTY!

ZERO *falls back, stunned for a moment by their vociferousness. The* JURORS *right-face in their places and file quickly out of the jury box and toward the door in a double column.*

ZERO [*recovering speech as the* JURORS *pass out at the door*]: Wait a minute. Jest a minute. You don't get me right. Jest give me a chance an' I'll tell you how it was. I'm all mixed up, see? On account of them lawyers. And the figgers in my head. But I'm goin' to tell you how it was. I was there twenty-five years, see? An' they gave her six months, see?

He goes on haranguing the empty jury box as the curtain falls.

Scene V[1]

In the middle of the stage is a large cage with bars on all four sides. The bars are very far apart and the interior of the cage is clearly visible. The floor of the cage is about six feet above the level of the stage. A flight of wooden steps leads up to it on the side facing the audience. ZERO *is discovered in the middle of the cage seated at a table above which is suspended a single naked electric light. Before him is an enormous platter of ham and eggs, which he eats voraciously with a large wooden spoon. He wears a uniform of very broad black and white horizontal stripes.*

A few moments after the rise of the curtain a man enters at left, wearing the blue uniform and peaked cap of a GUIDE. *He is followed by a miscellaneous crowd of* MEN, WOMEN, *and* CHILDREN*—about a dozen in all.*

THE GUIDE [*stopping in front of the cage*]: Now ladies and gentlemen, if you'll kindly step right this way! [THE CROWD *straggles up and forms a*

[1]This scene, which follows the courtroom scene, was part of the original script. It was omitted, however, when the play was produced, and was performed for the first time (in its present revised form) when the play was revived at the Phoenix Theatre in New York in February, 1956.

loose semicircle around him.] Step right up, please. A little closer so's everybody can hear. [*They move up closer.* ZERO *pays no attention whatever to them.*] This, ladies and gentlemen, is a very in-ter-est-in' specimen—the North American murderer, Genus *home sapiens,* Habitat North America. [*A titter of excitement. They all crowd up around the cage.*] Don't push. There's room enough for everybody.

A TALL LADY: Oh, how interesting!

A STOUT LADY [*excitedly*]: Look, Charley, he's eating!

CHARLEY [*bored*]: Yeh, I see him.

THE GUIDE [*repeating by rote*]: This specimen, ladies and gentlemen, exhibits the characteristics which are typical of his kind—

A SMALL BOY [*in a little Lord Fauntleroy suit, whiningly*]: Mama!

HIS MOTHER: Be quiet, Eustace, or I'll take you right home.

THE GUIDE: He has the opposable thumbs, the large cranial capacity, and the highly developed pre-frontal areas which distinguish him from all other species.

A YOUTH [*who has been taking notes*]: What areas did you say?

THE GUIDE [*grumpily*]: Pre-front-al areas. He learns by imitation and has a language which is said by some eminent philologists to bear many striking resemblances to English.

A BOY OF FOURTEEN: Pop, what's a philologist?

HIS FATHER: Keep quiet, can't you, and listen to what he's sayin'.

THE GUIDE: He thrives and breeds freely in captivity. This specimen was taken alive in his native haunts shortly after murdering his boss.

Murmurs of great interest.

THE TALL LADY:: Oh, how charming.

THE NOTE-TAKING YOUTH: What was that last? I didn't get it.

SEVERAL [*helpfully*]: Murdering his boss.

THE YOUTH: Oh—thanks.

THE GUIDE: He was tried, convicted, and sentenced in one hour, thirteen minutes, and twenty-four seconds, which sets a new record for his territory east of the Rockies and north of the Mason and Dixon line.

LITTLE LORD FAUNTLEROY [*whiningly*]: Ma-ma!

HIS MOTHER: Be quiet, Eustace, or Mama won't let you ride in the choo-choo.

THE GUIDE: Now take a good look at him, ladies and gents. It's his last day here. He's goin' to be executed at noon.

Murmurs of interest.

THE TALL LADY: Oh, how lovely!

A MAN: What's he eating?

THE GUIDE: Ham and eggs.

THE STOUT LADY: He's quite a big eater, ain't he?

THE GUIDE: Oh, he don't always eat that much. You see we always try to make 'em feel good on their last day. So about a week in advance we let them order what they want to eat on their last day. They can have eight courses and they can order anything they want—don't make no difference what it costs or how hard it is to get. Well, he couldn't make up his mind till last night, and then he ordered eight courses of ham and eggs.

They all push and stare.

THE BOY OF FOURTEEN: Look pop! He's eatin' with a spoon. Don't he know how to use a knife and fork?

THE GUIDE [*overhearing him*]: We don't dare trust him with a knife and fork, sonny. He might try to kill himself.

THE TALL LADY: Oh, how fascinating!

THE GUIDE [*resuming his official tone*]: And now, friends, if you'll kindly give me your attention for just a moment. [*He takes a bundle of folders from his pocket.*] I have a little souvenir folder which I'm sure you'll all want to have. It contains twelve beautiful colored views relating to the North American Murderer you have just been looking at. These include a picture of the murderer, a picture of the murderer's wife, the blood-stained weapon, the murderer at the age of six, the spot where the body was found, the little red schoolhouse where he went to school, and his vine-covered boyhood home in southern Illinois, with his sweet-faced white-haired old mother plainly visible in the foreground. And many other interesting views. I'm now going to distribute these little folders for your examination. [*Sotto voce.*] Just pass them back, will you? [*In louder tones.*] Don't be afraid to look at them. You don't have to buy them if you don't want to. It don't cost anything to look at them. [*To the* NOTE-TAKING YOUTH, *who is fumbling with a camera.*] Hey, there, young feller, no snapshots allowed. All right now, friends, if you'll just step this way. Keep close together and follow me. A lady lost her little boy here one time, and by the time we found him he was smoking cigarettes and hollering for a razor.

Much laughter as all follow him off left. ZERO *finishes eating and pushes away his plate. As* THE CROWD *goes at left,* MRS. ZERO *enters at right. She is dressed in mourning garments. She carries a large parcel. She goes up the steps to the cage, opens the door, and enters.* ZERO *looks up and sees her.*

MRS. ZERO: Hello.

ZERO: Hello, I didn't think you were comin' again.

MRS. ZERO: Well, I thought I'd come again. Are you glad to see me?

ZERO: Sure. Sit down. [*She complies.*] You're all dolled up, ain't you?

MRS. ZERO: Yeh, don't you like it? [*She gets up and turns about like a mannequin.*]

ZERO: Gee. Some class.

MRS. ZERO: I always look good in black. There's some weight to this veil though, I'll tell the world. I got a fierce headache.

ZERO: How much did all that set you back?

MRS. ZERO: Sixty-four dollars and twenty cents. And I gotta get a pin yet and some writin' paper—you know, with black around the edges.

ZERO: You'll be scrubbin' floors in about a year, if you go blowin' your coin like that.

MRS. ZERO: Well, I gotta do it right. It don't happen every day. [*She rises and takes up the parcel.*] I brought you somethin'.

ZERO [*interested*]: Yeh, what?

MRS. ZERO [*opening the parcel*]: You gotta guess.

ZERO: Er—er—gee, search me.

MRS. ZERO: Somethin' you like. [*She takes out a covered plate.*]

ZERO [*with increasing interest*]: Looks like somethin' to eat.

MRS. ZERO [*nodding*]: Yeh. [*She takes off the top plate.*] Ham an' eggs!

ZERO [*joyfully*]: Oh, boy! Just what I feel like eatin! [*He takes up the wooden spoon and begins to eat avidly.*]

MRS. ZERO [*pleased*]: Are they good?

ZERO [*his mouth full*]: Swell.

MRS. ZERO [*a little sadly*]: They're the last ones I'll ever make for you.

ZERO [*busily eating*]: Uh-huh.

MRS. ZERO: I'll tell you somethin'—shall I?

ZERO: Sure.

MRS. ZERO [*hesitantly*]: Well, all the while they were cookin' I was cryin!

ZERO: Yeh? [*He leans over and pats her hand.*]

MRS. ZERO: I just couldn't help it. The thought of it just made me cry.

ZERO: Well—no use cryin' about it.

MRS. ZERO: I just couldn't help it.

ZERO: Maybe this time next year you'll be fryin' eggs for some other bird.

MRS. ZERO: Not on your life.

ZERO: You never can tell.

MRS. ZERO: Not me. Once is enough for me.

ZERO: I guess you're right at that. Still, I dunno. You might just happen to meet some guy—

MRS. ZERO: Well, if I do, there'll be time enough to think about it. No use borrowin' trouble.

ZERO: How do you like bein' alone in the house?

MRS. ZERO: Oh, it's all right.

ZERO: You got plenty of room in the bed now, ain't you?

MRS. ZERO: Oh, yeh. [*A brief pause.*] It's kinda lonesome though—you know, wakin' up in the mornin' and nobody around to talk to.

ZERO: Yeh, I know. It's the same with me.

MRS. ZERO: Not that we ever did much talkin'.

ZERO: Well, that ain't it. It's just the idea of havin' somebody there in case you want to talk.

MRS. ZERO: Yeh, that's it. [*Another brief pause.*] I guess maybe I use t'bawl you out quite a lot, didn't I?

ZERO: Oh, well—no use talkin' about it now.

MRS. ZERO: We were always at it, weren't we?

ZERO: No more than any other married folks, I guess.

MRS. ZERO [*dubiously*]: I dunno—

ZERO: I guess I gave you cause, all right.

MRS. ZERO: Well—I got my faults too.

ZERO: None of us are perfect.

MRS. ZERO: We got along all right, at that, didn't we?

ZERO: Sure! Better'n most.

MRS. ZERO: Remember them Sundays at the beach, in the old days?

ZERO: You bet. [*With a laugh.*] Remember that time I ducked you. Gee, you was mad!

MRS. ZERO [*with a laugh*]: I didn't talk to you for a whole week.

ZERO [*chuckling*]: Yeh, I remember.

MRS. ZERO: And the time I had pneumonia and you brought me them roses. Remember?

ZERO: Yeh, I remember. And when the doctor told me maybe you'd pass out, I nearly sat down and cried.

MRS. ZERO: Did you?

ZERO: I sure did.

MRS. ZERO: We had some pretty good times at that, didn't we?

ZERO: I'll say we did!

MRS. ZERO [*with sudden soberness*]: It's all over now.

ZERO: All over is right. I ain't got much longer.

MRS. ZERO [*rising and going over to him*]: Maybe

—maybe—if we had to do it over again, it would be different.

ZERO [*taking her hand*]: Yeh. We live and learn.

MRS. ZERO [*crying*]: If we only had another chance.

ZERO: It's too late now.

MRS. ZERO: It don't seem right, does it?

ZERO: It ain't right. But what can you do about it?

MRS. ZERO: Ain't there somethin'—somethin' I can do for you—before—

ZERO: No. Nothin'. Not a thing.

MRS. ZERO: Nothin' at all?

ZERO: No. I can't think of anything. [*Suddenly.*] You're takin' good care of that scrapbook ain't you. With all the clippings in it?

MRS. ZERO: Oh, sure. I got it right on the parlor table. Right where everybody can see it.

ZERO [*pleased*]: It must be pretty near full, ain't it?

MRS. ZERO: All but three pages.

ZERO: Well, there'll be more tomorrow. Enough to fill it, maybe. Be sure to get them all, will you?

MRS. ZERO: I will. I ordered the papers already.

ZERO: Gee, I never thought I'd have a whole book full of clippings all about myself. [*Suddenly.*] Say, that's somethin' I'd like to ask you.

MRS. ZERO: What?

ZERO: Suppose you should get sick or be run over or somethin'—what would happen to the book?

MRS. ZERO: Well, I kinda thought I'd leave it to little Beatrice Elizabeth.

ZERO: Who? Your sister's kid?

MRS. ZERO: Yeh.

ZERO: What would she want with it?

MRS. ZERO: Well, it's nice to have, ain't it? And I wouldn't know who else to give it to.

ZERO: Well, I don't want her to have it. That fresh little kid puttin' her dirty fingers all over it.

MRS. ZERO: She ain't fresh and she ain't dirty. She's a sweet little thing.

ZERO: I don't want her to have it.

MRS. ZERO: Who do you want to have it?

ZERO: Well, I kinda thought I'd like Miss Devore to have it.

MRS. ZERO: Miss Devore?

ZERO: Yeh. You know. Down at the store.

MRS. ZERO: Why should she have it?

ZERO: She'd take good care of it. And anyhow, I'd like her to have it.

MRS. ZERO: Oh you would, would you?

ZERO: Yes.

MRS. ZERO: Well, she ain't goin' to have it. Miss Devore! Where does she come in, I'd like to know, when I got two sisters and a niece.

ZERO: I don't care nothin' about your sisters and your niece.

MRS. ZERO: Well, I do! And Miss Devore ain't goin' to get it. Now put that in your pipe and smoke it.

ZERO: What have you got to say about it? It's my book, ain't it?

MRS. ZERO: No, it ain't. It's mine now—or it will be tomorrow. And I'm goin' to do what I like with it.

ZERO: I should have given it to her in the first place—that's what I should have done.

MRS. ZERO Oh, should you? And what about me? Am I your wife or ain't I?

ZERO: Why remind me of my troubles?

MRS. ZERO: So it's Miss Devore all of a sudden, is it? What's been goin' on. I'd like to know, between you and Miss Devore?

ZERO: Aw, tie a can to that!

MRS. ZERO: Why didn't you marry Miss Devore, if you think so much of her?

ZERO: I would if I'd of met her first.

MRS. ZERO: [*Shrieking*] Ooh! A fine way to talk to me. After all I've done for you. You bum! You dirty bum! I won't stand for it! I won't stand for it!

In a great rage she takes up the dishes and smashes them on the floor. Then, crying hysterically, she opens the cage door, bangs it behind her, comes down the steps, and goes off toward left.

ZERO *stands gazing ruefully after her for a moment, and then with a shrug and a sigh begins picking up the pieces of broken crockery.*

As MRS. ZERO *exits at left, a door in the back of the cage opens and a man enters. He is dressed in a sky-blue, padded silk dressing-gown, which is fitted with innumerable pockets. Under this he wears a pink silk union-suit. His bare feet are in sandals. He wears a jaunty Panama hat with a red feather stuck in the brim. Wings are fastened to his sandals and to the shoulders of his dressing-gown.* ZERO, *who is busy picking up the broken crockery, does not notice him at first.* THE MAN *takes a gold toothpick and begins carefully picking his teeth, waiting for* ZERO *to notice him.* ZERO *happens to look up and suddenly sees* THE MAN. *He utters a cry of terror and shrinks into a corner of the cage, trembling with fear.*

ZERO: [*hoarsely*]. Who are you? Who are you?

THE MAN: [*calmly, as he pockets his toothpick*]. I'm the Fixer—from the Claim Department.

ZERO: Whaddya want?

THE FIXER: It's no use, Zero. There are no miracles.

ZERO: I don't know what you're talking about.

THE FIXER: Don't lie, Zero. [*Holding up his hand.*] And now that your course is run—now that the end is already in sight, you still believe that some thunderbolt, some fiery bush, some celestial apparition, will intervene between you and extinction. But it's no use, Zero. You're done for.

ZERO: [*vehemently*]. It ain't right! It ain't fair! I ain't gettin' a square deal!

THE FIXER: [*wearily*]. They all say that, Zero. [*Mildly.*] Now just tell me why you're not getting a square deal.

ZERO: Well, that addin' machine. Was that a square deal—after twenty-five years?

THE FIXER: Certainly—from any point of view, except a sentimental one. [*Looking at his wrist watch.*] The machine is quicker, it never makes a mistake, it's always on time. It presents no problems of housing, traffic congestion, water supply, sanitation.

ZERO: It costs somethin' to buy them machines, I'll tell you that!

THE FIXER: Yes, you're right there. In one respect you have the advantage over the machine—the cost of manufacture. But we've learned from many years' experience, Zero, that the original cost is an inconsequential item compared to upkeep. Take the dinosaurs, for example. They literally ate themselves out of existence. I held out for them to the last. They were damned picturesque—but when it came to a question of the nitrate supply, I simply had to yield. [*He begins to empty and clean his pipe.*] And so with you, Zero. It costs a lot to keep up all that delicate mechanism of eye and ear and hand and brain which you've never put to any use. We can't afford to maintain it in idleness—and so you've got to go.

ZERO: [*falling to his knees, supplicatingly*]. Gimme a chance, gimme another chance!

THE FIXER: What would you do if I gave you another chance?

ZERO: Well—first thing I'd go out and look for a job.

THE FIXER: Adding figures?

ZERO: Well—I ain't young enough to take up somethin' new.

THE FIXER *takes out a police whistle and blows shrilly. Instantly two guards enter.*

THE FIXER: Put the skids under him boys, and make it snappy.

He strolls away to the other side of the cage, and taking a nail clipper from a pocket, begins to clip his nails as the GUARDS *seize* ZERO.

ZERO: [*struggling and shrieking*]. No! No! Don't take me away! Don't kill me! Gimme a chance! Gimme another chance!

GUARD: [*soothingly*]. Ah, come on! Be a good fellow! It'll all be over in a minute!

ZERO: I don't want to die! I don't want to die! I want to live!

The GUARDS *look at each other dubiously. Then one of them walks rather timidly over to the* FIXER, *who is busy with his nails.*

GUARD: [*clearing his throat*], H'm!

THE FIXER: [*looking up*]. Well?

GUARD: [*timidly*]. He says he wants to live.

THE FIXER: No. He's no good.

GUARD: [*touching his cap, deferentially*]. Yes sir!

He goes back to his companion and the two of them drag ZERO *out at the back of the cage, still struggling and screaming.*

THE FIXER *puts away his nail clippers, yawns, then goes to the table and sits on the edge of it. From a pocket he takes an enormous pair of horn-rimmed spectacles. Then from another pocket he takes a folded newspaper, which he unfolds carefully. It is a colored comic supplement. He holds it up in front of him and becomes absorbed in it.*

A moment later the door at the back of the cage opens and a tall, brawny, bearded MAN *enters. He wears a red flannel undershirt and carries a huge blood-stained axe.* THE FIXER, *absorbed in the comic supplement, does not look up.*

MAN: [*hoarsely*]. O.K.

THE FIXER: [*looking up*]. What?

MAN: O.K.

THE FIXER: [*nodding*]. Oh, all right.

The MAN *bows deferentially and goes out at the back.* THE FIXER *puts away his spectacles and folds the comic supplement carefully. As he folds the paper:*

That makes a total of 2137 black eyes for Jeff.

He puts away the paper, turns out the electric light over his head, and leaves the cage by the front door. Then he takes a padlock from a pocket, attaches it to the door, and saunters off as the

CURTAIN FALLS

Scene VI

SCENE: *A graveyard in full moonlight. It is a second-rate graveyard—no elaborate tombstones or monu-*

*ments—just simple headstones and here and there a cross. At the back is an iron fence with a gate in the middle. At first no one is visible, but there are occasional sounds throughout: the hooting of an owl, the whistle of a distant whippoorwill, the croaking of a bullfrog, and the yowling of a serenading cat. After a few moments two figures appear outside the gate—a man and a woman. She pushes the gate and it opens with a rusty creak. The couple enter. They are now fully visible in the moonlight—*JUDY O'GRADY *and a* YOUNG MAN.

JUDY: [*advancing*]. Come on, this is the place.

YOUNG MAN: [*hanging back*]. This! Why this here is a cemetery.

JUDY: Aw, quit yer kiddin'!

YOUNG MAN: You don't mean to say—

JUDY: What's the matter with this place?

YOUNG MAN: A cemetery!

JUDY: Sure. What of it?

YOUNG MAN: You must be crazy.

JUDY: This place is all right, I tell you. I been here lots o' times.

YOUNG MAN: Nix on this place for me!

JUDY: Ain't this place as good as another? Whaddya afraid of? They're all dead ones here! They don't bother you. [*With sudden interest.*] Oh, look, here's a new one.

YOUNG MAN: Come on out of here.

JUDY: Wait a minute. Let's see what it says. [*She kneels on a grave in the foreground, and putting her face close to headstone, spells out the inscription.*] Z-e-r-o. Zero! Say, that's the guy—

YOUNG MAN: Zero? He's the guy killed his boss, ain't he?

JUDY: Yeh, that's him, all right. But what I'm thinkin' of is that I went to the hoosegow on account of him.

YOUNG MAN: What for?

JUDY: You know, same old stuff. Tenement House Law. [*Minicingly.*] Section blaa-blaa of the Penal Code. Third offense. Six months.

YOUNG MAN: And this bird—

JUDY: [*contemptuously*]. Him? He was mama's whitehaired boy. We lived in the same house. Across the airshaft, see? I used to see him lookin' in my window. I guess his wife musta seen him, too. Anyhow, they went and turned the bulls on me. And now I'm out and he's in. [*Suddenly.*] Say—say—[*She bursts into a peal of laughter.*]

YOUNG MAN: [*nervously*]. What's so funny?

JUDY: [*rocking with laughter*]. Say, wouldn't it be funny—if—if—[*She explodes again.*] That would be a good joke on him, all right. He can't do nothin' about it now, can he?

YOUNG MAN: Come on out of here. I don't like this place.

JUDY: Aw, you're a bum sport. What do you want to spoil my joke for? [*A cat yammers mellifluously.*]

YOUNG MAN: [*half-hysterically*]. What's that?

JUDY: It's only the cats. They seem to like it here all right. But come on if you're afraid. [*They go toward the gate. As they go out.*] You nervous men sure are the limit.

They go out through the gate. As they disappear, ZERO'S *grave opens suddenly and his head appears.*

ZERO: [*looking about*]. That's funny! I thought I heard her talkin' and laughin'. But I don't see nobody. Anyhow, what would she be doin' here? I guess I must 'a' been dreamin'. But how could I be dreamin' when I ain't been asleep? [*He looks about again.*] Well, no use goin' back. I can't sleep, anyhow. I might as well walk around a little. [*He rises out of the ground, very rigidly. He wears a fulldress suit of very antiquated cut and his hands are folded stiffly across his breast.*]

ZERO: [*walking woodenly*]. Gee! I'm stiff! [*He slowly walks a few steps, then stops.*] Gee, it's lonesome here! [*He shivers and walks on aimlessly.*] I should 'a' stayed where I was. But I thought I heard her laughin'.

A loud sneeze is heard. ZERO *stands motionless, quaking with terror. The sneeze is repeated.*

ZERO: [*hoarsely*]. What's that?

A MILD VOICE: It's all right. Nothing to be afraid of.

From behind a headstone SHRDLU *appears. He is dressed in a shabby and ill-fitting cutaway. He wears silver-rimmed spectacles and is smoking a cigarette.*

SHRDLU: I hope I didn't frighten you.

ZERO: [*still badly shaken*]. No-o. It's all right. You see, I wasn't expectin' to see anybody.

SHRDLU: You're a newcomer, aren't you?

ZERO: Yeh, this is my first night. I couldn't seem to get to sleep.

SHRDLU: I can't sleep, either. Suppose we keep each other company, shall we?

ZERO: [*eagerly*]. Yeh, that would be great. I been feelin' awful lonesome.

SHRDLU: [*nodding*]. I know. Let's make ourselves comfortable.

He seats himself easily on a grave. ZERO *tries to follow his example but he is stiff in every joint and groans with pain.*

ZERO: I'm kinda stiff.

SHRDLU: You mustn't mind the stiffness. It wears off in a few days. [*He seats himself on the grave beside* ZERO *and produces a package of cigarettes.*] Will you have a Camel?

ZERO: No, I don't smoke.

SHRDLU: I find it helps keep the mosquitoes away. [*He lights a cigarette.*]

SHRDLU: [*suddenly taking the cigarette out of his mouth*]. Do you mind if I smoke, Mr.—Mr.—?

ZERO: No, go right ahead.

SHRDLU: [*replacing the cigarette*]. Thank you. I didn't catch your name.

ZERO *does not reply.*

SHRDLU: [*mildly*]. I say I didn't catch your name.

ZERO: I heard you the first time. [*Hesitantly*]. I'm scared if I tell you who I am and what I done, you'll be off me.

SHRDLU: [*sadly*]. No matter what your sins may be, they are as snow compared to mine.

ZERO: You got another guess comin'. [*He pauses dramatically.*] My name's Zero. I'm a murderer.

SHRDLU: [*nodding calmly*]. Oh, yes, I remember reading about you, Mr. Zero.

ZERO: [*a little piqued*]. And you still think you're worse than me?

SHRDLU: [*throwing away his cigarette*]. Oh, a thousand times worse, Mr. Zero—a million times worse.

ZERO: What did you do?

SHRDLU: I, too, am a murderer.

ZERO: [*looking at him in amazement*]. Go on! You're kiddin' me!

SHRDLU: Every word I speak is the truth, Mr. Zero. I am the foulest, the most sinful of murderers! You only murdered your employer, Mr. Zero. But I—I murdered my mother. [*He covers his face with his hands and sobs.*]

ZERO: [*horrified*]. The hell yer say!

SHRDLU: [*sobbing*]. Yes, my mother!—my beloved mother!

ZERO: [*suddenly*]. Say, you don't mean to say you're Mr.—

SHRDLU: [*nodding*]. Yes. [*He wipes his eyes, still quivering with emotion.*]

ZERO: I remember readin' about you in the papers.

SHRDLU: Yes, my guilt has been proclaimed to all the world. But that would be a trifle if only I could wash the stain of sin from my soul.

ZERO: I never heard of a guy killin' his mother before. What did you do it for?

SHRDLU: Because I have a sinful heart—there is no other reason.

ZERO: Did she always treat you square and all like that?

SHRDLU: She was a saint—a saint, I tell you. She cared for me and watched over me as only a mother can.

ZERO: You mean to say you didn't have a scrap or nothin'?

SHRDLU: Never a harsh or an unkind word. Nothing except loving care and good advice. From my infancy she devoted herself to guiding me on the right path. She taught me to be thrifty, to be devout, to be unselfish, to shun evil companions, and to shut my ears to all the temptations of the flesh—in short, to become a virtuous, respectable, and God-fearing man. [*He groans.*] But it was a hopeless task. At fourteen I began to show evidence of my sinful nature.

ZERO: [*breathlessly*]. You didn't kill anybody else, did you?

SHRDLU: No, thank God, there is only one murder on my soul. But I ran away from home.

ZERO: You did!

SHRDLU: Yes. A companion lent me a profane book—the only profane book I have ever read, I'm thankful to say. It was called *Treasure Island.* Have you ever read it?

ZERO: No, I never was much on readin' books.

SHRDLU: It is a wicked book—a lurid tale of adventure. But it kindled in my sinful heart a desire to go to sea. And so I ran away from home.

ZERO: What did you do—get a job as a sailor?

SHRDLU: I never saw the sea— not to the day of my death. Luckily, my mother's loving intuition warned her of my intention and I was sent back home. She welcomed me with open arms. Not an angry word, not a look of reproach. But I could read the mute suffering in her eyes as we prayed together all through the night.

ZERO: [*sympathetically*]. Gee, that must 'a' been tough. Gee, the mosquitoes are bad, ain't they? [*He tries awkwardly to slap at them with his stiff hands.*]

SHRDLU: [*absorbed in his narrative*]. I thought that experience had cured me of evil and I began to think about a career. I wanted to go in foreign missions at first, but we couldn't bear the thought of the separation. So we finally decided that I should become a proofreader.

ZERO: Say, slip me one o' them Camels, will you? I'm gettin' all bit up.

SHRDLU: Certainly. [*He hands* ZERO *cigarettes and matches.*]

ZERO: [*lighting up*]. Go ahead. I'm listenin'.

SHRDLU: By the time I was twenty I had a good job reading proof for a firm that printed catalogues. After a year they promoted me and let me specialize in shoe catalogues.

ZERO: Yeh? That must 'a' been a good job.

SHRDLU: It was a very good job. I was on the shoe catalogues for thirteen years. I'd been on them yet, if I hadn't—[*He chokes back a sob.*]

ZERO: They oughta put a shot o' citronella in that embalmin'-fluid.

SHRDLU: [*he sighs*]. We were so happy together. I had my steady job. And Sundays we would go to morning, afternoon, and evening service. It was an honest and moral mode of life.

ZERO: It sure was.

SHRDLU: Then came that fatal Sunday. Dr. Amaranth, our minister, was having dinner with us—one of the few pure spirits on earth. When he had finished saying grace, we had our soup. Everything was going along as usual—we were eating our soup and discussing the sermon, just like every other Sunday I could remember. Then came the leg of lamb—[*He breaks off, then resumes in a choking voice.*] I see the whole scene before me so plainly—it never leaves me—Dr. Amaranth at my right, my mother at my left, the leg of lamb on the table in front of me and the cuckoo clock on the little shelf between the windows. [*He stops and wipes his eyes.*]

ZERO: Yeh, but what happened?

SHRDLU: Well, as I started to carve the lamb—Did you ever carve a leg of lamb?

ZERO: No, corned beef was our speed.

SHRDLU: It's very difficult on account of the bone. And when there's gravy in the dish there's danger of spilling it. So Mother always used to hold the dish for me. She leaned forward, just as she always did, and I could see the gold locket around her neck. It had my picture in it and one of my baby curls. Well, I raised my knife to carve the leg of lamb—and instead I cut my mother's throat! [*He sobs.*]

ZERO: You must 'a' been crazy!

SHRDLU: [*raising his head, vehemently*]. No! Don't try to justify me. I wasn't crazy. They tried to prove at the trial that I was crazy. But Dr. Amaranth saw the truth! He saw it from the first! He knew that it was my sinful nature—and he told me what was in store for me.

ZERO: [*trying to be comforting*]. Well, your troubles are over now.

SHRDLU: [*his voice rising*]. Over! Do you think this is the end?

ZERO: Sure. What more can they do to us?

SHRDLU: [*his tones growing shriller and shriller*]. Do you think there can ever be any peace for such as we are—murderers, sinners? Don't you know what awaits us—flames, eternal flames!

ZERO: [*nervously*]. Keep your shirt on, Buddy—they wouldn't do that to us.

SHRDLU: There's no escape—no escape for us, I tell you. We're doomed! We're doomed to suffer unspeakable torments through all eternity. [*His voice rises higher and higher.*]

A grave opens suddenly and a head appears.

THE HEAD: Hey, you birds! Can't you shut up and let a guy sleep? [ZERO *scrambles painfully to his feet.*]

ZERO: [*to* SHRDLU]. Hey, put on the soft pedal.

SHRDLU: [*too wrought up to attend.*] It won't be long now! We'll receive our summons soon.

THE HEAD: Are you goin' to beat it or not? [*He calls into the grave.*] Hey, Bill, lend me your head a minute. [*A moment later his arm appears holding a skull.*]

ZERO: [*warningly*]. Look out! [*He seizes* SHRDLU *and drags him away just as* THE HEAD *throws the skull.*]

THE HEAD: [*disgustedly*]. Missed 'em. Damn old tabby cats! I'll get 'em next time. [*A prodigious yawn.*] Ho-hum! Me for the worms!

THE HEAD *disappears as the curtain falls.*

Scene VII

SCENE: *A pleasant place. A scene of pastoral loveliness. A meadow dotted with fine old trees and carpeted with rich grass and field flowers. In the background are seen a number of tents fashioned of gaystriped silks, and beyond gleams a meandering river. Clear air and a fleckless sky. Sweet distant music throughout.*

At the rise of the curtain, SHRDLU *is seen seated under a tree in the foreground in an attitude of deep dejection. His knees are drawn up and his head is buried in his arms. He is dressed as in the preceding scene.*

A few minutes later, ZERO *enters at right. He walks slowly and looks about him with an air of half-suspicious curiosity. He, too, is dressed as in the preceding scene. Suddenly he sees* SHRDLU *seated under the tree. He stands still and looks at him half fearfully. Then, seeing something familiar in him, goes closer.* SHRDLU *is unaware of his presence. At last* ZERO *recognizes him and grins in pleased surprise.*

ZERO: Well, if it ain't—! [*He claps* SHRDLU *on the shoulder.*] Hello, Buddy!

SHRDLU looks up slowly; then, recognizing ZERO, he rises gravely and extends his hand courteously.

SHRDLU: How do you do, Mr. Zero? I'm very glad to see you again.

ZERO: Same here. I wasn't expectin' to see you, either. [*Looking about.*] This is a kinda nice place. I wouldn't mind restin' here a while.

SHRDLU: You may if you wish.

ZERO: I'm kinda tired. I ain't used to bein' outdoors. I ain't walked so much in years.

SHRDLU: Sit down here, under the tree.

ZERO: Do they let you sit on the grass?

SHRDLU: Oh, yes.

ZERO: [*seating himself*]. Boy, this feels good. I'll tell the world my feet are sore. I ain't used to so much walkin'. Say, I wonder would it be all right if I took my shoes off; my feet are tired.

SHRDLU: Yes. Some of the people here go barefoot.

ZERO: Yeh? They sure must be nuts. But I'm goin't' leave 'em off for a while. So long as it's all right. The grass feels nice and cool. [*He stretches out comfortably*]. Say, this is the life of Riley all right, all right. This sure is a nice place. What do they call this place, anyhow?

SHRDLU: The Elysian Fields.

ZERO: The which?

SHRDLU: The Elysian Fields.

ZERO: [*dubiously*]. Oh! Well, it's a nice place, all right.

SHRDLU: They say that this is the most desirable of all places. Only the most favoured remain here.

ZERO: Yeh? Well, that let's me out, I guess. [*Suddenly*]. But what are you doin' here? I thought you'd be burned by now.

SHRDLU: [*sadly*]. Mr. Zero, I am the most unhappy of men.

ZERO: [*in mild astonishment*]. Why, because you ain't bein' roasted alive?

SHRDLU: [*nodding*]. Nothing is turning out as I expected. I saw everything so clearly—the flames, the tortures, an eternity of suffering as the just punishment for my unspeakable crime. And it has all turned out so differently.

ZERO: Well, that's pretty soft for you, ain't it?

SHRDLU: [*wailingly*]. No, no, no! It's right and just that I should be punished. I could have endured it stoically. All through those endless ages of indescribable torment I should have exulted in the magnificence of divine justice. But this—this is maddening! What becomes of justice? What becomes of morality? What becomes of right and wrong? It's maddening—simply maddening! Oh, if Dr. Amaranth were only here to advise me! [*He buries his face and groans*].

ZERO: [*trying to puzzle it out*]. You mean to say they ain't called you for cuttin' your mother's throat?

SHRDLU: No! It's terrible—terrible! I was prepared for anything—anything but this.

ZERO: Well, what did they say to you?

SHRDLU: [*looking up*]. Only that I was to come here and remain until I understood.

ZERO: I don't get it. What do they want you to understand?

SHRDLU: [*despairingly*]. I don't know—I don't know! If I only had an inkling of what they meant—[*interrupting him*]. Just listen quietly for a moment; do you hear anything?

They are both silent, straining their ears.

ZERO: [*at length*]. Nope.

SHRDLU: You don't hear any music? Do you?

ZERO: Music? No, I don't hear nothin'.

SHRDLU: The people here say that the music never stops.

ZERO: They're kiddin' you.

SHRDLU: Do you think so?

ZERO: Sure thing. There ain't a sound.

SHRDLU: Perhaps. They're capable of anything. But I haven't told you of the bitterest of my disappointments.

ZERO: Well, spill it. I'm gettin' used to hearin' bad news.

SHRDLU: When I came to this place, my first thought was to find my dear mother. I wanted to ask her forgiveness. And I wanted her to help me to understand.

ZERO: An' she couldn't do it?

SHRDLU: [*with a deep groan*]. She's not here! Mr. Zero! Here where only the most favoured dwell, that wisest and purest of spirits is nowhere to be found. I don't understand it.

A WOMAN'S VOICE: [*in the distance*]. Mr. Zero! Oh, Mr. Zero!

ZERO raises his head and listens attentively.

SHRDLU: [*going on, unheedingly*]. If you were to see some of the people here—the things they do—

ZERO: [*interrupting*]. Wait a minute, will you? I think somebody's callin' me.

THE VOICE: [*somewhat nearer*]. Mr. Ze-ro! Oh! Mr. Ze-ro!

ZERO: Who the hell's that now? I wonder if the wife's on my trail already. That would be swell, wouldn't it? An' I figured on her bein' good for another twenty years, anyhow.

THE VOICE: [*nearer*]. Mr. Ze-ro! Yoo-hoo!

ZERO: No. That ain't her voice. [*calling, savagely.*] Yoo-hoo. [*To* SHRDLU.] Ain't that always the way? Just when a guy is takin' life easy an' havin' a good time! [*He rises and looks off left.*] Here she comes, whoever she is. [*In sudden amazement.*] Well, I'll be—! Well, what do you know about that!

He stands looking in wonderment, as DAISY DIANA DOROTHEA DEVORE *enters. She wears a much-beruffled white muslin dress which is a size too small and fifteen years too youthful for her. She is red-faced and breathless.*

DAISY: [*panting*]. Oh! I thought I'd never catch up to you. I've been followin' you for days—callin' an' callin'. Didn't you hear me?

ZERO: Not till just now. You look kinda winded.

DAISY: I sure am. I can't hardly catch my breath.

ZERO: Well, sit down an' take a load off your feet. [*He leads her to the tree.*]

[DAISY *sees* SHRDLU *for the first time and shrinks back a little.*]

ZERO: It's all right, he's a friend of mine. [*To* SHRDLU]. Buddy, I want you to meet my friend, Miss Devore.

SHRDLU: [*rising and extending his hand courteously*]. Howdoyoudo,MissDevore?

DAISY: [*self-consciously*]. How do!

ZERO: [*to* DAISY]. He's a friend of mine. [*To* SHRDLU.] I guess you don't mind if she sits here a while an' cools off, do you?

SHRDLU: No, no, certainly not.

They all seat themselves under the tree. ZERO *and* DAISY *are a little self-conscious.* SHRDLU *gradually becomes absorbed in his own thoughts.*

ZERO: I was just takin' a rest myself. I took my shoes off on account of my feet bein' so sore.

DAISY: Yeh, I'm kinda tired, too. [*Looking about.*] Say, ain't it pretty here, though?

ZERO: Yeh, it is at that.

DAISY: What do they call this place?

ZERO: Why—er—let's see. He was tellin' me just a minute ago. The—er—I don't know. Some kind o' fields. I forget now. [*To* SHRDLU]. Say, Buddy, what do they call this place again? [SHRDLU, *absorbed in his thoughts, does not hear him. To* DAISY]. He don't hear me. He's thinkin' again.

DAISY: [*sotto voce*]. What's the matter with him?

ZERO: Why, he's the guy that murdered his mother—remember?

DAISY: [*interested.*] Oh, yeh! Is that him?

ZERO: Yeh. An' he had it all figgered out how they was goin' t' roast him or somethin'. And now they ain't goin' to do nothin' to him an' it's kinda got his goat.

DAISY: [*sympathetically.*] Poor feller!

ZERO: Yeh. He takes it kinda hard.

DAISY: He looks like a nice young feller.

ZERO: Well, you sure are good for sore eyes. I never expected to see you here.

DAISY: I thought maybe you'd be kinda surprised.

ZERO: Surprised is right. I thought you was alive an' kickin'. When did you pass out?

DAISY: Oh, right after you did—a coupla days.

ZERO: [*interested.*] Yeh? What happened? Get hit by a truck or somethin'?

DAISY: No. [*Hesitantly.*] You see—it's this way. I blew out the gas.

ZERO: [*astonished.*] Go on! What was the big idea?

DAISY: [*falteringly.*] Oh, I don't know. You see, I lost my job.

ZERO: I'll bet you're sorry you did it now, ain't you?

DAISY: [*with conviction.*] No, I ain't sorry. Not a bit. [*Then hesitantly.*] Say, Mr. Zero, I been thinkin'—[*she stops.*]

ZERO: What?

DAISY: [*plucking up courage.*] I been thinkin' it would be kinda nice—if you an' me—if we could kinda talk things over.

ZERO: Yeh. Sure. What do you want to talk about?

DAISY: Well—I don't know—but you and me—we ain't really ever talked things over, have we?

ZERO: No, that's right, we ain't. Well let's go to it.

DAISY: I was thinkin' if we could be alone—just the two us, see?

ZERO: Oh, yeh! Yeh, I get you. [*He turns to* SHRDLU *and coughs loudly.* SHRDLU *does not stir.*]

ZERO: [*to* DAISY] He's dead to the world. [*He turns to* SHRDLU Say, Buddy [*No answer.*] Say, Buddy!

SHRDLU: [*looking up with a start.*] Were you speaking to me?

ZERO: Yeh. How'd you guess it? I was thinkin' that maybe you'd like to walk around a little and look for your mother.

SHRDLU: [*shaking his head.*] It's no use. I've looked everywhere. [*He relapses into thought again.*]

ZERO: Maybe over there they might know.

SHRDLU: No, no! I've searched everywhere. She's not here.

ZERO *and* DAISY *look at each other in despair.*

ZERO: Listen, old shirt, my friend here and me —see? we used to work in the same store. An' we got some things to talk over—business, see?—kinda confidential. So if it ain't askin' too much—

SHRDLU: [*springing to his feet.*] Why, certainly! Excuse me! [*He bows politely to Daisy and walks off.* DAISY *and* ZERO *watch him until he has disappeared.*]

ZERO: [*with a forced laugh.*] He's a good guy at that.

Now that they are alone, both are very self-conscious, and for a time they sit in silence.

DAISY: [*breaking the silence.*] It sure is pretty here, ain't it?

ZERO: Sure is.

DAISY: Look at the flowers! Ain't they just perfect! Why, you'd think they was artificial, wouldn't you?

ZERO: Yeh, you would.

DAISY: And the smell of them. Like perfume.

ZERO: Yeh.

DAISY: I'm crazy about the country, ain't you?

ZERO: Yeh. It's nice for a change.

DAISY: Them store picnics—remember?

ZERO: You bet. They sure was fun.

DAISY: One time—I guess you don't remember —the two of us—me and you—we sat down on the grass together under a tree—just like we're doin' now.

ZERO: Sure I remember.

DAISY: Go on! I'll bet you don't.

ZERO: I'll bet I do. It was the year the wife didn't go.

DAISY: [*her face brightening.*] That's right! I didn't think you'd remember.

ZERO: An' comin' home we sat together in the truck.

DAISY: [*eagerly, rather shamefacedly.*] Yeh! There's somethin' I've always wanted to ask you.

ZERO: Well, why didn't you?

DAISY: I don't know. It didn't seem refined. But I'm goin' to ask you now, anyhow.

ZERO: Go ahead. Shoot.

DAISY: [*falteringly.*] Well—while we was comin' home—you put your arm up on the bench behind me—and I could feel your knee kinda pressin' against mine. [*She stops.*]

ZERO: [*becoming more and more interested.*] Yeh—well—what about it?

DAISY: What I wanted to ask you was—was it just kinda accidental?

ZERO: [*with a laugh.*] Sure it was accidental. Accidental on purpose.

DAISY: [*eagerly.*] Do you mean it?

ZERO: Sure I mean it. You mean to say you didn't know it?

DAISY: No. I've been wantin' to ask you—

ZERO: Then why did you get sore at me?

DAISY: Sore? I wasn't sore! When was I sore?

ZERO: That night. Sure you was sore. If you wasn't sore why did you move away?

DAISY: Just to see if you meant it. I thought if you meant it you'd move up closer. An' then when you took your arm away I was sure you didn't mean it.

ZERO: An' I thought all the time you was sore. That's why I took my arm away. I thought if I moved up you'd hollar and then I'd be in a jam, like you read in the paper all the time about guys gettin' pulled in for annoyin' women.

DAISY: An' I was wishin' you'd put your arm around me—just sittin' there wishin' all the way home.

ZERO: What do you know about that? That sure is hard luck, that is. If I'd 'a' only knew! You know what I felt like doin'—only I didn't have the nerve?

DAISY: What?

ZERO: I felt like kissin' you.

DAISY: [*fervently.*] I wanted you to.

ZERO: [*astonished.*] You would 'a' let me?

DAISY: I wanted you to! I wanted you to! Oh, why didn't you—why didn't you?

ZERO: I didn't have the nerve. I sure was a dumbbell.

DAISY: I would 'a' let you all you wanted to. I wouldn't 'a' cared. I know it would 'a' been wrong but I wouldn't 'a' cared. I wasn't thinkin' about right an' wrong at all. I didn't care —see? I just wanted you to kiss me.

ZERO: [*feelingly.*] If I'd only knew. I wanted to do it, I swear I did. But I didn't think you cared nothin' about me.

DAISY: [*passionately.*] I never cared nothin' about nobody else.

ZERO: Do you mean it—on the level? You ain't kiddin' me, are you?

DAISY: No, I ain't kiddin'. I mean it. I'm telling you the truth. I ain't never had the nerve to tell you before—but now I don't care. It don't make no difference now. I mean it—every word of it.

ZERO: [*dejectedly.*] If I'd only knew it.

DAISY: Listen to me. There's somethin' else I wanted to tell you. I may as well tell you everything now. It don't make no difference now. About my blowin' out the gas—see? Do you know why I done it?

ZERO: Yeh, you told me—on account o' bein' canned.

DAISY: I just told you that. That ain't the real reason. The real reason is on account o' you.

ZERO: You mean to say on account o' me passin' out—?

DAISY: Yeh. That's it. I didn't want to go on livin'. What for? What did I want to go on livin' for? I didn't have nothin' to live for with you gone. I often thought of doin' it before. But I never had the nerve. An' anyhow I didn't want to leave you.

ZERO: An' me bawlin' you out, about readin' too fast an' readin' too slow.

DAISY: [*reproachfully.*] Why did you do it?

ZERO: I don't know, I swear I don't. I was always stuck on you. An' while I'd be addin' them figgers, I'd be thinkin' how if the wife died, you an' me could get married.

DAISY: I used to think o' that, too.

ZERO: An' then before I knew it, I was bawlin' you out.

DAISY: Them was the times I'd think o' blowin' out the gas. But I never did till you was gone. There wasn't nothin' to live for then. But it wasn't so easy to do, anyhow. I never could stand the smell o' gas. An' all the while I was gettin' ready, you know, stuffin' up all the cracks, the way you read about in the paper—I was thinkin' of you and hopin' that maybe I'd meet you again. An' I made up my mind if I ever did see you, I'd tell you.

ZERO: [*taking her hand.*] I'm sure glad you did. I'm sure glad. [*Ruefully.*] But it don't do much good now, does it?

DAISY: No, I guess it don't. [*Summoning courage.*] But there's one thing I'm goin' to ask you.

ZERO: What's that?

DAISY: [*in a low voice.*] I want you to kiss me.

ZERO: You bet I will! [*He leans over and kisses her cheek.*]

DAISY: Not like that. I don't mean like that. I mean really kiss me. On the mouth. I ain't never been kissed like that.

ZERO *puts his arms about and presses his lips to hers. A long embrace. At last they separate and sit side by side in silence.*

DAISY: [*putting her hands to her cheeks.*] So that's what it's like. I didn't know it could be like that. I didn't know anythin' could be like that.

ZERO: [*fondling her hand.*] Your cheeks are red. They're all red. And your eyes are shinin'. I never seen your eyes shinin' like that before.

DAISY: [*holding up her hand.*] Listen—do you hear it? Do you hear the music?

ZERO: No, I don't hear nothin'!

DAISY: Yeh—music. Listen an' you'll hear it.

They are both silent for a moment.

ZERO: [*excitedly.*] Yeh! I hear it! He said there was music but I didn't hear it till just now.

DAISY: Ain't it grand?

ZERO: Swell! Say, do you know what?

DAISY: What?

ZERO: It makes me feel like dancin'.

DAISY: Yeh? Me, too.

ZERO: [*springing to his feet.*] Come on! Let's dance! [*He seizes her hands and tries to pull her up.*]

DAISY: [*resisting laughingly.*] I can't dance. I ain't danced in twenty years.

ZERO: That's nothin'. I ain't neither.

He pulls her to her feet and seizes her about the waist.

DAISY: Wait a minute! Wait till I fix my skirt. [*She turns back her skirts and pins them above the ankles.*]

ZERO *seizes her about the waist. They dance clumsily but with gay abandon.* DAISY'S *hair becomes loosened and tumbles over her shoulders. She lends herself more and more to the spirit of the dance. But* ZERO *soon begins to tire and dances with less and less zest.*

ZERO: [*stopping at last, panting for breath.*] Wait a minute! I'm all winded.

He releases DAISY *but before he can turn away, she throws her arms about him and presses her lips to his.*

ZERO: [*freeing himself.*] Wait a minute! Let me get my wind!

He limps to the tree and seats himself under it, gasping for breath. DAISY *looks after him, her spirits rather dampened.*

ZERO: Whew! I sure am winded! I ain't used to dancin'. Gee, my heart's goin' a mile a minute.

He takes off his collar and tie and opens the neckband of his shirt. DAISY *sits under the tree near him, looking at him longingly. But he is busy catching his breath.* Gee, my heart's goin' a mile a minute.

DAISY: Why don't you lay down an' rest? You could put your head on my lap.

ZERO: That ain't a bad idea.

He stretches out, his head in DAISY'S *lap.*

DAISY: [*fondling his hair.*] It was swell, wasn't it?

ZERO: Yeh. But you gotta be used to it.

DAISY: Just imagine if we could stay here all the time—you an' me together—wouldn't it be swell?

ZERO: Yeh. But there ain't a chance.

DAISY: Won't they let us stay?

ZERO: No. This place is only for the good ones.

DAISY: Well, we ain't so bad, are we?

ZERO: Go on! Me a murderer an' you committin' suicide. Anyway, they wouldn't stand for this—the way we been goin' on.

DAISY: I don't see why.

ZERO: You don't! You know it ain't right. Ain't I got a wife?

DAISY: Not any more you ain't. When you're dead that ends it. Don't they always say "until death do us part?"

ZERO: Well, maybe you're right about that but they wouldn't stand for us here.

DAISY: It would be swell—the two of us together—we could make up for all them years.

ZERO: Yeh, I wish we could.

DAISY: We sure were fools. But I don't care. I've got you now. [*She kisses his forehead and cheeks and mouth.*]

ZERO: I'm sure crazy about you. I never saw you lookin' so pretty before, with your cheeks all red. An' you hair hangin' down. You got swell hair. [*He fondles and kisses her hair.*]

DAISY: [*ecstatically.*] We got each other now, ain't we?

ZERO: Yeh. I'm crazy about you. Daisy! That's a pretty name. It's a flower, ain't it? Well—that's what you are—just a flower.

DAISY: [*happily.*] We can always be together now, can't we?

ZERO: As long as they'll let us. I sure am crazy about you. [*Suddenly he sits upright.*] Watch your step!

DAISY: [*alarmed.*] What's the matter?

ZERO: [*nervously.*] He's comin' back.

DAISY: Oh, is that all? Well, what about it?

ZERO: You don't want him to see us layin' around like this, do you?

DAISY: I don't care if he does.

ZERO: Well, you oughta care. You don't want him to think you ain't a refined girl, do you? He's an awful moral bird, he is.

DAISY: I don't care nothin' about him. I don't care nothin' about anybody but you.

ZERO: Sure, I know. But we don't want people talkin' about us. You better fix your hair an' pull down your skirts.

DAISY *complies rather sadly. They are both silent as* SHRDLU *enters.*

ZERO: [*with feigned nonchalance*]. Well, you got back all right, didn't you?

SHRDLU: I hope I haven't returned too soon.

ZERO: No, that's all right. We were just havin' a little talk. You know—about business an' things.

DAISY: [*boldly.*] We were wishin' we could stay here all the time.

SHRDLU: You may if you like.

ZERO AND DAISY [*in astonishment*]. What!

SHRDLU: Yes. Any one who likes may remain—

ZERO: But I thought you were tellin' me—

SHRDLU: Just as I told you, only the most favored do remain. But anyone may.

ZERO: I don't get it. There's a catch in it somewheres.

DAISY: It don't matter as long as we can stay.

ZERO: [*to* SHRDLU]. We were thinkin' about gettin' married, see?

SHRDLU: You may or not, just as you like.

ZERO: You don't mean to say we could stay if we didn't, do you?

SHRDLU: Yes. They don't care.

ZERO: An' there's some here that ain't married?

SHRDLU: Yes.

ZERO: [*to* DAISY]. I don't know about this place, at that. They must be kind of a mixed crowd.

DAISY: It don't matter, so long as we got each other.

ZERO: Yeh, I know, but you don't want to mix with people that ain't respectable.

DAISY: [*to* SHRDLU]. Can we get married right away? I guess there must be a lot of ministers here, ain't there?

SHRDLU: Not as many as I had hoped to find. The two who seem most beloved are Dean Swift and the Abbé Rabelais. They are both much admired for some indecent tales which they have written.

ZERO: [*shocked*]. What! Ministers writin' smutty stories! Say, what kind of a dump is this, anyway?

SHRDLU: [*despairingly*]. I don't know, Mr. Zero. All these people here are so strange, so unlike the good people I've known. They seem to think of nothing but enjoyment or of wasting their time in profitless occupations. Some paint pictures from morning until night, or carve blocks of stone. Others write songs or put words together, day in and day out. Still others do nothing but lie under the trees and look at the sky. There are men who spend all their time reading books and women who think only of adorning themselves. And forever they are telling stories and laughing and singing and drinking and dancing. There are drunkards, thieves, vagabonds, blasphemers, adulterers. There is one—

ZERO: That's enough. I heard enough. [*He seats himself and begins putting on his shoes.*]

DAISY: [*anxiously*]. What are you goin' to do?

ZERO: I'm goin' to beat it, that's what I'm goin' to do.

DAISY: You said you liked it here.

ZERO: [*looking at her in amazement*]. Liked it! Say, you don't mean to say you want to stay here, do you, with a lot of rummies an' loafers an' bums?

DAISY: We don't have to bother with them. We can just sit here together an' look at the flowers an' listen to the music.

SHRDLU: [*eagerly*]. Music! Did you hear music?

DAISY: Sure. Don't you hear it?

SHRDLU: No, they say it never stops. But I've never heard it.

ZERO: [*listening*]. I thought I heard it before but I don't hear nothin' now. I guess I must 'a' been dreamin'. [*Looking about*]. What's the quickest way out of this place?

DAISY: [*pleadingly*]. Won't you stay just a little longer?

ZERO: Didn't yer hear me say I'm goin'? Good-bye, Miss Devore. I'm goin' to beat it.

He limps off at the right. DAISY *follows him slowly.*

DAISY: [*to* SHRDLU.] I won't ever see him again.

SHRDLU: Are you goin' to stay here?

DAISY: It don't make no difference now. Without him I might as well be alive.

She goes off right. SHRDLU *watches her a moment, then sighs, and seating himself under the tree, buries his head on his arm. Curtain falls.*

Scene VIII

SCENE: *Before the curtain rises the clicking of an adding machine is heard. The curtain rises upon an office similar in appearance to that in* SCENE TWO *except that there is a door in the back wall through which can be seen a glimpse of the corridor outside. In the middle of the room* ZERO *is seated completely absorbed in the operation of an adding machine. He presses the keys and pulls the lever with mechanical precision. He still wears his fulldress suit but he has added to it sleeve protectors and a green eyeshade. A strip of white paper-tape flows steadily from the machine as* ZERO *operates. The room is filled with this tape—streamers, festoons, billows of it everywhere. It covers the floor and the furniture, it climbs the walls and chokes the doorways. A few moments later,* LIEUTENANT CHARLES *and* JOE *enter at the left.* LIEUTENANT CHARLES *is middle-aged and inclined to corpulence. He has an air of world-weariness. He is bare-footed, wears a Panama hat, and is dressed in bright red tights which are a very bad fit—too tight in some places, badly wrinkled in others.* JOE *is a youth with a smutty face dressed in dirty blue overalls.*

CHARLES: [*after contemplating* ZERO *for a few moments*]. All right, Zero, cease firing.

ZERO: [*looking up, surprised.*] Whaddja say?

CHARLES: I said stop punching that machine.

ZERO: [*bewildered.*] Stop? [*He goes on working mechanically.*]

CHARLES: [*impatiently.*] Yes. Can't you stop? Here, Joe, give me a hand. He can't stop.

JOE *and* CHARLES *each take one of* ZERO'S *arms and with enormous effort detach him from the machine. He resists passively—mere inertia. Finally they succeed and swing him around on his stool.* CHARLES *and* JOE *mop their foreheads.*

ZERO: [*querulously*]. What's the idea? Can't you lemme alone?

CHARLES: [*ignoring the question*]. How long have you been here?

ZERO: Jes' twenty-five years. Three hundred months, ninety-one hundred and thirty-one days, one hundred thirty-six thousand—

CHARLES: [*impatiently*]. That'll do! That'll do!

ZERO: [*proudly.*] I ain't missed a day, not an hour, not a minute. Look at all I got done. [*He points to the maze of paper.*]

CHARLES: It's time to quit.

ZERO: Quit? Whaddye mean quit? I ain't goin' to quit!

CHARLES: You've got to.

ZERO: What for? What do I have to quit for?

CHARLES: It's time for you to go back.

ZERO: Go back where? Whaddya talkin' about?

CHARLES: Back to earth, you dub. Where do you think?

ZERO: Aw, go on, Cap, who are you kiddin'?

CHARLES: I'm not kidding anybody. And don't call me Cap. I'm a lieutenant.

ZERO: All right, Lieutenant, all right. But what's this you're tryin' to tell me about goin' back?

CHARLES: Your time's up, I'm telling you. You must be pretty thick. How many times do you want to be told a thing?

ZERO: This is the first time I heard about goin' back. Nobody ever said nothin' to me about it before.

CHARLES: You didn't think you were going to stay here forever, did you?

ZERO: Sure. Why not? I did my bit, didn't I? Forty-five years of it. Twenty-five years in the store. Then the boss canned me and I knocked him cold. I guess you ain't heard about that—

CHARLES: [*interrupting*]. I know all about that. But what's that got to do with it?

ZERO: Well, I done my bit, didn't I? That oughta let me out.

CHARLES: [*jeeringly*]. So you think you're all through, do you?

ZERO: Sure, I do. I did the best I could while I was there and then I passed out. And now I'm sittin' pretty here.

CHARLES: You've got a fine idea of the way they run things, you have. Do you think they're going to all the trouble of making a soul just to use it once?

ZERO: Once is often enough, it seems to me.

CHARLES: It seems to you, does it? Well, who are you? And what do you know about it? Why man, they use a soul over and over again—over and over until it's worn out.

ZERO: Nobody ever told me.

CHARLES: So you thought you were all through, did you? Well, that's a hot one, that is.

ZERO: [*sullenly*]. How was I to know?

CHARLES: Use your brains! Where would we put them all? We're crowded enough as it is. Why, this place is nothing but a kind of repair and service station—a sort of cosmic laundry, you might say. We get the souls in here by the bushelful. Then we get busy and clean them up. And you ought to see some of them. The muck and the slime. Phoo! And as full of holes as a floursifter. But we fix them up. We disinfect them and give them a kerosene rub and mend the holes and back they go—practically as good as new.

ZERO: You mean to say I've been here before—before the last time, I mean?

CHARLES: Been here before! Why, you poor boob—you've been here thousands of times—fifty thousand, at least.

ZERO: [*suspiciously*]. How is it I don't remember nothin' about it?

CHARLES: Well—that's partly because you're stupid, But it's mostly because that's the way they fix it. [*Musingly.*] They're funny that way—every now and then they'll do something white like that—when you'd least expect it. I guess economy's at the bottom of it, though. They figure that the souls would get worn out quicker—if they remembered.

ZERO: And don't any of 'em remember?

CHARLES: Oh, some do. You see there's different types: there's the type that gets a little better each time it goes back—we just give them a wash and send them right through. Then there's another type—the type that gets a little worse each time. That's where you belong!

ZERO: [*offended*]. Me? You mean to say I'm gettin' worse all the time?

CHARLES: [*nodding*]. Yes. A little worse each time.

ZERO: Well—what was I when I started? Somethin' big?—A king or somethin'?

CHARLES: [*laughing derisively*]. A king! That's a good one! I'll tell you what you were the first time—if you want to know so much—a monkey.

ZERO: [*shocked and offended*]. A monkey!

CHARLES: [*nodding*]. Yes, sir—just a hairy, chattering, long-tailed monkey.

ZERO: That must a been a long time ago.

CHARLES: Oh, not so long. A million years or so. Seems like yesterday to me.

ZERO: Then look here, whaddya mean by sayin' I'm gettin' worse all the time?

CHARLES: Just what I said. You weren't so bad as a monkey. Of course, you did just what all the other monkeys did, but still it kept you out in the open air. And you weren't women-shy—there was one little red-headed monkey—Well, never mind. Yes, sir, you weren't so bad then. But even in those days there must have been some bigger and brainier monkey that you kowtowed to. The mark of the slave was on you from the start.

ZERO: [*sullenly*]. You ain't very particular about what you call people, are you?

CHARLES: You wanted the truth, didn't you? If there ever was a soul in the world that was labeled slave it's yours. Why, all the bosses and kings that there ever were have left their trademarks on your backside.

ZERO: It ain't fair, if you ask me.

CHARLES: [*shrugging his shoulders*]. Don't tell me about it. I don't make the rules. All I know is you've been getting worse—worse each time. Why, even six thousand years ago you weren't so bad. That was the time you were hauling stones for one of those big pyramids in a place they call Africa. Ever hear of the pyramids?

ZERO: Them big pointy things?

CHARLES: [*nodding*]. That's it.

ZERO: I seen a picture of them in the movies.

CHARLES: Well, you helped build them. It was a

long step down from the happy days in the jungle, but it was a good job—even though you didn't know what you were doing and your back was striped by the foreman's whip. But you've been going down, down. Two thousand years ago you were a Roman galley-slave. You were on one of the triremes that knocked the Carthaginian fleet for a goal. Again the whip. But you had muscles then—chest muscles, back muscles, biceps. [*He feels* ZERO'S *arm gingerly and turns away in disgust*]. Phoo! A bunch of mush! [*He notices that* JOE *has fallen asleep. Walking over, he kicks him in the shin.*]

CHARLES: Wake up, you mutt! Where do you think you are! [*He turns to* ZERO *again.*] And then another thousand years and you were a serf—a lump of clay digging up other lumps of clay. You wore an iron collar then—white ones hadn't been invented yet. Another long step down. But where you dug, potatoes grew and that helped fatten the pigs. Which was something. And now—well, I don't want to rub it in —

ZERO: Rub it in is right! Seems to be I got a pretty healthy kick comin'. I ain't had a square deal! Hard work! That's all I've ever had!

CHARLES: [*callously*]. What else were you ever good for?

ZERO Well, that ain't the point. The point is I'm through! I had enough! Let 'em find somebody else to do the dirty work. I'm sick of bein' the goat! I quit right here and now! [*He glares about defiantly. There is a thunderclap and a bright flash of lightning.*]

ZERO: [*screaming*]. Ooh! What's that? [*He clings to* CHARLES]

CHARLES: It's all right. Nobody's going to hurt you. It's just their way of telling you that they don't like you to talk that way. Pull yourself together and calm down. You can't change the rules—nobody can—they've got it all fixed. It's a rotten system—but what are you going to do about it?

ZERO: Why can't they stop pickin' on me? I'm satisfied here—doin' my day's work. I don't want to go back.

CHARLES: You've got to, I tell you. There's no way out of it.

ZERO: What chance have I got—at my age? Who'll give me a job?

CHARLES: You big boob, you don't think you're going back the way you are, do you?

ZERO: Sure, how then?

CHARLES: Why, you've got to start all over.

ZERO: All over?

CHARLES: [*nodding*]. You'll be a baby again—a bald, red-faced little animal, and then you'll go through it all again. There'll be millions of others like you—all with their mouths open, squalling for food. And then when you get a little older you'll begin to learn things—and you'll learn all the wrong things and learn them all in the wrong way. You'll eat the wrong food and wear the wrong clothes and you'll live in swarming dens where there's no light and no air! You'll learn to be a liar and a bully and a braggart and a coward and a sneak. You'll learn to fear the sunlight and to hate beauty. By that time you'll be ready for school. There they'll tell you the truth about a great many things that you don't give a damn about and they'll tell you lies about all the things you ought to know—and about all the things you want to know they'll tell you nothing at all. When you get through you'll be equipped for your life-work. You'll be ready to take a job.

ZERO: [*eagerly*]. What'll my job be? Another adding machine?

CHARLES: Yes. But not one of these antiquated adding machines. It will be a superb, super-hyper-adding machine, as far from this old piece of junk as you are from God. It will be something to make you sit up and take notice, that adding machine. It will be an adding machine which will be installed in a coal mine and which will record the individual output of each miner. As each miner down in the lower galleries takes up a shovelful of coal, the impact of his shovel will automatically set in motion a graphite pencil in your gallery. The pencil will make a mark in white upon a blackened, sensitized drum. Then your work comes in. With the great toe of your right foot you release a lever which focuses a violet ray on the drum. The ray playing upon and through the white mark, falls upon a selenium cell which in turn sets the keys of the adding apparatus in motion. In this way the individual output of each miner is recorded without any human effort except the slight pressure of the great toe of your right foot.

ZERO: [*in breathless, round-eyed wonder*]. Say, that'll be some machine, won't it?

CHARLES: Some machine is right. It will be the culmination of human effort—the final triumph of the evolutionary process. For millions of years the nebulous gases swirled in space. For more millions of years the gases cooled and then through inconceivable ages they hardened into rocks. And then came life. Floating green things on the waters that covered the earth. More millions of years and a step upward—an animate organism in the ancient slime. And so on—step by step, down through the ages—a gain here, a gain there—the mollusc, the fish, the reptile, then mammal, man! And all so that you might sit in the gallery of a coal mine and operate the super-hyper-adding machine with the great toe of your right foot!

ZERO: Well, then—I ain't so bad, after all.

CHARLES: You're a failure, Zero, a failure. A waste product. A slave to a contraption of steel and iron. The animal's instincts, but not his strength and skill. The animal's appetites, but not his unashamed indulgence of them. True, you move and eat and digest and excrete and reproduce. But any microscopic organism can do as much. Well—time's up! Back you go—back to your sunless groove—the raw material of slums and wars—the ready prey of the first jingo or demagogue or political adventurer who takes the trouble to play upon your ignorance and credulity and provincialism. You poor, spineless, brainless boob—I'm sorry for you!

ZERO: [*falling to his knees*]. Then keep me here! Don't send me back! Let me stay!

CHARLES: Get up. Didn't I tell you I can't do anything for you? Come on, time's up!

ZERO: I can't! I can't! I'm afraid to go through it all again.

CHARLES: You've got to, I tell you. Come on, now!

ZERO: What did you tell me so much for? Couldn't you just let me go, thinkin' everythin' was goin' to be all right?

CHARLES: You wanted to know, didn't you?

ZERO: How did I know what you were goin' to tell me? Now I can't stop thinkin' about it! I can't stop thinkin'! I'll be thinkin' about it all the time.

CHARLES: All right! I'll do the best I can for you. I'll send a girl with you to keep you company.

ZERO: A girl? What for? What good will a girl do me?

CHARLES: She'll help make you forget.

ZERO: [*eagerly*]. She will? Where is she?

CHARLES: Wait a minute, I'll call her. [*He calls in a loud voice.*] Oh! Hope! Yoo-hoo! [*He turns his head aside and says in the manner of a ventriloquist imitating a distant feminine voice.*] Ye-es. [*Then in his own voice.*] Come here, will you? There's a fellow who wants you to take him back. [*Ventriloquously again.*] All right. I'll be right over, Charlie dear. [*He turns to* ZERO] Kind of familiar, isn't she? Charlie dear!

ZERO: What did you say her name is?

CHARLES: Hope. H-o-p-e.

ZERO: Is she good-lookin'?

CHARLES: Is she good-looking! Oh, boy, wait until you see her! She's a blonde with big blue eyes and red lips and little white teeth and—

ZERO: Say, that listens good to me. Will she be long?

CHARLES: She'll be here right away. There she is now! Do you see her?

ZERO: No. Where?

CHARLES: Out in the corridor. No, not there. Over farther. To the right. Don't you see her blue dress? And the sunlight on her hair?

ZERO: Oh, sure! Now I see her! What's the matter with me, anyhow? Say, she's some jane! Oh, you baby vamp!

CHARLES: She'll make you forget your troubles.

ZERO: What troubles are you talkin' about?

CHARLES: Nothing. Go on. Don't keep her waiting.

ZERO: You bet I won't! Oh, Hope! Wait for me! I'll be right with you! I'm on my way! [*He stumbles out eagerly.*]

JOE *bursts into uproarious laughter.*

CHARLES: [*eyeing him in surprise and anger*]. What in hell's the matter with you?

JOE: [*shaking with laughter.*] Did you get that? He thinks he saw somebody and he's following her! [*He rocks with laughter.*]

CHARLES: [*punching him in the jaw*]. Shut your face!

JOE: [*nursing his jaw*]. What's the idea? Can't I even laugh when I see something funny?

CHARLES: Funny! You keep your mouth shut or I'll show you something funny. Go on, hustle out of here and get something to clean up this mess with. There's another fellow moving in. Hurry now.

He makes a threatening gesture. JOE *exits hastily.* CHARLES *goes to chair and seats himself. He looks weary and dispirited.*

CHARLES: [*shaking his head*]. Hell, I'll tell the world this is a lousy job! [*He takes a flask from his pocket, uncorks it, and slowly drains it.*]

CURTAIN

Note: Copies of this play, in individual paper covered acting editions, are available from Samuel French, Inc., 25 W. 45th St., New York, N.Y. or 7623 Sunset Blvd., Hollywood, Calif. or in Canada Samuel French, (Canada) Ltd., 26 Grenville St., Toronto, Canada.

Jean-Claude van Italie

(1936–   )

Jean-Claude van Itallie was born in Brussels, raised in Great Neck, New York, and graduated from Harvard in 1958. He began writing plays for the Cafe La Mama Troupe, a contemporary drama work shop in New York, and The Open Theatre, another off-Broadway company. Van Itallie's plays, like many off-Broadway plays, are part of what is sometimes called "underground" theater. Underground theater rejects the customs of Broadway theater—of well-made plays with clear story lines, of professional actors working under the tutelage of established directors, of actors and directors and authors each working separately on their own part of the play, of stars whose names are familiar to all theater-goers, of realistic characters in realistic sets, of plays that amuse or educate the audience. Instead, the underground theater often assaults the viewers' sensibilities, sometimes with the actors physically moving into the audience and engaging viewers in conversation or slapstick, sometimes with caricatured symbols of ideas and people, sometimes with grotesquely staged scenes. Like the larger than life-size dolls who are the "characters" in van Itallie's "Motel," only the voice is human. Often the production represents an evolutionary collaboration among actors, director, and author, together helping to shape the final form of the play. The techniques of the underground theater are numerous, nearly as many different techniques as the hundreds of plays that have been produced. (Myrna Lamb's *Scyklon Z* is another example of this type of play.) But always there is the rejection of life as it is, of society as it is, and of art as it used to be.

Van Itallie, in his plays, gives dramatic shape to the criticism many young, idealistic counterculture-revolutionary spirits are making of modern America. He dramatizes gratuitous violence, wholesale apathy, deified materialism; he shows an effete era expiring under creature comforts. Suffocated by a "motel"-style culture of plastic neatness, sanitary glitter, and gaudy packaging, our nation of "hollow men" is ruthlessly captured by the things our gross national product generates. The plastic, ahuman environment is the extension into present time of the robotized environment of Elmer Rice's *The Adding Machine.* Today's robots have no heaven of green fields and dreams fulfilled. They have only the impersonal "Motel," "TV," and "Interview"—the titles of the three sections of *America Hurrah.*

In "Interview," van Itallie examines the mechanization of contemporary life where communication is spastic and dehumanized: "My" "fault" "Excuse" "me" "Can you" "help" "me?" exclaim the devitalized voices. The playwright's introductory note comments on the close collaboration among author, actors, and director: " 'Interview' would not exist in its present form . . . without the collaboration, in rehearsal, of Joseph Chaikin [the director] and the actors in *America Hurrah.*" In "TV," van Itallie juxtaposes the tired, trivial activities of three employees in a television rating room with typical melodramatic scenes from "the tube." By the end of the play the real-life employees have become indistinguishable from the fantasy characters of television. What, indeed, is reality?

"Motel,"originally called "America Hurrah" and first presented in the spring of 1965, is a transformation of reality into fantasy, a contemporary hallucination of the American Dream gone randomly spinning off. Beyond the superficial sheen, the playwright forces us to stare at the terrifying loneliness, at the sordid and savage in ourselves and in the life about us.

Robert Brustein, a distinguished critic of the modern stage, noted that in "Motel" van Itallie "discovered the deepest poetic function of the theater . . . : to invent metaphors which can poignantly suggest a nation's nightmares and afflictions." From the precision of the adding machine to the standardized efficiency of the spic and span motel, the American inheritance of progress spirals onward, the dramatist suggests, toward chaos.

Motel

A Masque for Three Dolls

. . . after all our subtle colour and nervous rhythm, after the faint mixed tints of Conder, what more is possible? After us the Savage God.

—W. B. Yeats

Characters

MOTEL-KEEPER
MAN
WOMAN
MOTEL—KEEPER'S VOICE
Music

Lights come up on the Motel-Keeper doll. The intensity of the light will increase as the play continues.

The Motel-Keeper doll is large, much larger than human size, but the impression of hugeness can come mainly from the fact that her head is at least three times larger than would be normal in proportion to her body. She is all gray. She has a large full skirt which reaches to the floor. She has squarish breasts. The hair curlers on her head suggest electronic receivers.

The Motel-Keeper doll has eyeglasses which are mirrors. It doesn't matter what these mirrors reflect at any given moment. The audience may occasionally catch a glimpse of itself, or be bothered by reflections of light in the mirrors. It doesn't matter; the sensory nerves of the audience are not to be spared.

The motel room in which the Motel-Keeper doll stands is anonymously modern, except for certain "homey" touches. A neon light blinks outside the window. The colors in the room, like the colors in the clothes on the Man and Woman dolls, are violent combinations of oranges, pinks, and reds against a reflective plastic background.

The Motel-Keeper's Voice, which never stops, comes from a loudspeaker, or from several loudspeakers in the theatre. The Voice will be, at first, mellow and husky and then, as the light grows harsher and brighter, the Voice will grow harsher too, more set in its pattern, hard finally, and patronizing and petty.

An actor on platform shoes works the Motel-Keeper doll from inside it. The actor can move only the doll's arms or its entire body. As the Voice begins, the arms move, and then the Motel-Keeper doll fusses about the room in little circles.

MOTEL-KEEPER'S VOICE: I am old. I am an old idea: the walls; that from which it springs forth. I enclose the nothing, making then a place in which it happens. I am the room; a Roman theatre where cheers break loose the lion; a railroad carriage in the forest at Compiègne, in 1918, and in 1941. I have been rooms of marble and rooms of cork, all letting forth an avalanche. Rooms of mud and rooms of silk. This room will be slashed too, as if by a scimitar, its contents spewed and yawned out. That is what happens. It is almost happening, in fact. I am this room.

As the Motel-Keeper's Voice continues, the doors at the back of the room open and headlights shine into the eyes of the audience; passing in front of the headlights, in silhouette, we see two more huge dolls, the Man and the Woman.

MOTEL-KEEPER'S VOICE: It's nice; not so fancy as some, but with all the conveniences. And a touch of home. The antimacassar comes from my mother's house in Boise. Boise, Idaho. Sits kind of nice, I think, on the Swedish swing. That's my own idea, you know. All modern, up-to-date, that's it—no motel on this route is more up-to-date. Or cleaner. Go look, then talk me a thing or two.

The Woman doll enters. Her shoulders are thrown way back, like a girl posing for a calendar. Her breasts are particularly large and perfect, wiggleable if possible. She has a cherry-lipstick smile, blond hair, and a garish patterned dress.

Both the Man and the Woman dolls are the same size as the Motel-Keeper doll, with heads at least three times larger than would be normal for their bodies. The Man and the Woman dolls, however, are flesh-colored and have more mobility. The actors inside these dolls are also on platform shoes. There is absolutely no rapport between the Motel-Keeper and the Man and Woman. All of the Motel-Keeper's remarks are addressed generally. She is never directly motivated by the actions of the Man and Woman dolls.

As the Woman doll enters, she puts down her purse and inspects the room. Then she takes off her dress, revealing lace panties and bra.

MOTEL-KEEPER'S VOICE: All modern here, as I say, with the tang of home. Do you understand? When folks are fatigued, in a strange place? Not that it's old-fashioned. No. Not in the wrong way. There's a pushbutton here for TV. The toilet flushes of its own accord. All you've got to do is get off. Pardon my mentioning it, but you'll have to go far before you see a thing like that on this route. Oh, it's quite a room. Yes. And reasonable. Sign here. Pardon the pen leak. I can see you're fatigued.

The Woman doll goes into the bathroom.

MOTEL-KEEPER'S VOICE: Any children? Well, that's nice. Children don't appreciate travel. And rooms don't appreciate children. As it happens it's the last one I've got left. I'll just flip my vacancy switch. Twelve dollars, please. In advance that'll be. That way you can go any time you want to go, you know, get an early start. On a trip to see sights, are you? That's nice. You just get your luggage while I unlock the room. You can see the light.

The Man doll enters carrying a suitcase. He has a cigar and a loud Florida shirt. He closes the door, inspects the room, and takes off his clothes, except for his loudly patterned shorts.

MOTEL-KEEPER'S VOICE: There now. What I say doesn't matter. You can see. It speaks for itself. The room speaks for itself. You can see it's a perfect 1966 room. But a taste of home. I've seen to that. A taste of home.
Comfy, cozy, nice, but a taste of newness. That's what. You can see it. The best stop on route Six Sixty-Six. Well, there might be others like it, but this is the best stop. You've arrived at the right place. This place. And a hooked rug. I don't care what, but I've said no room IS without a hooked rug.

Sound of the toilet flushing

MOTEL-KEEPER'S VOICE: No complaints yet. Never. Modern people like modern places. Oh yes. I can tell. They tell me. And reasonable. Very very reasonable rates. No cheaper rates on the route, not for this. You receive what you pay for.

Sound of the toilet flushing again

MOTEL-KEEPER'S VOICE: All that driving and driving and driving. Fatigued. You must be. I would be. Miles and miles and miles.

The Man doll begins an inspection of the bed. He pulls at the bedspread, testing its strength.

MOTEL-KEEPER'S VOICE: Fancy. Fancy your ending up right here. You didn't know and I didn't know. But you did. End up right here. Respectable and decent and homelike. Right here.

The Woman doll comes back from the bathroom to get her negligee from her purse. She returns to the bathroom.

MOTEL-KEEPER'S VOICE: All folks everywhere sitting in the very palm of God. Waiting, whither, whence.

The Man doll pulls the bedspread, blankets, and sheets off the bed, tearing them apart. He jumps hard on the bed.

MOTEL-KEEPER'S VOICE: Any motel you might have come to on Six Sixty-Six. Any motel. On that vast network of roads Whizzing by, whizzing by. Trucks too. And cars from everywhere. Full up with folks, all sitting in the very palm of God. I can tell proper folks when I get a look at them. All folks.

The Man doll rummages through the suitcase, throwing clothes about the room.

MOTEL-KEEPER'S VOICE: Country roads, state roads, United States roads. It's a big world and here you are. I noticed you got a license plate. I've not been to there myself. I've not been to anywhere myself, excepting town for supplies, and Boise. Boise, Idaho.

Toilet articles and bathroom fixtures, including toilet paper and the toilet seat, are thrown out of the bathroom. The Man doll casually tears pages out of the Bible.

MOTEL-KEEPER'S VOICE: The world arrives to me, you'd say. It's a small world. These plastic flowers here: "Made in Japan" on the label. You noticed? Got them from the catalogue. Cat-al-ogue. Every product in this room is ordered.

The Man doll pulls down some of the curtains. Objects continue to be thrown from the bathroom.

MOTEL-KEEPER'S VOICE: Ordered from the catalogue. Excepting the antimacassars and the hooked rug. Made the hooked rug myself. Tang of home. No room is a room without. Course the bedspread, hand-hooked, hooked near here at town. Mrs. Harritt. Betsy Harritt gets materials through another catalogue. Cat-al-ogue.

The Woman doll comes out of the bathroom wearing her negligee over her panties and bra. When the Man doll notices her, he stops his other activities and goes to her.

MOTEL-KEEPER'S VOICE: Myself, I know it from the catalogue: bottles, bras, breakfasts, refrigerators, cast iron gates, plastic posies,

The Woman doll opens her negligee and the Man doll pulls off her bra. The Man and Woman dolls embrace. The Woman doll puts lipstick on her nipples.

MOTEL-KEEPER'S VOICE: paper subscriptions, Buick trucks, blankets, forks, clitter-clack darning hooks, transistors and antimacassar, vinyl plastics,

The Man doll turns on the TV. It glares viciously and plays loud rock and roll music.

MOTEL-KEEPER'S VOICE: Crazy quilts, paper hairpins, cats, catnip, club feet, canisters, banisters, holy books, tattooed toilet articles, tables, tea cozies,

The Man doll writes simple obscene words on the wall. The Woman doll does the same with her lipstick.

MOTEL-KEEPER'S VOICE: pickles, bayberry candles, South Dakotan Kewpie Dolls, fiberglass hair, polished milk, amiable grandpappies, colts, Galsworthy books, cribs, cabinets, teeter-totters,

The Woman doll has turned to picture-making. . . .

MOTEL-KEEPER'S VOICE: and television sets. Oh I tell you it, I do. It's a wonder. Full with things, the world, full up. Shall I tell you my thought? Next year there's a shelter to be built by me, yes. Shelter motel. Everything to be placed under the ground. Signs up in every direction up and down Six Sixty-Six.

The Man and Woman dolls twist.

MOTEL-KEEPER'S VOICE: Complete Security, Security While You Sleep Tight, Bury Your Troubles At This Motel, Homelike, Very Comfy, and Encased In Lead, Every Room Its Own Set, Fourteen Day Emergency Supplies $5.00 Extra,

The rock and roll music gets louder and louder. A civil-defense siren, one long wail, begins to build. The Man and Woman dolls proceed methodically to greater and greater violence. They smash the TV screen and picture frames. They pull down the remaining curtains, smash the window, throw bits of clothing and bedding around, and finally tear off the arms of the Motel-Keeper doll.

MOTEL-KEEPER'S VOICE: Self-Contained Latrine Waters, Filters, Counters, Periscopes and Mechanical Doves, Hooked Rugs, Dearest Little Picture Frames for Loved Ones—Made in Japan—though the catalogue. Cat-a-logue. You can pick items and products: cablecackles—so nice—cuticles, twice-twisted combs with corrugated calisthenics, meat-beaters, fish-tackles, bug bombs, toasted terra-cotta'd Tanganyikan switch blades, ochre closets, ping-pong balls, didies, Capricorn and Cancer prognostics, crackers, total uppers, stick pins, basting tacks . . .

The Motel-Keeper's Voice is drowned out by the other sounds—siren and music—which have built to a deafening pitch and come from all parts of the theatre.

The door opens again and headlights shine into the eyes of the audience.

The actor inside the Motel-Keeper doll has slipped out of it. The Man and Woman dolls tear off the head of the Motel-Keeper doll, then throw her body aside.

Then, one by one, the Man and Woman dolls leave the motel room and walk down the aisle. Fans blow air through the debacle on stage onto the audience.

After an instant more of excruciatingly loud noise: blackout and silence.

It is preferable that the actors take no bow after this play.

Counterculture Revolutionaries

Maxwell Anderson

(1888–1959)

"Unless you and your play have a dream—or a conviction," wrote Maxwell Anderson, " . . . and unless you can defend that conviction against death and hell and the wiles of experienced tricksters, your play isn't worth producing." This statement, indicative of the consummate integrity Maxwell Anderson and his plays have characteristically brought to the American stage, keeps faith not only with Anderson the social critic, but also with Anderson the dramatic poet. When he was a graduate student at Stanford University in California, Anderson chose verse as his medium; and in his earliest published writings the fusion of poetry and social commentary are evident. His poem "Youth" accepts—and lauds—rebellion as part of the natural order of society:

I am the render of chains;
I am the filcher of fire;
Rebellion flows in my veins;
I may not rest for desire.
You have made me a law? I shall break it.
You have set me a bound? I shall pass.
You choose this your own? I shall take it.
*Your bonds are of glass!**

Another poem, "Kings," exults in the decadence and inevitable overthrow of the established, effete organization:

The kings are failing;
Their race is old;
They need more madmen,
They must have gold.

. . .

With broken nations,
With bleeding things,
With hate and darkness
Bolster your kings.†

His first major success in the theater was the war play he wrote with Lawrence Stallings, *What Price Glory* (1924); from that "hit" onward Anderson's work in prose and verse established him in twentieth-century American theater as a thoughtful, challenging dramatist intent on issues rather than mere entertainment. Political corruption occupied Anderson's attention in *Both Your Houses,* which won him the Pulitzer Prize in 1933. *High Tor* (1937) examines the significance of freedom in a society where industrialism appears at variance with personal liberty and seeks to destroy it. *Night Over Taos* (1932) dramatizes the coming of the Americanos ("*gringos*") like "locusts" to end the "old civilization"

**A Stanford Book of Verse,* 1912–1916 (English Club, Stanford University, 1916), p. 84.
†*ibid.,* p. 75.

of Spain in New Mexico. Versatile and inventive, Anderson wrote history plays (*Mary of Scotland* [1933] and *Anne of the Thousand Days* [1948]), dramas of World War II (*Candle in the Wind* [1941] and *Storm Operation* [1944]), and musical productions with Kurt Weill (*Knickerbocker Holiday* [1938] and *Lost in the Stars* [1948], the latter based upon Alan Paton's novel of South African apartheid *Cry, the Beloved Country*).

Anderson's heart and loyalties, nevertheless, were always in verse drama. He once said: " . . . I have a strong and chronic hope that the theater of this country will outgrow the phase of journalistic social comment and reach occasionally into the upper air of poetic tragedy. I believe with Goethe that dramatic poetry is man's greatest achievement on his earth so far. . . . " *Winterset* combines Anderson's dual vision: it is probably America's most famous verse drama; and its theme, the need for social justice and individual forgiveness, is still contemporary.

In 1928 Anderson had collaborated with Harold Hickerson on *Gods of the Lightning,* a play dealing with the Sacco-Vanzetti case. In *Winterset* (1935) he returned to the subject of that notorious trial, imagining what might be its after-effects years later. The Sacco-Vanzetti case began in April, 1920, with the murder of the paymaster of a New England shoe company during a robbery. Shortly after the crime, Nicola Sacco and Bartolomeo Vanzetti were arrested when they claimed ownership of the automobile authorities had connected with the killing. Although numerous witnesses placed Sacco and Vanzetti miles away from the murder scene, the two were convicted. After much litigation and public protest they were executed in 1927. It is interesting to note that Sacco and Vanzetti, perennial favorites in radical literature, also appear in Elvie A. Moore's black drama *Angela Is Happening.*

Gods of the Lightning, written shortly after these controversial men were executed, presents the final statements of James Macready and Dante Capraro, two anarchists convicted of murder, in this way:

> MACREADY: "I'm not guilty as charged but I am guilty—I'm guilty of being a radical—and that's what I was convicted for and that's what you're sentencing me for. I'm guilty of thinking like a free man and talking like a free man and acting like a free man. . . . I'm guilty of spreading unrest among the slaves and raising hell with slave morality. I'm guilty of exercising my rights under the constitution. . . . "
>
> CAPRARO: "All my life I have worked against crime, against the murder of war, against oppression of the poor, against the great crime which is government. [to Judge Vail]: "I know that you have been an unjust judge to us, that you have fear for us, and therefore hate for us —that you have wanted us dead and have taken advantage to kill us. . . . But you are an old man, and wearier than we, even if we have been in prison; and you too will die sometime even if you kill us first. . . . [and] in my silence I will silence you."

Sacco and Vanzetti, prototypes for Macready and Capraro, were admitted radicals, labor agitators, and social incendiaries. It is clear that Anderson believed they had been murdered for their political beliefs.

Winterset picks up in time several years after the convicted anarchist Capraro's address to the judge.‡ The characters are different, but their creation stems from the same historical event. Distinguished theater critic Joseph Wood Krutch has given an accurate evaluation of Anderson's verse treatment of the passions of this somber episode in American history:

> *"Probably 'Winterset' would never have been written if Mr. Anderson had not concerned himself with the famous [Sacco-Vanzetti] case. But if the earlier play [Gods of Lightning] represents the immediate reaction of the citizen, 'Winterset' is the product of a poet's brooding. It represents no change of opinion; the social protest is still there. . . . But here also is that deeper penetration into thoughts and passions and souls which it is the dramatist's business to achieve."*§

Winterset, a modern classic of the American stage, depicts the uncertainty and anger that grows out of a basic social problem: What is justice for the disinherited in America? Is political heresy to be hunted down and its proponents eliminated like the "witches" of Salem were in 1692? In Anderson's own words, written more than a dozen years after his play appeared: "*Winterset* . . . treats a contemporary tragic theme." The theme is still contemporary, still tragic.

Winterset

Characters

TROCK	HERMAN
SHADOW	LUCIA
GARTH	PINY
MIRIAMNE	A SAILOR
ESDRAS	STREET URCHIN
THE HOBO	POLICEMAN
1ST GIRL	RADICAL
2ND GIRL	SERGEANT
JUDGE GAUNT	*Non-speaking*
MIO	URCHINS
CARR	TWO MEN IN BLUE SERGE

ACT I

Scene I

The scene is the bank of a river under a bridgehead. A gigantic span starts from the rear of the stage and appears to lift over the heads of the audience and out to the left. At the right rear is a wall of solid supporting masonry. To the left an apartment building abuts against the bridge and forms the left wall of the stage with a dark basement window and a door in the brick wall. To the right, and in the foreground, an outcropping of original rock makes a barricade behind which one may enter through a cleft. To the rear, against the masonry, two sheds have been built by waifs and strays for shelter. The river bank, in the foreground, is black rock worn smooth by years of trampling. There is room for exit and entrance to the left around the apartment house, also around the rock to the right. A single street lamp is seen at the left—and a glimmer of apartment lights in the background beyond. It is an early, dark December morning.

TWO YOUNG MEN IN SERGE *lean against the masonry, matching bills.* TROCK *and* SHADOW *come in from the left.*

TROCK: Go back and watch the car.

---

‡At the actual sentencing of Sacco and Vanzetti, April 9, 1927, Bartolomeo Vanzetti delivered a long, eloquent statement which playwright Anderson used as source for the Capraro address: "Not only am I innocent . . . but in all my life I have never stole [sic], never killed, never spilled blood, but I have struggled all my life, since I began to reason, to eliminate crime from the earth."

§ *The Nation,* CXLI (October 9, 1935), p. 420.

The TWO YOUNG MEN *go out.* TROCK *walks to the corner and looks toward the city.*

You roost of punks and gulls! Sleep, sleep it off,
whatever you had last night, get down in warm,
one big ham-fat against another—sleep,
cling, sleep and rot! Rot out your pasty guts
with diddling, you had no brain to begin. If you had
there'd be no need for us to sleep on iron
who had too much brains for you.

SHADOW: Now look, Trock, look what would the warden say to talk like that?

TROCK: May they die as I die!
By God, what life they've left me
they shall keep me well! I'll have that out of them—
these pismires that walk like men!

SHADOW: Because, look, chief,
it's all against science and penology
for you to get out and begin to cuss that way
before your prison vittles are out of you. Hell,
you're supposed to leave the pen full of high thought,
kind of noble-like, loving toward all mankind,
ready to kiss their feet—or whatever parts
they stick out toward you. Look at me!

TROCK: I see you.
And even you may not live as long as you think.
You think too many things are funny. Well, laugh.
But it's not so funny.

SHADOW: Come on, Trock, you know me.
Anything you say goes, but give me leave
to kid a little.

TROCK: Then laugh at somebody else!
it's a lot safer! They've soaked me once too often
in that vat of poisoned hell they keep up-state
to soak men in, and I'm rotten inside, I'm all
one liquid puke inside where I had lungs
once, like yourself! And now they want to get me
and stir me in again—and that'd kill me—
and that's fine for them. But before that happens to me
a lot of these healthy boys'll know what it's like
when you try to breathe and have no place to put air—
they'll learn it from me!

SHADOW: They've got nothing on you, chief.

TROCK: I don't know yet. That's what I'm here to find out.
If they've got what they might have.
It's not a year this time—
no, nor ten. It's screwed down under a lid.—
I can die quick enough, without help.

SHADOW: You're the skinny kind
that lives forever.

TROCK: He gave me a half a year,
the doc at the gate.

SHADOW: Jesus.

TROCK: Six months I get,
and the rest's dirt, six feet.

LUCIA, *the street-piano man, comes in right from behind the rock and goes to the shed where he keeps his piano.* PINY, *the apple-woman, follows and stands in the entrance.* LUCIA *speaks to* ESTRELLA, *who still stands facing* SHADOW.

LUCIA: Morning.

TROCK *and* SHADOW *go out round the apartment house without speaking.*

PINY: Now what would you call them?

LUCIA: Maybe something da river washed up.

PINY: Nothing ever washed him—that black one.

LUCIA: Maybe not, maybe so. More like his pa and ma raise-a heem in da cellar. [*He wheels out the piano.*]

PINY: He certainly gave me a turn. [*She lays a hand on the rock.*]

LUCIA: You don' live-a right, ol' gal. Take heem easy. Look on da bright-a side. Never say-a die. Me, every day in every way I getta be da regular heller. [*He starts out.*]

CURTAIN

Scene II

A cellar apartment under the apartment building, floored with cement and roofed with huge boa constrictor pipes that run slantwise from left to right, dwarfing the room. An outside door opens to the left and a door at the right rear leads to the interior of the place. A low squat window to the left. A table at the rear and a few chairs and books make up the furniture. GARTH, *son of* ESDRAS, *sits alone, holding a violin upside down to inspect a crack at its base. He lays the bow on the floor and runs his fingers over the joint.* MIRIAMNE *enters from the rear, a girl of fifteen.* GARTH *looks up, then down again.*

MIRIAMNE: Garth—

GARTH: The glue lets go. It's the steam, I guess
It splits the hair on your head.

MIRIAMNE: It can't be mended?

GARTH: I can't mend it.

No doubt there are fellows somewhere
who'd mend it for a dollar—and glad to do it.
That is if I had a dollar.—Got a dollar?
No, I thought not.

MIRIAMNE: Garth, you've sat at home here
three days now. You haven't gone out at all.
Something frightens you.

GARTH: Yes?

MIRIAMNE: And father's frightened.
He reads without knowing where. When a shadow falls
across the page he waits for a blow to follow
after the shadow. Then in a little while
he puts his book down softly and goes out
to see who passed.

GARTH: A bill collector, maybe.
We haven't paid the rent.

MIRIAMNE: No.

GARTH: You're a bright girl, sis.—
You see too much. You run along and cook.
Why don't you go to school?

MIRIAMNE: I don't like school.
They whisper behind my back.

GARTH: Yes? about what?

MIRIAMNE: What did the lawyer mean
that wrote to you?

GARTH [*rising*]:
What lawyer?

MIRIAMNE: I found a letter
on the floor of your room. He said, "Don't get me wrong,
but stay in out of the rain the next few days
just for instance."

GARTH: I thought I burned that letter.

MIRIAMNE: Afterward you did. And then what was printed
about the Estrella gang—you hid it from me,
you and father. What is it—about this murder—?

GARTH: Will you shut up, you fool!

MIRIAMNE: But if you know
why don't you tell them, Garth?
If it's true—what they say—
you knew all the time Romagna wasn't guilty,
and could have said so—

GARTH: Everybody knew
Romagna wasn't guilty! But they weren't listening
to evidence in his favor. They didn't want it.
They don't want it now.

MIRIAMNE: But was that why
they never called on you?—

GARTH: So far as I know
they never'd heard of me—and I can assure you
I knew nothing about it—

MIRIAMNE: But something's wrong—
and it worries father—

GARTH: What could be wrong?

MIRIAMNE: I don't know.

A pause.

GARTH: And I don't know. You're a good kid, Miriamne,
but you see too many movies. I wasn't mixed up
in any murder, and I don't mean to be
If I had a dollar to get my fiddle fixed
and another to hire a hall, by God I'd fiddle
some of the prodigies back into Sunday School
where they belong, but I won't get either, and so
I sit here and bite my nails—but if you hoped
I had some criminal romantic past
you'll have to look again!

MIRIAMNE: Oh, Garth, forgive me—
But I want you to be so far above such things
nothing could frighten you. When you seem to shrink
and be afraid, and you're the brother I love,
I want to run there and cry, if there's any question
they care to ask, you'll be quick and glad to answer,
for there's nothing to conceal!

GARTH: And that's all true—

MIRIAMNE: But then I remember—
how you dim the lights—
and we go early to bed—and speak in whispers—
and I could think there's a death somewhere behind us—
an evil death—

GARTH [*hearing a step*]:
Now for God's sake, be quiet!

ESDRAS, *an old rabbi with a kindly face, enters from the outside. He is hurried and troubled.*

ESDRAS: I wish to speak alone with someone here
if I may have this room. Miriamne—

MIRIAMNE [*turning to go*]:
Yes, father.

The outer door is suddenly thrown open. TROCK *appears.*

TROCK [*after a pause*]:
You'll excuse me for not knocking.
[SHADOW *follows* TROCK *in.*]
Sometimes it's best to come in quiet. Sometimes
it's a good way to go out. Garth's home, I see.

He might not have been here if I made a point
of knocking at doors.

GARTH: How are you, Trock?

TROCK: I guess
you can see how I am.
[*To* MIRIAMNE.] Stay here. Stay where you are.
We'd like to make your acquaintance.
—If you want the facts
I'm no better than usual, thanks. Not enough sun,
my physician tells me. Too much close confinement.
A lack of exercise and an overplus
of beans in the diet. You've done well, no doubt?

GARTH: I don't know what makes you think so.

TROCK: Who's the family?

GARTH: My father and my sister.

TROCK: Happy to meet you.
Step inside a minute. The boy and I
have something to talk about.

ESTRAS: No, no—he's said nothing— nothing, sir, nothing!

TROCK: When I say go out, you go—

ESDRAS [*pointing to the door*]:
Miriamne—

GARTH: Go on out, both of you!

ESDRAS: Oh, sir—I'm old—
old and unhappy—

GARTH: Go on!

MIRIAMNE *and* ESDRAS *go inside.*

TROCK: And if you listen
I'll riddle that door!
[SHADOW *shuts the door behind them and stands against it.*]
I just got out, you see,
and I pay my first call on you.

GARTH: Maybe you think
I'm not in the same jam you are.

TROCK: That's what I do think.
Who started looking this up?

GARTH: I wish I knew,
and I wish he was in hell! Some damned professor
with nothing else to do. If you saw his stuff
you know as much as I do.

TROCK: It wasn't you
turning state's evidence?

GARTH: Hell, Trock, use your brain!
The case was closed. They burned Romagna for it
and that finished it. Why should I look for trouble
and maybe get burned myself?

TROCK: Boy, I don't know,
but I just thought I'd find out.

GARTH: I'm going straight, Trock.
I can play this thing, and I'm trying to make a living.
I haven't talked and nobody's talked to me.
Christ—it's the last thing I'd want!

TROCK: Your old man knows.

GARTH: That's where I got the money that last time
when you needed it. He had a little saved up,
but I had to tell him to get it. He's as safe
as Shadow there.

TROCK [*looking at* SHADOW]:
There could be people safer
than that son-of-a-bitch.

SHADOW: Who?

TROCK: You'd be safer dead
along with some other gorillas.

SHADOW: It's beginning to look
as if you'd feel safer with everybody dead,
the whole god-damn world.

TROCK: I would. These Jesus-bitten
professors! Looking up their half-ass cases!
We've got enough without that.

GARTH: There's no evidence
to reopen the thing.

TROCK: And suppose they called on you
and asked you to testify?

GARTH: Why then I'd tell 'em
that all I know is what I read in the papers.
And I'd stick to that.

TROCK: How much does your sister know?

GARTH: I'm honest with you, Trock. She read my name
in the professor's pamphlet, and she was scared
the way anybody would be. She got nothing
from me, and anyway she'd go to the chair
herself before she'd send me there.

TROCK: Like hell.

GARTH: Besides, who wants to go to trial again
except the radicals?—You and I won't spill
and unless we did there's nothing to take to court
as far as I know. Let the radicals go on howling
about getting a dirty deal. They always howl
and nobody gives a damn. This professor's red—
everybody knows it.

TROCK: You're forgetting the judge.
Where's the damn judge?

GARTH: What judge?

TROCK: Read the morning papers.
It says Judge Gaunt's gone off his nut. He's got

that damn trial on his mind, and been going round
proving to everybody he was right all the time
and the radicals were guilty—stopping people
in the street to prove it—and now he's nuts entirely
and nobody knows where he is.

GARTH: Why don't they know?

TROCK: Because he's on the loose somewhere! They've got
the police of three cities looking for him.

GARTH: Judge Gaunt?

TROCK: Yes. Judge Gaunt.

SHADOW: Why should that worry you?
He's crazy, ain't he? And even if he wasn't
he's arguing on your side. You're jittery, chief.
God, all the judges are looney. You've got the jitters,
and you'll damn well give yourself away some time
peeing yourself in public.
[TROCK *half turns toward* SHADOW *in anger.*]
Don't jump the gun now,
I've got pockets in my clothes, too.
[*His hand is in his coat pocket.*]

TROCK: All right. Take it easy.

He takes his hand from his pocket, and SHADOW *does the same.*

[*To* GARTH.]
Maybe you're lying to me and maybe you're not.
Stay at home a few days.

GARTH: Sure thing. Why not?

TROCK: And when I say stay home I mean stay home.
If I have to go looking for you you'll stay a long time
wherever I find you.
[*To* SHADOW.] Come on. We'll get out of here.
[*To* GARTH.] Be seeing you.

SHADOW *and* TROCK *go out. After a pause* GARTH *walks over to his chair and picks up the violin. Then he puts it down and goes to the inside door, which he opens.*

GARTH: He's gone.

MIRIAMNE *enters,* ESDRAS *behind her.*

MIRIAMNE [*going up to* GARTH]:
Let's not stay here.
[*She puts her hands on his arms.*]
I thought he'd come for something—horrible.
Is he coming back?

GARTH: I don't know.

MIRIAMNE: Who is he, Garth?

GARTH: He'd kill me if I told you who he is,
that is, if he knew.

MIRIAMNE: Then don't say it—

GARTH: Yes, and I'll say it! I was with a gang one time
that robbed a pay roll. I saw a murder done,
and Trock Estrella did it. If that got out
I'd go to the chair and so would he—that's why
he was here today—

MIRIAMNE: But that's not true—

ESDRAS: He says it
to frighten you, child.

GARTH: Oh, no I don't! I say it
because I've held it in too long! I'm damned
if I set here forever and look at the door,
waiting for Trock with his submachine gun, waiting
for police with a warrant!—I say I'm damned, and I am,
no matter what I do! These piddling scales
on a violin—first position, third, fifth,
arpeggios in E—and what I'm thinking
is Romagna dead for the murder—dead while I sat here
dying inside—dead for the thing Trock did
while I looked on—and I could have saved him, yes—
but I sat here and let him die instead of me
because I wanted to live! Well, it's no life,
and it doesn't matter who I tell, because
I mean to get it over!

MIRIAMNE: Garth, it's not true!

GARTH: I'd take some scum down with me if I died—
that'd be one good deed—

ESDRAS: Son, son, you're mad—
someone will hear—

GARTH: Then let them hear! I've lived
with ghosts too long, and lied too long. God damn you
if you keep me from the truth!—
[*He turns away.*] Oh, God damn the world!
I don't want to die!

ESDRAS: I should have known.
I thought you hard and sullen,
Garth, my son. And you were a child, and hurt
with a wound that might be healed.
—All men have crimes,
and most of them are hidden, and many are heavy
as yours must be to you.
[GARTH *sobs.*] They walk the streets
to buy and sell, but a spreading crimson stain

tinges the inner vestments, touches flesh,
and burns the quick. You're not alone.

GARTH: I'm alone
in this.

ESDRAS: Yes, if you hold with the world that only
those who die suddenly should be revenged.
But those whose hearts are cancered, drop by drop
in small ways, little by little, till they've borne
all they can bear, and die—these deaths will go
unpunished now as always. When we're young
we have faith in what is seen, but when we're old
we know that what is seen is traced in air
and built on water. There's no guilt under heaven,
just as there's no heaven, till men believe it—
no earth, till men have seen it, and have a word
to say this is the earth.

GARTH: Well, I say there's an earth,
and I say I'm guilty on it, guilty as hell.

ESDRAS: Yet till it's known you bear no guilt at all—
unless you wish. The days go by like film,
like a long written scroll, a figured veil
unrolling out of darkness into fire
and utterly consumed. And on this veil,
running in sounds and symbols of men's minds
reflected back, life flickers and is shadow
going toward flame. Only what men can see
exists in that shadow. Why must you rise and cry out:
That was I, there in the ravelled tapestry,
there, in that pistol flash, when the man was killed.
I was there, and was one, and am bloodstained!
Let the wind
and fire take that hour to ashes out of time
and out of mind! This thing that men call justice,
this blind snake that strikes men down in the dark,
mindless with fury, keep your hand back from it,
pass by in silence—let it be forgotten, forgotten!—
Oh, my son, my son—have pity!

MIRIAMNE: But if it was true
and someone died—then it was more than shadow—
and it doesn't blow away—

GARTH: Well, it was true.

ESDRAS: Say it if you must. If you have heart to die,
say it, and let them take what's left—there was little
to keep, even before—

GARTH: Oh, I'm a coward—
I always was. I'll be quiet and live. I'll live
even if I have to crawl. I know.
[*He gets up and goes into the inner room.*]

MIRIAMNE: Is it better
to tell a lie and live?

ESDRAS: Yes, child. It's better.

MIRIAMNE: But if I had to do it—
I think I'd die.

ESDRAS: Yes, child. Because you're young.

MIRIAMNE: Is that the only reason?

ESDRAS: The only reason.

CURTAIN

Scene III

Under the bridge, evening of the same day. When the curtain rises MIRIAMNE *is sitting alone on the ledge at the rear of the apartment house. A spray of light falls on her from a street lamp above. She shivers a little in her thin coat, but sits still as if heedless of the weather. Through the rocks on the other side a* TRAMP *comes down to the river bank, hunting a place to sleep. He goes softly to the apple-woman's hut and looks in, then turns away, evidently not daring to preëmpt it. He looks at* MIRIAMNE *doubtfully. The door of the street-piano man is shut. The vagabond passes it and picks carefully among some rags and shavings to the right.* MIRIAMNE *looks up and sees him but makes no sign. She looks down again, and the man curls himself up in a makeshift bed in the corner, pulling a piece of sacking over his shoulders.* TWO GIRLS *come in round the apartment house.*

1ST GIRL: Honest, I never heard of anything so romantic. Because you never liked him.

2ND GIRL: I certainly never did.

1ST GIRL: You've got to tell me how it happened. You've got to.

2ND GIRL: I couldn't. As long as I live I couldn't. Honest, it was terrible. It was terrible.

1ST GIRL: What was so terrible?

2ND GIRL: The way it happened.

1ST GIRL: Oh, please—not to a soul, never.

2ND GIRL: Well, you know how I hated him because he had such a big mouth. So he reached over and grabbed me, and I began all falling to pieces inside, the way you do—and I said, "Oh no you don't mister," and started screaming and kicked a hole through the windshield and lost a shoe, and he let go and was cursing and growling because he borrowed the car and didn't have money to pay for the windshield, and he started to cry, and I got so sorry for him I let him, and now he wants to marry me.

1ST GIRL: Honest, I never heard of anything so romantic! [*She sees the sleeping* TRAMP.] My God, what you won't see!

They give the TRAMP *a wide berth, and go out right. The* TRAMP *sits up looking about him.* JUDGE GAUNT, *an elderly, quiet man, well dressed but in clothes that have seen some weather, comes in undertainly from the left. He holds a small clipping in his hand and goes up to the* HOBO.

GAUNT [*tentatively*]: Your pardon, sir. Your pardon, but perhaps you can tell me the name of this street.

HOBO: Huh?

GAUNT: The name of this street?

HOBO: This ain't no street.

GAUNT: There, where the street lamps are.

HOBO: That's the alley.

GAUNT: Thank you. It has a name, no doubt?

HOBO: That's the alley.

GAUNT: I see. I won't trouble you. You wonder why I ask, I daresay.—I'm a stranger.—Why do you look at me? [*He steps back.*] I—I'm not the man you think. You've mistaken me, sir.

HOBO: Huh?

JUDGE: Perhaps misled by a resemblance. But you're mistaken—I had an errand in this city. It's only by accident that I'm here—

HOBO [*muttering*]: You go to hell.

JUDGE [*going nearer to him, bending over him*]: Yet why should I deceive you? Before God, I held the proofs in my hands. I hold them still. I tell you the defense was cunning beyond belief, and unscrupulous in its use of propaganda—they gagged at nothing—not even—[*He rises.*] No, no—I'm sorry—this will hardly interest you. I'm sorry. I have an errand.

He looks toward the street. ESDRAS *enters from the basement and goes to* MIRIAMNE. *The* JUDGE *steps back into the shadows.*

ESDRAS: Come in, my daughter. You'll be cold here.

MIRIAMNE: After a while.

ESDRAS: You'll be cold. There's a storm coming.

MIRIAMNE: I didn't want him to see me crying. That was all.

ESDRAS: I know.

MIRIAMNE: I'll come soon.

ESDRAS *turns reluctantly and goes out the way he came.* MIRIAMNE *rises to go in, pausing to dry her eyes.* MIO *and* CARR, *road boys of seventeen or so, come round the apartment house. The* JUDGE *has disappeared.*

CARR: Thought you said you were never coming east again.

MIO: Yeah, but—I heard something changed my mind.

CARR: Same old business?

MIO: Yes, just as soon not talk about it.

CARR: Where did you go from Portland?

MIO: Fishing—I went fishing. God's truth.

CARR: Right after I left?

MIO: Fell in with a fisherman's family on the coast and went after the beautiful mackerel fish that swim in the beautiful sea. Family of Greeks—Aristides Marinos was his lovely name. He sang while he fished. Made the pea-green Pacific ring with his bastard Greek chanties. Then I went to Hollywood High School for a while.

CARR: I'll bet that's a seat of learning.

MIO: It's the hind end of all wisdom. They kicked me out after a time.

CARR: For cause?

MIO: Because I had no permanent address, you see. That means nobody's paying school taxes for you, so out you go. [*To* MIRIAMNE.] What's the matter, Kid?

MIRIAMNE: Nothing. [*She looks up at him, and they pause for a moment.*] Nothing.

MIO: I'm sorry.

MIRIAMNE: It's all right. [*She withdraws her eyes from his and goes out past him. He turns and looks after her.*]

CARR: Control your chivalry.

MIO: A pretty kid.

CARR: A baby.

MIO: Wait for me.

CARR: Be a long wait? [MIO *steps swiftly out after* MIRIAMNE, *then returns.*] Yeah?

MIO: She's gone.

CARR: Think of that.

MIO: No, but I mean—vanished. Presto—into nothing—prodigioso.

CARR: Damn good thing, if you ask me. The homely ones are bad enough, but the lookers are fatal.

MIO: You exaggerate, Carr.

CARR: I doubt it.

MIO: Well, let her go. This river bank's loaded with typhus rats, too. Might as well die one death as another.

CARR: They say chronic alcoholism is nice but expensive. You can always starve to death.

MIO: Not always. I tried it. After the second day I walked thirty miles to Niagara Falls and made a tour of the plant to get the sample of shredded wheat biscuit on the way out.

CARR: Last time I saw you you couldn't think of anything you wanted to do except curse God and pass out. Still feeling low?

MIO: Not much different. [*He turns away, then comes back.*] Talk about the lost generation, I'm the only one fits that title. When the State executes your father, and your mother dies of grief, and you know damn well he was innocent, and the authorities of your home town politely inform you they'd consider it a favor if you lived somewhere else—that cuts you off from the world—with a meat-axe.

CARR: They asked you to move?

MIO: It came to that.

CARR: God, that was white of them.

MIO: It probably gave them a headache just to see me after all that agitation. They knew as well as I did my father never staged a holdup. Anyway, I've got a new interest in life now.

CARR: Yes—I saw her.

MIO: I don't mean the skirt.—No, I got wind of something, out west, some college professor investigating the trial and turning up new evidence. Couldn't find anything he'd written out there, so I beat it east and arrived on this blessed island just in time to find the bums holing up in the public library for the winter. I know now what the unemployed have been doing since the depression started. They've been catching up on their reading in the main reference room. Man, what a stench! Maybe I stank, too, but a hobo has the stench of ten because his shoes are poor.

CARR: Tennyson.

MIO: Right. Jeez, I'm glad we met up again! Never knew anybody else that could track me through the driven snow of Victorian literature.

CARR: Now you're cribbing from some half-forgotten criticism of Ben Jonson's Roman plagiarisms.

MIO: Where did you get your education, sap?

CARR: Not in the public library, sap. My father kept a news-stand.

MIO: Well, you're right again. [*There is a faint rumble of thunder.*] What's that? Winter thunder?

CARR: Or Mister God, beating on His little tocsin. Maybe announcing the advent of a new social order.

MIO: Or maybe it's going to rain coffee and doughnuts.

CARR: Or maybe it's going to rain.

MIO: Seems more likely. [*Lowering his voice.*] Anyhow, I found Professor Hobhouse's discussion of the Romagna case. I think he has something. It occurred to me I might follow it up by doing a little sleuthing on my own account.

CARR: Yes;

MIO: I have done a little. And it leads me to somewhere in that tenement house that backs up against the bridge. That's how I happen to be here.

CARR: They'll never let you get anywhere with it, Mio. I told you that before.

MIO: I know you did.

CARR: The State can't afford to admit it was wrong, you see. Not when there's been that much of a row kicked up over it. So for all practical purposes the State was right and your father robbed the pay roll.

MIO: There's still such a thing as evidence.

CARR: It's something you can buy. In fact, at the moment I don't think of anything you can't buy, including life, honor, virtue, glory, public office, conjugal affection and all kinds of justice, from the traffic court to the immortal nine. Go out and make yourself a pot of money and you can buy all the justice you want. Convictions obtained, convictions averted. Lowest rates in years.

MIO: I know all that.

CARR: Sure.

MIO: This thing didn't happen to you.
They've left you your name
and whatever place you can take. For my heritage
They've left me one thing only, and that's to be
my father's voice crying up out of the earth
and quicklime where they stuck him. Electrocution
doesn't kill, you know. They eviscerate them
with a turn of the knife in the dissecting room
The blood spurts out. The man was alive. Then into
the lime pit, leave no trace. Make it short shrift
and chemical dissolution. That's what they thought
of the man that was my father. Then my mother—
I tell you these county burials are swift

and cheap and run for profit! Out of the house
and into the ground, you wife of a dead dog.
Wait,
here's some Romagna spawn left.
Something crawls here—
something they called a son. Why couldn't he die
along with his mother? Well, ease him out of town
ease him out, boys, and see you're not too gentle.
He might come back. And, by their own living Jesus,
I will go back, and hang the carrion
around their necks that made it!
Maybe I can sleep then.
Or even live.

CARR: You have to try it?

MIO: Yes.
Yes, It won't let me alone. I've tried to live
and forget it—but I was birthmarked with hot iron
into the entrails. I've got to find out who did it
and make them see it till it scalds their eyes
and make them admit it till their tongues are blistered
with saying how black they lied!

HERMAN, *a gawky shoe salesman, enters from the left.*

HERMAN: Hello. Did you see a couple of girls go this way?

CARR: Couple of girls? Did we see a couple of girls?

MIO: No.

CARR: No. No girls.

HERMAN *hesitates, then goes out right.* LUCIA *comes in from the left, trundling his piano.* PINY *follows him, weeping.*

PINY: They've got no right to do it—

LUCIA: All right, hell what, no matter, I got to put him away, I got to put him away, that's what the hell! [TWO STREET URCHINS *follow him in.*]

PINY: They want everybody on the relief rolls and nobody making a living?

LUCIA: The cops, they do what the big boss say. The big boss, that's the mayor, he says he heard it once too often, the sextette——

PINY: They want graft, that's all. It's a new way to get graft——

LUCIA: Oh, no, no, no! He's a good man, the mayor. He's just don't care for music, that's all.

PINY: Why shouldn't you make a living on the street? The National Biscuit Company ropes off Eighth Avenue—and does the mayor do anything? No, the police hit you over the head if you try to go through!

LUCIA: You got the big dough, you get the pull, fine. No big dough, no pull, what the hell, get off the city property! Tomorrow I start cooking chestnuts . . . [*He strokes the piano fondly. The* TWO GIRLS *and* HERMAN *come back from the right.*] She's a good little machine, this baby. Cost plenty—and two new records I only played twice. See this one. [*He starts turning the crank, talking while he plays.*] Two weeks since they play this one in a picture house. [A SAILOR *wanders in from the left. One of the* STREET URCHINS *begins suddenly to dance a wild rumba, the others watch.*] Good boy—see, it's a lulu—it itches in the feet!

HERMAN, *standing with his girl, tosses the boy a penny. He bows and goes on dancing; the other* URCHIN *joins him. The* SAILOR *tosses a coin.*

SAILOR: Go it, Cuba! Go it!

LUCIA *turns the crank, beaming.*

2ND GIRL: Oh, Herman! [*She throws her arms round* HERMAN *and they dance.*]

1ST URCHIN: Hey, pipe the professionals!

1ST GIRL: Do your glide, Shirley! Do your glide!

LUCIA: Maybe we can't play in front, maybe we can play behind! [*The* HOBO *gets up from his nest and comes over to watch.* A YOUNG RADICAL *wanders in.*] Maybe you don't know, folks! Tonight we play good-bye to the piano! Good-bye forever! No more piano on the streets! No more music! No more money for the music-man! Last time, folks! Good-bye to the piano—good-bye forever! [MARIAMNE *comes out the rear door of the apartment and stands watching. The* SAILOR *goes over to the* 1ST GIRL *and they dance together.*] Maybe you don't know, folks! Tomorrow will be sad as hell, tonight we dance! Tomorrow no more Verdi, no more rumba, no more good time! Tonight we play good-bye to the piano, good-bye forever! [*The* RADICAL *edges up to* MARIAMNE *and asks her to dance. She shakes her head and he goes to* PINY, *who dances with him. The* HOBO *begins to do a few lonely curvets on the side above.*] Hoy! Hoy! Pick 'em up and take 'em around! Use the head, use the feet! Last time forever! [*He begins to sing to the air.*]

MIO: Wait for me, will you?

CARR: Now's your chance.

MIO *goes over to* MIRIAMNE *and holds out a hand, smiling. She stands for a moment uncertain, then dances with him.* ESDRAS *comes out to watch.* JUDGE GAUNT *comes in from the left. There is a rumble of thunder.*

LUCIA: Hoy Hoy! Maybe it rains tonight, maybe it snows tomorrow! Tonight we dance good-bye. [*He sings the air lustily.* A POLICEMAN *comes in from the left and looks on.* TWO OR THREE PEDESTRIANS *follow him.*]

POLICEMAN: Hey you! [LUCIA *goes on singing.*] Hey, you!

LUCIA [*still playing*]: What you want?

POLICEMAN: Sign off!

LUCIA: What you mean? I get off the street!

POLICEMAN: Sign off!

LUCIA [*still playing*]: What you mean? [*The* POLICEMAN *walks over to him.* LUCIA *stops playing and the* DANCERS *pause.*]

POLICEMAN: Cut it.

LUCIA: Is this a street?

POLICEMAN: I say cut it out.

The HOBO *goes back to his nest and sits in it, watching.*

LUCIA: It's the last time. We dance good-bye to the piano.

POLICEMAN: You'll dance good-bye to something else if I catch you cranking that thing again.

LUCIA: All right.

PINY: I'll bet you don't say that to the National Biscuit Company!

POLICEMAN: Lady, you've been selling apples on my beat for some time now, and I said nothing about it——

PINY: Selling apples is allowed——

POLICEMAN: You watch yourself—[*He takes a short walk around the place and comes upon the* HOBO.] What are you doing here? [*The* HOBO *opens his mouth, points to it, and shakes his head.*] Oh, you are, are you? [*He comes back to* LUCIA] So you trundle your so called musical instrument to wherever you keep it, and don't let me hear it again.

The RADICAL *leaps on the base of the rock at right. The* 1ST GIRL *turns away from the* SAILOR *toward the* 2ND GIRL *and* HERMAN.

SAILOR: Hey, captain, what's the matter with the music?

POLICEMAN: Not a thing, admiral

SAILOR: Well, we had a little party going here—

POLICEMAN: I'll say you did.

2ND GIRL: Please, officer, we want to dance.

POLICEMAN: Go ahead. Dance.

2ND GIRL: But we want music!

POLICEMAN [*turning to go*]. Sorry. Can't help you.

RADICAL: And there you see it, the perfect example of capitalistic oppression! In a land where music should be free as air and the arts should be encouraged, a uniformed minion of the rich, a guardian myrmidon of the Park Avenue pleasure hunters, steps in and puts a limit on the innocent enjoyments of the poor! We don't go to theatres! Why not? We can't afford it! We don't go to night clubs, where women dance naked and the music drips from saxophones and leaks out of Rudy Vallee—we can't afford that either!—But we might at least dance on the river bank to the strains of a barrel organ—!

GARTH *comes out of the apartment and listens.*

POLICEMAN: It's against the law!

RADICAL: What law? I challenge you to tell me what law of God or man—what ordinance—is violated by this spontaneous diversion? None! I say none! An official whim of the masters who should be our servants!——

POLICEMAN: Get down! Get down and shut up!

RADICAL: By what law, by what ordinance do you order me to be quiet?

POLICEMAN: Speaking without a flag. You know it.

RADICAL [*pulling out a small American flag*]. There's my flag! There's the flag of this United States which used to guarantee the rights of man—the rights of man now violated by every statute of the commonweal——

POLICEMAN: Don't try to pull tricks on me! I've seen you before! You're not making any speech, and you're climbing down——

JUDGE GAUNT [*who has come quietly forward*]. One moment, officer. There is some difference of opinion even on the bench as to the elasticity of police power when applied in minor emergencies to preserve civil order. But the weight of authority would certainly favor the defendant in any equable court, and he would be upheld in his demand to be heard.

POLICEMAN: Who are you?

GAUNT: Sir, I am not accustomed to answer that question.

POLICEMAN: I don't know you.

GAUNT: I am a judge of some standing, not in your city but in another with similar statutes.

You are aware, of course, that the Bill of Rights is not to be set aside lightly by the officers of any municipality——

POLICEMAN [*looking over* GAUNT'S *somewhat bedraggled costume*]: Maybe they understand you better in the town you come from, but I don't get your drift.—[*To the* RADICAL.] I don't want any trouble, but if you ask for it you'll get plenty. Get down!

RADICAL: I'm not asking for trouble, but I'm staying right here. [*The* POLICEMAN *moves towards him.*]

GAUNT [*taking the* POLICEMAN'S *arm, but shaken off roughly*]: I ask this for yourself, truly, not for the dignity of the law nor the maintenance of precedent. Be gentle with them when their threats are childish—be tolerant while you can—for your least harsh word will return on you in the night—return in a storm of cries!—[*He takes the* POLICEMAN'S *arm again.*] Whatever they may have said or done, let them disperse in peace! It is better that they go softly, lest when they are dead you see their eyes pleading, and their outstretched hands touch you, fingering cold on your heart!—I have been harsher than you. I have sent men down that long corridor into blinding light and blind darkness! [*He suddenly draws himself erect and speaks defiantly.*] And it was well that I did so! I have been an upright judge! They are all liars! Liars!

POLICEMAN [*shaking* GAUNT *off so that he falls*]:
Why, you fool, you're crazy!

GAUNT: Yes, and there are liars on the force! They came to me with their shifty lies! [*He catches at the* POLICEMAN, *who pushes him away with his foot.*]

POLICEMAN: You think I've got nothing better to do than listen to a crazy fool?

1ST GIRL: Shame, shame!

POLICEMAN: What have I got to be ashamed of? And what's going on here, anyway? Where in hell did you all come from?

RADICAL: Tread on him! That's right! Tread down the poor and the innocent! [*There is a protesting murmur in the crowd.*]

SAILOR [*moving in a little*]: Say, big boy, you don't have to step on the guy.

POLICEMAN [*facing them, stepping back*]:
What's the matter with you! I haven't stepped on anybody!

MIO [*at the right, across from the* POLICEMAN]:
Listen now, fellows, give the badge a chance.
He's doing his job, what he gets paid to do,
the same as any of you. They're all picked men,
these metropolitan police, hand picked
for loyalty and a fine up-standing pair
of shoulders on their legs—it's not so easy
to represent the law. Think what he does
for all of us, stamping out crime!
Do you want to be robbed and murdered in your beds?

SAILOR: What's eating you?

RADICAL: He must be a capitalist.

MIO: They pluck them fresh,
from Ireland, and a paucity of headpiece
is a prime prerequisite. You from Ireland, buddy?

POLICEMAN [*surly*]:
Where are you from?

MIO: Buddy, I tell you flat
I wish I was from Ireland, and could boast
some Tammany connections. There's only one drawback
about working on the force. It infects the brain,
it eats the cerebrum. There've been cases known,
fine specimens of manhood, too, where autopsies,
conducted in approved scientific fashion,
revealed conditions quite incredible
in policemen's upper layers. In some, a trace,
in others, when they've swung a stick too long,
there was nothing there!—but nothing! Oh, my friends,
this fine athletic figure of a man
that stands so grim before us, what will they find
when they saw his skull for the last inspection?
I fear me a little puffball dust will blow away
rejoining earth, our mother—and this same dust,
this smoke, this ash on the wind, will represent
all he had left to think with!

THE HOBO: Hooray!

The POLICEMAN *turns on his heel and looks hard at the* HOBO, *who slinks away.*

POLICEMAN: Oh, yeah?

MIO: My theme
gives ears to the deaf and voice to the dumb! But now
forgive me if I say you were most unkind
in troubling the officer. He's a simple man
of simple tastes, and easily confused
when faced with complex issues. He may reflect

on returning home, that is, so far as he is capable of reflection, and conclude that he was kidded out of his uniform pants,
and in his fury when this dawns on him
may smack his wife down!

POLICEMAN: That'll be about enough from you, too, professor!

MIO: May I say that I think you have managed this whole situation rather badly, from the beginning?——

POLICEMAN: You may not!

TROCK *slips in from the background. The* TWO YOUNG MEN IN SERGE *come with him.*

MIO: Oh, but your pardon, sir! It's apparent to the least competent among us that you should have gone about your task more subtly—the glove of velvet, the hand of iron, and all that sort of thing——

POLICEMAN: Shut that hole in your face!

MIO: Sir, for that remark I shall be satisfied with nothing less than an unconditional apology! I have an old score to settle with policeman, brother, because they're fools and fat-heads, and you're one of the most fatuous fat-heads that ever walked his feet flat collecting graft! Tell that to your sergeant back in the booby-hatch.

POLICEMAN: Oh, you want an apology, do you? You'll get an apology out of the other side of your mouth! [*He steps toward* MIO. CARR *suddenly stands in his path.*] Get out of my way! [*He pauses and looks round him; the crowd looks less and less friendly. He lays a hand on his gun and backs to a position where there is nobody behind him.*] Get out of here, all of you! Get out! What are you trying to do—start a riot?

MIO: There now, that's better! That's in the best police tradition. Incite a riot yourself and then accuse the crowd.

POLICEMAN: It won't be pleasant if I decide to let somebody have it! Get out!

The onlookers begin to melt away. The SAILOR *goes out left with the* GIRLS *and* HERMAN. CARR *and* MIO *go out right,* CARR *whistling "The Star Spangled Banner." The* HOBO *follows them. The* RADICAL *walks past with his head in the air.* PINY *and* LUCIA *leave the piano where it stands and slip away to the left. At the end the* POLICEMAN *is left standing in the center, the* JUDGE *near him.* ESDRAS *stands in the doorway.* MIRIAMNE *is left sitting half in shadow and unseen by* ESDRAS.

JUDGE GAUNT [*to the* POLICEMAN]: Yes, but should a man die, should it be necessary that one man die for the good of many, make not yourself the instrument of death, lest you sleep to wake sobbing! Nay, it avails nothing that you are the law—this delicate ganglion that is the brain, it will not bear these things—!

The POLICEMAN *gives the* JUDGE *the onceover, shrugs, decides to leave him there and starts out left.* GARTH *goes to his father—a fine sleet begins to fall through the street lights.* TROCK *is still visible.*

GARTH: Get him in here, quick.

ESDRAS: Who, son?

GARTH: The Judge, damn him!

ESDRAS: Who did you think it was? He's crazy as a bedbug and telling the world. Get him inside! [*He looks round.*]

ESDRAS [*going up to* GAUNT]: Will you come in, sir?

GAUNT: You will understand, sir. We old men know how softly we must proceed with these things.

ESDRAS: Yes, surely, sir.

GAUNT: It was always my practice—always. They will tell you that of me where I am known. Yet even I am not free of regret—even I. Would you believe it?

ESDRAS: I believe we are none of us free of regret.

GAUNT: None of us? I would it were true. I would I thought it were true.

ESDRAS: Shall we go in, sir? This is sleet that's falling.

GAUNT: Yes. Let us go in.

ESDRAS, GAUNT *and* GARTH *enter the basement and shut the door.* TROCK *goes out with his men. After a pause* MIO *comes back from the right, alone. He stands at a little distance from* MIRIAMNE.

MIO: Looks like rain. [*She is silent.*] You live around here? [*She nods gravely.*] I guess
you thought I meant it—about waiting here to meet me. [*She nods again.*]
I'd forgotten about it till I got that winter
across the face. You'd better go inside. I'm not your kind. I'm nobody's kind but my own.
I'm waiting for this to blow over.
[*She rises.*] I lied. I meant it—
I meant it when I said it—but there's too much black
whirling inside me—for any girl to know.
So go on in. You're somebody's angel child
and they're waiting for you.

MIRIAMNE: Yes. I'll go. [*She turns.*]

MIO: And tell them
when you get inside where it's warm,
And you love each other,

and mother comes to kiss her darling, tell them
to hang on to it while they can, believe while they can
it's a warm safe world, and Jesus finds his lambs
and carries them in his bosom.—I've seen some lambs
that Jesus missed. If they ever want the truth
tell them that nothing's guaranteed in this climate
except it gets cold in winter, nor on this earth
except you die sometime.
[*He turns away.*]

MIRIAMNE: I have no mother.
And my people are Jews.

MIO: Then you know something about it.

MIRIAMNE: Yes.

MIO: Do you have enough to eat?

MIRIAMNE: Not always.

MIO: What do you believe in?

MIRIAMNE: Nothing.

MIO: Why?

MIRIAMNE: How can one?

MIO: It's easy if you're a fool. You see the words
in books. Honor, it says there, chivalry, freedom,
heroism, enduring love—and these
are words on paper. It's something to have them there.
You'll get them nowhere else.

MIRIAMNE: What hurts you?

MIO: Just that.
You'll get them nowhere else.

MIRIAMNE: Why should you want them;

MIO: I'm alone, that's why. You see those lights,
along the river, cutting across the rain—?
those are the hearths of Brooklyn, and up this way
the love-nests of Manhattan—they turn their points
like knives against me—outcast of the world,
snake in the streets.—I don't want a hand-out.
I sleep and eat.

MIRIAMNE: Do you want me to go with you?

MIO: Where?

MIRIAMNE: Where you go.

A pause. He goes nearer to her.

MIO: Why, you god-damned little fool—
what made you say that?

MIRIAMNE: I don't know.

MIO: If you have a home
stay in it. I ask for nothing. I've schooled myself
to ask for nothing, and take what I can get,
and get along. If I fell for you, that's my lookout,
and I'll starve it down.

MIRIAMNE: Wherever you go, I'd go.

MIO: What do you know about loving?
How could you know?
Have you ever had a man?

MIRIAMNE [*after a slight pause*]: No. But I know.
Tell me your name.

MIO: Mio. What's yours?

MIRIAMNE: Miriamne.

MIO: There's no such name.

MIRIAMNE: But there's no such name as Mio!
M.I.O. It's no name.

MIO: It's for Bartolomeo.

MIRIAMNE: My mother's name was Miriam,
so they called me Miriamne.

MIO: Meaning little Miriam?

MIRIAMNE: Yes.

MIO: So now little Miriamne will go in
and take up quietly where she dropped them all
her small housewifely cares.—When I first saw you,
not a half-hour ago, I heard myself saying.
this is the face that launches ships for me—
and if I owned a dream—yes, half a dream—
we'd share it. But I have no dream. This earth
came tumbling down from chaos, fire and rock,
and bred up worms, blind worms that sting each other
here in the dark. These blind worms of the earth
took out my father—and killed him, and set a sign
on me—the heir of the serpent—and he was a man
such as men might be if the gods were men—
but they killed him—
as they'll kill all others like him
till the sun cools down to the stabler molecules,
yes, till men spin their tent-worm webs to the stars
and what they think is done, even in the thinking,
and they are the gods, and immortal, and constellations
turn for them all like mill wheels—still as they are
they will be, worms and blind. Enduring love,
oh gods and worms, what mockery!—And yet
I have blood enough in my veins. It goes like music,
singing, because you're here. My body turns

as if you were the sun, and warm. This men called love
in happier times, before the Freudians taught us
to blame it on the glands. Only go in
before you breathe too much of my atmosphere
and catch death from me.

MIRIAMNE: I will take my hands
and weave them to a little house, and there
you shall keep a dream——

MIO: God knows I could use a dream
and even a house.

MIRIAMNE: You're laughing at me, Mio!

MIO: The worms are laughing.
I tell you there's death about me
and you're a child! And I'm alone and half mad
with hate and longing. I shall let you love me
and love you in return, and then, why then
God knows what happens!

MIRIAMNE: Something most unpleasant?

MIO: Love in a box car—love among the children.
I've seen too much of it. Are we to live in this
same house you make with your two hands
mystically, out of air?

MIRIAMNE: No roof, nor mortgage!
Well, I shall marry a baker out in Flatbush,
it gives hot bread in the morning! Oh, Mio, Mio,
in all the unwanted places and waste lands
that roll up into the darkness out of sun
and into sun out of dark, there should be one empty
for you and me.

MIO: No.

MIRIAMNE: Then go now and leave me.
I'm only a girl you saw in the tenements,
and there's been nothing said.

MIO: Miriamne.

She takes a step toward him.

MIRIAMNE: Yes. [*He kisses her lips lightly.*]

MIO: Why, girl, the transfiguration on the mount
was nothing to your face. It lights from within—
a white chalice holding fire, a flower in flame,
this is your face.

MIRIAMNE: And you shall drink the flame
and never lessen it. And round your head
the aureole shall burn that burns there now,
forever. This I can give you. And so forever
the Freudians are wrong.

MIO: They're well-forgotten
at any rate.

MIRIAMNE: Why did you speak to me
when you first saw me?

MIO: I knew then.

MIRIAMNE: And I came back
because I must see you again. And we danced together
and my heart hurt me. Never, never, never,
though they should bind me down and tear out my eyes,
would I ever hurt you now. Take me with you, Mio,
let them look for us, whoever there is to look,
but we'll be away.

MIO *turns away toward the tenement.*

MIO: When I was four years old
we climbed through an iron gate, my mother and I,
to see my father in prison. He stood in the death-cell
and put his hand through the bars and said, My Mio,
I have only this to leave you, that I love you,
and will love you after I die. Love me then, Mio,
when this hard thing comes on you, that you must live
a man despised for your father. That night the guards,
walking in flood-lights brighter than high noon,
led him between them with his trousers slit
and a shaven head for the cathodes. This sleet and rain
that I feel cold here on my face and hands
will find him under thirteen years of clay
in prison ground. Lie still and rest, my father,
for I have not forgotten. When I forget
may I lie blind as you. No other love,
time passing, nor the spaced lightyears of suns
shall blur your voice, or tempt me from the path
that clears your name—
till I have these rats in my grip
or sleep deep where you sleep.
[*To* MIRIAMNE.] I have no house,
nor home, nor love of life, nor fear of death,
nor care for what I eat, or who I sleep with,
or what color of calcimine the Government
will wash itself this year or next to lure
the sheep and feed the wolves. Love somewhere else,

and get your children in some other image
more acceptable to the State! This face of mine
is stamped for sewage!

She steps back, surmising.

MIRIAMNE: Mio——

MIO: My road is cut
in rock, and leads to one end. If I hurt you, I'm sorry.
One gets over hurts.

MIRIAMNE: What was his name—
your father's name?

MIO: Bartolomeo Romagna.
I'm not ashamed of it.

MIRIAMNE: Why are you here?

MIO: For the reason
I've never had a home, Because I'm a cry
out of a shallow grave, and all roads are mine
that might revenge him!

MIRIAMNE: But Mio—why here—why here?

MIO: I can't tell you that.

MIRIAMNE: No—but—there's someone
lives here—lives not far—and you mean to see him—
you mean to ask him—[*She pauses.*]

MIO: Who told you that?

MIRIAMNE: His name
is Garth—Garth Esdras——

MIO [*after a pause, coming nearer*]:
Who are you, then? You seem
to know a good deal about me.— Were you sent
to say this?

MIRIAMNE: You said there was death about you! Yes,
but nearer than you think! Let it be as it is—
let it all be as it is, never see this place
nor think of it—forget the streets you came
when you're away and safe! Go before you're seen
or spoken to!

MIO: Will you tell me why?

MIRIAMNE: As I love you
I can't tell you—and I can never see you——

MIO: I walk where I please——

MIRIAMNE: Do you think it's easy for me
to send you away? [*She steps back as if to go.*]

MIO: Where will I find you then
if I should want to see you?

MIRIAMNE: Never—I tell you
I'd bring you death! Even now. Listen!

SHADOW *and* TROCK *enter between the bridge and the tenement house.* MIRIAMNE *pulls* MIO *back into the shadow of the rock to avoid being seen.*

TROCK: Why, fine.

SHADOW: You watch it now—just for the record, Trock—
you're going to thank me for staying away from it
and keeping you out. I've seen men get that way,
thinking they had to plug a couple of guys
and then a few more to cover it up, and then
maybe a dozen more. You can't own all
and territory adjacent, and you can't
slough all the witnesses, because every man
you put away has friends——

TROCK: I said all right.
I said fine.

SHADOW: They're going to find this judge,
and if they find him dead it's just too bad,
and I don't want to know anything about it—
and you don't either.

TROCK: You all through?

SHADOW: Why sure.

TROCK: All right.
We're through, too, you know.

SHADOW: Yeah? [*He becomes wary.*]

TROCK: Yeah, we're through.

SHADOW: I've heard that said before, and afterwards
somebody died.
TROCK *is silent.*] Is that what you mean?

TROCK: You can go.
I don't want to see you.

SHADOW: Sure, I'll go.
Maybe you won't mind if I just find out
what you've got on you. Before I turn my back.
I'd like to know.
[*Silently and expertly he touches* TROCK'S *pockets, extracting a gun.*]
Not that I'd distrust you,
but you know how it is. [*He pockets the gun.*]
So long, Trock.

TROCK: So long.

SHADOW: I won't talk.
You can be sure of that.

TROCK: I know you won't.

SHADOW *turns and goes out right, past the rock and along the bank. As he goes the* TWO YOUNG MEN IN BLUE SERGE *enter from the left and walk slowly after* SHADOW. *They look toward* TROCK *as they enter and he motions with his thumb in the direction taken by* SHADOW. *They follow* SHADOW *out without haste.* TROCK *watches them disappear, then slips out the way he came.* MIO *comes a step forward, looking after the two men. Two or three shots are heard, then silence.* MIO *starts to run after* SHADOW.

MIRIAMNE: Mio!
MIO: What do you know about this?
MIRIAMNE: The other way,
Mio—quick!

CARR *slips in from the right, in haste.*

CARR: Look, somebody's just been shot.
He fell in the river. The guys that did the shooting
ran up the bank.
MIO: Come on.

MIO *and* CARR *run out right.* MIRIAMNE *watches uncertainly, then slowly turns and walks to the rear door of the tenement. She stands there a moment, looking after* MIO, *then goes in, closing the door.* CARR *and* MIO *return.*

CARR: There's a rip tide past the point. You'd never find him.
MIO: No.
CARR: You know a man really ought to carry insurance living around here.—God, it's easy, putting a fellow away. I never saw it done before.
MIO [*looking at the place where* MIRIAMNE *stood*]: They have it all worked out.
CARR: What are you doing now?
MIO: I have a little business to transact in this neighborhood.
CARR: You'd better forget it.
MIO: No.
CARR: Need any help?
MIO: Well, if I did I'd ask you first. But I don't see how it would do any good. So you keep out of it and take care of yourself.
CARR: So long, then.
MIO: So long, Carr.
CARR [*looking down-stream*]: He was drifting face up. Must be halfway to the island the way the tide runs. [*He shivers.*] God, it's cold here. Well——

He goes out to the left. MIO *sits on the edge of the rock.* LUCIA *comes stealthily back from between the bridge and the tenement, goes to the street-piano and wheels it away.* PINY *comes in. They take a look at* MIO, *but say nothing.* LUCIA *goes into his shelter and* PINY *into hers.* MIO *rises, looks up at the tenement, and goes out to the left.*

CURTAIN

ACT II

The basement as in Scene Two of Act I. The same evening. ESDRAS *sits at the table reading,* MIRIAMNE *is seated at the left, listening and intent. The door of the inner room is half open and* GARTH'S *violin is heard. He is playing the theme from the third movement of Beethoven's Archduke Trio.* ESDRAS *looks up.*

ESDRAS: I remember when I came to the end
of all the Talmud said, and the commentaries,
then I was fifty years old—and it was time
to ask what I had learned. I asked this question
and gave myself the answer. In all the Talmud
there was nothing to find but the names of things,
set down that we might call them by those names
and walk without fear among things known. Since then
I have had twenty years to read on and on
and end with Ecclesiastes. Names of names,
evanid days, evanid nights and days
and words that shift their meaning. Space is time,
that which was is now—the men of tomorrow
live, and this is their yesterday. All things
that were and are and will be, have their being
then and now and to come. If this means little
when you are young, remember it. It will return
to mean more when you are old.
MIRIAMNE: I'm sorry—I
was listening for something.
ESDRAS: It doesn't matter.
It's a useless wisdom. It's all I have,
but useless. It may be there is no time,
but we grow old. Do you know his name?
MIRIAMNE: Whose name?
ESDRAS: Why, when we're young and listen for a step
the step should have a name——

MIRIAMNE, *not hearing, rises and goes to the window.* GARTH *enters from within, carrying his violin and carefully closing the door.*

GARTH [*as* ESDRAS *looks at him*]: Asleep.
ESDRAS: He may
sleep on through the whole night—then in the morning
we can let them know.
GARTH: We'd be wiser to say nothing—
let him find his own way back.
ESDRAS: How did he come here?
GARTH: He's not too crazy for that. If he wakes again
we'll keep him quiet and shift him off tomorrow.
Somebody'd pick him up.
ESDRAS: How have I come

to this sunken end of a street, at a life's end——?

GARTH: It was cheaper here—not to be transcendental—
So—we say nothing——?

ESDRAS: Nothing.

MIRIAMNE: Garth, there's no place
in this whole city—not one—
where you would be safer
than here—tonight—or tomorrow.

GARTH [*bitterly*]: Well, that may be.
What of it?

MIRIAMNE: If you slipped away and took
a place somewhere where Trock couldn't find you——

GARTH: Yes—
using what for money? and why do you think
I've sat here so far—because I love my home
so much? No, but if I stepped round the corner
it'd be my last corner and my last step.

MIRIAMNE: And yet—
if you're here—they'll find you here—
Trock will come again—
and there's worse to follow——

GARTH: Do you want to get me killed?

MIRIAMNE: No.

GARTH: There's no way out of it. We'll wait
and take what they send us.

ESDRAS: Hush! You'll wake him.

GARTH: I've done it.
I hear him stirring now.

They wait quietly. JUDGE GAUNT *opens the door and enters.*

GAUNT [*in the doorway*]: I beg your pardon—
no, no, be seated—keep your place—I've made
your evening difficult enough, I fear;
and I must thank you doubly for your kindness,
for I've been ill—I know it.

ESDRAS: You're better, sir?

GAUNT: Quite recovered, thank you. Able, I hope,
to manage nicely now. You'll be rewarded
for your hospitality—though at this moment
[*He smiles.*] I'm low in funds.
[*He inspects his billfold.*] Sir, my embarrassment
is great indeed—and more than monetary,
for I must own my recollection's vague
of how I came here—how we came together—
and what we may have said. My name is Gaunt,
Judge Gaunt, a name long known in the criminal courts,
and not unhonored there.

ESDRAS: My name is Esdras—
and this is Garth, my son. And Miriamne,
the daughter of my old age.

GAUNT: I'm glad to meet you.
Esdras. Garth Esdras.
[*He passes a hand over his eyes.*] It's not a usual name.
Of late it's been connected with a case—
a case I knew. But this is hardly the man.
Though it's not a usual name.
[*They are silent.*] Sir, how I came here,
as I have said, I don't well know. Such things
are sometimes not quite accident.

ESDRAS: We found you
outside our door and brought you in.

GAUNT: The brain
can be overworked, and weary, even when the man
would swear to his good health. Sir, on my word
I don't know why I came here, nor how, nor when,
nor what would explain it. Shall we say the machine
begins to wear? I felt no twinge of it.—
You will imagine how much more than galling
I feel it, to ask my way home—and where I am—
but I do ask you that.

ESDRAS: This is New York City—
or part of it.

GAUNT: Not the best part, I presume?
[*He smiles grimly.*] No, not the best.

ESDRAS: Not typical, no.

GAUNT: And you—[*To* GARTH.]
you are Garth Esdras?

GARTH: That's my name.

GAUNT: Well, sir, [*To* ESDRAS.]
I shall lie under the deepest obligation
if you will set an old man on his path,
for I lack the homing instinct, if the truth
were known. North, east and south mean nothing to me
here in this room.

ESDRAS: I can put you in your way.

GARTH: Only you'd be wiser to wait a while—
if I'm any judge.——

GAUNT: It happens I'm the judge—
[*With stiff humor.*]
in more ways than one. You'll forgive me if I say
I find this place and my predicament
somewhat distasteful.
[*He looks round him.*]

GARTH: I don't doubt you do;
but you're better off here.

GAUNT: Nor will you find it wise

to cross my word as lightly as you seem
inclined to do. You've seen me ill and shaken—
and you presume on that.

GARTH: Have it your way.

GAUNT: Doubtless what information is required
we'll find nearby.

ESDRAS: Yes, sir—the terminal,—
if you could walk so far.

GAUNT: I've done some walking—
to look at my shoes.
[*He looks down, then puts out a hand to steady himself.*] That—that was why I came—
never mind—it was there—and it's gone.
[*To* GARTH.] Professor Hobhouse—
that's the name—he wrote some trash about you
and printed it in a broadside.
—Since I'm here I can tell you
it's a pure fabrication—lacking facts
and legal import. Senseless and impudent,
written with bias—with malicious intent
to undermine the public confidence
in justice and the courts. I knew it then—
all he brings out about this testimony
you might have given. It's true I could have called you,
but the case was clear—Romagna was known guilty,
and there was nothing to add. If I've endured
some hours of torture over their attacks
upon my probity—and in this torture
have wandered from my place, wandered perhaps
in mind and body—and found my way to face you—
why, yes, it is so—I know it—I beg of you
say nothing. It's not easy to give up
a fair name after a full half century
of service to a state. It may well rock
the surest reason. Therefore I ask of you
say nothing of this visit.

GARTH: I'll say nothing.

ESDRAS: Nor any of us.

GAUNT: Why, no—for you'd lose, too.
You'd have nothing to gain.

ESDRAS: Indeed we know it.

GAUNT: I'll remember you kindly. When I've returned,
there may be some mystery made of where I was—
we'll leave it a mystery?

GARTH: Anything you say.

GAUNT: Why, now I go with much more peace
of mind—if I can call you friends.

ESDRAS: We shall be grateful
for silence on your part, Your Honor.

GAUNT: Sir—
if there were any just end to be served
by speaking out, I'd speak! There is none. No—
bear that in mind!

ESDRAS: We will, Your Honor.

GAUNT: Then—
I'm in some haste. If you can be my guide,
we'll set out now.

ESDRAS: Yes, surely.

There is a knock at the door. The four look at each other with some apprehension. MIRIAMNE *rises.*

I'll answer it.

MIRIAMNE: Yes.

She goes into the inner room and closes the door. ESDRAS *goes to the outer door. The knock is repeated. He opens the door.* MIO *is there.*

ESDRAS: Yes, sir.

MIO: May I come in?

ESDRAS: Will you state your business, sir?
It's late—and I'm not at liberty——

MIO: Why, I might say
that I was trying to earn my tuition fees
by peddling magazines. I could say that,
or collecting old newspapers—paying cash—
highest rates—no questions asked—
[*He looks round sharply.*]

GARTH: We've nothing to sell.
What do you want?

MIO: Your pardon, gentlemen.
My business is not of an ordinary kind,
and I felt the need of this slight introduction
while I might get my bearings. Your name is Esdras,
or they told me so outside.

GARTH: What do you want?

MIO: Is that the name?

GARTH: Yes.

MIO: I'll be quick and brief.
I'm the son of a man who died many years ago
for a pay roll robbery in New England. You
should be Garth Esdras, by what I've heard. You have
some knowledge of the crime, if one can believe
what he reads in the public prints, and it might be
that your testimony, if given, would clear my father
of any share in the murder. You may not care
whether he was guilty or not. You may not know.

But I do care—and care deeply, and I've come
to ask you face to face.

GARTH: To ask me what?

MIO: What do you know of it?

ESDRAS: This man Romagna,
did he have a son?

MIO: Yes, sir, this man Romagna,
as you choose to call him, had a son, and I
am that son, and proud.

ESDRAS: Forgive me.

MIO: Had you known him,
and heard him speak, you'd know why I'm proud, and why
he was no malefactor.

ESDRAS: I quite believe you.
If my son can help he will. But at this moment,
as I told you—could you, I wonder, come tomorrow,
at your own hour?

MIO: Yes.

ESDRAS: By coincidence
we too of late have had this thing in mind—
there have been comments printed, and much discussion
which we could hardly avoid.

MIO: Could you tell me then
in a word?—What you know—
is it for him or against him?—
that's all I need.

ESDRAS: My son knows nothing.

GARTH: No.
The picture-papers lash themselves to a fury
over any rumor—make them up when they're short
of bedroom slops.—This is what happened. I
had known a few members of a gang one time
up there—and after the murder they picked me up
because I looked like someone that was seen
in what they called the murder car. They held me
a little while, but they couldn't identify me
for the most excellent reason I wasn't there
when the thing occurred. A dozen years later now
a professor comes across this, and sees red
and asks why I wasn't called on as a witness
and yips so loud they syndicate his picture
in all the rotos. That's all I know about it.
I wish I could tell you more.

ESDRAS: Let me say too
that I have read some words your father said,
and you were a son fortunate in your father,
whatever the verdict of the world.

MIO: There are few
who think so, but it's true, and I thank you. Then—
that's the whole story?

GARTH: All I know of it.

MIO: They cover their tracks well, the inner ring
that distributes murder. I came three thousand miles
to this dead end.

ESDRAS: If he was innocent
and you know him so, believe it, and let the others
believe as they like.

MIO: Will you tell me how a man's
to live, and face his life, if he can't believe
that truth's like a fire,
and will burn through and be seen
though it takes all the years there are?
While I stand up and have breath in my lungs
I shall be one flame of that fire;
it's all the life I have.

ESDRAS: Then you must live so.
One must live as he can.

MIO: It's the only way
of life my father left me.

ESDRAS: Yes? Yet it's true
the ground we walk on is impacted down
and hard with blood and bones of those who died
unjustly. There's not one title to land or life,
even your own, but was built on rape and murder,
back a few years. It would take a fire indeed
to burn out all this terror.

MIO: Then let it burn down,
all of it!

ESDRAS: We ask a great deal of the world
at first—then less—and then less.
We ask for truth
and justice. But this truth's a thing unknown
in the lightest, smallest matter—and as for justice,
who has once seen it done? You loved your father,
and I could have loved him, for every word he spoke
in his trial was sweet and tolerant, but the weight
of what men are and have, rests heavy on
the graves of those who lost. They'll not rise again,
and their causes lie there with them.

GAUNT: If you mean to say
that Bartolomeo Romagna was innocent,
you are wrong. He was guilty.
There may have been injustice

from time to time, by regrettable chance, in our courts,
but not in that case, I assure you.

MIO: Oh, you assure me!
You lie in your scrag teeth, whoever you are!
My father was murdered!

GAUNT: Romagna was found guilty
by all due process of law, and given his chance
to prove his innocence.

MIO: What chance? When a court
panders to mob hysterics, and the jury
comes in loaded to soak an anarchist
and a foreigner, it may be due process of law
but it's also murder!

GAUNT: He should have thought of that
before he spilled blood.

MIO: He?

GAUNT: Sir, I know too well
that he was guilty.

MIO: Who are you? How do you know?
I've searched the records through, the trial and what
came after, and in all that million words
I found not one unbiased argument
to fix the crime on him.

GAUNT: And you yourself,
were you unprejudiced?

MIO: Who are you?

ESDRAS: Sir,
this gentleman is here, as you are here,
to ask my son, as you have asked, what ground
there might be for this talk of new evidence
in your father's case. We gave him the same answer
we've given you.

MIO: I'm sorry. I'd supposed
his cause forgotten except by myself. There's still
a defense committee then?

GAUNT: There may be. I
am not connected with it.

ESDRAS: He is my guest,
and asks to remain unknown.

MIO [*after a pause, looking at* GAUNT]:
The judge at the trial
was younger, but he had your face. Can it be
that you're the man?—Yes—Yes.—The jury charge—
I sat there as a child and heard your voice,
and watched that Brahminical mouth. I knew even then
you meant no good to him. And now you're here
to winnow out truth and justice—the fountain-head
of the lies that slew him! Are you Judge Gaunt?

GAUNT: I am.

MIO: Then tell me what damnation to what inferno
would fit the toad that sat in robes and lied
when he gave the charge, and knew he lied! Judge that,
and then go to your place in that hell!

GAUNT: I know and have known
what bitterness can rise against a court
when it must say, putting aside all weakness,
that a man's to die. I can forgive you that,
for you are your father's son, and you think of him
as a son thinks of his father. Certain laws
seem cruel in their operation; it's necessary
that we be cruel to uphold them. This cruelty
is kindness to those I serve.

MIO: I don't doubt that.
I know who it is you serve.

GAUNT: Would I have chosen
to rack myself with other men's despairs,
stop my ears, harden my heart, and listen only
to the voice of law and light, if I had hoped
some private gain for serving? In all my ears
on the bench of a long-established commonwealth
not once has my decision been in question
save in this case. Not once before or since.
For hope of heaven or place on earth, or power
or gold, no man has had my voice, nor will
while I still keep the trust that's laid on me
to sentence and define.

MIO: Then why are you here?

GAUNT: My record's clean. I've kept it so. But suppose
with the best intent, among the myriad tongues
that come to testify, I had missed my way
and followed a perjured tale to a lethal end
till a man was forsworn to death? Could I rest or sleep
while there was doubt of this,
even while there was question in a layman's mind?
For always, night and day,
there lies on my brain like a weight, the admonition:
see truly, let nothing sway you; among all functions
there's but one godlike, to judge. Then see to it
you judge as a god would judge, with clarity,
with truth, with what mercy is found consonant

with order and law. Without law men are beasts,
and it's a judge's task to lift and hold them
above themselves. Let a judge be once mistaken
or step aside for a friend, and a gap is made
in the dykes that hold back anarchy and chaos,
and leave men bond but free.

MIO: Then the gap's been made,
and you made it.

GAUNT: I feared that too. May you be a judge
sometime, and know in what fear,
through what nights long
in fear, I scanned and verified and compared
the transcripts of the trial.

MIO: Without prejudice,
no doubt. It was never in your mind to prove
that you'd been right.

GAUNT: And conscious of that, too—
that that might be my purpose—watchful of that,
and jealous as his own lawyer of the rights
that should hedge the defendant!
And still I found no error,
shook not one staple of the bolts that linked
the doer to the deed! Still following on from
step to step, I watched all modern comment,
and saw it centered finally on one fact—
Garth Esdras was not called. This is Garth Esdras,
and you have heard him. Would his deposition
have justified a new trial?

MIO: No. It would not.

GAUNT: And there I come, myself. If the man were still
in his cell, and waiting, I'd have no faint excuse
for another hearing.

MIO: I've told you that I read
the trial from beginning to end. Every word you spoke
was balanced carefully to keep the letter
of the law and still convict—convict, by Christ,
if it tore the seven veils! You stand here now
running cascades of casuistry, to prove
to yourself and me that no judge of rank and breeding
could burn a man out of hate! But that's what you did
under all your varnish!

GAUNT: I've sought for evidence,
and you have sought. Have you found it? Can you cite
one fresh word in defence?

MIO: The trial itself
was shot full of legerdemain, prearranged to lead
the jury astray——

GAUNT: Could you prove that?

MIO: Yes!

GAUNT: And if
the jury were led astray, remember it's
the jury, by our Anglo-Saxon custom,
that finds for guilt or innocence. The judge
is powerless in that matter.

MIO: Not you! Your charge
misled the jury more than the evidence,
accepted every biased meaning, distilled
the poison for them!

GAUNT: But if that were so
I'd be the first, I swear it, to step down
among all men, and hold out both my hands
for manacles—yes, publish it in the streets,
that all I've held most sacred was defiled
by my own act. A judge's brain becomes
a delicate instrument to weigh men's lives
for good and ill—too delicate to bear
much tampering. If he should push aside
the weights and throw the beam, and say, this once
the man is guilty, and I will have it so
though his mouth cry out from the ground,
and all the world
revoke my word, he'd have a short way to go
to madness. I think you'd find him in the squares,
stopping the passers-by with arguments,—
see, I was right, the man was guilty there—
this was brought in against him, this—and this—
and I was left no choice! It's no light thing
when a long life's been dedicate to one end
to wrench the mind awry!

MIO: By your own thesis
you should be mad, and no doubt you are.

GAUNT: But my madness
is only this—that I would fain look back
on a life well spent—without one stain—one breath
of stain to flaw the glass—not in men's minds
nor in my own. I take my God as witness
I meant to earn that clearness, and believe
that I have earned it. Yet my name is clouded
with the blackest, fiercest scandal of our age
that's touched a judge. What I can do to wipe
that smutch from my fame I will. I think you know
how deeply I've been hated, for no cause
that I can find there. Can it not be—and I ask this

quite honestly—that the great injustice lies
on your side and not mine? Time and time again
men have come before me perfect in their lives,
loved by all who knew them, loved at home,
gentle, not vicious, yet caught so ripe red-handed
in some dark violence there was no denying
where the onus lay.

MIO: That was not so with my father!

GAUNT: And yet it seemed so to me. To other men
who sat in judgment on him. Can you be sure—
I ask this in humility—that you,
who were touched closest by the tragedy,
may not have lost perspective—may have brooded
day and night on one theme—till your eyes are tranced
and show you one side only?

MIO: I see well enough.

GAUNT: And would that not be part of the malady—
to look quite steadily at the drift of things
but see there what you wish—not what is there—
not what another man to whom the story
was fresh would say is there?

MIO: You think I'm crazy.
Is that what you meant to say?

GAUNT: I've seen it happen
with the best and wisest men. I but ask the question.
I can't speak for you. Is is not true wherever
you walk, through the little town where you knew him well,
or flying from it, inland or by the sea,
still walking at your side, and sleeping only
when you too sleep, a shadow not your own
follows, pleading and holding out its hands
to be delivered from shame?

MIO: How you know that
by God I don't know.

GAUNT: Because one spectre haunted you and me—
and haunts you still, but for me it's laid to rest
now that my mind is satisfied. He died
justly and not by error. [*A pause.*]

MIO [*stepping forward*]: Do you care to know
you've come so near to death it's miracle
that pulse still beats in your splotchy throat?
Do you know
there's murder in me?

GAUNT: There was murder in your sire,
and it's to be expected! I say he died
justly, and he deserved it!

MIO: Yes, you'd like too well
to have me kill you! That would prove your case
and clear your name, and dip my father's name
in stench forever! You'll not get that from me!
Go home and die in bed, get it under cover,
your lux-et-lex putrefaction of the right thing,
you man that walks like a god!

GAUNT: Have I made you angry
by coming too near the truth?

MIO: This sets him up,
this venomous slug, this sets him up in a gown,
deciding who's to walk above the earth
and who's to lie beneath! And giving reasons!
The cobra giving reasons; I'm a god,
by Buddha, holy and worshipful my fang,
and can I sink it in!
[*He pauses, turns as if to go, then sits.*] This is no good. This won't help much.

The JUDGE *and* ESDRAS *look at each other.*

GAUNT: We should be going.

ESDRAS: Yes [*They prepare to go.*] I'll lend you my coat.

GAUNT [*looking at it with distaste*].
No, keep it. A little rain
shouldn't matter to me.

ESDRAS: It freezes as it falls,
and you've a long way to go.

GAUNT: I'll manage, thank you.

GAUNT *and* ESDRAS *go out,* ESDRAS *obsequious, closing the door.*

GARTH [*looking at* MIO'S *back*]: Well?

MIO [*not moving*]: Let me sit here a moment.

GARTH *shrugs his shoulders and goes toward the inner door.* MIRIAMNE *opens it and comes out.* GARTH *looks at her, then at* MIO, *then lays his fingers on his lips. She nods.* GARTH *goes out.* MIRIAMNE *sits and watches* MIO. *After a little he turns and sees her.*

MIO: How did you come here?

MIRIAMNE: I live here.

MIO: Here?

MIRIAMNE: My name is Esdras. Garth
is my brother. The walls are thin.
I heard what was said.

MIO [*stirring wearily*]: I'm going. This is no place for me.

MIRIAMNE: What place would be better?

MIO: None. Only it's better to go.
Just to go.

She comes over to him, puts her arm around him and kisses his forehead.

MIRIAMNE: Mio.
MIO: What do you want?
Your kisses burn me—and your arms. Don't offer
what I'm never to have! I can have nothing. They say
they'll cross the void sometime to the other planets
and men will breathe in that air.
Well, I could breathe there,
but not here now. Not on this ball of mud.
I don't want it.
MIRIAMNE: They can take away so little
with all their words. For you're a king among them.
I heard you, and loved your voice.
MIO: I thought I'd fallen
so low there was no further, and now a pit
opens beneath. It was bad enough that he
should have died innocent, but if he were guilty—
then what's my life—what have I left to do—?
The son of a felon—and what they spat on me
was earned—and I'm drenched with the stuff.
Here on my hands
and cheeks, their spittle hanging! I liked my hands
because they were like his. I tell you I've lived
by his innocence, lived to see it flash
and blind them all—
MIRIAMNE: Never believe them, Mio,
never. [*She looks toward the inner door.*]
MIO: But it was truth I wanted, truth—
not the lies you'd tell yourself, or tell a woman,
or a woman tells you! The judge with his cobra mouth
may have spat truth—and I may be mad! For me—
your hands are too clean to touch me. I'm to have
the scraps from hotel kitchens—and instead of love
those mottled bodies that hitch themselves through alleys
to sell for dimes or nickels. Go, keep yourself chaste
for the baker bridegroom—baker and son of a baker,
let him get his baker's dozen on you!
MIRIAMNE: No—
say once you love me—say it once; I'll never
ask to hear it twice, nor for any kindness,
and you shall take all I have!

GARTH *opens the inner door and comes out.*

GARTH: I interrupt
a love scene, I believe. We can do without
your adolescent mawkishness.
[*To* MIRIAMNE.] You're a child.
You'll both remember that.
MIRIAMNE: I've said nothing to harm you—
and will say nothing.
GARTH: You're my sister, though,
and I take a certain interest in you. Where
have you two met?
MIRIAMNE: We danced together.
GARTH: Then
the dance is over, I think.
MIRIAMNE: I've always loved you
and tried to help you, Garth. And you've been kind.
Don't spoil it now.
GARTH: Spoil it how?
MIRIAMNE: Because I love him.
I didn't know it would happen. We danced together.
And the world's all changed. I see you through a mist,
and our father, too. If you brought this to nothing
I'd want to die.
GARTH [*to* MIO]: You'd better go.
MIO: Yes, I know.

He rises. There is a trembling knock at the door. MIRIAMNE *goes to it. The* HOBO *is there shivering.*

HOBO: Miss, could I sleep under the pipes tonight, miss?
Could I, please?
MIRIAMNE: I think—not tonight.
HOBO: There won't be any more nights—
if I don't get warm, miss.
MIRIAMNE: Come in.

The HOBO *comes in, looks round deprecatingly, then goes to a corner beneath a huge heating pipe, which he crawls under as if he'd been there before.*

HOBO: Yes, miss, thank you.
GARTH: Must we put up with that?
MIRIAMNE: Father let him sleep there—
last winter.
GARTH: Yes, God, yes.
MIO: Well, good night.
MIRIAMNE: Where will you go?
MIO: Yes, where? As if it mattered.

GARTH: Oh, sleep here, too.
We'll have a row of you under the pipes.
MIO: No, thanks.
MIRIAMNE: Mio, I've saved a little money. It's only
some pennies, but you must take it.
[*She shakes some coins out of a box into her hand.*]
MIO: No, thanks.
MIRIAMNE: And I love you.
You've never said you love me.
MIO: Why wouldn't I love you
when you're clean and sweet,
and I've seen nothing sweet or clean
this last ten years? I love you. I leave you that
for what good it may do you. It's none to me.
MIRIAMNE: Then kiss me.
MIO [*looking at* GARTH]:
With that scowling over us? No.
When it rains, some spring
on the planet Mercury, where the spring comes often,
I'll meet you there, let's say. We'll wait for that.
It may be some time till then.

The outside door opens and ESDRAS *enters with* JUDGE GAUNT, *then, after a slight interval,* TROCK *follows.* TROCK *surveys the interior and its occupants one by one, carefully.*

TROCK: I wouldn't want to cause you inconvenience,
any of you, and especially the Judge.
I think you know that. You've all got things to do—
trains to catch, and so on. But trains can wait.
Hell, nearly anything can wait, you'll find,
only I can't. I'm the only one that can't
because I've got no time. Who's all this here?
Who's that? [*He points to the* HOBO.]
ESDRAS: He's a poor half-wit, sir,
that sometimes sleeps there.
TROCK: Come out. I say come out,
whoever you are.
[*The* HOBO *stirs and looks up.*]
Yes, I mean you. Come out.
[*The* HOBO *emerges.*]
What's your name?
HOBO: They mostly call me Oke.
TROCK: What do you know?
HOBO: No, sir.
TROCK: Where are you from?
HOBO: I got a piece of bread.
[*He brings it out, trembling.*]
TROCK: Get back in there!
[*The* HOBO *crawls back into his corner.*]
Maybe you want to know why I'm doing this.
Well, I've been robbed, that's why—
robbed five or six times;
the police can't find a thing—so I'm out for myself—
if you want to know.
[*To* MIO.] Who are you?
MIO: Oh, I'm a half-wit,
came in here by mistake. The difference is
I've got no piece of bread.
TROCK: What's your name?
MIO: My name?
Theophrastus Such. That's respectable.
You'll find it all the way from here to the coast
on the best police blotters.
Only the truth is we're a little touched in the head,
Oke and me. You'd better ask somebody else.
TROCK: Who is he?
ESDRAS: His name's Romagna. He's the son.
TROCK: Then what's he doing here? You said you were on the level.
GARTH: He just walked in. On account of the stuff in the papers. We didn't ask him.
TROCK: God, we are a gathering. Now if we had Shadow we'd be all here, huh? Only I guess we won't see Shadow. No, that's too much to ask.
MIO: Who's Shadow?
TROCK: Now you're putting questions. Shadow was just nobody, you see. He blew away. It might happen to anyone. [*He looks at* GARTH.] Yes, anyone at all.
MIO: Why do you keep your hand in your pocket, friend?
TROCK: Because I'm cold, punk. Because I've been outside and it's cold as the tomb of Christ. [*To* GARTH.] Listen, there's a car waiting up at the street to take the Judge home. We'll take him to the car.
GARTH: That's not necessary.
ESDRAS: No.
TROCK: I say it is, see? You wouldn't want to let the Judge walk, would you? The Judge is going to ride where he's going, with a couple of chauffeurs, and everything done in style. Don't you worry about the Judge. He'll be taken care of. For good.
GARTH: I want no hand in it.
TROCK: Anything happens to me happens to you too, musician.
GARTH: I know that.
TROCK: Keep your mouth out of it then. And you'd better keep the punk here tonight, just for luck. [*He turns toward the door. There is a*

brilliant lightning flash through the windows, followed slowly by dying thunder. TROCK *opens the door. The rain begins to pour in sheets.*] Jesus, somebody tipped it over again! [*A cough racks him.*] Wait till it's over. It takes ten days off me every time I step into it. [*He closes the door.*] Sit down and wait.

Lightning flashes again. The thunder is fainter. ESDRAS, GARTH *and the* JUDGE *sit down.*

GAUNT: We were born too early. Even you who are young
are not of the elect. In a hundred years
man will put his finger on life itself, and then
he will live as long as he likes. For you and me
we shall die soon—one day, one year more or less,
when or where, it's no matter. It's what we call
an indeterminate sentence. I'm hungry.

GARTH *looks at* MIRIAMNE.

MIRIAMNE: There was nothing left tonight.

HOBO: I've got a piece of bread.

He breaks his bread in two and hands half to the JUDGE.

GAUNT: I thank you, sir. [*He eats.*]
This is not good bread. [*He rises.*] Sir, I am used
to other company. Not better, perhaps, but their clothes
were different. These are what it's the fashion to call
the underprivileged.

TROCK: Oh, hell!
[*He turns toward the door.*]

MIO [*to* TROCK]: It would seem that you and the Judge know each other.

TROCK *faces him.*

TROCK: I've been around.

MIO: Maybe you've met before.

TROCK: Maybe we have.

MIO: Will you tell me where?

TROCK: How long do you want to live?

MIO: How long? Oh, I've got big ideas about that.

TROCK: I thought so. Well, so far I've got nothing against you but your name, see? You keep it that way.

He opens the door. The rain still falls in torrents. He closes the door. As he turns from it, it opens again, and SHADOW, white, bloodstained and dripping, stands in the doorway. GARTH *rises.* TROCK *turns.*

GAUNT [*to the* HOBO]: Yet if one were careful of his health, ate sparingly, drank not at all, used himself wisely, it might be that even an old man could live to touch immortality. They may come on the secret sooner than we dare hope. You see? It does no harm to try.

TROCK [*backing away from* SHADOW]: By God, he's out of his grave!

SHADOW [*leaning against the doorway, holding a gun in his hands*]: Keep your hands where they belong, Trock.
You know me.

TROCK: Don't! Don't! I had nothing to do with it!
[*He backs to the opposite wall.*]

SHADOW: You said the doctor gave you six months to live—well, I don't give you that much. That's what you had, six months, and so you start bumping off your friends to make sure of your damn six months. I got it from you.
I know where I got it.
Because I wouldn't give it to the Judge.
So he wouldn't talk.

TROCK: Honest to God—

SHADOW: What God?
The one that let you put three holes in me
when I was your friend? Well, He let me get up again
and walk till I could find you. That's as far as I get,
but I got there, by God! And I can hear you
even if I can't see!
[*He takes a staggering step forward.*] A man needs blood
to keep going.—I got this far.—And now I can't see!
It runs out too fast—too fast—
when you've got three slugs
clean through you.
Show me where he is, you fools! He's here!
I got here! [*He drops the gun.*] Help me! Help me! Oh, God! Oh, God!
I'm going to die! Where does a man lie down?
I want to lie down!

MIRIAMNE *starts toward* SHADOW. GARTH *and* ESDRAS *help him into the next room,* MIRIAMNE *following.* TROCK *squats in his corner, breathing hard, looking at the door.* MIO *stands, watching* TROCK. GARTH *returns, wiping his hand with a handkerchief.* MIO *picks up and pockets the gun.* MIRIAMNE *comes back and leans against the door jamb.*

GAUNT: You will hear it said that an old man makes a good judge, being calm, clear-eyed, without passion. But this is not true. Only the young love truth and justice. The old are savage, wary, violent, swayed by maniac desires, cynical of friendship or love, open to bribery and the temptations of lust, corrupt and dastardly to the heart. I know these old men. What have they left to believe, what have they left to lose? Whorers of daughters, lickers of girls' shoes, contrivers of nastiness in the night, purveyors of perversion, worshippers of possession! Death is the only radical. He comes late, but he comes at last to put away the old men and give the young their places. It was time. [*He leers.*]

Here's one I heard yesterday:

Marmaduke behind the barn
got his sister in a fix;
he says damn instead of darn;
ain't he cute? He's only six!

THE HOBO: He, he, he!

GAUNT:

And the hoot-owl hoots all night,
and the cuckoo cooks all day,
and what with a minimum grace of
God
we pass the time away.

THE HOBO: He, he, he—I got ya!

[*He makes a sign with his thumb.*]

GAUNT [*sings*]:

And he led her all around
and laid her on the ground
and he ruffled up the feathers of
her cuckoo's nest!

HOBO: Ho, ho, ho!

GAUNT: I am not taken with the way you laugh. You should cultivate restraint.

ESDRAS *reënters.*

TROCK: Shut the door.

ESDRAS: He won't come back again.

TROCK: I want the door shut! He was dead, I tell you! [ESDRAS *closes the door.*] And Romagna was dead, too, once! Can't they keep a man under ground?

MIO: No. No more! They don't stay under ground any more, and they don't stay under water! Why did you have him killed?

TROCK: Stay away from me! I know you!

MIO: Who am I, then?

TROCK: I know you, damn you! Your name's Romagna!

MIO: Yes! And Romagna was dead, too, and Shadow was dead, but the time's come when you can't keep them down, these dead men! They won't stay down! They come in with their heads shot off and their entrails dragging! Hundreds of them! One by one—all you ever killed! Watch the door! See!—It moves!

TROCK [*looking, fascinated, at the door*]: Let me out of here! [*He tries to rise.*]

MIO [*the gun in his hand*]: Oh, no! You'll sit there and wait for them! One by one they'll come through that door, pulling their heads out of the gunny-sacks where you tied them—glauming over you with their rotten hands! They'll see without eyes and crawl over you—Shadow and the paymaster and all the rest of them—putrescent bones without eyes! Now! Look! Look! For I'm first among them!

TROCK: I've done for better men than you! And I'll do for you!

GAUNT [*rapping on the table*]: Order, gentlemen, order! The witness will remember that a certain decorum is essential in the court-room!

MIO: By God, he'll answer me!

GAUNT [*thundering*]: Silence! Silence! Let me remind you of courtesy toward the witness! What case is this you try?

MIO: The case of the state against Bartolomeo Romagna for the murder of the paymaster!

GAUNT: Sir, that was disposed of long ago!

MIO: Never disposed of, never, not while I live!

GAUNT: Then we'll have done with it now! I deny the appeal! I have denied the appeal before and I do so again!

HOBO: He, he!—He think's he's in the moving pictures! [*A flash of lightening.*]

GAUNT: Who set that flash! Bailiff, clear the court! This is not Flemington, gentlemen! We are not conducting this case to make a journalistic holiday! [*The thunder rumbles faintly.* GARTH *opens the outside door and faces a solid wall of rain.*] Stop that man! He's one of the defendants!

GARTH *closes the door.*

MIO: Then put him on the stand!

GARTH: What do you think you're doing?

MIO: Have you any objection?

GAUNT: The objection is not sustained. We will hear the new evidence. Call your witness.

MIO: Garth Esdras!

GAUNT: He will take the stand!

GARTH: If you want me to say what I said before I'll say it!

MIO: Call Trock Estrella then!

GAUNT: Trock Estrella to the stand!

TROCK: No, by God!

MIO: Call Shadow, then! He'll talk! You thought he was dead, but he'll get up again and talk!

TROCK [*screaming*]: What do you want of me?

MIO: You killed the paymaster! You!
TROCK: You lie! It was Shadow killed him!
MIO: And now I know! Now I know!
GAUNT: Again I remind you of courtesy toward the witness!
MIO: I know them now!
Let me remind you of courtesy toward the dead!
He says that Shadow killed him! If Shadow were here
he'd say it was Trock! There were three men involved
in the new version of the crime for which
my father died! Shadow and Trock Estrella
as principals in the murder—Garth as witness!—
Why are they here together?—and you—the Judge—
why are you here? Why, because you were all afraid
and you drew together out of that fear to arrange
a story you could tell! And Trock killed Shadow
and meant to kill the Judge out of that same fear—
to keep them quiet! This is the thing I've hunted
over the earth to find out, and I'd be blind
indeed if I missed it now!
[*To* GAUNT.] You heard what he said:
It was Shadow killed him! Now let the night conspire
with the sperm of hell! It's plain beyond denial
even to this fox of justice—and all his words
are curses on the wind! You lied! You lied!
You knew this too!
GAUNT [*low*]: Let me go. Let me go!
MIO: Then why
did you let my father die?
GAUNT: Suppose it known,
but there are things a judge must not believe
though they should head and fester underneath
and press in on his brain. Justice once rendered
in a clear burst of anger, righteously,
upon a very common laborer,
confessed an anarchist, the verdict found
and the precise machinery of law
invoked to know him guilty—think what furor
would rock the state if the court then flatly said:
all this was lies—must be reversed? It's better,
as any judge can tell you, in such cases,
holding the common good to be worth more
than small injustice, to let the record stand,
let one man die. For justice, in the main,
is governed by opinion. Communities
will have what they will have, and it's quite as well,
after all, to be rid of anarchists. Our rights
as citizens can be maintained as rights
only while we are held to be the peers
of those who live about us. A vendor of fish
is not protected as a man might be
who kept a market. I own I've sometimes wished
this was not so, but it is. The man you defend
was unfortunate—and his misfortune bore
almost as heavily on me.—I'm broken—
broken across. You're much too young to know
how bitter it is when a worn connection chars
and you can't remember—can't remember.
[*He steps forward.*] You
will not repeat this? It will go no further?
MIO: No.
No further than the moon takes the tides—no further
than the news went when he died—
when you found him guilty
and they flashed that round the earth. Wherever men
still breathe and think, and know what's done to them
by the powers above, they'll know. That's all I ask.
That'll be enough.

TROCK *has risen and looks darkly at* MIO.

GAUNT: Thank you. For I've said some things
a judge should never say.
TROCK: Go right on talking.
Both of you. It won't get far, I guess.
MIO: Oh, you'll see to that?
TROCK: I'll see to it. Me and some others.
Maybe I lost my grip there just for a minute.
That's all right.
MIO: Then see to it! Let it rain!
What can you do to me now when the night's on fire
with this thing I know? Now I could almost wish
there was a god somewhere—I could almost think
there was a god—and he somehow brought me here
and set you down before me here in the rain
where I could wring this out of you! For it's said,

and I've heard it, and I'm free! He was as I thought him,
true and noble and upright, even when he went
to a death contrived because he was as he was
and not your kind! Let it rain! Let the night speak fire
and the city go out with the tide, for he was a man
and I know you now, and I have my day!

There is a heavy knock at the outside door. MIRIAMNE *opens it, at a glance from* GARTH. *The* POLICEMAN *is there in oilskins.*

POLICEMAN: Evening. [*He steps in, followed by a* SERGEANT, *similarly dressed.*]
We're looking for someone
might be here. Seen an old man around
acting a little off?
[*To* ESDRAS.] You know the one
I mean. You saw him out there. Jeez! You've got
a funny crowd here!
[*He looks round. The* HOBO *shrinks into his corner.*] That's the one I saw.
What do you think?
SERGEANT: That's him. You mean to say
you didn't know him by his pictures?
[*He goes to* GAUNT.] Come on, old man.
You're going home.
GAUNT: Yes, sir. I've lost my way.
I think I've lost my way.
SERGEANT: I'll say you have.
About three hundred miles. Now don't you worry.
We'll get you back.
GAUNT: I'm a person of some rank
in my own city.
SERGEANT: We know that. One look at you
and we'd know that.
GAUNT: Yes, sir.
POLICEMAN: If it isn't Trock!
Trock Estrella. How are you, Trock?
TROCK: Pretty good,
Thanks.
POLICEMAN: Got out yesterday again, I hear?
TROCK: That's right.
SERGEANT: Hi'ye, Trock?
TROCK: O. K.
SERGEANT: You know we got orders
to watch you pretty close. Be good now, baby,
or back you go. Don't try to pull anything,
not in my district.
TROCK: No, sir.
SERGEANT: No bumping off.
If you want my advice quit carrying a gun.
Try earning your living for once.
TROCK: Yeah.
SERGEANT: That's an idea.
Because if we find any stiffs on the river bank
we'll know who to look for.
MIO: Then look in the other room!
I accuse that man of murder! Trock Estrella!
He's a murderer!
POLICEMAN: Hello. I remember you.
SERGEANT: Well, what murder?
MIO: It was Trock Estrella
that robbed the pay roll thirteen years ago
and did the killing my father died for! You know
the Romagna case! Romagna was innocent,
and Trock Estrella guilty!
SERGEANT [*disgusted*]: Oh, what the hell!
That's old stuff—the Romagna case.
POLICEMAN: Hey, Sarge!
[*The* SERGEANT *and* POLICEMAN *come closer together.*]
The boy's a professional kidder. He took me over
about half an hour ago. He kids the police
and then ducks out!
SERGEANT: Oh, yeah?
MIO: I'm not kidding now.
You'll find a dead man there in the next room
and Estrella killed him!
SERGEANT: Thirteen years ago?
And nobody smelled him yet?
MIO [*pointing*]: I accuse this man
of two murders! He killed the paymaster long ago
and had Shadow killed tonight. Look, look for yourself!
He's there all right!
POLICEMAN: Look boy. You stood out there
and put the booby sign on the dumb police
because they're fresh out of Ireland. Don't try it twice.
SERGEANT [*to* GARTH]: Any corpses here?
GARTH: Not that I know of.
SERGEANT: I thought so.
[MIO *looks at* MIRIAMNE.]
[*To* MIO.] Think up a better one.
MIO: Have I got to drag him
out here where you can see him?
[*He goes toward the inner door.*] Can't you scent a murder
when it's under your nose? Look in!
MIRIAMNE: No, no—there's no one—there's no one there!
SERGEANT [*looking at* MIRIAMNE]: Take a look inside.

POLICEMAN: Yes sir.
[*He goes into the inside room. The* SERGEANT *goes up to the door. The* POLICEMAN *returns.*]
He's kidding, Sarge. If there's a cadaver
in here I don't see it.

MIO: You're blind then!
[*He goes into the room, the* SERGEANT *following him.*]

SERGEANT: What do you mean?
[*He comes out,* MIO *following him.*]
When you make a charge of murder it's better to have
the corpus delicti, son. You're the kind puts in
fire alarms to see the engine!

MIO: By God, he was there.
He went in there to die.

SERGEANT: I'll bet he did.
And I'm Haile Selassie's aunt! What's your name?

MIO: Romagna. [*To* GARTH.] What have you done with him?

GARTH: I don't know what you mean.

SERGEANT [*to* GARTH]: What's he talking about?

GARTH: I wish I could tell you.
I don't know.

SERGEANT: He must have seen something.

POLICEMAN: He's got
the Romagna case on the brain. You watch yourself,
chump, or you'll get run in.

MIO: Then they're in it together!
All of them!
[*To* MIRIAMNE.] Yes, and you!

GARTH: He's nuts, I say.

MIRAIMNE [*gently*]:
You have dreamed something—isn't it true?
You've dreamed—
But truly, there was no one—
[MIO *looks at her comprehendingly.*]

MIO: You want me to say it. [*He pauses.*]
Yes, by God, I was dreaming.

SERGEANT [*to* POLICEMAN]: I guess you're right.
We'd better be going. Haven't you got a coat?

GAUNT: No, sir.

SERGEANT: I guess I'll have to lend you mine.
[*He puts his oilskins on* GAUNT.] Come on, now. It's getting late.

GAUNT, *the* POLICEMAN *and the* SERGEANT *go out.*

TROCK: They're welcome to him.
His fuse is damp. Where is that walking fool
with the three slugs in him?

ESDRAS: He fell in the hall beyond
and we left him there.

TROCK: That's lucky for some of us. Is he out this time
or is he still butting around?

ESDRAS: He's dead.

TROCK: That's perfect.
[*To* MIO.] Don't try using your firearms, amigo baby,
the Sarge is outside. [*He turns to go.*] Better ship that carrion
back in the river! The one that walks when he's dead;
maybe he'll walk the distance for you.

GARTH: Coming back?

TROCK: Well, if I come back
you'll see me. If I don't, you won't. Let the punk
go far as he likes. Turn him loose and let him go.
And may you all rot in hell.

He pulls his coat around him and goes to left. MIRIAMNE *climbs up to look out a window.*

MIRAIMNE: He's climbing up the street,
along the bridgehead.
[*She turns.*] Quick, Mio! It's safe now! Quick!

GARTH: Let him do as he likes.

MIRAIMNE: What do you mean? Garth! He means to kill him!
You know that!

GARTH: I've no doubt Master Romagna can run his own campaign.

MIRAIMNE: But he'll be killed!

MIO: Why did you lie about Shadow?
[*There is a pause.* GARTH *shrugs, walks across the room, and sits.*] You were one of the gang!

GARTH: I can take a death if I have to! Go tell your story,
only watch your step, for I warn you, Trock's out gunning
and you may not walk very far. Oh, I could defend it
but it's hardly worth while.
If they get Trock they get me too.
Go tell them. You owe me nothing.

ESDRAS: This Trock you saw,
no one defends him. He's earned his death so often
there's nobody to regret it. But his crime,
his same crime that has dogged you, dogged us down
from what little we had, to live here among the drains,
where the waterbugs break out like a scrofula
on what we eat—and if there's lower to go

we'll go there when you've told your story. And more
that I haven't heart to speak—

MIO [*to* GARTH]: My father died
in your place. And you could have saved him!
You were one of the gang!

GARTH: Why, there you are.
You certainly owe me nothing.

MIRIAMNE [*moaning*]: I want to die.
I want to go away.

MIO: Yes, and you lied!
And trapped me into it!

MIRIAMNE: But Mio, he's my brother.
I couldn't give them my brother.

MIO: No. You couldn't.
You were quite right. The gods were damned ironic
tonight, and they've worked it out.

ESDRAS: What will be changed
if it comes to trial again? More blood poured out
to a mythical justice, but your father lying still
where he lies now.

MIO: The bright, ironical gods!
What fun they have in heaven! When a man prays hard
for any gift, they give it, and then one more
to boot that makes it useless.
[*To* MIRIAMNE.] You might have picked
some other stranger to dance with!

MIRIAMNE: I know.

MIO: Or chosen
some other evening to sit outside in the rain.
But no, it had to be this. All my life long
I've wanted only one thing, to say to the world
and prove it: the man you killed was clean and true
and full of love as the twelve-year-old that stood
and taught in the temple. I can say that now
and give my proofs—and now you stick a girl's face
between me and the rites I've sworn the dead
shall have of me! You ask too much! Your brother
can take his chance! He was ready enough to let
an innocent man take certainty for him
to pay for the years he's had. That parts us, then,
but we're parted anyway, by the same dark wind
that blew us together. I shall say what I have to say.
[*He steps back.*] And I'm not welcome here.

MIRIAMNE: But don't go now! You've stayed too long! He'll be waiting!

MIO: Well, is this any safer?
Let the winds blow, the four winds of the world,
and take us to the four winds.

The three are silent before him. He turns and goes out.

CURTAIN

ACT III

The river banks outside the tenement, a little before the close of the previous act. The rain still falls through the street lamps. The TWO NATTY YOUNG MEN IN SERGE AND GRAY *are leaning against the masonry in a ray of light, concentrating on a game of chance. Each holds in his hand a packet of ten or fifteen crisp bills. They compare the numbers on the top notes and immediately a bill changes hands. This goes on with varying fortune until the tide begins to run toward the* 1ST GUNMAN, *who has accumulated nearly the whole supply. They play on in complete silence, evidently not wishing to make any noise. Occasionally they raise their heads slightly to look carefully about. Luck begins to favor the* 2ND GUNMAN, *and the notes come his way. Neither evinces the slightest interest in how the game goes. They merely play on, bored, half-absorbed. There is a slight noise at the tenement door. They put the bills away and watch.* TROCK *comes out, pulls the door shut and comes over to them. He says a few words too low to be heard, and without changing expression the* YOUNG MEN *saunter toward the right.* TROCK *goes out to the left, and the* 2ND PLAYER, *catching that out of the corner of his eye, lingers in a glimmer of light to go on with the game. The* 1ST, *with an eye on the tenement door, begins to play without ado, and the bills again shift back and forth, then concentrate in the hands of the* 1ST GUNMAN. *The* 2ND *shrugs his shoulders, searches his pockets, finds one bill, and playing with it begins to win heavily. They hear the door opening, and putting the notes away, slip out in front of the rock.* MIO *emerges, closes the door, looks around him and walks to the left. Near the corner of the tenement he pauses, reaches out his hand to try the rain, looks up toward the street, and stands uncertainly a moment. He returns and leans against the tenement wall.* MIRIAMNE *comes out.* MIO *continues to look off into space as if unaware of her. She looks away.*

MIO: This rather takes one off his high horse.—What I mean, tough weather for a hegira. You see, this is my sleeping suit, and if I get it wet—basta!

MIRIAMNE: If you could only hide here.

MIO: Hide?

MIRIAMNE: Lucia would take you in. The street-piano man.

MIO: At the moment I'm afflicted with claustrophobia. I prefer to die in the open, seeking air.

MIRIAMNE: But you could stay there till daylight.

MIO: You're concerned about me.

MIRIAMNE: Shall I ask him?

MIO: No. On the other hand there's a certain reason in your concern. I looked up the street and our old friend Trock hunches patiently under the warehouse eaves.

MIRIAMNE: I was sure of that.

MIO: And here I am, a young man on a cold night, waiting the end of the rain. Being read my lesson by a boy, a blind boy—you know the one I mean. Knee-deep in the salt-marsh, Miriamne, bitten from within, fought.

MIRIAMNE: Wouldn't it be better if you came back in to the house?

MIO: You forget my claustrophobia.

MIRIAMNE: Let me walk with you, then. Please. If I stay beside you he wouldn't dare.

MIO: And then again he might.—We don't speak the same language, Miriamne.

MIRIAMNE: I betrayed you. Forgive me.

MIO: I wish I knew this region. There's probably a path along the bank.

MIRIAMNE: Yes, Shadow went that way.

MIO: That's true, too. So here I am, a young man on a wet night, and blind in my weather eye. Stay and talk to me.

MIRIAMNE: If it happens—it's my fault.

MIO: Not at all, sweet. You warned me to keep away. But I would have it. Now I have to find a way out. It's like a chess game. If you think long enough there's always a way out.—For one or the other.—I wonder why white always wins and black always loses in the problems. White to move and mate in three moves. But what if white were to lose—ah, what then? Why, in that case, obviously black would be white and white would be black.—As it often is.—As we often are.—Might makes white. Losers turn black. Do you think I'd have time to draw a gun?

MIRIAMNE: No.

MIO: I'm a fair shot. Also I'm fair game.

The door of the tenement opens and GARTH *comes out to look about quickly. Seeing only* MIO *and* MIRIAMNE *he goes in and comes out again almost immediately carrying one end of a door on which a body lies covered with a cloth. The* HOBO *carries the other end. They go to the right with their burden.*

This is the buriel of Shadow, then;
feet first he dips, and leaves the haunts of men.
Let us make mourn for Shadow, wetly lying,
in elegiac stanzas and sweet crying.
Be gentle with him, little cold waves and fishes;
nibble him not, respect his skin and tissues—

MIRIAMNE: Must you say such things?

MIO: My dear, some requiem is fitting over the dead, even
for Shadow. But the last rhyme was bad.
Whittle him not, respect his dying wishes.
That's better. And then to conclude;
His aromatic virtues, slowly rising
will circumnamb the isle, beyond disguising.
He clung to life beyond the wont of men.
Time and his silence drink us all. Amen.
How I hate these identicals. The French allow them, but the French have no principles anyway. You know, Miriamne, there's really nothing mysterious about human life. It's purely mechanical, like an electric appliance. Stop the engine that runs the generator and the current's broken. When we think the brain gives off a small electrical discharge—quite measurable, and constant within limits. But that's not what makes your hair stand up when frightened.

MIRIAMNE: I think it's a mystery.

MIO: Human life? We'll have to wear veils if we're to keep it a mystery much longer. Now if Shadow and I were made up into sausages we'd probably make very good sausages.

MIRIAMNE: Don't——

MIO: I'm sorry. I speak from a high place, far off, long ago, looking down. The cortège returns. [GARTH *and the* HOBO *return, carrying the door, the cloth lying loosely over it.*] I hope you placed an obol in his mouth to pay the ferryman? Even among the Greeks a little money was prerequisite to Elysium. [GARTH *and the* HOBO *go inside, silent.*] No? It's grim to think of Shadow lingering among lesser shades on the hither side. For lack of a small gratuity.

ESDRAS *comes out the open door and closes it behind him.*

ESDRAS: You must wait here, Mio, or go inside. I know
you don't trust me, and I haven't earned your trust

You're young enough to seek truth—
and there is no truth;
and I know that—
but I shall call the police and see that you get safely off.

MIO: It's a little late for that.

ESDRAS: I shall try.

MIO: And your terms? For I daresay you make terms?

ESDRAS: No.

MIO: Then let me remind you what will happen.
The police will ask some questions.
When they're answered
they'll ask more, and before they're done with it
your son will be implicated.

ESDRAS: Must he be?

MIO: I shall not keep quiet.

A pause.

ESDRAS: Still, I'll go.

MIO: I don't ask help, remember. I made truce. truce.
He's not on my conscience, and I'm not on yours.

ESDRAS: But you
could make it easier, so easily.
He's my only son. Let him live.

MIO: His chance of survival's
better than mine, I'd say.

ESDRAS: I'll go.

MIO: I don't urge it.

ESDRAS: No, I put my son's life in your hands.
When you're gone,
that may come to your mind.

MIO: Don't count on it.

ESDRAS: Oh.
I count on nothing.
[*He turns to go.* MIRIAMNE *runs over to him and silently kisses his hands.*]
Not mine, not mine, my daughter!
They're guilty hands.
[*He goes out left.* GARTH'S *violin is heard within.*]

MIO: There was a war in heaven
once, all the angels on one side, and all
the devils on the other, and since that time
disputes have raged among the learned, concerning
whether the demons won, or the angels. Maybe
the angels won, after all.

MIRIAMNE: And again, perhaps
there are no demons or angels.

MIO: Oh, there are none.
But I could love your father.

MIRIAMNE: I love him. You see,
he's afraid because he's old. The less one has
to lose the more he's afraid.

MIO: Suppose one had
only a short stub end of life, or held
a flashlight with the batteries run down
till the bulb was dim, and knew that he could live
while the glow lasted. Or suppose one knew
that while he stood in a little shelter of time
under a bridgehead, say, he could live, and then,
from then on, nothing. Then to lie and turn
with the earth and sun, and regard them not in the least
when the bulb was extinguished or he stepped beyond
his circle into the cold? How could he live
that last dim quarter-hour, before he went,
minus all recollection, to grow in grass
between cobblestones?

MIRIAMNE: Let me put my arms round you, Mio.
Then if anything comes, it's for me, too. [*She puts both arms round him.*]

MIO: Only suppose
this circle's charmed! To be safe until he steps
from this lighted space into dark! Time pauses here
and high eternity grows in one quarter-hour
in which to live.

MIRIAMNE: Let me see if anyone's there—
there in the shadows.
[*She looks toward the right.*]

MIO: It might blast our eternity—
blow it to bits. No, don't go. This is forever,
here where we stand. And I ask you, Miriamne,
how does one spend a forever?

MIRIAMNE: You're frightened?

MIO: Yes.
So much that time stands still.

MIRIAMNE: Why didn't I speak—
tell them—when the officers were here? I failed you
in that one moment!

MIO: His life for mine? Oh, no.
I wouldn't want it, and you couldn't give it.
And if I should go on living we're cut apart
by that brother of yours.

MIRIAMNE: Are we?

MIO: Well, think about it.
A body lies between us, buried in quicklime.
Your allegiance is on the other side of that grave and not to me.

MIRIAMNE: No, Mio! Mio, I love you!

MIO: I love you, too, but in case my life went on

beyond that barrier of dark—then Garth
would run his risk of dying.

MIRIAMNE: He's punished, Mio.
His life's been torment to him. Let him go,
for my sake, Mio.

MIO: I wish I could. I wish
I'd never seen him—or you. I've steeped too long
in this thing. It's in my teeth and bones. I can't
let go or forget. And I'll not add my lie
to the lies that cumber his ground. We live our days
in a storm of lies that drifts the truth too deep
for path or shovel; but I've set my foot on a truth
for once, and I'll trail it down!

A silence. MIRIAMNE *looks out to the right.*

MIRIAMNE: There's someone there—
I heard—

CARR *comes in from the right.*

MIO: It's Carr.

CARR: That's right. No doubt about it.
Excuse me.

MIO: Glad to see you. This is Miriamne.
Carr's a friend of mine.

CARR: You're better employed
than when I saw you last.

MIO: Bow to the gentleman,
Miriamne. That's meant for you.

MIRIAMNE: Thank you, I'm sure.
Should I leave you, Mio? You want to talk?

MIO: Oh, no.
we've done our talking.

MIRIAMNE: But—

CARR: I'm the one's out of place—
I wandered back because I got worried about you,
that's the truth.—Oh—those two fellows with the hats
down this way, you know, the ones that ran
after we heard the shooting—they're back again,
lingering or malingering down the bank,
revisiting the crime, I guess. They may
mean well.

MIO: I'll try to avoid them.

CARR: I didn't care
for the way they looked at me.—No luck, I suppose,
with that case history? The investigation
you had on hand?

MIO: I can't say. By the way,
the stiff that fell in the water and we saw swirling
down the eddy, he came trudging up, later on,
long enough to tell his name. His name was Shadow
but he's back in the water now. It's all in an evening.
These things happen here.

CARR: Good God!

MIO: I know.
I wouldn't believe it if you told it.

CARR: But—
the man was alive?

MIO: Oh, not for long! He's dunked
for good this time. That's all that's happened.

CARR: Well,
if you don't need me——

MIRIAMNE: You had a message to send—
have you forgotten——?

MIO: I?—Yes, I had a message—
but I won't send it—not now.

MIRIAMNE: Then I will——!

MIO: No.
Let it go the way it is! It's all arranged
another way. You've been a good scout, Carr,
the best I ever knew on the road.

CARR: That sounds
like making your will.

MIO: Not yet, but when I do
I've thought of something to leave you. It's the view
of Mt. Rainier from the Seattle jail,
snow over cloud. And the rusty chain in my pocket from a pair of handcuffs my father wore. That's all the worldy goods I'm seized of.

CARR: Look, Mio—hell—
if you're in trouble——

MIO: I'm not. Not at all. I have
a genius that attends me where I go,
and guards me now. I'm fine.

CARR: Well, that's good news.
He'll have his work cut out.

MIO: Oh, he's a genius.

CARR: I'll see you then.
I'll be at the Grand Street place. I'm lucky tonight,
and I can pay. I could even pay for two.

MIO: Thanks, I may take you up.

CARR: Good night.

MIO: Right, Carr.

CARR [*to* MIRIAMNE]: Good night.

MIRIAMNE: [*after a pause*]. Good night.

CARR *goes out to the left.*

Why did you do that? He's your genius, Mio,
and you let him go.

MIO: I couldn't help it.

MIRIAMNE: Call him,
Run after him and call him!
MIO: I tried to say it
and it strangled in my throat. I might have known
you'd win in the end.
MIRIAMNE: Is it for me?
MIO: For you?
It stuck in my throat, that's all I know.
MIRIAMNE: Oh, Mio,
I never asked for that! I only hoped
Garth could go clear.
MIO: Well, now he will.
MIRIAMNE: But you—
It was your chance!
MIO: I've lost
my taste for revenge if it falls on you. Oh, God,
deliver me from the body of this death
I've dragged behind me all these years! Miriamne!
Miriamne!
MIRIAMNE: Yes!
MIO: Miriamne, if you love me
teach me a treason to what I am, and have been,
till I learn to live like a man! I think I'm waking
from a long trauma of hate and fear and death
that's hemmed me from my birth—and glimpse a life
to be lived in hope—but it's young in me yet, I can't
get free, or forgive! But teach me how to live
and forget to hate!
MIRIAMNE: He would have forgiven.
MIO: He?
MIRIAMNE: Your father. [*A pause.*]
MIO: Yes. [*Another pause.*]
You'll think it strange, but I've never
remembered that.
MIRIAMNE: How can I help you?
MIO: You have.
MIRIAMNE: If I were a little older—if I knew
the things to say! I can only put out my hands
and give you back the faith you bring to me
by being what you are. Because to me
you are all hope and beauty and brightness drawn
across what's black and mean!
MIO: He'd have forgiven—
Then there's no more to say—I've groped long enough
through this everglades of old revenges—here
the road ends.—Miriamne, Miriamne,
the iron I wore so long—it's eaten through
and fallen from me. Let me have your arms.
They'll say we're children—Well—the world's made up of children.
MIRIAMNE: Yes.
MIO: But it's too late for me.
MIRIAMNE: No.
[*She goes into his arms, and they kiss for the first time.*]
Then we'll meet again?
MIO: Yes.
MIRIAMNE: Where?
MIO: I'll write—
or send Carr to you.
MIRIAMNE: You won't forget?
MIO: Forget?
Whatever streets I walk, you'll walk them, too,
from now on, and whatever roof or stars
I have to house me, you shall share my roof
and stars and morning. I shall not forget.
MIRIAMNE: God keep you!
MIO: And keep you. And this to remember!
if I should die, Miriamne, this half-hour
is our eternity. I came here seeking
light in darkness, running from the dawn,
and stumbled on a morning.

One of the YOUNG MEN IN SERGE *strolls in casually from the right, looks up and down without expression, then, seemingly having forgotten something, retraces his steps and goes out.* ESDRAS *comes in slowly from the left. He has lost his hat, and his face is bleeding from a slight cut on the temple. He stands abjectly near the tenement.*

MIRIAMNE: Father—what is it?
[*She goes toward* ESDRAS.]
ESDRAS: Let me alone.
[*He goes nearer to*] MIO. He wouldn't let me pass.
The street's so icy up along the bridge
I had to crawl on my knees—he kicked me back
three times—and then he held me there—I swear
what I could do I did! I swear to you
I'd save you if I could.
MIO: What makes you think
that I need saving?
ESDRAS: Child, save yourself if you can!
He's waiting for you.
MIO: Well, we knew that before.
ESDRAS: He won't wait much longer. He'll come here—
he told me so. Those damned six months of his—
he wants them all—and you're to die—you'd spread
his guilt—I had to listen to it——

MIO: Wait—
[*He walks forward and looks casually to the right, then returns.*]
There must be some way up through the house and out
across the roof——

ESDRAS: He's watching that. But come in—
and let me look.——

MIO: I'll stay here, thanks. Once in and I'm a rat
in a deadfall—I'll stay here—
look for me if you don't mind.

ESDRAS: Then watch for me—
I'll be on the roof——
[*He goes in hurriedly.*]

MIO [*looking up*]: Now all you silent powers
that make the sleet and dark, and never yet
have spoken, give us a sign, let the throw be ours
this once, on this longest night, when the winter sets
his foot on the threshold leading up to spring
and enters with remembered cold—let fall
some mercy with the rain. We are two lovers
here in your night, and we wish to live.

MIRIAMNE: Oh, Mio—
if you pray that way, nothing good will come!
You're bitter, Mio.

MIO: How many floors has this building?

MIRAIMNE: Five or six. It's not as high as the bridge.

MIO: No, I thought not. How many pomegranate seeds did you eat, Persephone?

MIRIAMNE: Oh, darling, darling,
if you die, don't die alone.

MIO: I'm afraid I'm damned
to hell, and you're not damned at all. Good God,
how long he takes to climb!

MIRIAMNE: The stairs are steep.
[*A slight pause.*]

MIO: I'll follow him.

MIRIAMNE: He's there—at the window—now.
He waves you to go back, not to go in.
Mio, see, that path between the rocks—
they're not watching that—they're out at the river—
I can see them there—they can't watch both—
it leads to a street above.

MIO: I'll try it, then.
Kiss me. You'll hear. But if you never hear—
then I'm the king of hell, Persephone,
and I'll expect you.

MIRIAMNE: Oh, lover, keep safe.

MIO: Good-bye.

He slips out quickly between the rocks. There is a quick machine gun rat-tat. The violin stops. MIRIAMNE *runs toward the path.* MIO *comes back slowly, a hand pressed under his heart.*

It seems you were mistaken.

MIRIAMNE: Oh, God, forgive me!
[*She puts an arm around him. He sinks to his knees.*]
Where is it, Mio? Let me help you in! Quick, quick, let me help you!

MIO: I hadn't thought to choose—this—ground—
but it will do. [*He slips down.*]

MIRIAMNE: Oh, God, forgive me!

MIO: Yes?
The king of hell was not forgiven then,
Dis[1] is his name and Hades is his home—
and he goes alone——

MIRIAMNE: Why does he bleed so? Mio, if you go
I shall go with you.

MIO: It's better to stay alive.
I wanted to stay alive—because of you—
I leave you that—and what he said to me dying:
I love you, and will love you after I die.
Tomorrow, I shall still love you, as I've loved
the stars I'll never see, and all the mornings
that might have been yours and mine. Oh, Miriamne,
you taught me this.

MIRIAMNE: If only I'd never seen you
then you could live——

MIO: That's blasphemy—Oh, God,
there might have been some easier way of it.
You didn't want me to die, did you, Miriamne—?
You didn't send me away——?

MIRIAMNE: Oh, never, never——

MIO: Forgive me—kiss me—I've got blood on your lips—
I'm sorry—it doesn't matter—I'm sorry——

ESDRAS *and* GARTH *come out.*

MIRIAMNE: Mio—
I'd have gone to die myself—you must hear this, Mio,
I'd have died to help you—you must listen, sweet,

---

[1]Dis: the god of the underworld in Roman mythology.

you must hear it—[*She rises.*]
I can die, too, see! You! There!
You in the shadows!—You killed him to silence him!
[*She walks toward the path.*]
But I'm not silenced! All that he knew I know,
and I'll tell it tonight! Tonight—
tell it and scream it
through all the streets—that Trock's a murderer
and he hired you for this murder!
Your work's not done—
and you won't live long! Do you hear?
You're murderers, and I know who you are!

The machine gun speaks again. She sinks to her knees. GARTH *runs to her.*

GARTH: You little fool!
[*He tries to lift her.*]
MIRIAMNE: Don't touch me!
[*She crawls toward* MIO.]
Look, Mio! They killed me, too. Oh, you can believe me
now, Mio. You can believe I wouldn't hurt you,
because I'm dying! Why doesn't he answer me?
Oh, now he'll never know!

She sinks down, her hand over her mouth, choking. GARTH *kneels beside her, then rises, shuddering. The* HOBO *comes out.* LUCIA *and* PINY *look out.*

ESDRAS: It lacked only this.
GARTH: Yes.
[ESDRAS *bends over* MIRIAMNE, *then rises slowly.*]
Why was the bastard born? Why did he come here?
ESDRAS: Miriamne—Miriamne—yes, and Mio,
one breath shall call you now—forgive us both—
forgive the ancient evil of the earth
that brought you here——
GARTH: Why must she be a fool?
ESDRAS: Well, they were wiser than you and I. To die
when you are young and untouched, that's beggary
to a miser of years, but the devils locked in synod
shake and are daunted when men set their lives
at hazard for the heart's love, and lose. And these,
who were yet children, will weigh more than all
a city's elders when the experiment
is reckoned up in the end. Oh, Miriamne,
and Mio—Mio, my son—know this where you lie,
this is the glory of earth-born men and women,
not to cringe, never to yield, but standing,
take defeat implacable and defiant,
die unsubmitting. I wish that I'd died so,
long ago; before you're old you'll wish
that you had died as they have. On this star,
in this hard star-adventure, knowing not
what the fires mean to right and left, nor whether
a meaning was intended or presumed,
man can stand up, and look out blind, and say:
in all these turning lights I find no clue,
only a masterless night, and in my blood
no certain answer, yet is my mind my own,
yet is my heart a cry toward something dim
in distance, which is higher than I am
and makes me emperor of the endless dark
even in seeking! What odds and ends of life
men may live otherwise, let them live, and then
go out, as I shall go, and you. Our part
is only to bury them. Come, take her up.
They must not lie here.

LUCIA *and* PINY *come near to help.* ESDRAS *and* GARTH *stoop to carry* MIRIAMNE.

CURTAIN

Introduction to

The Tales of Hoffman

One of the most bizarre trials of our era ran for five months in the Federal District Courthouse in Chicago, beginning December 26, 1969, and accumulating a massive 22,000 pages of official transcript. Brought to trial on charges of conspiracy to commit riot were eight counterculture revolutionaries who had been arrested during confrontations with the Chicago police during the Democratic National Convention in the summer of 1968. Called to witness was a cross section of radicalized America versus their conservative opponents.

Passed by Congress in 1968, the Anti-Riot Act made it a federal offense to cross state lines with the intention of inciting, promoting, encouraging, or participating in a riot. That such a law is well meaning (the aim of protecting lives and property is certainly an admirable one) but ambiguous (how can one determine "intention"?) was dramatized by a trial which mirrored vividly American polarization, a virtual breakdown in the ability of citizens to talk to and understand one another. The radical, alienated Students for a Democratic Society (SDS), Yippies, Black Panthers, and their youthful supporters were aligned against the austere middle class American establishment, which had on its side the clout and power of the law.

The trial looked like absurdist theater, amply grotesque. Defendant Bobby Seale, a black revolutionary, was chained and gagged in his chair. Fellow-defendants Abbie Hoffman and Jerry Rubin interrupted the proceedings with outbursts like "Gestapo!" "[Judge] Julius Hoffman equals Adolf Hitler today," and "Fascist!" "RIGHT ON," echoed frequently from all corners of the courtroom. Guru-poet Allan Ginsberg chanted. Psychedelic drug prophet and former Harvard professor Dr. Timothy Leary revealed with painful clarity the wide divergence between hip and straight in America, with differences evidently irreconcilable.

Was the trial a series of skits in neovaudeville? Were there episodes actually worthy of a dramatist's skill? Clearly, some moments approached tragic and comic art. The sudden evocation of nostalgia in lawyer William Kunstler when he hears himself referred to as "Billy" fuses the carefree, irresponsible era of childhood with the fierce exigencies of the moment. Dr. Leary's reference to wife, cow, and lantern brings to the scene the mythology of Mrs. Leary's part in the famous Chicago Fire: the cow kicked over the lantern and the conflagration began. Such effective comic allusion is theater.

At one time, however, Judge Hoffman asked for order, declaring that the courtroom "isn't a theater." Jerry Rubin wryly observed, though, "I like being here. It is interesting. . . . It is good theater, your Honor."

On February 18, 1970, the Chicago "rioters" were fined $5,000 and sentenced to five years in prison for having violated the federal anti-riot statute, the so-called "H. Rap Brown Amendment." As an epilogue to this grim courtroom drama, however, the 7th U.S. Circuit Court of Appeals on November 21, 1972, reversed the convictions, citing errors in jury selection as well as improper communication between judge and jurors. Specifically, the appeals magistrates criticized Judge Hoffman for displaying "a deprecatory and often antagonistic attitude toward the defense."

From The Tales of Hoffman*

Direct examination of Defense Witness Allen Ginsberg, poet, by Mr. Weinglass

Q. Could you indicate for the Court and jury what the area of your studies consisted of?

A. Mantra Yoga, meditation exercises, chanting, and sitting quietly, stilling the mind and breathing exercises to calm the body and to calm the mind, but mainly a branch called Mantra Yoga, which is a yoga which involves prayer and chanting.

* * *

Q. Now, calling your attention to the month of February 1968, did you have occasion in that month to meet with Abbie Hoffman?

A. Yeah.

. . .

Q. Do you recall what Mr. Hoffman said in the course of that conversation?

A. Yippie—among other things. He said that politics had become theater and magic; that it was the manipulation of imagery through mass media that was confusing and hypnotizing the people in the United States and making them accept a war which they did not really believe in; that people were involved in a life style which was intolerable to the younger folk, which involved brutality and police violence as well as a larger violence in Vietnam, and that ourselves might be able to get together in Chicago and invite teachers to present different ideas of what is wrong with the planet, what we can do to solve the pollution crisis, what we can do to solve the Vietnam war, to present different ideas for making the society more sacred and less commercial, less materialistic, what we could do to uplevel or improve the whole tone of the trap that we all felt ourselves in as the population grew and as politics became more and more violent and chaotic.

* * *

Q. After he spoke to you, what, if anything, was your response to his suggestion?

A. I was worried as to whether or not the whole scene would get violent. I was worried whether we would be allowed to put on such a situation. I was worried whether, you know, the Government would let us do something that was funnier or prettier or more charming than what was going to be going on in the convention hall.

* * *

Q. Would you explain what your statement was.

A. My statement was that the planet Earth at the present moment was endangered by violence, overpopulation, pollution, ecological destruction brought about by our own greed; that the younger children in America and other countries of the world might not survive the next 30 years, that it was a planetary crisis that had not been recognized by any government of the world . . . [T]he more selfish elder politicians . . . were not thinking in terms of what their children would need in future generations or even in the generation immediately coming or even for themselves in their own life-time and were continuing to threaten the planet with violence, with war, with mass murder, with germ warfare. . . . The desire for preservation of the planet and the planet's

* *The Tales of Hoffman* is a series of excerpts from the "Chicago Conspiracy" trial, *The United States of America, Plaintiff, vs. David T. Dellinger et al., Defendants, No. 69 Crim. 180.*

In the Forward to *The Tales of Hoffman,* editors Mark L. Levine, George C. McNamee, and Daniel Greenberg have explained their use of asterisks and ellipses. The transcript is divided into segments, with three asterisks separating the segments, and unnecessary dialogue deleted at that point; two asterisks dividing the segments indicate a pause in the dialogue, but no material has been deleted; and ellipses between paragraphs indicate the deletion of irrelevant dialogue.

form, that we do continue to be, to exist on this planet instead of destroy the planet, was manifested to my mind by the great Mantra from India to the preserver God Vishnu whose Mantra is Hare Krishna, and then I chanted the Hare Krishna Mantra for ten minutes to the television cameras and it goes:

"Hare Krishna, Hare Krishna, Krishna, Krishna, Hare, Hare, Rama, Hare, Rama, Rama, Rama, Hare, Hare."

* * *

Q. Mr. Ginsberg, I show you an object marked 150 for identification, and I ask you to examine that object.

A. Yes.

MR. FORAN: All right.

Your Honor, that is enough. I object to it, your Honor. I think that it is outrageous for counsel to—

THE COURT: You asked him to examine it and instead of that he played a tune on it.

MR. FORAN: I mean, counsel is so clearly—

THE COURT: I sustain the objection.

MR. FORAN:—talking about things that have no conceivable materiality to this case, and it is improper, your Honor.

THE WITNESS: It adds spirituality to this case, sir.

December 12, 1969

Continued direct testimony of Defense Witness Allen Ginsberg by Defense Attorney Weinglass

Q. Did you hear the defendant, Jerry Rubin, say anything at this meeting?

A. Jerry Rubin said that he didn't think the police would attack the kids who were in the park at night if there were enough kids there, that he didn't think it would be a good thing to fight over the park if the police started fighting with the kids, if the police attacked the kids and tried to drive them out of the park as the police had announced at 11 o'clock, that as far as he was concerned, he wanted to leave the park at 9:00 and would not encourage anybody to fight and get hurt that evening if the police did physically try to force everybody out of the park. That was on Saturday night, the first night when the people would be in the park.

* * *

Q. Did the defendant, Abbie Hoffman, say anything at this meeting?

A. Abbie Hoffman said the park wasn't worth fighting for, that we had on our responsibility invited many thousands of kids to Chicago for a happy festival of life, for an alternative proposition to the festival of death that the politicians were putting on, and that it wasn't right to lead them or encourage them to get into a violent argument with the police over staying in the park overnight. He didn't know, he said he didn't know what to say to those who wanted to stay and fight for what they felt was their liberty, but he wasn't going to encourage anybody to fight, and he was going to leave when forced himself.

. . .

Q. Now, do you recall what, if anything, occurred at 10:30?

A. There was a sudden burst of lights in the center of the park, and a group of policemen moved in fast to where the bonfires were and kicked over the bonfires.

Q. That what—

A. There was a great deal of consternation and movement and shouting among the crowd in the park, and I turned, surprised, because it was early. . . .

. . .

Q. Without relating what you said to another person, Mr. Ginsberg, what did you do at the time you saw the police do this?

A. I started the chant, O-o-m-m-m-m-m-m, O-o-m-m-m-m-m-m.

Q. Did you finish your answer?

A. I am afraid I will be in contempt if I continue to Om. . . .

. . .

Q. What did you do when you saw the policemen in the center of the crowd?

A. Adrenalin ran through my body. I sat down on a green hillside with a group of younger people that were walking with me at about 3:30 in the afternoon, 4 o'clock, sat, crossed my leg and began chanting O-o-m—O-o-m-m-m, O-o-m-m-m, O-o-m-m-m.

MR. FORAN: I gave him four that time.

THE WITNESS: I continued chanting for seven hours.

MR. WEINGLASS: I am sorry, I did not hear the answer.

THE COURT: He said he continued chanting for seven hours. Seven hours, was it, sir?

THE WITNESS: Until 10:30.

THE COURT: I wanted to know what your answer was. Did you say you continued chanting for seven hours?

THE WITNESS: Seven hours, yes.

. . .

Q. Now, when you left the Coliseum, where, if anywhere, did you go?

A. The group I was with, Mr. Genet, Mr. Burroughs and Mr. Seaver, and Terry Southern, all went back to Lincoln Park.

Q. What time did you arrive in the park?

A. 11:00, 11:30.

Q. What was occurring at the park as you got there?

A. There was a great crowd lining the outskirts of the park and a little way into the park on the inner roads, and there was a larger crowd moving in toward the center. We all moved in toward the center and at the center of the park, there was a group of ministers and rabbis who had elevated a great cross about ten-foot high in the middle of a circle of people who were sitting around, quietly, listening to the ministers conduct a ceremony.

. . .

Q. After the ministers moved the cross to another location which you have indicated, what happened?

A. After, I don't know, a short period of time, there was a burst of smoke and tear gas around the cross, and the cross was enveloped with tear gas, and the people who were carrying the cross were enveloped with tear gas which began slowly drifting over the crowd.

. . .

Q. And when you saw the persons with the cross and the cross being gassed, what if anything did you do?

A. I turned to Burroughs and said, "They have gassed the cross of Christ."

MR. FORAN: Objection, if the Court please. I ask that the answer be stricken.

THE COURT: I sustain the objection.

December 19, 1969

Direct examination of Defense Witness, Dr. Timothy Leary, former Harvard professor, by Mr. Kunstler

Q. Prior to this press conference had you had any other meetings with Jerry and Abbie?

A. Yes, we had met two or three times during the spring in which we were planning the Chicago Convention love-in.

MR. FORAN: Your Honor, I object to the constant use of the diminutives in the references to the defendants.

THE COURT: Yes, I think it is better courtroom form, Mr. Kunstler, to refer to the defendants by their surnames.

MR. KUNSTLER: Your Honor, sometimes it is hard because we work together in this case, we use first names constantly.

THE COURT: I know, but if I knew you that well, and I don't, how would it seem for me to say, "Now Billy . . ."

. . .

MR. KUNSTLER: I was just thinking I hadn't been called "Billy" since my mother used that word the first time.

THE COURT: I haven't called you that.

MR. KUNSTLER: I know, but you used it.

THE COURT: I used it . . .

MR. KUNSTLER: It evokes some memories.

THE COURT: I was trying to point out to you how absurd it sounds in a courtroom.

MR. KUNSTLER: It didn't sound . . .

THE COURT: Oh, let's get on. Let's examine this witness. He seems eager to get away.

* * *

Q. Dr. Leary, tell what people said.

A. Yes. Mr. Hoffman continued to say that we should set up a series of political meetings throughout the country, not just for the coming summer but for the coming years. Mr. Hoffman suggested that we have love-ins or be-ins in which thousands of young people and freedom-loving people throughout the country could get together on Sunday afternoons, listen to music which represented the new point of view, the music of love and peace and harmony, and try to bring about a political change in this country that would be nonviolent in people's minds and in their hearts, and this is the concept of the love-in which Mr. Hoffman was urging upon us and this was the first time that the coming to Chicago was mentioned.

. . .

I also told Jerry that my wife and I had had a press conference about the Yippie meetings and the Convention the day we were in Chicago. I told Jerry we had that press conference at the Model Farm, I think it is in Lincoln Park, where my wife, whose name is Mrs. Leary, had a lantern by a cow, and we were announcing that we were going to come to Chicago in August, not with fire, but to bring light and peace.

* * *

Dr. Leary testifying to another conversation

DR. LEARY: . . . Both Mr. Hoffman and Mr. Rubin at that time said to me before I left that they were not sure whether we should come to

Chicago, and that we would watch what happened politically. At that time, Jerry Rubin pointed out that Robert Kennedy was still alive, and many of us felt that he represented the aspirations of young people, so we thought we would wait. I remember Mr. Rubin saying, "Let's wait and see what Robert Kennedy come out with as far as peace is concerned. Let's wait to see if Robert Kennedy does speak to young people, and if Robert Kennedy does seek to represent the peaceful, joyous, erotic feelings of young people . . ."

THE COURT: "Erotic," did you say?

THE WITNESS: Erotic.

THE COURT: E-r-o-t-i-c?

THE WITNESS: Eros. That means love, your Honor.

THE COURT: I know; I know. I wanted to be sure I didn't mishear you.

THE WITNESS: Because Mr. Rubin pointed out that Mr. Robert Kennedy did represent a youthful, healthy, masculine approach that was lacking in most of our other politicians, and we felt that young people would respond to a person like Mr. Kennedy, who seemed to enjoy life as opposed to the pessimistic uptight older politicians.

So Mr. Rubin suggested that we hold off the decision as to whether we come to Chicago until we saw how Mr. Kennedy's campaign developed, and at that point, I think most of us would have gladly, joyously called off the Chicago meeting.

MR. FORAN: Oh, I object to this, your Honor.

* * *

Direct examination of Defendant Abbott H. Hoffman by Defense Attorney Weinglass.

Q. Will you please identify yourself for the record.

A. My name is Abbie. I am an orphan of America.

. . .

Q. Where do you reside?

A. I live in Woodstock Nation.

Q. Will you tell the Court and jury where it is.

A. Yes. It is a nation of alienated young people. We carry it around with us as a state of mind in the same way the Sioux Indians carried the Sioux nation around with them. It is a nation dedicated to cooperation versus competition, to the idea that people should have better means of exchange than property or money, that there should be some other basis for human interaction. It is a nation dedicated to—

THE COURT: Excuse me, sir. Read the question to the witness, please.

Question read

THE COURT: Just where it is, that is all.

THE WITNESS: It is in my mind and in the minds of my brothers and sisters. We carry it around with us in the same way that the Sioux Indians carried around the Sioux nation. It does not consist of property or material but, rather, of ideas and certain values, those values being cooperation versus competition, and that we believe in a society—

MR. SCHULTZ: This doesn't say where Woodstock Nation, whatever that is, is.

MR. WEINGLASS: Your Honor, the witness has identified it as being a state of mind and he has, I think, a right to define that state of mind.

THE COURT: No, we want the place of residence, if he has one, place of doing business, if you have a business, or both if you desire to tell them both. One address will be sufficient. Nothing about philosophy or India, sir. Just where you live, if you have a place to live.

Now you said Woodstock. In what state is Woodstock?

THE WITNESS: It is in the state of mind, in the mind of myself and my brothers and sisters. It is a conspiracy . . .

. . .

Q. Can you tell the Court and jury your present age?

A. My age is 33. I am a child of the 60's.

Q. When were you born?

A. Psychologically, 1960.

. . .

Q. Can you tell the Court and jury what is your present occupation?

A. I am a cultural revolutionary. Well, I am really a defendant—

Q. What do you mean?

A. —full time.

* * *

Elvie A. Moore

(1942–   )

When in March, 1971, *Angela Is Happening* opened in Los Angeles, critics unanimously regarded it as a total theatrical experience reminiscent of the Agit-prop staging of the 1930's. An unconventional experiment in people's theater, the drama was said to cross symbol and reality with the fervor and passion of an old-time revival meeting. Called to speak by playwright Elvie A. Moore are voices past and present that challenge the American establishment: Nat Turner, Harriet Tubman, and John Brown; Martin Luther King, Frederick Douglass, Susan B. Anthony, Sacco and Vanzetti, and Malcolm X. Miss Moore has composed a "happening" fashioned from the historical chaos of our time. Her dramatic zeal matches the anger and passions inherent in the complex issues which permeate the play.

In August, 1970, Angela Yvonne Davis (born 1944), a black university instructor, doctoral candidate in philosophy, controversial revolutionary, and avowed Marxist, was indicted for conspiracy, kidnapping, and murder. The charges grew out of the following episode: Miss Davis had become active in the cause of three prison inmates, the Soledad Brothers, who had been charged with killing a guard. As their trial began in the Marin County courthouse, San Rafael, California, Jonathan Jackson, a young black, appeared in the courtroom with four weapons he had been able to smuggle past the security guards. Hostages, including the judge, were taken from the Hall of Justice. There was a bloody shootout. Two of the prisoners and Judge Harold Haley were killed. The hand guns, rifle, and shotgun used by the prisoners in their attempted escape were all registered to Miss Davis. One day before this episode, Miss Davis was reported seen in the area. After the gunfight, she vanished. A fugitive for three months, Miss Davis was taken into custody by the FBI in October, 1970. Under California law, a person abetting a murderer before the act is considered as guilty as the killer himself. All during the lengthy trial, her supporters regarded her as a true martyr; her antagonists saw her as an absolute criminal and champion of sedition. It was not until June, 1972, that Angela Davis was found not guilty—and was finally free.

As a student of political philosophy, Miss Davis appeared on the American scene as "a breath of new life in the doddering American Communist Party." (*Newsweek,* October 26, 1970). She has never attempted to hide her unpopular revolutionary opinions:

> *Why is it that the masses of the people in this country have to work eight hours a day every day and somehow or another what they produce goes to some people who are sitting out at a country club, on a golf course, and not doing a damn thing? That tells me that something is wrong and it tells me that maybe the real criminals in this society are not all the people who populate the prisons across the state but those people who have stolen the wealth of the world from the people.* *

* *Life* (September 11, 1970), p. 27.

Black and radical, Angela Davis was the focus of gnawing doubts and unresolved suspicions: Was she really a victim of the oppression, and hatred in white America? Was she held a political prisoner because of her radical, controversial views? Was the case against her, as her attorney put it, "a gigantic hoax"? A spokesman for violence and revolution she was, but did she knowingly commit herself to this direct action which terminated in such carnage? Whatever the viewpoint, one fact looms clear: the Angela Davis controversy marks a major confrontation of the revolutionary spirit and law in America. The trial's end has not diminished the passions surrounding the issues behind it all.

Actually, *Angela Is Happening* does not concern itself with the legal questions surrounding Miss Davis's indictment. A significant point made by Elvie A. Moore is that Angela Davis's innocence or guilt hardly matters at all. Some of the historical figures brought back to life in Miss Moore's play protested injustice through lawful acts of passive resistance and moral persuasion; others resorted to total revolution. When they come to "white" courts of justice, however, the result is always the same: defeat, punishment, and death seem inevitable. Yet after an emotionally-charged trial of more than thirteen weeks, Miss Davis was acquitted.

Miss Moore encompasses these trying social dilemmas with Absurdist theater: the fantasy is angry; the trial is rigged. The judge is a clown, no matter how compassionate, fervent, and rational the defense may be. White law, supported by white society and condoned by the black bourgeoisie, will ultimately triumph. Her documentary drama, which details the roiling passions that continue to seethe in America, is hard brutal theater for hard brutal times. One of the Soledad Brothers, George Jackson, Jonathan's older brother, activist and author† admired by Angela Davis, was killed in San Quentin prison August 21, 1971, during an attempt to escape in which three guards and two other inmates lost their lives. Already a folk ballad has been written about this incident. For years to come the national conscience will be confronted by it. Elvie A. Moore, who has committed herself to writing for freedom and liberation, has molded these challenging contemporary materials into a dramatic warhead.

Angela Is Happening

ACT I

OPENING SCENE: *The* JUDGE sits stage right, on high podium . . . Jury box [*empty*] *is at extreme stage left, on center stage there is a jail cell. Church music plays softly in the background.* JUDGE enters, sits himself on podium, pounds gavel.

JUDGE: THE DEFENDANT WILL COME FORTH. Nicolla Sacco, you have been charged with first degree murder. You are a strike organizer, you have raised money to fight FRAME UPS, YOU HAVE BEEN ARRESTED FOR DEMONSTRATING, you have been active in the defense of the foreign born, you have organized protest meetings. Now it seems that you were also involved in a payroll robbery. There were two guards killed in that robbery; therefore, the state finds you guilty. Do you have anything to say?

SACCO: I would not wish a dog or a snake, the

†*Soledad Brother: The Prison Letters of George Jackson* (Coward, McCann: New York, 1970).

most low and unfortunate creature of the earth to suffer what I suffer. I would not wish to say of them that which I have had to suffer for things that I am not guilty of. I am suffering because I am radical and indeed I am radical ... I have suffered because I am an Italian, and indeed I am an Italian. I have suffered more for my family and for my beloved country than for myself; but I am so convinced to be right that if you could execute me two times and I could be reborn two other times, I would live again to do what I have done already.

JUDGE: The State of Massachusetts sentences you to death. You will be hanged by the neck until dead. [SACCO *is hanged on stage.* JUDGE *turns collar, claps hands, beckons children to him and takes up Bible. Children enter from rear of auditorium singing, clapping hands to very spirited music. Jubilation, the old revival spirit, fills the auditorium. Suddenly a bomb explosion goes off, leaving the four children lying dead at* ANGELA'S *feet.*]

ANGELA: THE DAY OF MY POLITICAL BIRTH BEGAN WITH THE DEATH OF THESE YOUNG FRIENDS ... CYNTHIA WESTLEY, 14; DENISE McNAIR, 11; CAROL ROBERTSON, 14; ADDIE MAY COLLINS, 14.[1]

JURY *enters wearing grotesque makeup. They chant in unison as they remove the bodies of the children.*

JURY: We hold these truths to be self-evident: That all men are created equal; that they are endowed by their Creator with certain unalienable Rights; that among these are Life, Liberty, and the pursuit of Happiness. That, to secure these rights, Governments are instituted among Men, deriving their just powers from the consent of the governed; That, whenever any form of Government becomes destructive of these ends, it is the right of the People to alter or to abolish it, and to institute a new Government, laying its foundations on such principles, and organizing its powers in such form, as to them shall seem most likely to effect their Safety and Happiness.

JUDGE: Order ... order in the Court. We are here today to indict the fugitive, Angela Yvonne Davis.

ACTORS AND AUDIENCE [*Protesting loudly*]: Wait, the trial hasn't begun yet, etc.

JUDGE: It has begun, and I say we have found Angela Davis GUILTY.

ACTORS AND AUDIENCE [*Loud protest*]: No ... No, WE DEMAND TO BE HEARD. WE SPEAK FOR ANGELA, etc.

JUDGE: We will proceed.

ACTORS AND AUDIENCE [*Furiously*]: NO, WE WILL BE HEARD ...

BOURGEOISE JUROR: Judge, in the interest of international relations, I feel that we should listen to them. After all, what would Russia and Red China think if we denied our citizens the right to free speech!

JUDGE [*Nods head*]: All right, it is in the interest of the Court to have a fair and impartial trial. We will allow pertinent testimony from the public at large. Your comments must be clear and to the point, do you understand? Now, we will continue. We have found the defendant guilty of conspiring against us.

JURY: Against us, against us, against us.

JUDGE: We, the Citizens of Marin County charge you with conspiracy to commit murder. [*Becomes very personal and anger builds.*] My very close friend, Judge Harold Haley, was kidnapped at the point of a gun by one of three Black convicts, and the guns they used were registered to the fugitive Davis.

BLACK MILITANT ACTOR: How do we know those were Angela's guns? How do we know that she gave Jonathan those guns?

YOUNG MILITANT ACTOR: Yeah, prove it, man ... you gotta show that Angela talked and plotted the kidnapping with Jonathan, that she was in on it from the gitgo.

JUDGE [*Enraged*]: Contempt, contempt. Get his name. Get his name.

BLACK MILITANT ACTOR [*Yelling*]: PROVE IT. Prove that Angela and Jonathan did more than just breathe together in this funky world. You gotta show she knew what was on Jonathan's mind the day he gave up his life to your bullet.

JUDGE: Silence. We'll prove these charges in due time, without any trouble at all. We have a criminal here. This fugitive is charged with kidnapping and interstate flight; besides that, she's a known Black Communist who by her color and political views has corrupted the youth of this land.

YOUNG MILITANT ACTOR: You're not trying a criminal. She's being tried as a political prisoner and you know it, you slimy, mealy-mouth old liar.

JUDGE [*Enraged*]: Contempt, arrest him. We don't have political prisoners in this country, they're all criminals. Take him out.

---

[1]Youngsters killed in the bombing of a black Sunday School in Birmingham, Alabama, September 15, 1963.

GUARD *takes actor out of audience at gun point, disturbing audience around him. Actor resists and is hit over head with butt of gun and dragged out. Blood drips from the side of his face.*

BLACK MILITANT ACTOR [*Screams*]: Let him alone. You don't have to hit the brother like that, etc.

JURY: He broke the law by wilfully resisting arrest.

ACTORS AND AUDIENCE: Liars . . . Liars . . . Liars . . .

JUDGE [*Pounds wildly with gavel*]: ORDER IN THE COURT . . . ORDER IN THIS COURTROOM.

JURY [*Screaming berserkly*]: CRIMINALLLLLLLLLLLLLLS. CRIM-MIN-ALS.

BLACK MILITANT ACTRESS [*Crying with vehemence*]: What about the Soledad Brothers, Martin Sostre,[2] the Panther 21; You know they're being held captive because of their political views. You've set them up as examples to the rest of the people.

JURY: Let that be a lesson to you.

JUDGE: Be seated and confine your remarks to the issue at hand.

BLACK MILITANT ACTRESS: I am . . . FREE ANGELA.

JUDGE: Another outburst and you will have a cell of your own. Let us continue.

JOHN BROWN[3] [*Standing, stooped shouldered*]: I protest this trial.

JUDGE: John Brown, what is the meaning of this intrusion?

JURY: HAVE YOU COME TO FREE THE SLAVES AGAIN? HAHAHAHAHA.

JOHN BROWN: The cry of distress from the oppressed is my reason and the only thing that prompted me to come here. Moral suasion is hopeless. I don't think the people of these slave states will ever consider the subject of slavery in its true light till some argument is resorted to other than moral suasion. I wish to say, furthermore, that you had better—all of you people, prepare yourselves for a settlement of that question that must come up for settlement sooner than you are prepared for it. I am nearly disposed of now; but this question is still to be settled, this Negro question, I mean; the end of that is not yet. Now, if it is deemed necessary that I should forfeit my blood further with the blood of my children and with the blood of millions in this slave country whose rights are disregarded by wicked, cruel and unjust enactments, I submit. So let it be done.

JURY: Hang him . . . hang him . . . Never another Harper's Ferry. Never another Harper's Ferry.

JUDGE: John Brown, your confessions justify the presumption that you will be found guilty. Even now you are committing a felony by uttering such sentiments as these. It is better you should turn your attention to your eternal future than be dealing in denunciations which can only injure you.

JOHN BROWN: There is an eternity behind and an eternity before, and the little speck in the center, however long, it is but comparatively a minute. The difference between your tenure and mine is trifling, and I therefore tell you to be prepared; I am prepared. We shall free Angela.

JURY: Free—hahahahahaha. Suppose you had every nigger in the United States, John Brown, what would you do with them? To set them free would sacrifice the life of every man in this community.

JOHN BROWN: These are men . . . people, who love and breathe as you and I, only probably more profoundly in the face of such great adversity.

JURY: Fanatic—John Brown is a fanatic . . . HANG HIM . . . HANG HIM HIGH. . . . HANG HIM HIGH.

JUDGE: Tomorrow, Brown, your body will be lying cold on a slab. Take him out.

GUARDS *push and drag* BROWN *out of Courtroom, as he stumbles and falters.*

JURY [*Sings, then laughs heinously*]: John Brown's body lies a-mouldering in the grave. John Brown's body lies a-mouldering in the grave. Hahahahahaha.

ANGELA [*Yelling*]: Free the oppressed . . . freedom.

ACTORS AND AUDIENCE [*Goes wild stomping feet and screaming*]: FREEDOM! FREEDOM! FREEDOM!

JUDGE [*Pounding gavel*]: Silence, you are on trial. Now let us proceed, under California law anyone who aids or abets a major crime is as guilty as the direct participant, and it was a gun regis-

---

[2]Martin Gonzalez Sostre, Afro-Puerto Rican radical bookstore owner in Buffalo, New York, who in 1967 was arrested, tried, and convicted of possession of narcotics, riot, arson, and assault. Sostre asserted that police conspiracy and harassment stemmed from his political activities.

[3]John Brown (1800–1859), militant white abolitionist who organized a guerrilla band and led an attack on a U.S. Government arsenal. Captured and indicted for treason, he was hanged.

tered in your name that was involved in the crime.

BANDAGED WOMAN[4] [*White woman in early forties, dressed pedestrian, her arm and head in bandages, rises and hobbles out to central isle, and yells at* JUDGE]: How did her gun get into the hands of the prison guards? I was there . . . right inside that van. We were all right until the guards opened fire and then there was blood everywhere. They didn't care about us . . . no, they didn't give a damn, so busy worrying about shooting up that colored kid. I was so scared, I yelled, "Don't shoot," but they did . . . our lives meant nothing to them . . . nothing. Look at me [*puts hand to head in agonizing pain.*]
My head hurts, I can't sleep at night. [*Then vicious.*] Who hired those guards? I want to know . . . I've got some rights here. I want to know who was the real participant in this crime.

JUDGE [*Stands up crazed and yells into audience . . .*]: Out of order . . . be seated. Strike that off the record.

JURY [*Yelling like hyenas*]: Sit down, old woman.

BANDAGED WOMAN: I have a right TO SPEAK THE TRUTH. YOU'RE NOT GOING TO TAKE AWAY MY FREEDOM TO SPEAK AND BELIEVE WHAT I WANT. I'M A CITIZEN. I've GOT RIGHTS.

JUDGE: Take her out.

GUARD *pushes woman out roughly.*

FREDERICK DOUGLASS[5] [*Rises to feet*]: I oppose this slavery. I feel at liberty to speak on this subject. I have on my back the marks of the lash; I have four sisters and one brother now under the galling chain, I feel it my duty to cry aloud and spare not. I am not adverse to being kindly regarded by all men; but I am bound, even at the hazard of making a large class of religionists in this country hate me, oppose me and malign me as they have done. I expose slavery in this country, because to expose it, is to kill it. Slavery is one of those monsters of darkness to whom the light of truth is death. Expose slavery, and it dies. All the slaveholder asks of me is silence. They want the hatchway shut down, that the monster may crawl in his den of darkness, crushing human hopes and happiness, destroying the bondman at will, and having no one to reprieve or rebuke him.

JURY [*To* JUDGE]: WATCH HIM, JUDGE, HE'S STIRRING UP THE PEOPLE.

DOUGLASS: I want the slaveholder surrounded, as by a wall of antislavery fire, so that he may see the condemnation of himself and his system glaring down in letters of lights. I want him to feel that the voice of the civilized, aye, and savage world is against him.

JURY [*Prodding the bourgeoise* JUROR, *urging her to speak*]: Say something to him for us.

BOURGEOISE JUROR: Frederick, you are teaching those people to act like savages. The reason we haven't gotten anywhere is because we don't know how to be civilized. We have to learn how to clean our homes, wash our cars, teach our children how to be polite first before we start raving and carrying on about freedom.

BLACK MILITANT ACTOR: Oreo,[6] chocolate covered mint, Aunt Jemina, Julia, Thomasina, etc.

JURY [*Pets* BOURGEOISE]: Good girl, love, good girl.

WELFARE WOMAN: They're using you, Sister Sadie. You ain't no better than nobody else. Don't you know that every time they look at you all they see is black—nigga.

JUDGE: You be quiet, Miss. Now confine your remarks, Douglass, to this fugitive's defense or be quiet.

DOUGLASS: The slave finds more of the milk of human kindness in the bosom of the Indian than in the heart of his Christian master. He loves the man of the Bible and takes refuge with the man of the tomahawk. He rushes from the praying slaveholder to the paws of the bear. He quits the homes of men for the haunt of wolves. He prefers to encounter a life of trial, however bitter; or death, however terrible, to dragging out his existence under the dominion of these kind masters.

ACTORS AND AUDIENCE: Right on, Brother Douglass.

JUDGE [*Enraged*]: Silence! this is a court of law. Another emotional outburst from you people and I shall cite you with contempt of court. You speak of freedom, but freedom comes within the confines of the law.

JURY: We are the law.

DOUGLASS: I will be heard. Mankind is on trial

[4]A hostage in the shoot-out.

[5]Douglas (1817–1895), an escaped slave who established *The North Star,* America's first anti-slavery newspaper, and who published in 1845 his well-known autobiography.

[6]Oreo cookie: black on outside, white on inside.

here today. These men who profess to favor freedom, and yet deprecate agitation, are men who want crops without plowing up the ground. They want rain without thunder and lightning. They want the ocean without the awful roar of its waters. This struggle may be a moral one or it may be a physical one, it may be both moral and physical; but it must be a struggle. Power concedes nothing without a demand. It never did, and it never will. Find out just what people will submit to, and you have found out the exact amount of injustice and wrong which will be imposed upon them, and these will continue till they are resisted with either words or blows, or with both. The limits of tyrants are prescribed by the endurance of those whom they oppress.

ACTORS AND AUDIENCE: Right on . . . tell it like it is.

JURY: He's an agitator. Stop him.

DOUGLASS: We'll make a way for Angela.

JURY [*To* JUDGE]: Stop this agitator! We must have law and order. Dissension leads to anarchy.

JUDGE [*Stern and serious*]: This court will not tolerate Southerners coming up north and stirring up trouble. Outside agitators, Frederick Douglass, are the basis of all our problems. Our country can no longer abide this internal chaos. Southerners coming up north, bringing their local problems with them; while Northerners are going south taking their imaginary grievances with them is giving our country a bad image. We'd have peace if each person just minded his own business.

JURY [*Chants*]: OUTSIDE AGITATOR—OUTSIDE AGITATOR—GO HOME—GO HOME.

DOUGLASS: I have no home. We have drunk to the dregs the bitter cup of slavery. We have worn the heavy yoke; we have sighed beneath our bonds, and writhed beneath the bloody lash. Remember, that we are one. That our cause is one, and that we must help each other, if we would succeed.

ACTORS AND AUDIENCE: Run, Brother Douglass, RUN, RUN. Run, Brother Douglass, RUN, RUN.

JURY: No, we want him dead. We want him dead.

JUDGE: Arrest Douglass.

JURY: Catch him . . . Catch him . . .

GUARDS *chase* DOUGLASS *out.*

HARRIET TUBMAN:[7] Frederick Douglass not gonna let you take him in.

JURY [*To* JUDGE]: That's crazy Harriet Tubman. She's harmless. Let her talk.

TUBMAN: Frederick Douglass will talk about freedom till we all move to TAKE our freedom. People shouldn't have to feel like prisoners and slaves no more, but they do. All my life I felt like the man who was put in a state prison for twenty-five years. All these years he was always thinking of his home, and counting by years, months and days, the time till he should be free and see his family and friends once more. The years roll on, the time of imprisonment is over, the man is free. He leaves the prison gates, he makes his way to his old home, but his old home is not there. The house in which he had dwelt in his childhood had been torn down, and a new one had been put up in its place; his family were gone, their very name was forgotten, there was no one to take him by the hand to welcome him back to life. So it was with me. I had crossed the line of which I had so long been dreaming, I was free, but there was no one to welcome me to de land of freedom, I was a stranger in a strange land, and my home after all was down in the old cabin quarters, with all the ole folks, and my brudders and sister. But to dis solemn resolution I came. I was free, and they should be free also, I would make a home for them in the North, and the Lord helping me, I would bring them all here. I'll make a way also for Angela in this land.

ACTORS AND AUDIENCE: We'll make a way for Angela. We'll make a way for Angela.

BOURGEOISE JUROR: The only thing that's holding us back is ourselves. Even when we get a chance, we don't know what to do with it. Look at Angela. Look at her. She had everything, status, prestige and ends up like some common criminal . . . Oh God, I'm so ashamed.

Sits down, shaking her head in despair

ANGELA [*Raises clenched fist*]: Power, power to the people. The first condition of freedom is the open act of resistance—physical resistance, violent resistance. In that act of resistance, the rudiments of freedom are already present. The violent retaliation signifies much more than the physical act; it is refusal not only to submit

---

[7]Harriet Tubman (1826–1913), called the "Black Moses" of her race, was the leading "conductor' of the Underground Railroad over which countless slaves fled from Southern bondage to freedom.

to floggings, but refusal to accept the definitions of the slavemaster, it is implicitly a rejection of the institution of slavery, a microcosmic effort towards liberation. Freedom is not a fact, but rather something to be fought for; it can exist only through a process of struggle.

ACTORS AND AUDIENCE: Right on!

JURY: You people struggle. Learn to pull yourselves up by your bootstraps.

JURY MEMBER: Like I did!!!

SLAVE: Praise the Lord . . . The Lord will show us the way.

JURY: We are the Lords of this land.

HARRIET TUBMAN: King Jesus is not just the abstract Christ; he is whoever helps the oppressed and the disfranchised, or gives him a right to his life.

JUDGE: Contempt . . . Contempt. Jesus Christ has no place in this courtroom. Get to the point.

TUBMAN: I tell you, you'll see it, and you'll see it soon. My people are free. My people are free. I'm coming up to get you, Angela.

SLAVE [*Following* HARRIET]: I'm coming up there with you. Wait on me, Moses . . . wait.

TUBMAN: No time to wait . . . move along. There's two things I've got a right to and these are death or liberty. One or the other I mean to have. No one will take me back alive. I shall fight for my liberty, and when the time has come for me to go, the Lord will let them kill me.

HARRIET *moves toward stage.*

ANGELA [*Clenching bars and yelling*]: POWER TO THE PEOPLE . . . POWER TO THE PEOPLE—Fight the brave fight, Harriet.

SLAVE [*Beginning to retreat*]: Look at them people. Look at 'em. They's vicious. I don't think I can make this . . . let me go back.

TUBMAN: Dead niggers tell no tales, you go or you die. I never run my train off the track, and I never lost a passenger.

Takes the revolver out of satchel, and points it at slave's head.

JURY: Stop her. She may be crazy, but she's mighty dangerous.

GUARD: No further, old fool.

TUBMAN *falls to the floor, her head bleeding.* GUARDS *drag her out.*

JURY: DEAD NIGGERS TELL NO TALES . . . HAHAHAHAHAHA.

TOM PAINE:[8] STOP this tyranny.

ACTORS AND AUDIENCE: Justice—Justice—Justice. . . .

JUDGE: Order, order in this courtroom.

BLACK MILITANT ACTRESS [*Yells*]: WE DEMAND JUSTICE. We want justice now.

JURY: WE ARE JUSTICE. Our greatest desire is for law, on the streets, in the classrooms, and in the courts of this, Our America.

PAINE: Stop this tyranny . . . stop it.

JURY: HAHAHAHAHAHAHAHA

ALL AMERICAN RACIST: Sit down up there, I can't see the Judge. You people mouthing off are only making things worse for yourselves.

PAINE: I will not sit down. These are the times that try men's souls. Tyranny, like hell, is not easily conquered; yet we have this consolation with us that the harder the conflict, the more glorious the triumph. The circumstances of the world are continually changing and the opinions of men change also; as government is for the living and not for the dead. That which may be thought right in one age, may be found wrong and inconvenient in another. In such cases, who is to decide, the living or the dead?

JUDGE: What is your name?

PAINE: Thomas Paine, your Honor.

JUDGE: Well, Mr. Tommy Plain, your remarks are irresponsible and without any intellectual merit.

JURY: You are decadent. HaHaHaHa

PAINE: The name is Tom Paine, your Honor, and I beg to differ with you.

JUDGE: You may be silent, Painbrain.

JURY: Hahahahahaha. You're hot tonight, your Honor.

PAINE: Is my name uncommon in this part of the country?

JURY: Oh, no, it isn't. Hahahaha

JUDGE: On the contrary, it is unusually common. Now to proceed, this case is not concerned with the state of cadavers. The Court concedes that we are all living, breathing people and as such have decided which laws are for the common good and *we are* the living sitting on this bench.

JURY: Yes, we are the living. We decide who comes and who goes.

PAINE: You have missed the point. There never did, there never will exist a parliament or any

[8]Thomas Paine (1737–1809)—free thinker, patriot, and propagandist in behalf of the American Revolutionary War—was a strong opponent of tyranny in government and orthodoxy in religion.

description of men or any generation of men, in any country, possessed of the right of commanding forever how the world shall be governed or who shall govern it, and therefore, all such clauses in which the makers of them attempt to do what they have neither the right nor the power to execute, are in themselves null and void.

JURY: He is an anarchist. He is an anarchist. He is an anarchist.

JUDGE: You are an anarchist!!

JURY [*Hold their fists in air and yell wildly*]: Silence him . . . Silence him.

JUDGE: Silence, Mr. Paine, another irresponsible outburst and you shall be restrained.

JURY: We'll gag you!

BLACK MILITANT ACTOR: I see your racist attitudes have no regard for color.

JURY: The law is no respecter of people when they all act like niggers!

PAINE: The rights of men are the rights of all generations of men, and cannot be monopolized by any. Government ought to be as much open to improvement as anything which appertains to man, instead of which it has been monopolized from age to age, by the most ignorant and vicious of the human race.

JUDGE: You are in contempt, Mr. Blaine. Now be seated. [GUARD *pushes* PAINE *down into chair.*] This is a court of law, and I warn everyone here that it is to be respected.

JURY: It is time that the people of these states moved to what is right.

BLACK MILITANT ACTRESS: Right wing, you mean.

JURY: The problem is, no matter how you label it, civil disobedience, protest, moral duty or conscience, it's all against the law.

ALL AMERICAN RACIST: Men's law—white men's law. Blacks are still children, not men or women, so how can they demand rights?

SOJOURNER TRUTH:[9] Aren't I a woman? Look at me. Look at my arm. I have ploughed and I have planted. I have gathered harvests into barns. And no man could head me. Aren't I a woman? I could work as much and eat as much as any man when I could get it, and bear the lash as well. I have borne children and seen them sold into slavery and when I cried a mother's grief, none but Jesus heard me. Aren't I a woman? I heard Lincoln read the Emancipation Proclamation into a law that was supposed to be the end of slavery, but we weren't free then and we're not free now. We must get behind the law. Freedom is not in the law. Freedom is in the most perishable of all materials, the human heart.

ALL AMERICAN RACIST: If God had wanted you to have rights, he would have made you white —and a man.

SOJOURNER TRUTH: Where did Christ come from? From God and a woman! Man had nothing to do with it.

JURY: Lock her up. Lock her up. Put her in Jail.

SOJOURNER TRUTH: If you lock me up in the guardhouse I'll make the United States rock like a baby in a cradle. My people must have their rights restored for they have been toiling and yet have no reward. They dwell in so-called freedom's land, a race that has no abiding place, subjected to the whims and wishes of man. It's time to change. Get behind the law, make Angela free.

JUDGE [*Looks at watch and yawns*]: Enough of these emotional statements. Let's get back to the facts. We the citizens of Marin County, charge you, Angela Davis, with conspiracy to commit murder. On August 7, 1970, Jonathan Jackson did willfully enter a courtroom and seize my colleague . . . [*He is interrupted by* BOURGEOISE JUROR *who stands and pronounces charges.*]

BOURGEOISE JUROR: We, the citizens of these United States, charge you, Angela Davis, with having made our schools seed beds of sedition. Academic freedom should not provide a sanctuary for so-called intellectuals to actively work against our country. There is a limit to what is protected by the First Amendment.

ANGELA: I think that if we look around us we see that somehow or another a very small minority of people in this country have all the wealth in their hands and to top that, we don't even see them out working. We do not see them in the factories. We don't see them in the fields. We don't see them using their labor to produce the products which they then present. That tells me that something is wrong. Why is it that the masses of the people in this country have to work eight hours a day every day and somehow or another what they produce goes to some people who are sitting at a country club, on a golf course, and not doing a damn thing. That tells me something is wrong, and it

[9]Sojourner Truth (1797–1885), the first Black woman orator to speak out against slavery, felt herself to be a "Pilgrim of God" with a mission to preach freedom.

tells me that the real criminals in this society are not all the people who populate the prisons across the state, but those people who have stolen the wealth of the world from the people. Those are the criminals. And that means the Rockefellers, the Kennedys, and that means that state that is designed to protect their property, because that's what Nixon is doing, that's what Reagan's doing, that's what they're all doing. And so every time a black child in this city dies, we should indict them for murder, because they're the ones who killed that black child.

ACTORS AND AUDIENCE: Power to the People.

WELFARE WOMAN: RIGHT ON . . . RIGHT ON . . . I'm on welfare . . . been on it for two years. I know what you're talking about. When I first came here, my husband was sick, couldn't work, he'd been in a job accident, so we didn't have no money, no place to sleep. The welfare people put us up near Skid Row for two nights; with the rats and the roaches. My husband died, and I got no help, can't find anyone to take my kids while I work. Even if I find a job, there's no help. Found one as an aid in the hospital and didn't have money to buy a uniform. Worker said there wasn't any money in the budget for it. I get $221 a month for the four of us. This damn system must hate me, can't find no kinda work anymore. What the hell am I to do to live, sleep with any man who'll pop a five into my palm?

ALL AMERICAN RACIST: You being on welfare is just another excuse to drain my pockets. I'm a taxpayer and my taxes are so high that I might have to take my kid out of private school next year. You people are always bellyaching about the system, but you don't do a damn thing to support it. If you get paid for sleeping with every bum that comes along, we shouldn't be held responsible for your lascivious sex habits.

WELFARE WOMAN: You racist! You're not going to make slurs at me. I don't give a shit if you're white or not.

JUDGE: TAKE HER OUT . . . TAKE HER OUT.

GUARDS *push* WOMAN *hit her and drag her out.*

ACTORS AND AUDIENCE [*Going wild*]: Stop the guards. This is tyranny . . . fascism.

JUDGE: This is a court of law, and we will have order if I have to put everyone here in jail. Now we have heard the fugitive's seditious statements, which are indicative of her guilt.

JURY: She's guilty . . . she's guilty. She is guilty.

ANGELA: I now declare before the Court, before the people of this country that I am innocent of all charges which have been leveled against me by the State of California. I am innocent and therefore maintain that my presence in this courtroom today is unrelated to any criminal act.

JURY: You are a murderer . . . MURDERER.

ANGELA: I stand before this Court as a target of a political frame-up which, far from pointing to my culpability, implicates the State of California as an agent of political repression . . . indeed, the state reveals its own role by introducing as evidence against me my participation in the struggles of my people, black people, against the many injustices of this society . . . specifically, my involvement with the Soledad Brothers Defense Committee. The American people have been led to believe that such involvement is Constitutionally protected.

JURY: The Soledad Brothers are guilty . . . Gas 'em, gas 'em.

JUDGE: We will discuss the charges against those men later, the Court will now recess.

ACTORS AND AUDIENCE: We want freedom Now. FREEDOM . . . FREEDOM . . . FREE ANGELA.

JUDGE [*Angry*]: SILENCE. Justice will reign. We owe it to the cause of justice that a trial should be afforded this fugitive. If guilty, she will pay the extreme penalty of that guilt and when thus inflicted by virtue of law will be more efficacious for our protection than any torture to which pure passion would subject her. We will recess until 9:30. This evening we shall sentence Angela . . . ummph, I mean render our verdict. [*Raises fist.*] POWER TO THE COURTS.

JUDGES *and* JURY *rise.* JUDGE *exits, followed by* JURY. JURY *chants Declaration of Independence excerpt ". . . We hold these truths . . ." etc.* GUARDS *remove* ANGELA *from the Court. Freedom song.*

ACT II

Music is playing. ANGELA, *the* JUDGE *and* JURY *are in their places. The stage is dark. Action begins in the audience.*

ALL AMERICAN RACIST: You people, stop getting yourselves upset. Your Angela will get a fair trial. This is a land of law. We're not living in the days of the Klan. Running up and down like that is only gonna make you hot and sweaty.

BLACK MILITANT ACTOR: We're hot and angry all right and sweaty with the tears of injustice. I want my sister free.

ALL AMERICAN RACIST: He'll give her her freedom in due time. You blacks need to know how to live in a civilized culture. We don't live by the rules of the jungle in this country.

DRUNKEN WINO: [*sipping on Thunderbird wine.*] Say, man:

Since you a so-called
master of common sense
let's us talk grass-roots
politics.

Look, don't come
stomping on my culture
'cause I didn't come on
the Mayflower.
I couldn't ride—
there was no place to hide.

Naw, don't be labeling my handiwork.
You bundled it together
trying to smother it out
with your law and order; self
Law for me, 'en order for you.

Naw, man.
GIT the hell offa my culture.
Lemme be.
I walk my walk
'en talk my talk
'cause it pleases me.

I bees happy in a way
You'll never unna stand,
'en don't be knocking me
'cause I'm a mixture
Of a whole heapa thangs.

I got patience,
story, and art
all rolled up into one.

It's mine, all mine
En it's a part of me.
Yeah, Yeah:
You leave my black culture be.

We done slaved more'n 400 years.
It high time some changes made; you'al
Man, we gonna walk tall
in our black culture
AND BE LIKE HE WHO IS
FREEEEEEEEEEEEEEEEEEE[10]

JUDGE: Get that drunken bum out of here. Guards, throw him out.

GUARDS *drag him out roughly.*

DRUNKEN WINO: Don't be messin' with my Thunderbird. You gonna break my bottle. Fool, what's wrong wit' you?

BLACK MILITANT ACTRESS: This ain't gonna get it . . . this just ain't gonna get it, brothers and sisters. You can't get freedom from no broken bottles. If that's the way we're going to try to liberate ourselves, there just ain't no hope for us and that's all there is to it.

MARCUS GARVEY:[11] We should renew our hope and find our strength in each other, my dear sister. We came from a great people. People here remember the day when Egypt, Ethiopia, Timbuctoo towered in their civilizations, towered above Europe, towered above Asia. When Europe was inhabited by a race of cannibals, a race of savage, naked, heathens and pagans, Africa was peopled with a race of cultured black men who were masters in art, science and literature, men who were cultured and refined; men who were Gods. Black men, you were once great; you shall be great again. Lose not courage, lose not faith, go forward. The thing to do is to get organized; keep separated and you will be exploited, robbed, killed. If the world fails to give you consideration, because you are black men, because you are Negroes, four hundred million of you shall, through organization, shake the pillars of the universe and bring down creation, even as Samson brought down the temple upon his head and upon the heads of the Philistines.

ALL AMERICAN RACIST: Let him take his people back to his savage jungles. Christian democracy and white supremacy are the greatest things we've got going and it's gonna stay that way.

JURY: He is a racist . . . expel him.

JUDGE: Marcus, you speak of culture but your acts betray you. I charge you with extortion . . . you may now leave and go to your beloved wild Africa.

JURY: [*mockingly*] HAHAHAHAHAHAHAHA Swing low . . . sweet chariot . . . comin' for to carry YOU home . . . HAHAHAHAHAHAHAHA.

ACTORS AND AUDIENCE: We want freedom . . . FREEDOM . . . FREEDOM . . . FREEDOM.

---

[10]Song "Don't Stomp on My Black Culture" by Joann Bruno. Used by permission.

[11]Marcus A. Garvey (1887–1940), Black nationalist leader and founder of the Universal Negro Improvement Association, argued that the solution of the "Negro Problem" was the return of blacks to Africa.

JUDGE: This court will come to order. This is a court of law, and it will be treated as such. Let us continue. Now, according to the record, on January 18, 1970, a guard at the Soledad prison was found dead. The treatment of these so-called "brothers" has been just, yet this woman was inciting others to disobey the law by deliberately defending these known, hardened criminals.

JACKSON: [*bound in chains*] I don't think it necessary for me to burden myself with listing the strains we've endured. You are intelligent enough to know. At each phase of this long train of tyrannies, we have conducted ourselves in a very meek and civilized manner, with only polite pleas for justice and moderation, all to no avail; but any fool should be able to see that this cannot be allowed to continue. We have remonstrated, supplicated, demonstrated and prostrated ourselves before the feet of our self-appointed administrators. The point of no return in our relationship has long been passed.

ALL AMERICAN RACIST: You're there because you're guilty . . .

JURY: Guilty . . . guilty . . . Our peers found you GUILTY.

JACKSON: [*Angry*] Guilty? What guilt does my manhood speak of? I was captured and brought to prison when I was eighteen years old because they said I couldn't adjust. I was accused of robbing a gas station of seventy dollars. I accepted a deal. I agreed to confess and spare the county court costs in return for a light jail sentence. I confessed but when the time for sentencing came, they tossed me into the penitentiary with one year to life.

JURY: [*Begins chanting*] Life . . . life . . . life . . . life . . .

JACKSON: That was in 1960, I've been here ever since . . . I met Marx, Lenin, Trotsky, Engles and Mann. When I entered prison they redeemed me. I met black guerillas, George "Big Jack" Lewis and James Carr, and many, many others. We attempted to transform the black criminal mentality into a revolutionary mentality.

JURY: Oooohh!

JACKSON: As a result, each of us has been subjected to years of the most vicious reactionary violence by the State. Our mortality rate is almost what you would expect to find in the history of Dachau. Three of us were murdered several months ago by a pig shooting from thirty feet above our heads with a military rifle.

JUDGE: All this is irrelevant . . .

BLACK MILITANT ACTOR: That's right! We ain't nothing but irrelevant to you. Go on and talk, brother.

JACKSON: I'm being tried in Court right now with two other brothers, John Cluchette and Fleeta Drumgo, for the alleged slaying of a prison guard. This charge carries an automatic death penalty for me.

JURY: Life . . . life . . . life . . . life . . .etc.

JACKSON: [*Looks at* JURY] I can't get life; I already have it.

JURY: OHHHHHHHHHHHH . . . DEATH . . . DEATH . . . DEATH . . . DEATH . . .

JUDGE: Guard, take him out.

GUARD: Shut up and come with me. Can't you see they want you dead, nigger?

JACKSON: [*resisting*] I may not live but another five minutes, but it will be five minutes definitely on my terms.

GEORGE *pushes the* GUARD *and scuffle ensues as he is brutally removed from the Court.*

BLACK MILITANT ACTOR: Angela was telling us the truth.

ALL AMERICAN RACIST: We're not trying the Soledad Brothers.

JURY: The Soledad Brothers are guilty. Our peers found them guilty; so Angela is guilty—guilty by association.

JUDGE: Guilty . . . All those who subvert the law are GUILTYYYYYYYY.

WOMAN AT LYNCHING: Guilty . . . Yes, I was there . . . I saw that little boy Emmet Till's[12] body burning. He was guilty, the little bastard whistling at me like that. I saw them take the hot poker and burn out those brown moody eyes till the sockets ran with pus and blood and his tongue yelled out to the hot branding iron. I was there, I saw that black smelly body receive the hot tar and feathers . . . Hahahaha [*completely hysterical now*] as it dripped down that long, thick, groin between his legs . . . CUT IT OFF . . . the crowd yelled . . . RIP IT OFF . . . but it remained there to remind him of what it could have been . . . I saw his thick matted head go under the water that we tied and pulled and tore till the tufts fell on our fingers and we smeared that hair over his bloody body while it waded in the water . . .

[12]Black fourteen-year-old boy lynched by a Southern mob in 1955.

BLACK MILITANT ACTOR: Take her out. Get her out of here.

WOMAN AT LYNCHING: I was there ... hahahahaha. You can't take me out ... 'cause I saw it all ... hahahahahaha.

JUDGE: Shhh, quiet please, somebody get her some water. Remove her from the courtroom.

KENT STATE AND JACKSON UNIVERSITY STUDENTS:

We protest
Injustice
Political prisoners
War
Political prisoners
Racism
Poverty
Political prisoners
Political prisoners

This refrain louder and louder till the audience and students are in a frenzy as the students try to make their way on stage. The GUARDS *at the front of the stage back them off with their guns. There is pandemonium as the students begin to run, some freeze, the* GUARDS *shoot, the students fall in the aisles. Lights are colored in audience. Students die in slow motion, blood dripping on faces and hands.* GUARDS *quickly drag their bodies up the aisles.*

ACTORS AND AUDIENCE: My son ... my daughter ... my brother ... my sister ... my brother ... my sister ...etc.

Music builds, a slow chant, very low goes through the audience.

ALL AMERICAN RACIST: We are in a time when things are a little bit difficult, but that's just part of the way democracy works. We've had peace and prosperity before and we must continue to work towards greater peace and prosperity in the future.

SUSAN B. ANTHONY:[13] What is this about "restoring our country to peace and prosperity, to the blessed conditions which existed before the war?" I ask you, what sort of peace, what sort of prosperity have we had? Since the first slave ship sailed up the James River with its human cargo and there on the soil of the Old Dominion the first slave was sold to the highest bidder, we have had nothing but war. When that pirate captain landed on the shores of Africa and there kidnapped the first Negro and fastened the first manacle, the struggle between that captain and that Negro was the commencement of the terrible war in the midst of which we are today. Between the slave and the master there has been war and war only. This is but a new form of it. No, no, we ask for no return of the old conditions. We demand something better. We have been bound, in case of insurrection, to go to the aid, not of those struggling for liberty, but of the oppressors. It was politicians who made this pledge and who have renewed it from year to year. Woman must now assume her God-given responsibilities and make herself what she was clearly designed to be, the educator of the race. Had the women of this land studied to know and to teach their sons the law of justice, they would not now be called upon to offer the loved of their households to the bloody Moloch of war.

ALL AMERICAN RACIST: You should be home in bed, baby, and not worrying your little head about a thing.

ANTHONY: Bed is for the likes of you, and a better world for the strong, like me.

ALL AMERICAN RACIST: Hahahahaha, a spitfire. That's real cute! You should be home making babies instead of worrying about some blacks. Let the black women do their own crusading. Our women are ladies, not washwomen.

W.E.B. DUBOIS:[14] You will not put our women down. The uplift of woman is, next to the problem of the color line and peace movement, our greatest modern cause. In other years woman's way was clear; to be beautiful, to be petted, to bear children. The revolt of white women against this preordained destiny has in latter days reached splendid proportions, but it is the revolt of an aristocracy of brains and ability—the middle class and rank and file still plod the appointed path, paid by the almost mocking homage of men. Some few women are born free, and some through insult and scarlet letters achieve freedom; but, our women in black had freedom thrust contemptuously upon them. With that freedom they are buying an untrammeled independence and dear as is the price they pay for it, it will in the end be worth every taunt and groan. I honor the women of my race. No other women on earth could have emerged from the Hell of force and temptation which once engulfed and

[13]Susan B. Anthony (1820–1906), one of the earlier champions of women's rights who, in 1869, organized the National Woman Suffrage Association.

[14]W.E.B. DuBois (1868–1963), black scholar, teacher, writer who helped found the NAACP and who published at least two influential works: *The Souls of Black Folk* (1903) and *Black Reconstruction* (1935).

still surrounds black women in America with half the modesty and womanliness that they retain. I have never known more sweetly feminine, more unswervingly loyal, more desperately earnest and more instinctively pure in soul than the daughters of my black mothers.

JUDGE: Mr. Dubois, your remarks are subversive and are to be stricken from the record. Be seated.

JURY: Sit down, Pinky. Hahahahaha.

ALL AMERICAN RACIST: That's right. You've got to learn some respect. And stay in your place.

BLACK MILITANT ACTRESS: Our place has been picking your cotton, suckling your babies, mopping your floors, but we're tired and we're going to make a place up front. You hear, Peckerwood?

DUBOIS: This is the America the Negro knows. His fight here is a fight to the finish. Either he wins or he dies. If he wins it will be no subterfuge or evasion or amalgamation. He will enter modern civilization in America as a black man on terms of unlimited equality with any white man or he won't enter it at all.

JURY: The point is, she's black, she's militant, she's intelligent. She's a criminallllllllllll.

FRANCES E. HARPER:[15] She's a courageous sister. You're trying to dig graves for our leaders.

ACTORS AND AUDIENCE: Teach on, poet Harper.

JURY: We'll make a grave for you.

HARPER: Make me a grave wher'er you will,
In a lowly paling or a lofty hill,
Make it among earth's humblest graves
But not in a land where men are slaves.

JURY: This is a land of freedom. Slavery is a dead issue. You are insane, woman.

HARPER:

I could not rest if around my grave
I heard the steps of a trembling slave;
His shadow above my silent tomb
Would make it a place of fearful gloom

I could not rest if I heard the tread
Of a coffle[16] gang to a shambles led,
And the mother's shreik of wild despair
Rise like a curse on the trembling air.

I could not sleep if I saw the lash
Drinking her blood at each fearful gash,
And I saw her babes torn from her breast
Like trembling doves from their parents' nest.

JURY: Ooh, ugly—take her out.

HARPER:

I would sleep, dear friends, where bloated might
Can rob no man of his dearest right;
My rest shall be calm in any grave
Where none can call his brother a slave.

I ask no monument, proud and high
To arrest the gaze of the passerby;
All that my yearning spirit craves
Is bury me not in a land of slaves.

JUDGE: Get this maniac out of here.

GUARD *grabs* FRANCES, *she resists. A second* GUARD *runs to assist. The two* GUARDS *lift* FRANCES *up in the air and carry her out. She yells the last stanza of the poem as they trudge out.*

HARPER: [*repeats until she is out of hearing distance*]

ALL THAT MY YEARNING SPIRIT CRAVES IS BURY ME NOT IN A LAND OF SLAVES . . .

JURY: She's insane . . . hahahahaha.

BLACK MILITANT ACTOR: Take your hands off her. Frances Harper is cursed because of her color and talent.

JURY: [*vicious*] Bury her talent in the ground.

BLACK MILITANT ACTOR: Are all Blacks guilty? Are you crucifying her because of her color?

ALL AMERICAN RACIST: It's not her color anyone here is concerned with; it's the fact that she doesn't have the American Spirit. If you don't love this country GODDAMMIT, why don't you leave it?

BLACK MILITANT ACTOR: Yeah, well, we're gonna leave it and we're gonna take your ass with us . . . [*Heads for racist, racist moves away.*]

MALCOLM X:[17] No, we won't leave it because we've paid for it with the blood of our fathers. We don't love it because this so-called American Spirit dies when you're born just another black child, to walk another bleak and heartbroken mile down a rickety, mysterious, one-way road called life. Yes, I was born in poverty, but my trials and tribulations and denials came from being black in this prejudiced, funky, pit of hell called America, highly infested with this sick, inhuman, bloodsucking beast, the devil himself called whiteman. As a black child I was then known as Malcolm Little, and

---

[15]Frances Ellen Watkins Harper (1825–1911), black lyric poet and lecturer who captured Negro speech patterns in her work. *Poems on Miscellaneous Subjects* (1854) went through many popular editions.

[16]A group of slaves chained together (as when travelling).

[17]Malcolm X, assassinated in 1965, was a Balck Nationalist leader and founder of the Organization of Afro-American Unity.

through innocence and ignorance I managed to survive the nightmare-like terror of having uncles lynched and beheaded by this horrible beast. I, a black child, was forced to endure the pain and agony that comes from having a father shot in the back and his body placed on the railroad tracks to be mutilated almost beyond human recognition. Yes, at an early age I came in contact with this beast, the incompetent machine, who brainwashes himself as being superior by looking at blackfolks as being things, property to be bought and sold at will. While his woman under the title of Social Worker, with her false smile and deceptive eyes, planted lies in my head. Lies, which destroyed our family and made me think my mother was insane; when it was them and their funky ideas that were sick and corrupted. It was these same little lies, planted by so-called legality and cultivated by violence, I had come to witness as a child. These lies grew as I grew and these same little lies became monstrous lies which subconsciously kept me in line and made my life an easy prey for this white man's corruption. For as I grew up and began to mature, I started putting konk in my hair. My pride became a Cadillac, my status quo a white woman. Then I started dropping bennies and reds, shooting smack into my veins due to the lies he had instilled into my brain. These values made me swindle my black brothers and misuse my sisters, because I had become a typical house nigger. I acquired street names such as Flashy Red, Little Red, the Gamer, me, a fool thinking I was cool; but it was these lies, these same lies that led me to the penitentiary, because I didn't know my real enemy. But while there I didn't play checkers with my time, I pulled his lies out of my mind and planted fresh seeds of truth and got myself together, and doing this I forgot about legality and started looking at reality and found I wasn't the criminal—HE WAS. As I came to myself, I dropped my slave name and became Malcolm X, a Muslim, a freedom fighter, a FIELD NIGGER. Now, I said all that, all sisters and brothers, just to say this: We must forget about legality and look at reality! The Mosque wasn't shot up in the sixties because we were Muslims or lawbreakers. The Panthers aren't attacked because they are lawbreakers or Panthers; and Angela isn't being persecuted because she's Communist or because she's guilty of a rogue crime, but because she's Black and knows her real enemy and refuses to lie to her people. I know she's not guilty. You know she's not guilty; but the white man's laws are like tin—they bend, like rubber—they stretch, like rope—they hang, whenever he wants them to. But to me, to you they are a sentence of death. This stonehearted, merciless, unjust beast must be stopped, because Angela must be saved, Angela must be saved. She must go free.

ACTORS AND AUDIENCE: Free her. Free Angela.

ALL AMERICAN RACIST: This is America. We can't let Criminals run loose in the streets. You Blacks, Chicanos, smelling Yippies are the limit. We gonna clean this country up, if it's the last thing we do.

H. RAP BROWN[18]: What is this? This country says, "Yes, you may be Black, but, you must be American," which means we are as responsible for oppression as whites . . . This country says, "Yeah, you may have Black heroes; but we must approve of them." Do they publicize Negroes who have been beneficial to this country? The tactic of co-opting is being used to its fullest. Today niggers are tomming and don't even know they're tomming. We must say as Fidel Castro says, "No liberalism whatsoever. A revolutionary people, a political people, a strong people . . . this is what is needed throughout these years."

ACTORS AND AUDIENCE:

Right on, Rap.
Rap, brother Rap.
Tell it like it is.

CHE[19]: Arise, you sleeping heads and free Angela. The revolution is made by man, but man must forge his revolutionary spirit from day to day. It does not matter if these are the times when the bad winds blow, when the pirate attacks are unleashed against us and other countries of the world. If we are able to fulfill our duty and place at the disposal of this struggle whatever little of ourselves we are permitted to give, our lives, our sacrifices; and if some

---

[18]H. Rap Brown, advocate of Black Power, former Chairman of the Student Nonviolent Coordination Committee (SNCC) and Minister of Justice of the Black Panther Party, published the manifesto *Die Nigger Die!* (Dial Press: New York, 1969).

[19]Ernesto (Ché) Guevara (1928–1967), Argentine-born Cuban revolutionary leader and Communist whose guerrilla warfare strategies played an important role in Premier Fidel Castro's success. Guevara was killed by Bolivian soldiers while leading rebels against the government.

day we be known that we have measured the scope of our actions and that we only consider ourselves elements in the great army of the people, but that we are proud of having learned from the Cuban revolution and from its maximum leader, the great lesson emanating from his attitude. What do the dangers or the sacrifices of a man or of a nation matter when the destiny of humanity is at stake?

ACTORS AND AUDIENCE: Freedom . . . Freedom . . . We want Freedom.

MARTIN LUTHER KING[20]: [*standing*] I say there is another way. Yes, there is another way to climb the top of the mountain. We can do it through love. Let us love together. There is a power in this way. I've firmly planted in the roots of my mind and heart and soul, the principles and teaching of our savior Jesus Christ and practice, with all sincerity, the art of loving my enemy as I do myself. I know the same questions which plague my father have plagued me when my children ask, "Daddy, why do white folks treat colored folks so mean?" I have marched up freedom trails, I've seen little children attacked by trained vicious dogs, set on in the name of the law. I've seen bombs thrown in black churches by white Christians, I've been jailed for exercising my right of freedom of speech, I've been jailed for making a peaceful assembly in a country that supposedly guarantees these rights to every man, but I know I wasn't jailed for breaking the law, but I was jailed for being a thinking honest black man. For being a fighter for justice! I know we all begin to ask, "How long will we have to live with this system?" And I know we're all asking, "How long will prejudice blind the vision of men, darken their understanding and drive bright-eyed wisdom from her sacred throne?" Yes, when will wounded justice, lying prostrate on the streets of our cities, be lifted from this dust of shame to reign supreme among the children of men? When will the radiant star of hope be plunged against the nocturnal bosom of this lonely night, and pluck from weary souls the manacles of death and chain of fear? How long will justice be crucified and truth buried, how long? All I can answer—not long—not long! Today, we're going to transform this courtroom from a dungeon of hell and shame to a peaceful heaven of freedom and human dignity. Now is the time to make real the promises of democracy. Now is the time to rise from the dark and desolate valley of racial prejudice to the sunlit path of racial justice. Now is the time to lift our nation from the quicksands of racial injustice to the solid rock of brotherhood. I know there is a way we can move together. I do feel and know within my heart and mind that sister Angela Davis is another victim of this country's shrewd, intricate political plots and we will not allow her to face the atrocities that Medgar Evers[21] and Emmet Till had to face. The whirlwinds of revolt will continue to shake the foundations of our nation until the bright day of justice emerges. We can never be satisfied as long as the Negro is the victim of the unspeakable horrors of police brutality. No, no, we are not satisfied, and will not be satisfied, until justice rolls down, running like waters and righteousness like a mighty stream. I beg you now in this hour of gloom, I appeal to your conscience and heart and soul in the name of justice, FREE ANGELA, FREE ANGELA. "This is our hope. This is the faith with which we come to this trial today. With this faith we will be able to hew out of the mountain of despair a stone of hope. With this faith we will be able to transform the jangling discords of our nation into a beautiful symphony of brotherhood. With this faith we will struggle together to free Angela, stand up for freedom together, knowing that we will be free one day." This is our challenge. This is the way we must grapple with this dilemma. So I say to you today, "walk together chullen, don't ya git wearied; there is a great camp meeting in the promised land today!" We Americans have long aspired to the glories of freedom while we compromise with prejudice and servitude. Today the Negro is fighting for a finer America, and we will inevitably win the majority of nations to this side because our hard-won heritage of freedom is ultimately more powerful than our traditions of cruelty and injustice. We shall overcome because the arc of the moral universe is long but it bends toward justice: "truth crushed to earth shall rise again." We shall overcome because James Russell Lowell was right, "truth forever on the scaffold, wrong forever on the throne; yet that scaffold

[20]Martin Luther King (1929–1968), minister, preacher of non-violence, organizer of bus boycott and freedom marches, winner of the Nobel Peace Prize in 1964, was assassinated April 4, 1968.

[21]Southern black political leader, Secretary of the NAACP in Mississippi, killed in 1963 by a sniper.

sways the future, and, behind the dim unknown, standeth God within the shadow, keeping watch above his own." We shall overcome . . . we shall overcome because the Bible is right, no lie can live forever, you shall reap what you sow. We shall overcome, because deep in my heart I do believe that we shall overcome: and with this faith we will get out and adjourn the councils of despair, and bring bright new light into the dark chambers of pessimism and we will be able to rise from the fatigues of despair to the buoyance of hope . . . so I say to you today, let us set Sister Davis free and in doing so you shall free yourselves; then this will be a greater America and this will be the day when she can say, "Free at last; free at last, thank God Almighty, I'm free at last." Let us all stand and sing, "We shall overcome."

ACTORS AND AUDIENCE: Yes, ah yes. Free at last.

MARTIN: Let us all sing . . . We shall overcome.

Actors and audience begin to sing and hum, "We Shall Overcome."

MALCOLM X: Whoever heard of angry revolutionaries harmonizing, "WE SHALL OVERCOME SOMEDAY," while tripping and swaying along arm-in-arm with the very people they are supposed to be angrily revolting against?

JURY: Malcolm, you are full of violence and hate.

MALCOLM X: If you notice, the people who are sicking the dogs on the Black people are never accused of violence; they are never accused of hate. It is only when the Black man begins to explode and erupt after he has had too much that they say that the Black man is violent, and as long as these whites are putting out a doctrine that paves the way to justify their mistreatment of Blacks, this is never called hate.

MARTIN: We'll go our separate ways. Everybody sing "We Shall Overcome" as we free our sister Angela.

MALCOLM: We'll release our sister Angela now. Brothers, sisters, follow me.

There is a series of shots. Malcolm and Martin fall. Screams! Total darkness. RAP BROWN *exits during excitement.*

BLACK MILITANT ACTOR: Where's Rap . . . Where's Rap?

ACTORS AND AUDIENCE: Justice . . . Justice . . . Justice . . .

ANGELA: It is obvious that democracy in America is helplessly deteriorated when the Courts, allegedly guardians of the right of the people, have been enlisted to play an active role in the genocidal war against Black people. We must reject the right of the Courts to further oppress us. The only way we can get justice is to demand it and to create a mass movement which will use all means at our disposal to secure justice for our people. This is the only way we can expect to free all our brothers and sisters held in captivity in America's dungeons. This is the only way we can expect to ultimately gain total liberation.

NAT TURNER:[22] REBEL YOU NIGGERS. GOD ALMIGHTY HAS SENT ME, AND THE TIME IS NOW.

ACTORS AND AUDIENCE: Nat is here . . . Nat is here . . .

TURNER: If I had a second chance, even if I knew it meant certain death, even if I knew I could be free and safe if I ran away right now. I would smite another blow for my poor people. I would smite the rock with such a force that its sounds would reach a thousand miles. If we wait for the whites to give us our God-given right, we will wait until the sun grows cold. If we wait until the whites decide to treat black people like human beings, we will wait until the ocean is dry. The Black man will only get as much as he is willing to fight for. For a man to be free he must be ready to die for that same freedom.

SLAVE: [*Runs through aisles and out door.*] Nat Turner's getting the slaves together. Nat Turner's getting the slaves together.

JUDGE: Hang him!

GUARDS *take* NAT *and place him on the scaffold right off stage.*

ACTORS AND AUDIENCE: Freedom . . . Freedom . . . We want Freedom.

BLACK MILITANT ACTOR: We have seen enough. For too long we have been witnesses to the historical genocide of our people. For too long we have sat and waited for liberation while our leaders' blood has covered this fallowed earth. It is we the people that must break the tyrant's whip and move towards our own liberation.

[22]Nat Turner (1800–1831), leader in 1831 of an unsuccessful slave rebellion in Virginia, was captured in The Dismal Swamp and hanged.

We have the power together. Feel the strength that flows from our veins into each other and unites us into one People. WE THE PEOPLE WILL FREE OUR SISTER ANGELA NOW.

Rise up.
Free yourselves.
Free Angela.

ACTORS AND AUDIENCE: [*Move towards stage chanting*] Power to the people! Power to the people! Power to the people!

TO BE CONTINUED!!!

Nigger, Negro, Black

Eugene O'Neill

(1888–1953)

Only in very recent years has the concept of Negritude and Black Power begun to emerge as a literary force in the professional American theater. From the year 1858 when ex-slave William Wells Brown began to give public readings of his play *The Escape* until 1959 when *A Raisin in the Sun* by Lorraine Hansberry began a Broadway run of 530 performances, the black dramatist had been almost totally upstaged, not only by his white counterpart, but also by stereotyped "coon" shows in the tradition of "minstrel" theater vaudeville. Only on rare occasions would a white dramatist attempt to give a serious and, to his view, realistic portrait of the life and psychology of the American Negro. And even then, it was, of course, for white audiences. Edward Brewster Sheldon (1886–1946), a minor playwright whose forte was melodrama, produced *The Nigger* (1909), which shows the moral and spiritual complications that follow the shocking discovery of Negro blood in the ancestry of a prominent Southern politician. Subsequently, this theme of "crossing-over" or "passing" became cliché.

In 1921, Eugene O'Neill, the Nobel Prize winner (1936) with whose work critics date the beginnings of modern drama in the United States, began to explore the stage possibilities of the black and produced his famous expressionistic drama *The Emperor Jones.* Four years later O'Neill brought to the stage *All God's Chillun Got Wings,* a naturalistic picture of miscegenation and the psychological problems that may stem from it. Arthur and Barbara Gelb, authors of the definitive biography of O'Neill, note: "Treating a marriage between a Negro and a White in stage terms, without giving a thought to the incendiary reaction this was bound to evoke was something only O'Neill would have dared attempt in 1923."

The disinherited, black and white, appealed to O'Neill as dramatic materials, and a number of his famous plays reflect this interest. In *Beyond the Horizon,* which won a Pulitzer Prize in 1920, the playwright portrays poverty down on the farm. *Anna Christie* (1921 and another Pulitzer Prize winner) is a waterfront drama about a prostitute. *The Hairy Ape* (1922) studies the bizarre life of Yank, a stupid, brutal stoker, deep in the infernal hold of a ship; having adapted himself to the animalized environment of his hellish world, when he enters the more genteel atmosphere of the upper earth, Yank recognizes himself as the ultimate disinherited, kin only to the ape in the zoo. *Desire Under the Elms* (1924) traces the disintegration of a rural New England family through greed, sensuality, and, finally, murder. O'Neill's strategy included the portrayal of distinctive characters as grotesque. This technique was made famous by Sherwood Anderson in *Winesburg, Ohio* (1919), a collection of tales in which each character embodies with monomaniacal passion a single viewpoint, theory, or idea.

In *All God's Chillun* O'Neill tried to present a sympathetic picture of the Negro contrasted with the degenerate poor white of the urban ghetto. Jim Harris —bright, ambitious, and black—remains from childhood deeply in love with Ella Downey, who marries him only after she is deserted by Mickey, a white thug. Ella is Jim's intellectual inferior; she simultaneously loves him and hates his blackness; she fears being ostracized by the white bigots of the racially mixed slum neighborhood. At length, the psychological explosions of the "mixed" marriage make for bitter disappointment and chaotic failure. Paradoxially, love and commitment lead to a destructive, anguish-filled relationship. O'Neill, simply but passionately, poses the question, Why? Despite his romanticizing of Jim and Ella and tumbling at times into the theatrical melodrama prevalent on the stage of the 1920's, O'Neill, from the white side of the line, succeeds in making a strong social statement that provokes powerful emotions.

All God's Chillun Got Wings

Characters

JIM HARRIS
MRS. HARRIS, *his mother*
HATTIE, *his sister*
ELLA DOWNEY
SHORTY
JOE
MICKEY
Whites and Negroes

ACT I

SCENE I: *A corner in lower New York. Years ago. End of an afternoon in Spring.*

SCENE II: *The same. Nine years later. End of an evening in Spring.*

SCENE III: *The same. Five years later. A night in Spring.*

SCENE IV: *The street before a church in the same ward. A morning some weeks later.*

ACT II

SCENE I: *A flat in the same ward. A morning two years later.*

SCENE II: *The same. At twilight some months later.*

SCENE III: *The same. A night some months later.*

ACT I

Scene I

A corner in lower New York, at the edge of a colored district. Three narrow streets converge. A triangular building in the rear, red brick, four-storied, its ground floor a grocery. Four-story tenements stretch away down the skyline of the two streets. The fire escapes are crowded with people. In the street leading left, the faces are all white; in the street leading right, all black. It is hot Spring. On the sidewalk are eight children, four boys and four girls. Two of each sex are white, two black. They are playing marbles. One of the black boys is JIM HARRIS. *The little blonde girl, her complexion rose and white, who sits behind his elbow and holds his marbles is* ELLA DOWNEY. *She is eight. They play the game with concentrated attention for a while. People pass, black and white, the Negroes frankly participants in the spirit of Spring, the whites laughing constrainedly, awkward in natural emotion. Their words are lost. One hears only their laughter. It expresses the difference in race. There are street noises—the clattering roar of the Elevated, the puff of its locomotives, the ruminative lazy sound of a horse-car, the hooves of its team clacking on the cobbles. From the street of the whites, a high-pitched, nasal tenor sings the chorus of "Only a Bird in a Gilded Cage." On the street of the blacks a Negro strikes up the chorus of: "I Guess I'll Have to Telegraph My Baby." As this singing ends, there is laughter, distinctive in quality, from both streets. Then silence. The light in the street begins to grow brilliant with the glow of the setting sun. The game of marbles goes on.*

WHITE GIRL: [*tugging at the elbow of her brother*]. Come on, Mickey!

HER BROTHER: [*roughly*]. Aw, gwan, youse!

WHITE GIRL: Aw right den. You kin git a lickin' if you wanter. [*Gets up to move off*].

HER BROTHER: Aw, git off de eart'!

WHITE GIRL: De old woman'll be madder'n hell!

HER BROTHER: [*worried now*]. I'm comin', ain't I? Hold your horses.

BLACK GIRL [*to a black boy*]: Come on, you Joe. We gwine git frailed too, you don't hurry.

JOE: Go long!

MICKEY: Bust up de game, huh? I gotta run! [*Jumps to his feet*].

OTHER WHITE BOY: Me, too! [*Jumps up*].

OTHER BLACK GIRL: Lawdy, it's late!

JOE: Me for grub!

MICKEY: [*to* JIM HARRIS]. You's de winner, Jim Crow. Yeh gotta play tomorrer.

JIM: [*readily*]. Sure t'ing, Mick. Come one, come all! [*He laughs*].

OTHER WHITE BOY: Me, too! I gotta git back at yuh.

JIM: Aw right, Shorty.

LITTLE GIRL: Hurry! Come on, come on! [*The six start off together. Then they notice that* JIM *and* ELLA *are hesitating, standing awkwardly and shyly together. They turn to mock*].

JOE: Look at dat Jim Crow! Land sakes, he got a gal! [*He laughs. They all laugh*].

JIM: [*ashamed*]. Ne'er mind, you Chocolate!

MICKEY: Look at de two softies, will yeh! Mush! Mush! [*He and the two other boys take this up*].

LITTLE GIRLS: [*pointing their fingers at* ELLA]. Shame! Shame! Everybody knows your name! Painty Face! Painty Face!

ELLA: [*hanging her head*]. Shut up!

LITTLE WHITE GIRL: He's been carrying her books!

COLORED GIRL: Can't you find nuffin' better'n him, Ella? Look at de big feet he got!

She laughs. They all laugh. JIM *puts one foot on top of the other, looking at* ELLA.

ELLA: Mind yer own business, see!

She strides toward them angrily. They jump up and dance in an ecstasy, screaming and laughing.

ALL: Found yeh out! Found yeh out!

MICKEY: Mush-head! Jim Crow de Sissy! Stuck on Painty Face!

JOE: Will Painty Face let you hold her doll, boy?

SHORTY: Sissy! Softy!

ELLA *suddenly begins to cry. At this they all howl.*

ALL: Cry-baby! Cry-baby! Look at her! Painty Face!

JIM: [*suddenly rushing at them, with clenched fists, furiously*]. Shut yo' moufs! I kin lick de hull of you!

They all run away, laughing, shouting, and jeering, quite triumphant now that they have made him, too, lose his temper. He comes back to ELLA, *and stands beside her sheepisly, stepping on one foot after the other. Suddenly he blurts out:*

Don't bawl no more. I done chased 'em.

ELLA: [*comforted, politely*]. T'anks.

JIM: [*swelling out*]. It was a cinch. I kin wipe up de street wid any one of dem. [*He stretches out his arms, trying to bulge out his biceps*]. Feel dat muscle!

ELLA: [*does so gingerly—then with admiration*]. My!

JIM: [*protectingly*]. You mustn't never be scared when I'm hanging round, Painty Face.

ELLA: Don't call me that, Jim—please!

JIM [*contritely*]: I didn't mean nuffin'. I didn't know you'd mind.

ELLA: I do—more'n anything.

JIM: You oughtn't to mind. Dey's jealous, dat's what.

ELLA: Jealous? Of what?

JIM: [*pointing to her face*]. Of dat. Red 'n' white. It's purty.

ELLA: I hate it!

JIM: It's purty. Yes, it's—it's purty. It's—outa sight!

ELLA: I hate it. I wish I was black like you.

JIM: [*sort of shrinking*]. No you don't. Dey'd call you Crow, den—or Chocolate—or Smoke.

ELLA: I wouldn't mind.

JIM: [*somberly*]. Dey'd call you nigger sometimes, too.

ELLA: I wouldn't mind.

JIM: [*humbly*]. You wouldn't mind?

ELLA: No, I wouldn't mind. [*An awkward pause*].

JIM: [*suddenly*]. You know what, Ella? Since I been tuckin' yo' books to school and back, I been drinkin' lots o' chalk 'n' water three times a day. Dat Tom, de barber, he tole me dat make me white, if I drink enough. [*Pleadingly*] Does I look whiter?

ELLA: [*comfortingly*]. Yes—maybe—a little bit—

JIM: [*trying a careless tone*]. Reckon dat Tom's a liar, an' de joke's on me! Dat chalk only makes me feel kinder sick inside.

ELLA: [*wonderingly*]. Why do you want to be white?

JIM: Because—just because—I lak dat better.

ELLA: I wouldn't. I like black. Let's you and me swap. I'd like to be black. [*Clapping her hands*] Gee, that'd be fun, if we only could!

JIM: [*hesitatingly*]. Yes—maybe—

ELLA: Then they'd call me Crow, and you'd be Painty Face!

JIM: They wouldn't never dast call you nigger, you bet! I'd kill 'em!

A long pause. Finally she takes his hand shyly. They both keep looking as far away from each other as possible.

ELLA: I like you.

JIM: I like you.

ELLA: Do you want to be my feller?

JIM: Yes.

ELLA: Then I'm your girl.

JIM: Yes. [*Then grandly*] You kin bet non o' de gang gwine call you Painty Face from dis out! I lam' 'em good!

The sun has set. Twilight has fallen on the street. An organ grinder comes up to the corner and plays "Annie Rooney." They stand hand-in-hand and listen. He goes away. It is growing dark.

ELLA: [*suddenly*]. Golly, it's late! I'll git a lickin'!

JIM: Me, too.

ELLA: I won't mind it much.

JIM: Me nuther.

ELLA: See you going to school tomorrow?

JIM: Sure.

ELLA: I gotta skip now.

JIM: Me, too.

ELLA: I like you, Jim.

JIM: I like you.

ELLA: Don't forget.

JIM: Don't you.

ELLA: Good-by.

JIM: So long. [*They run away from each other—then stop abruptly, and turn as at a signal*].

ELLA: Don't forget.

JIM: I won't, you bet!

ELLA: Here! [*She kisses her hand at him, then runs off in frantic embarrassment*].

JIM: [*overcome*]. Gee! [*Then he turns and darts away as*

THE CURTAIN FALLS

Scene II

The same corner. Nine years have passed. It is again late Spring at a time in the evening which immediately follows the hour of SCENE ONE. *Nothing has changed much. One street is still all white, the other all black. The fire escapes are laden with drooping human beings. The grocery store is still at the corner. The street noises are now more rhythmically mechanical, electricity having taken the place of horse and steam. People pass, white and black. They laugh as in* SCENE ONE. *From the street of the whites the high-pitched nasal tenor sings: "Gee, I Wish That I Had a Girl," and the Negro replies with "All I Got Was Sympathy." The singing is followed again by laughter from both streets. Then silence. The dusk grows darker. With a spluttering flare the arc-lamp at the corner is lit and sheds a pale glare over the street. Two young roughs slouch up to the corner, as tough in manner as they can make themselves. One is the* SHORTY *of* SCENE ONE; *the other the* NEGRO, JOE. *They stand loafing. A boy of seventeen or so passes by, escorting a girl of about the same age. Both are dressed in their best, the boy in black with stiff collar, the girl in white.*

SHORTY: [*scornfully*]. Hully cripes! Pipe who's here. [*To the girl, sneeringly*] Wha's matter, Liz? Don't yer recernize yer old fr'ens?

GIRL: [*frightenedly*] Hello, Shorty.

SHORTY: Why de glad rags? Goin' to graduation? [*He tries to obstruct their way, but, edging away from him, they turn and run*].

JOE: Har-har! Look at dem scoot, will you! [SHORTY *grins with satisfaction*].

SHORTY: [*looking down other street*]. Here comes Mickey.

JOE: He won de semi-final last night easy?

SHORTY: Knocked de bloke out in de thoid.

JOE: Dat boy's suah a-comin'! He'll be de champeen yit.

SHORTY: [*judicially*]. Got a good chanct—if he leaves de broads alone. Dat's where he's wide open.

MICKEY *comes in from the left. He is dressed loudly, a straw hat with a gaudy band cocked over one cauliflower ear. He has acquired a typical "pug's" face, with the added viciousness of a natural bully. One of his eyes is puffed, almost closed, as a result of his battle the night before. He swaggers up.*

BOTH: Hello, Mickey.

MICKEY: Hello.

JOE: Hear you knocked him col'.

MICKEY: Sure. I knocked his block off. [*Changing the subject*]. Say. Seen 'em goin' past to de graduation racket?

SHORTY: [*with a wink*]. Why? You int'rested?

JOE: [*chuckling*]. Mickey's gwine roun' git a good conduct medal.

MICKEY: Sure. Dey kin pin it on de seat o' me pants. [*They laugh*] Listen. Seen Ella Downey goin'?

SHORTY: Painty Face? No, she ain't been along.

MICKEY: [*with authority*]. Can dat name, see! Want a bunch o' fives in yer kisser? Den nix! She's me goil, understan'?

JOE: [*venturing to joke*]. Which one? Yo' number ten?

MICKEY: [*flattered*]. Sure. De real K. O. one.

SHORTY: [*pointing right—sneeringly*]. Gee! Pipe Jim Crow all dolled up for de racket.

JOE: [*with disgusted resentment*]. You mean tell me dat nigger's graduatin'?

SHORTY: Ask him.

JIM HARRIS *comes in. He is dressed in black, stiff white collar, etc.—a quiet-mannered Negro boy with a queerly-baffled, sensitive face.*

JIM: [*pleasantly*]. Hellow, fellows.

They grunt in reply, looking over him scornfully.

JOE: [*staring resentfully*]. Is you graduatin' tonight?

JIM: Yes.

JOE: [*spitting disgustedly*]. Fo' Gawd's sake! You *is* gittin' highfalutin'!

JIM: [*smiling deprecatingly*]. This is my second try. I didn't pass last year.

JOE: What de hell does it git you, huh? Whatever is you gwine do wid it now you gits it? Live lazy on yo' ol' woman?

JIM: [*assertively*]. I'm going to study and become a lawyer.

JOE: [*with a snort*]. Fo' Chris' sake, nigger!

JIM: [*fiercely*]. Don't you call me that—not before them!

JOE: [*pugnaciously*]. Does you deny you's a nigger? I shows you—

MICKEY: [*gives them both a push—truculently*]. Cut it out, see! I'm runnin' dis corner. [*Turning to* JIM *insultingly*] Say you! Painty Face's gittin' her ticket tonight, ain't she?

JIM: You mean Ella—

MICKEY: Painty Face Downey, dat's who I mean! I don't have to be perlite wit' her. She's me goil!

JIM: [*glumly*]. Yes, she's graduating.

SHORTY: [*winks at* MICKEY]. Smart, huh?

MICKEY: [*winks back—meaningly*]. Willin' to loin, take it from me!

JIM *stands tensely as if a struggle were going on in him.*

JIM: [*finally blurts out*]. I want to speak to you, Mickey—alone.

MICKEY: [*surprised—insultingly*]. Aw, what de hell—!

JIM: [*excitedly*]. It's important, I tell you!

MICKEY: Huh? [*Stares at him inquisitively—then motions the others back carelessly and follows* JIM *down front.*]

SHORTY: Some noive!

JOE: [*vengefully*]. I gits dat Jim alone, you wait!

MICKEY: Well, spill de big news. I ain't got all night. I got a date.

JIM: With—Ella?

MICKEY: What's dat to you?

JIM: [*the words trumbling out*]. What—I wanted to say! I know—I've heard—all the stories—what you've been doing around the ward—with other girls—it's none of my business, with them—but she—Ella—it's different—she's not that kind—

MICKEY: [*insultingly*]. Who told yuh so, huh?

JIM: [*draws back his fist threateningly*]. Don't you dare—!

MICKEY *is so paralyzed by this effrontery that he actually steps back.*

MICKEY: Say, cut de comedy! [*Beginning to feel insulted*] Listen, you Jim Crow! Ain't you wise I could give yuh one poke dat'd knock yoh into next week?

JIM: I'm only asking you to act square, Mickey.

MICKEY: What's it to yuh? Why, yuh lousy goat, she wouldn't spit yuh even! She hates de sight of a coon.

JIM: [*in agony*]. I—I know—but once she didn't mind—we were kids together—

MICKEY: Aw, ferget dat! Dis is *now!*

JIM: And I'm still her friend always—even if she don't like colored people—

MICKEY: *Coons,* why don't yuh say it right! De trouble wit' you is yeh're gettin' stuck up, dat's what! Stay where yeh belong, see! Yer old man made coin at de truckin' game and yuh're trying to buy yerself white—graduatin' and law, for Christ sake! Yuh're gettin' yerself in Dutch wit' everyone in de ward—and it ain't cause yer a coon neider. Don't de gang all train wit'

Joe dere and lots of others? But yuh're tryin' to buy white and it won't git yuh no place, see!

JIM: [*trembling*]. Some day—I'll show you—

MICKEY: [*turning away*]. Aw, gwan!

JIM: D'you think I'd change—be you—your dirty white—!

MICKEY: [*whirling about*]. What's dat?

JIM: [*with hysterical vehemence*]. You act square with her—or I'll show you up—I'll report you —I'll write to the papers—the sporting writers —I'll let them know how white you are!

MICKEY: [*infuriated*]. Yuh damn nigger, I'll bust yer jaw in! [*Assuming his ring pose he weaves toward* JIM, *his face set in a cruel scowl.* JIM *waits helplessly but with a certain dignity*].

SHORTY: Cheese it! A couple bulls! And here's de Downey skoit comin', too.

MICKEY: I'll get yuh de next time!

ELLA DOWNEY *enters from the right. She is seventeen, still has the same rose and white complexion, is pretty but with a rather repelling bold air about her.*

ELLA: [*smiles with pleasure when she sees* MICKEY]. Hellow, Mick. Am I late? Say, I'm so glad you won last night. [*She glances from one to the other as she feels something in the air*] Hello! What's up?

MICKEY: Dis boob. [*He indicates* JIM *scornfully*].

JIM: [*diffidently*]. Hello, Ella.

ELLA: [*shortly, turning away*]. Hello. [*Then to* MICKEY] Come on, Mick. Walk down with me. I got to hurry.

JIM: [*blurts out*]. Wait—just a second. [*Painfully*] Ella, do you hate—colored people?

MICKEY: Aw, shut up!

JIM: Please answer.

ELLA: [*forcing a laugh*]. Say! What is this—another exam?

JIM: [*doggedly*]. Please answer.

ELLA: [*irritably*]. Of course I don't! Haven't I been brought up alongside—Why, some of my oldest—the girls I've been to public school the longest with—

JIM: Do you hate me, Ella?

ELLA: [*confusedly and more irritably*]. Say, is he drunk? Why should I? I don't hate anyone.

JIM: Then why haven't you ever hardly spoken to me—for years?

ELLA: [*resentfully*]. What would I speak about? You and me've got nothing in common any more.

JIM: [*desperately*]. Maybe not any more—but—right on this corner—do you remember once—?

ELLA: I don't remember nothing! [*Angrily*] Say! What's got into you to be butting into my business all of a sudden like this? Because you finally managed to graduate, has it gone to your head?

JIM: No, I—only want to help you, Ella.

ELLA: Of all the nerve! You're certainly forgetting your place! Who's asking you for help, I'd like to know? Shut up and stop bothering me!

JIM: [*insistently*]. If you ever need a friend—a true friend—

ELLA: I've got lots of friends among my own—kind, I can tell you. [*Exasperatedly*] You make me sick! Go to the devil!

She flounces off. The three men laugh. MICKEY *follows her.* JIM *is stricken. He goes and sinks down limply on a box in front of the grocery store.*

SHORTY: I'm going to shoot a drink. Come on, Joe, and I'll blow yuh.

JOE: [*who has never ceased to follow every move of* JIM'S *with angry, resentful eyes*] Go long. I'se gwine stay here a secon'. I got a lil' argyment. [*He points to* JIM].

SHORTY: Suit yerself. Do a good job. See yuh later. [*He goes, whistling*].

JOE: [*stands for a while glaring at* JIM, *his fierce little eyes peering out of his black face. Then he spits on his hands aggressively and strides up to the oblivious* JIM. *He stands in front of him, gradually working himself into a fury at the other's seeming indifference to his words*]. Listen to me, nigger: I got a heap on whisper in yo' ear! Who is you, anyhow? Who does you think you is? Don't yo' old man and mine work on de docks togidder befo' yo' old man gits his own truckin' business? Yo' ol' man swallers his nickels, my ol' man buys him beer wid dem and swallers dat—dat's the on'y diff'rence. Don't you 'n' me drag up togidder?

JIM: [*dully*]. I'm your friend, Joe.

JOE: No, you isn't! I ain't no fren o' yourn! I don't even know who you is! What's all dis schoolin' you doin'? What's all dis dressin' up and graduatin' an' sayin' you gwine study be a lawyer? What's all dis fakin' an' pretendin' and swellin' out grand an' talkin' soft and perlite? What's all dis denyin' you's a nigger—an' wid de white boys listenin' to you say it! Is you aimin' to buy white wid yo' ol' man's dough like Mickey say? What is you? [*In a rage at the other's silence*] You don't talk? Den I takes it out o' yo' hide! [*He grabs* JIM *by the throat with one hand and draws the other fist back*] Tell me befo' I wrecks yo' face in! Is you a nigger or isn't you? [*Shaking him*] Is you a nigger, Nigger? Nigger, is you a nigger?

JIM: [*looking into his eyes—quietly*]. Yes. I'm a nigger. We're both niggers.

They look at each other for a moment. JOE'S *rage vanishes. He slumps onto a box beside* JIM'S. *He offers him a cigarette.* JIM *takes it.* JOE *scratches a match and lights both their cigarettes.*

JOE: [*after a puff, with full satisfaction*]. Man, why didn't you splain dat in de fust place?

JIM: We're both niggers.

The same hand-organ man of SCENE ONE *comes to the corner. He plays the chorus of "Bon-bon Buddie The Chocolate Drop." They both stare straight ahead listening. Then the organ man goes away. A silence.* JOE *gets to his feet.*

JOE: I'll go get me a cold beer. [*He starts to move off—then turns*] Time you was graduatin', ain't it?

He goes. JIM *remains sitting on his box staring straight before him as*

THE CURTAIN FALLS

Scene III

The same corner five years later. Nothing has changed much. It is a night in Spring. The arc-lamp discovers faces with a favorless cruelty. The street noises are the same but more intermittent and dulled with a quality of fatigue. Two people pass, one black and one white. They are tired. They both yawn, but neither laughs. There is no laughter from the two streets. From the street of the whites the tenor, more nasal than ever and a bit drunken, wails in high barber-shop falsetto the last half of the chorus of "When I Lost You." The Negro voice, a bit maudlin in turn, replies with the last half of "Waitin' for the Robert E. Lee." Silence. SHORTY *enters. He looks tougher than ever, the typical gangster. He stands waiting, singing a bit drunkenly, peering down the street.*

SHORTY: [*indignantly*]. Yuh bum! Ain't yuh ever comin'? [*He begins to sing: "And sewed up in her yeller kimona, She had a blue-barreled forty-five gun, For to get her man Who'd done her wrong." Then he comments scornfully*] Not her, dough! No gat for her. She ain't got de noive. A little sugar. Dat'll fix her.

ELLA *enters. She is dressed poorly, her face is pale and hollow-eyed, her voice cold and tired.*

SHORTY: Yuh got de message?

ELLA: Here I am.

SHORTY: How yuh been?

ELLA: All right. [*A pause. He looks at her puzzledly*].

SHORTY: [*a bit embarrassedly*]. Well, I s'pose yuh'd like me to give yuh some dope on Mickey, huh?

ELLA: No.

SHORTY: Mean to say yuh don't wanter know where he is or what he's doin'?

ELLA: No.

SHORTY: Since when?

ELLA: A long time.

SHORTY: [*after a pause—with a rat-like viciousness*]. Between you'n me, kid, you'll get even soon—you'n all de odder dames he's tossed. I'm on de inside. I've watched him trainin'. His next scrap, watch it! He'll go! It won't be de odder guy. It'll be all youse dames he's kidded—and de ones what's kidded him. Youse'll all be in de odder guy's corner. He won't need no odder seconds. Youse'll trow water on him, and sponge his face, and take de kinks out of his socker—and Mickey'll catch it on de button—and he won't be able to take it no more—'cause all your weight—you and de odders—'ll be behind dat punch. Ha ha! [*He laughs an evil laugh*] And Mickey'll go—down to his knees first—[*He sinks to his knees in the attitude of a groggy boxer*].

ELLA: I'd like to see him on his knees!

SHORTY: And den—flat on his pan—dead to de world—de boidies singin' in de trees—ten—out! [*He suits his action to the words, sinking flat on the pavement, then rises and laughs the same evil laugh*].

ELLA: He's been out—for me—a long time. [*A pause*] Why did you send for me?

SHORTY: He sent me.

ELLA: Why?

SHORTY: To slip you dis wad o' dough. [*He reluctantly takes a roll of bills from his pocket and holds it out to her*].

ELLA: [*looks at the money indifferently*]. What for?

SHORTY: For you.

ELLA: No.

SHORTY: For de kid den.

ELLA: The kid's dead. He took diphtheria.

SHORTY: Hell yuh say! When?

ELLA: A long time.

SHORTY: Why didn't you write Mickey—?

ELLA: Why should I? He'd only be glad.

SHORTY: [*after a pause*]. Well—it's better.

ELLA: Yes.

SHORTY: You made up wit yer family?

ELLA: No chance.

SHORTY: Livin' alone?

ELLA: In Brooklyn.

SHORTY: Workin'?

ELLA: In a factory.

SHORTY: You're a sucker. There's lots of softer snaps fer you, kid—

ELLA: I know what you mean. No.

SHORTY: Don't yuh wanter step out no more—have fun—live?

ELLA: I'm through.

SHORTY: [*mockingly*]. Jump in de river, huh? T'ink it over, baby. I kin start yuh right in my stable. No one'll bodder yuh den. I got influence.

ELLA: [*without emphasis*]. You're a dirty dog. Why doesn't someone kill you?

SHORTY: Is dat so! What're you? They say you been travelin' round with Jim Crow.

ELLA: He's been my only friend.

SHORTY: A nigger!

ELLA: The only white man in the world! Kind and white. You're all black—black to the heart.

SHORTY: Nigger-lover! [*He throws the money in her face. It falls to the street*] Listen, you! Mickey says he's off of yuh for keeps. Dis is de finish! Dat's what he sent me to tell you. [*Glances at her searchingly—a pause*] Yuh won't make no trouble?

ELLA: Why should I? He's free. The kid's dead. I'm free. No hard feelings—only—I'll be there in spirit at his next fight, tell him! I'll take your tip—the other corner—second the punch—nine—ten—out! He's free! That's all. [*She grins horribly at* SHORTY] Go away, Shorty.

SHORTY: [*looking at her and shaking his head—maudlinly*]. Groggy! Groggy! We're all groggy! Gluttons for punishment! Me for a drink. So long.

He goes. A Salvation army band comes toward the corner. They are playing and singing "Till We Meet at Jesus' Feet." They reach the end as they enter and stop before ELLA. THE CAPTAIN *steps forward.*

CAPTAIN: Sister—

ELLA: [*picks up the money and drops it in his hat—mockingly*]. Here. Go save yourself. Leave me alone.

A WOMAN SALVATIONIST: Sister—

ELLA: Never mind that. I'm not in your line—yet. [*As they hesitate, wonderingly*] I want to be alone.

To the thud of the big drum they march off. ELLA *sits down on a box, her hands hanging at her sides. Presently* JIM HARRIS *comes in. He has grown into a quietly-dressed, studious-looking Negro with an intelligent yet queerly-baffled face.*

JIM: [*with a joyous but bewildered cry*]. Ella! I just saw Shorty—

ELLA: [*smiling at him with frank affection*]. He had a message from Mickey.

JIM: [*sadly*]. Ah!

ELLA: [*pointing to the box behind her*]. Sit down. [*He does so. A pause—then she says indifferently*] It's finished. I'm free, Jim.

JIM: [*wearily*]. We're never free—except to do what we have to do.

ELLA: What are you getting gloomy about all of a sudden?

JIM: I've got the report from the school. I've flunked again.

ELLA: Poor Jim.

JIM: Don't pity me. I'd like to kick myself all over the block. Five years—and I'm still plugging away where I ought to have been at the end of two.

ELLA: Why don't you give it up?

JIM: No!

ELLA: After all, what's being a lawyer?

JIM: A lot—to me—what it means. [*Intensely*] Why, if I was a Member of the Bar right now, Ella, I believe I'd almost have the courage to—

ELLA: What?

JIM: Nothing. [*After a pause—gropingly*] I can't explain—just—but it hurts like fire. It brands me in my pride. I swear I know more'n any member of my class. I ought to, I study harder. I work like the devil. It's all in my head—all fine and correct to a T. Then when I'm called on—I stand up—all the white faces looking at me—and I can feel their eyes—I hear my own voice sounding funny, trembling—and all of a sudden it's all gone in my head—there's nothing remembered—and I hear myself stuttering—and give up—sit down— They don't laugh, hardly ever. They're kind. They're good people. [*In a frenzy*] They're considerate, damn them! But I feel branded!

ELLA: Poor Jim.

JIM: [*going on painfully*]. And it's the same thing in the written exams. For weeks before I study all night. I can't sleep anyway. I learn it all, I see it, I understand it. Then they give me the paper in the exam room. I look it over, I know each answer—perfectly. I take up my pen. On all sides are white men starting to write. They're so sure—even the ones that I know know nothing. But I know it all—but I can't remember any more—it fades—it goes—it's gone. There's a blank in my head—stupidity—

I sit like a fool fighting to remember a little bit here, a little bit there—not enough to pass—not enough for anything—when I know it all!

ELLA: [*compassionately*]. Jim. It isn't worth it. You don't need to—

JIM: I need it more than anyone ever needed anything. I need it to live.

ELLA: What'll it prove?

JIM: Nothing at all much—but everything to me.

ELLA: You're so much better than they are in every other way.

JIM: [*looking up at her*]. Then—you understand?

ELLA: Of course. [*Affectionately*] Don't I know how fine you've been to me! You've been the only one in the world who's stood by me—the only understanding person—and all after the rotten way I used to treat you.

JIM: But before that—way back so high—you treated me good. [*He smiles*].

ELLA: You've been white to me, Jim. [*She takes his hand*].

JIM: White—to you!

ELLA: Yes.

JIM: All love is white. I've always loved you. [*This with the deepest humility.*]

ELLA: Even now—after all that's happened!

JIM: Always.

ELLA: I like you, Jim—better than anyone else in the world.

JIM: That's more than enough, more than I ever hoped for. [*The organ grinder comes to the corner. He plays the chorus of "Annie Laurie." They sit listening, hand in hand*] Would you ever want to marry me, Ella?

ELLA: Yes, Jim.

JIM [*as if this quick consent alarmed him*]: No, no, don't answer now. Wait! Turn it over in your mind! Think what it means to you! Consider it—over and over again! I'm in no hurry, Ella. I can wait months—years—

ELLA: I'm alone. I've got to be helped. I've got to help someone—or it's the end—one end or another.

JIM [*eagerly*]: Oh, I'll help—I know I can help—I'll give my life to help you—that's what I've been living for—

ELLA:: But can I help you? Can I help you?

JIM: Yes! Yes! We'll go abroad where a man is a man—where it don't make that difference—where people are kind and wise to see the soul under skins. I don't ask you to love me—I don't dare to hope nothing like that! I don't want nothing—only to wait—to know you like me—to be near you—to keep harm away—to make up for the past—to never let you suffer any more—to serve you—to lie at your feet like a dog that loves you—to kneel by your bed like a nurse that watches over you sleeping—to preserve and protect and shield you from evil and sorrow—to give my life and my blood and all the strength that's in me to give you peace and joy—to become your slave!—yes, be your slave—your black slave that adores you as sacred! [*He has sunk to his knees. In a frenzy of self-abnegation, as he says the last words he beats his head on the flagstones.*]

ELLA [*overcome and alarmed*]: Jim! Jim! You're crazy! I want to help you, Jim—I want to help—

CURTAIN

Scene IV

Some weeks or so later. A street in the same ward in front of an old brick church. The church sets back from the sidewalk in a yard enclosed by a rusty iron railing with a gate at center. On each side of this yard are tenements. The buildings have a stern, forbidding look. All the shades on the windows are drawn down, giving an effect of staring, brutal eyes that pry callously at human beings without acknowledging them. Even the two tall, narrow church windows on either side of the arched door are blanked with dull green shades. It is a bright sunny morning. The district is unusually still, as if it were waiting, holding its breath.

From the street of the blacks to the right a Negro tenor sings in a voice of shadowy richness—the first stanza with a contented, childlike melancholy—

Sometimes I feel like a mourning dove,
Sometimes I feel like a mourning dove,
Sometimes I feel like a mourning dove,
I feel like a mourning dove.
Feel like a mourning dove.

The second with a dreamy, boyish exultance—

Sometimes I feel like an eagle in the air,
Sometimes I feel like an eagle in the air,
Sometimes I feel like an eagle in the air,
I feel like an eagle in the air.
Feel like an eagle in the air.

The third with a brooding, earthbound sorrow—

Sometimes I wish that I'd never been born,
Sometimes I wish that I'd never been born,
Sometimes I wish that I'd never been born,

I wish that I'd never been born.
Wish that I'd never been born.

As the music dies down there is a pause of waiting stillness. This is broken by one startling, metallic clang of the church-bell. As if it were a signal, people —men, women, children—pour from the two tenements, whites from the tenement to the left, blacks from the one to the right. They hurry to form into two racial lines on each side of the gate, rigid and unyielding, staring across at each other with bitter hostile eyes. The halves of the big church door swing open and JIM *and* ELLA *step out from the darkness within into the sunlight. The doors slam behind them like wooden lips of an idol that has spat them out.* JIM *is dressed in black.* ELLA *in white, both with extreme plainness. They stand in the sunlight, shrinking and confused. All the hostile eyes are now concentrated on them. They become aware of the two lines through which they must pass; they hesitate and tremble; then stand there staring back at the people as fixed and immovable as they are. The organ grinder comes in from the right. He plays the chorus of "Old Black Joe." As he finishes the bell of the church clangs one more single stroke, insistently dismissing.*

JIM [*as if the sound had awakened him from a trance, reaches out and takes her hand*]: Come. Time we got to the steamer. Time we sailed away over the sea. Come, Honey! [*She tries to answer but her lips tremble; she cannot take her eyes off the eyes of the people; she is unable to move. He sees this and, keeping the same tone of profound, affectionate kindness, he points upward in the sky, and gradually persuades her eyes to look up*] Look up, Honey! See the sun! Feel his warm eye lookin' down! Feel how kind he looks! Feel his blessing deep in your heart, your bones! Look up, Honey!

Her eyes are fixed on the sky now. Her face is calm. She tries to smile bravely back at the sun. Now he pulls her by the hand, urging her gently to walk with him down through the yard and gate, through the lines of people. He is maintaining an attitude to support them through the ordeal only by a terrible effort, which manifests itself in the hysteric quality of ecstasy which breaks into his voice.

And look at the sky! Ain't it kind and blue! Blue for hope. Don't they say blue's for hope? Hope! That's for us, Honey. All those blessings in the sky! What's it the Bible says? Falls on just and unjust alike? No, that's the sweet rain. Pshaw, what am I saying? All mixed up. There's no unjust about it. We're all the same —equally just—under the sky—under the sun —under God—sailing over the sea—to the other side of the world—the side where Christ was born—the kind side that takes count of the soul—over the sea—the sea's blue, too—. Let's not be late—let's get that steamer!

They have reached the curb now, passed the lines of people. She is looking up to the sky with an expression of trance-like calm and peace. He is on the verge of collapse, his face twitching, his eyes staring. He calls hoarsely:

Taxi! Where is he! Taxi!

CURTAIN

ACT II

Scene I

Two years later. A flat of the better sort in the Negro district near the corner of Act One. This is the parlor. Its furniture is a queer clash. The old pieces are cheaply ornate, naively, childishly gaudy—the new pieces give evidence of a taste that is diametrically opposed, severe to the point of somberness. On one wall, in a heavy gold frame, is a colored photograph—the portrait of an elderly Negro with an able, shrewd face but dressed in outlandish lodge regalia, a get-up adorned with medals, sashes, a cocked hat with frills—the whole effect as absurd to contemplate as one of Napoleon's Marshals in full uniform. In the left corner, where a window lights it effectively, is a Negro primitive mask from the Congo—a grotesque face, inspiring obscure, dim connotations in one's mind, but beautifully done, conceived in a true religious spirit. In this room, however, the mask acquires an arbitrary accentuation. It dominates by a diabolical quality that contrast imposes upon it.

There are two windows on the left looking out in the street. In the rear, a door to the hall of the building. In the right, a doorway with red and golf portières leading into the bedroom and the rest of the flat. Everything is cleaned and polished. The dark brown wall paper is new, the brilliantly figured carpet also. There is a round mahogany table at center. In a rocking chair by the table MRS. HARRIS *is sitting. She is a mild-looking, gray-haired Negress of sixty-five, dressed in an old-fashioned Sunday-best dress. Walking about the room nervously is* HATTIE, *her daughter,* JIM'S *sister, a woman of about thirty with a high-strung, defiant face—an intelligent head showing both power and courage. She is dressed severely, mannishly.*

It is a fine morning in Spring. Sunshine comes through the windows at the left.

MRS. HARRIS: Time dey was here, ain't it?

HATTIE [*impatiently*]: Yes.

MRS. H. [*worriedly*]: You ain't gwine ter kick up a fuss, is you—like you done wid Jim befo' de weddin'?

HATTIE: No. What's done is done.

MRS. H.: We mustn't let her see we hold it agin' her—de bad dat happened to her wid dat no-count fighter.

HATTIE: I certainly never give that a thought. It's what she's done to Jim—making him run away and give up his fight—!

MRS. H.: Jim loves her a powerful lot, must be.

HATTIE [*after a pause—bitterly*]: I wonder if she loves Jim!

MRS. H.: She must, too. Yes, she must, too. Don't you forget dat it was hard for her—mighty, mighty hard—harder for de white dan for de black!

HATTIE [*indignantly*]: Why should it be?

MRS. H. [*shaking her head*]: I ain't talkin' of shoulds. It's too late for shoulds. Dey's o'ny one should. [*Solemnly*] De white and de black shouldn't mix dat close. Dere's one road where de white goes on alone; dere's anudder road where de black goes on alone—

HATTIE: Yes, if they'd only leave us alone!

MRS. H.: Dey leaves your Pa alone. He comes to de top till he's got his own business, lots o' money in de bank, he owns a building even befo' he die. [*She looks up proudly at the picture.* HATTIE *sighs impatiently—then her mother goes on*] Dey leaves me alone. I bears four children into dis worl', two dies, two lives, I helps you two grow up fine an' healthy and eddicated wid schoolin' and money fo' yo' comfort—

HAIITE [*impatiently*]: Ma!

MRS. H.: I does de duty God set for me in dis worl'. Dey leaves me alone.

HATTIE *goes to the window to hide her exasperation.*

The mother broods for a minute—then goes on.

The worl' done change. Dey ain't no satisfaction wid nuffin' no more.

HATTIE: Oh! [*Then after a pause*] They'll be here any minute now.

MRS. H.: Why didn't you go meet 'em at de dock like I axed you?

HATTIE: I couldn't. My face and Jim's among those hundreds of white faces— [*With a harsh laugh*] It would give her too much advantage!

MRS. H. [*impatiently*]: Don't talk dat way! What makes you so proud? [*Then after a pause—sadly*] Hattie.

HATTIE [*turning*]: Yes, Ma.

MRS. H.: I want to see Jim again—my only boy—but—all de same I'd ruther he stayed away. He say in his letter he's happy, she's happy, dey likes it dere, de folks don't think nuffin' but what's natural at seeing 'em married. Why don't dey stay?

HATTIE [*vehemently*]: No! They were cowards to run away. If they believe in what they've done, then let them face it out, live it out here, be strong enough to conquer all prejudice!

MRS. H.: Strong? Dey ain't many strong. Dey ain't many happy neider. Dey was happy ovah yondah.

HATTIE: We don't deserve happiness till we've fought the fight of our race and won it!

In the pause that follows there is a ring from back in the flat.

It's the door bell! You go, Ma. I--I—I'd rather not.

Her mother looks at her rebukingly and goes out agitatedly through the portières. HATTIE *waits, nervously walking about, trying to compose herself. There is a long pause. Finally the portières are parted and* JIM *enters. He looks much older, graver, and worried.*

JIM: Hattie!

HATTIE: Jim!

They embrace with great affection.

JIM: It's great to see you again! You're looking fine.

HATTIE [*looking at him searchingly*]: You look well, too—thinner maybe—and tired. [*Then as she sees him frowning*] But where's Ella?

JIM: With Ma. [*Apologetically*] She sort of—broke down—when we came in. The trip wore her out.

HATTIE [*coldly*]: I see.

JIM: Oh, it's nothing serious. Nerves. She needs a rest.

HATTIE: Wasn't living in France restful?

JIM: Yes, but—too lonely—especially for her.

HATTIE [*resentfully*]: Why? Didn't the people there want to associate—?

JIM [*quickly*]: Oh, no indeedy, they didn't think anything of that. [*After a pause*] But—she did. For the first year it was all right. Ella liked everything a lot. She went out with French folks and got so she could talk it a little—and I learned it—a little. We were having a right nice time. I never thought then we'd ever want to come back here.

HATTIE [*frowning*]: But—what happened to change you?

JIM [*after a pause—haltingly*]: Well—you see first year—she and I were living around—like friends—like a brother and sister—like you and I might.

HATTIE [*her face becoming more and more drawn and tense*]: You mean—then—? [*She shudders—then after a pause*] She loves you, Jim?

JIM: If I didn't know that I'd have to jump in the river.

HATTIE: Are you sure she loves you?

JIM: Isn't that why she's suffering?

HATTIE [*letting her breath escape through her clenched teeth*]: Ah!

JIM [*suddenly springs up and shouts almost hysterically*]: Why d'you ask me all those damn questions? Are you trying to make trouble between us?

HATTIE [*controlling herself—quietly*]: No, Jim.

JIM [*after a pause—contritely*]: I'm sorry, Hattie. I'm kind of on edge today. [*He sinks down on his chair—then goes on as if something forced him to speak*] After that we got to living housed in. Ella didn't want to see nobody, she said just the two of us was enough. I was happy then—and I really guess she was happy, too—in a way—for a while. [*Again a pause*] But she never did get to wanting to go out any place again. She got to saying she felt she'd be sure to run into someone she knew—from over here. So I moved us out to the country where no tourist ever comes—but it didn't make any difference to her. She got to avoiding the French folks the same as if they were Americans and I couldn't get it out of her mind. She lived in the house and got paler and paler, and more and more nervous and scary, always imagining things—until I got to imagining things, too. I got to feeling blue. Got to sneering at myself that I wasn't any better than a quitter because I sneaked away right after getting married, didn't face nothing, gave up trying to become a Member of the Bar—and I got to suspecting Ella must feel that way about me, too—that I wasn't a *real man!*

HATTIE: [*indignantly*]. She couldn't!

JIM [*with hostility*]: You don't need to tell me! All this was only in my mind. We never quarreled a single bit. We never said a harsh word. We were as close to each other as could be. We were all there was in the world to each other. We were alone together! [*A pause*] Well, one day I got so I couldn't stand it. I could see she couldn't stand it. So I just up and said: Ella, we've got to have a plain talk, look everything straight in the face, hide nothing, come out with the exact truth of the way we feel.

HATTIE: And you decided to come back!

JIM: Yes. We decided the reason we felt sort of ashamed was we'd acted like cowards. We'd run away from the thing—and taken it with us. We decided to come back and face it and live it down in ourselves, and prove to ourselves we were strong in our love—and then, and that way only, by being brave we'd free ourselves, and gain confidence, and be really free inside and able then to go anywhere and live in peace and equality with ourselves and the world without any guilty uncomfortable feeling coming up to rile us. [*He has talked himself now into a state of happy confidence.*]

HATTIE [*bending over and kissing him*]: Good for you! I admire you so much, Jim! I admire both of you! And are you going to begin studying right away and get admitted to the Bar?

JIM: You bet I am!

HATTIE: You must, Jim! Our race needs men like you to come to the front and help— [*As voices are heard approaching she stops, stiffens, and her face grows cold.*]

JIM [*noticing this—warningly*]: Remember Ella's been sick! [*Losing control—threateningly*] You be nice to her, you hear!

MRS. HARRIS *enters, showing* ELLA *the way. The colored woman is plainly worried and perplexed.* ELLA *is pale, with a strange, haunted expression in her eyes. She runs to* JIM *as to a refuge, clutching his hands in both of hers, looking from* MRS. HARRIS *to* HATTIE *with a frightened defiance.*

MRS. H.: Dere he is, child, big's life! She was afraid we'd done kidnapped you away, Jim.

JIM [*patting her hand*]: This place ought to be familiar, Ella. Don't you remember playing here with us sometimes as a kid?

ELLA [*queerly—with a frown of effort*]: I remember playing marbles one night—but that was on the street.

JIM: Don't you remember Hattie?

HATTIE [*coming forward with a forced smile*]: It was a long time ago—but I remember Ella. [*She holds out her hand.*]

ELLA [*taking it—looking at* HATTIE *with the same queer defiance*]: I remember. But you've changed so much.

HATTIE [*stirred to hostility by* ELLA'S *manner—condescendingly*]: Yes, I've grown older, naturally. [*Then in a tone which, as if in spite of herself, becomes bragging*] I've worked so hard. First I went away to college, you know—then I took up post-graduate study—when suddenly I decided I'd accomplish more good if I gave up learning and took up teaching. [*She suddenly checks herself, ashamed, and stung by* ELLA'S *indifference*] But this sounds like stupid boasting. I don't mean that. I was only explaining—

ELLA [*indifferently*]: I didn't know you'd been to school so long. [*A pause*] Where are you teaching? In a colored school, I suppose. [*There is an indifferent superiority in her words that is maddening to* HATTIE.]

HATTIE [*controlling herself*]: Yes. A private school endowed by some wealthy members of our race.

ELLA [*suddenly—even eagerly*]: Then you must have taken lots of examinations and managed to pass them, didn't you?

HATTIE [*biting her lips*]: I always passed with honors!

ELLA: Yes, we both graduated from the same High School, didn't we? That was dead easy for me. Why I hardly even looked at a book. But Jim says it was awfully hard for him. He failed one year, remember?

She turns and smiles at JIM—*a tolerant, superior smile but one full of genuine love.* HATTIE *is outraged, but* JIM *smiles.*

JIM: Yes, it was hard for me, Honey.

ELLA: And the law school examinations Jim hardly ever could pass at all. Could you? [*She laughs lovingly.*]

HATTIE [*harshly*]: Yes, he could! He can! He'll pass them now—if you'll give him a chance!

JIM [*angrily*]: Hattie!

MRS. HARRIS: Hold yo' fool tongue!

HATTIE [*sullenly*]: I'm sorry.

ELLA *has shrunk back against* JIM. *She regards* HATTIE *with a sort of wondering hatred. Then she looks away about the room. Suddenly her eyes fasten on the primitive mask and she gives a stifled scream.*

JIM: What's the matter, Honey?

ELLA [*pointing*]: That! For God's sake, what is it?

HATTIE [*scornfully*]: It's a Congo mask. [*She goes and picks it up*] I'll take it away if you wish. I thought you'd like it. It was my wedding present to Jim.

ELLA: What is it?

HATTIE: It's a mask which used to be worn in religious ceremonies by my people in Africa. But, aside from that, it's beautifully made, a work of Art by a real artist—as real in his way as your Michaelangelo. [*Forces* ELLA *to take it*] Here. Just notice the workmanship.

ELLA: [*defiantly*]. I'm not scared of it if you're not. [*Looking at it with disgust*] Beautiful? Well, some people certainly have queer notions! It looks ugly to me and stupid—like a kid's game—making faces! [*She slaps it contemptuously*] Pooh! You needn't look hard at me. I'll give you the laugh. [*She goes to put it back on the stand*].

JIM: Maybe, if it disturbs you, we better put it in some other room.

ELLA [*defiantly aggressive*]: No. I want it here where I can give it the laugh! [*She sets it there again—then turns suddenly on* HATTIE *with aggressive determination*] Jim's not going to take any more examinations! I won't let him!

HATTIE [*bursting forth*]: Jim! Do you hear that? There's white justice!—their fear for their superiority!—

ELLA [*with a terrified pleading*]: Make her go away, Jim!

JIM [*losing control—furiously to his sister*]: Either you leave here—or we will!

MRS. H [*weeping—throws her arms around* HATTIE]: Let's go, chile! Let's go!

HATTIE [*calmly now*]: Yes, Ma. All right.

They go through the portières. As soon as they are gone, JIM *suddenly collapses into a chair and hides his head in his hands.* ELLA *stands beside him for a moment. She stares distractedly about her, at the portrait, at the mask, at the furniture, at* JIM. *She seems fighting to escape from some weight on her mind. She throws this off and, completely her old self for the moment, kneels by* JIM *and pats his shoulder.*

ELLA [*with kindness and love*]: Don't, Jim! Don't cry, please! You don't suppose I really meant that about the examinations, do you? Why, of course, I didn't mean a word! I couldn't mean it! I want you to take the examinations! I want you to pass! I want you to be a lawyer! I want you to be the best lawyer in the country! I want you to show 'em—all the dirty sneaking, gossiping liars that talk behind our backs—what a man I married. I want the whole world to know you're the whitest of the white! I want you to climb and climb—and step on 'em, stamp right on their mean faces! I love you, Jim. You know that!

JIM [*calm again—happily*]: I hope so, Honey—and I'll make myself worthy.

HATTIE [*appears in the doorway—quietly*]: We're going now, Jim.

ELLA: No. Don't go.

HATTIE: We were going to, anyway. This is your house—Mother's gift to you, Jim.

JIM [*astonished*]: But I can't accept—Where are you going?

HATTIE: We've got a nice flat in the Bronx—

[*with bitter pride*] in the heart of the Black Belt—the Congo—among our own people!

JIM [*angrily*]: You're crazy—I'll see Ma—

He goes out. HATTIE *and* ELLA *stare at each other with scorn and hatred for a moment, then* HATTIE *goes.* ELLA *remains kneeling for a moment by the chair, her eyes dazed and strange as she looks about her. Then she gets to her feet and stands before the portrait of* JIM'S *father—with a sneer.*

ELLA: It's his Old Man—all dolled up like a circus horse! Well, they can't help it. It's in the blood, I suppose. They're ignorant, that's all there is to it. [*She moves to the mask—forcing a mocking tone*] Hello, sport! Who d'you think you're scaring? Not me! I'll give you the laugh. He won't pass, you wait and see. Not in a thousand years! [*She goes to the window and looks down at the street and mutters*] All black! Every one of them! [*Then with sudden excitement*] No, there's one. Why, it's Shorty! [*She throws the window open and calls*] Shorty! Shorty! Hello, Shorty! [*She leans out and waves—then stops, remains there for a moment looking down, then shrinks back on the floor suddenly as if she wanted to hide—her whole face in an anguish*] Say! Say! I wonder?—No, he didn't hear you. Yes, he did, too! He must have! I yelled so loud you could hear me in Jersey! No, what are you talking about? How would he hear with all the kids yelling down there? He never heard a word, I tell you! He did, too! He didn't want to hear you! He didn't want to let anyone know he knew you! Why don't you acknowledge it? What are you lying about? I'm not! Why shouldn't he? Where does he come in to—for God's sake, who is Shorty, anyway? A pimp! Yes, and a dope-peddler, too! D'you mean to say he'd have the nerve to hear me call him and then deliberately—? Yes, I mean to say it! I do say it! And it's true, and you know it, and you might as well be honest for a change and admit it! He heard you but he didn't want to hear you! He doesn't want to know you any more. No, not even him! He's afraid it'd get him in wrong with the old gang. Why? You know well enough! Because you married a—a—a—well, I won't say it, but you know without my mentioning names! [ELLA *springs to her feet in horror and shakes off her obsession with a frantic effort*] Stop! [*Then whimpering like a frightened child*] Jim! Jim! Jim! Where are you? I want you, Jim! [*She runs out of the room as*

THE CURTAIN FALLS

Scene II

The same. Six months later. It is evening. The walls of the room appear shrunken in, the ceiling lowered, so that the furniture, the portrait, the mask look unnaturally large and domineering. JIM *is seated at the table studying, law books piled by his elbows. He is keeping his attention concentrated only by a driving physical effort which gives his face the expression of a runner's near the tape. His forehead shines with perspiration. He mutters one sentence from Blackstone over and over again, tapping his forehead with his fist in time to the rhythm he gives the stale words. But, in spite of himself, his attention wanders, his eyes have an uneasy, hunted look, he starts at every sound in the house or from the street. Fnally, he remains rigid, Blackstone forgotten, his eyes fixed on the portières with tense grief. Then he groans, slams the book shut, goes to the window and throws it open and sinks down beside it, his arms on the sill, his head resting wearily on his arms, staring out into the night, the pale glare from the arc-lamp on the corner throwing his face into relief. The portières on the right are parted and* HATTIE *comes in.*

HATTIE [*not seeing him at the table*]: Jim! [*Discovering him*] Oh, there you are. What're you doing?

JIM [*turning to her*]: Resting. Cooling my head. [*Forcing a smile*] These law books certainly are a sweating proposition! [*Then, anxiously*] How is she?

HATTIE: She's asleep now. I felt it was safe to leave her for a minute. [*After a pause*] What did the doctor tell you, Jim?

JIM: The same old thing. She must have rest, he says, her mind needs rest— [*Bitterly*] But he can't tell me any prescription for that rest—leastways not any that'd work.

HATTIE [*after a pause*]: I think you ought to leave her, Jim—or let her leave you—for a while, anyway.

JIM [*angrily*]: You're like the doctor. Everything's so simple and easy. Do this and that happens. Only it don't. Life isn't simple like that—not in this case, anyway—no, it isn't simple a bit. [*After a pause*] I can't leave her. She can't leave me. And there's a million little reasons combining to make one big reason why we can't. [*A pause*] For her sake—if it'd do her good—I'd go—I'd leave—I'd do anything—because I love her. I'd kill myself even—jump out of this window this second—I've thought it over, too—but that'd only make matters worse for her. I'm all she's got in the world! Yes, that isn't bragging or fooling myself. I know that for a fact! Don't you know that's true? [*There is a pleading for the certainty he claims.*]

HATTIE: Yes, I know she loves you, Jim. I know that now.

JIM [*simply*]: Then we've got to stick together to the end, haven't we, whatever comes—and hope and pray for the best? [*A pause—then hopefully*] I think maybe this is the crisis in her mind. Once she settles this in herself, she's won to the other side. And me—once I become a Member of the Bar—then I win, too! We're both free—by our own fighting down our own weakness! We're both really, truly free! Then we can be happy with ourselves here or anywhere. She'll be proud then! Yes, she's told me again and again, she says she'll be actually proud!

HATTIE [*turning away to conceal her emotion*]: Yes, I'm sure—but you mustn't study too hard, Jim! You mustn't study too awfully hard!

JIM [*gets up and goes to the table and sits down wearily*]: Yes, I know. Oh, I'll pass easily. I haven't got any scary feeling about that any more. And I'm doing two years' work in one here alone. That's better than schools, eh?

HATTIE [*doubtfully*]: It's wonderful, Jim.

JIM [*his spirit evaporating*]: If I can only hold out! It's hard! I'm worn out. I don't sleep. I get to thinking and thinking. My head aches and burns like fire with thinking. Round and round my thoughts go chasing like crazy chickens hopping and flapping before the wind. It gets me crazy mad—'cause I can't stop!

HATTIE [*watching him for a while and seeming to force herself to speak*]: The doctor didn't tell you all, Jim.

JIM [*dully*]: What's that?

HATTIE: He told me you're liable to break down too, if you don't take care of yourself.

JIM [*abjectly weary*]: Let 'er come! I don't care what happens to me. Maybe if I get sick she'll get well. There's only so much bad luck allowed to one family, maybe. [*He forces a wan smile.*]

HATTIE [*hastily*]: Don't give in to that idea, for the Lord's sake!

JIM: I'm tired—and blue—that's all.

HATTIE [*after another long pause*]: I've got to tell you something else, Jim.

JIM [*dully*]: What?

HATTIE: The doctor said Ella's liable to be sick like this a very long time.

JIM: He told me that too—that it'd be a long time before she got back her normal strength. Well, I suppose that's got to be expected.

HATTIE [*slowly*]: He didn't mean convalescing—what he told me. [*A long pause*].

JIM [*evasively*]: I'm going to get other doctors in to see Ella—specialists. This one's a damn fool.

HATTIE: Be sensible, Jim. You'll have to face the truth—sooner or later.

JIM [*irritable*]: I know the truth about Ella better'n any doctor.

HATTIE [*persuasively*]: She'd get better so much sooner if you'd send her away to some nice sanitarium—

JIM: No! She'd die of shame there!

HATTIE: At least until after you've taken your examinations—

JIM: To hell with me!

HATTIE: Six months. That wouldn't be long to be parted.

JIM: What are you trying to do—separate us? [*He gets to his feet—furiously*] Go on out! Go on out!

HATTIE [*calmly*]: No, I won't. [*Sharply*] There's something that's got to be said to you and I'm the only one with the courage— [*Intensely*] Tell me, Jim, have you heard her raving when she's out of her mind?

JIM [*with a shudder*]: No!

HATTIE: You're lying, Jim. You must have—if you don't stop your ears—and the doctor says she may develop a violent mania, dangerous for you—get worse and worse until—Jim, you'll go crazy too—living this way. Today she raved on about "Black! Black!" and cried because she said her skin was turning black—that you had poisoned her—

JIM [*in anguish*]: That's only when she's out of her mind.

HATTIE: And then she suddenly called me a dirty nigger.

JIM: No! She never said that ever! She never would!

HATTIE: She did—and kept on and on! [*A tense pause*] She'll be saying that to you soon.

JIM [*torturedly*]: She don't mean it! She isn't responsible for what she's saying!

HATTIE: I know she isn't—yet she is just the same. It's deep down in her or it wouldn't come out.

JIM: Deep down in her people—not deep in her.

HATTIE: I can't make such distinctions. The race in me, deep in me, can't stand it. I can't play nurse to her any more, Jim,—not even for your sake. I'm afraid—afraid of myself—afraid sometime I'll kill her dead to set you free! [*She loses control and begins to cry*].

JIM [*after a long pause—somberly*]: Yes, I guess you'd better stay away from here. Good-by.

HATTIE: Who'll you get to nurse her, Jim,—a white woman?

JIM: Ella'd die of shame. No, I'll nurse her myself.

HATTIE: And give up your studies?

JIM: I can do both.

HATTIE: You can't! You'll get sick yourself! Why, you look terrible even as it is—and it's only beginning!

JIM: I can do anything for her! I'm all she's got in the world! I've got to prove I can be all to her! I've got to prove worthy! I've got to prove she can be proud of me! I've got to prove I'm the whitest of the white!

HATTIE [*stung by this last—with rebellious bitterness*]: Is that the ambition she's given you? Oh, you soft, weak-minded fool, you traitor to your race! And the thanks you'll get—to be called a dirty nigger—to hear her cursing you because she can never have a child because it'll be born black—!

JIM [*in a frenzy*]: Stop!

HATTIE: I'll say what must be said even though you kill me, Jim. Send her to an asylum before you both have to be sent to one together.

JIM [*with a sudden wild laugh*]: Do you think you're threatening me with something dreadful now? Why, I'd like that. Sure, I'd like that! Maybe she'd like it better, too. Maybe we'd both find it all simple then—like you think it is now. Yes. [*He laughs again*].

HATTIE [*frightenedly*]: Jim!

JIM: Together! You can't scare me even with hell fire if you say she and I go together. It's heaven then for me! [*With sudden savagery*] You go out of here! All you've ever been aiming to do is to separate us so we can't be together!

HATTIE: I've done what I did for your own good.

JIM: I have no own good. I only got a good together with her. I'm all she's got in the world! Let her call me nigger! Let her call me the whitest of the white! I'm all she's got in the world, ain't I? She's all I've got! You with your fool talk of the black race and the white race! Where does the human race get a chance to come in? I suppose that's simple for you. You lock it up in asylums and throw away the key! [*With fresh violence*] Go along! There isn't going to be no more people coming in here to separate—excepting the doctor. I'm going to lock the door and it's going to stay locked, you hear? Go along, now!

HATTIE [*confusedly*]: Jim!

JIM [*pushes her out gently and slams the door after her—vaguely*]: Go along! I got to study. I got to nurse Ella, too. Oh, I can do it! I can do anything for her!

He sits down at the table and, opening the book, begins again to recite the line from Blackstone in a meaningless rhythm, tapping his forehead with his fist. ELLA *enters noiselessly through the portières. She wears a red dressinggown over her night-dress but is in her bare feet. She has a carving-knife in her right hand. Her eyes fasten on* JIM *with a murderous mania. She creeps up behind him. Suddenly he senses something and turns. As he sees her he gives a cry, jumping up and catching her wrist. She stands fixed, her eyes growing bewildered and frightened.*

JIM [*aghast*]: Ella! For God's sake! Do you want to murder me?

She does not answer. He shakes her.

ELLA [*whimperingly*]: They kept calling me names as I was walking along—I can't tell you what, Jim—and then I grabbed a knife—

JIM: Yes! See! This! [*She looks at it frightenedly*].

ELLA: Where did I—? I was having a nightmare — Where did they go—I mean, how did I get here? [*With sudden terrified pleading—like a little girl*] Oh, Jim—don't ever leave me alone! I have such terrible dreams, Jim—promise you'll never go away!

JIM: I promise, Honey.

ELLA [*her manner becoming more and more childishly silly*]: I'll be a little girl—and you'll be old Uncle Jim who's been with us for years and years— Will you play that?

JIM: Yes, Honey. Now you better go back to bed.

ELLA [*like a child*]: Yes, Uncle Jim.

She turns to go. He pretends to be occupied by his book. She looks at him for a second—then suddenly asks in her natural woman's voice

Are you studying hard. Jim?

JIM: Yes, Honey. Go to bed now. You need to rest, you know.

ELLA [*stands looking at him, fighting with herself. A startling transformation comes over her face. It grows mean, vicious, full of jealous hatred. She cannot contain herself but breaks out harshly with a cruel, venomous grin*] You dirty nigger!

JIM [*starting as if he'd been shot*]: Ella! For the good Lord's sake!

ELLA [*coming out of her insane mood for a moment,*

aware of something terrible, frightened]: Jim! Jim! Why are you looking at me like that?

JIM: What did you say to me just then?

ELLA [*gropingly*]: Why, I—I said—I remember saying, are you studying hard, Jim? Why? You're not mad at that, are you?

JIM: No, Honey. What made you think I was mad? Go to bed now.

ELLA [*obediently*]: Yes, Jim.

She passes behind the portières. JIM *stares before him. Suddenly her head is thrust out at the side of the portières. Her face is again that of a vindictive maniac.*

Nigger!

The face disappears—she can be heard running away, laughing with cruel satisfaction. JIM *bows his head on his outstretched arms but he is too stricken for tears.*

CURTAIN

Scene III

The same, six months later. The sun has just gone down. The Spring twilight sheds a vague, gray light about the room, picking out the Congo mask on the stand by the window. The walls appear shrunken in still more, the ceiling now seems barely to clear the people's heads, the furniture and the characters appear enormously magnified. Law books are stacked in two great piles on each side of the table. ELLA *comes in from the right, the carving-knife in her hand. She is pitifully thin, her face is wasted, but her eyes glow with a mad energy, her movements are abrupt and springlike. She looks stealthily about the room, then advances and stands before the mask, her arms akimbo, her attitude one of crazy mockery, fear and bravado. She is dressed in the red dressing-gown, grown dirty and ragged now, and is in her bare feet.*

ELLA: I'll give you the laugh, wait and see! [*Then in a confidential tone*] He thought I was asleep! He called, Ella, Ella—but I kept my eyes shut, I pretended to snore. I fooled him good. [*She gives a little hoarse laugh*] This is the first time he's dared to leave me alone for months and months. I've been wanting to talk to you every day but this is the only chance— [*With sudden violence—flourishing her knife*] What're you grinning about, you dirty nigger, you? How dare you grin at me? I guess you forget what you are! That's always the way. Be kind to you, treat you decent, and in a second you've got a swelled head, you think you're somebody, you're all over the place putting on airs; why, it's got so I can't even walk down the street without seeing niggers, niggers everywhere. Hanging around, grinning, grinning—going to school—pretending they're white—taking examinations— [*She stops, arrested by the word, then suddenly*] That's where he's gone—down to the mail-box—to see if there's a letter from the Board—telling him—But why is he so long? [*She calls pitifully*] Jim! [*Then in a terrified whimper*] Maybe he's passed! Maybe he's passed! [*In a frenzy*] No! No! He can't! I'd kill him! I'd kill myself! [*Threatening the Congo mask*] It's you who're to blame for this! Yes, you! Oh, I'm on to you! [*Then appealingly*] But why d'you want to do this to us? What have I ever done wrong to you? What have you got against me? I married you, didn't I? Why don't you let Jim alone? Why don't you let him be happy as he is—with me? Why don't you let me be happy? He's white, isn't he—the whitest man that ever lived? Where do you come in to interfere? Black! Black! Black as dirt! You've poisoned me! I can't wash myself clean! Oh, I hate you! I hate you! Why don't you let Jim and I be happy?

She sinks down in his chair, her arms outstretched on the table. The door from the hall is slowly opened and JIM *appears. His bloodshot, sleepless eyes stare from deep hollows. His expression is one of crushed numbness. He holds an open letter in his hand.*

JIM [*seeing* ELLA—*in an absolutely dead voice*]: Honey—thought you were asleep.

ELLA [*Starts and wheels about in her chair*]: What's that? You got—you got a letter—?

JIM [*turning to close the door after him*]: From the Board of Examiners for admission to the Bar, State of New York—God's country! [*He finishes up with a chuckle of ironic self-pity so spent as to be barely audible.*]

ELLA [*writhing out of her chair like some fierce animal, the knife held behind her—with fear and hatred*]: You didn't—you didn't—you didn't pass, did you?

JIM [*looking at her widely*]: Pass? Pass? [*He begins to chuckle and laugh between sentences and phrases, rich, Negro laughter but heart-breaking in its mocking grief*] Good Lord, child, how come you can ever imagine such a crazy idea? Pass? Me? Jim Crow Harris? Nigger Jim Harris—become a full-fledged Member of the Bar! Why the mere notion of it is enough to kill you with laughing! It'd be against all natural laws, all human right and justice. It'd be miraculous, there'd be earthquakes and catastrophes, the seven Plagues'd come again and locusts'd devour all the money in the banks, the second Flood'd come roaring and Noah'd fall overboard, the sun'd drop out of the sky like a ripe fig, and the Devil'd perform miracles, and God'd be tipped head first right out of the Judgment seat! [*He laughs, maudlinly uproarious.*]

ELLA [*her face beginning to relax, to light up*]: Then you—you didn't pass?

JIM [*spent—giggling and gasping idiotically*]: Well, I should say not! I should certainly say not!

ELLA [*with a cry of joy, pushes all the law books crashing to the floor—then with childish happiness she grabs* JIM *by both hands and dances up and down*] Oh, Jim, I knew it! I knew you couldn't! Oh, I'm so glad, Jim! I'm so happy! You're still my old Jim—and I'm so glad! [*He looks at her dazedly, a fierce rage slowly gathering on his face. She dances away from him. His eyes follow her. His hands clench. She stands in front of the mask—triumphantly*] There! What did I tell you? I told you I'd give you the laugh! [*She begins to laugh with wild unrestraint, grabs the mask from its place, sets it in the middle of the table and plunging the knife down through it pins it to the table*] There! Who's got the laugh now?

JIM [*his eyes bulging—hoarsely*]: You devil! You white devil woman! [*In a terrible roar, raising his fists above her head*] You devil!

ELLA [*looking up at him with a bewildered cry of terror*]: Jim!

Her appeal recalls him to himself. He lets his arms slowly drop to his sides, bowing his head. ELLA *points tremblingly to the mask.*

It's all right, Jim! It's dead. The devil's dead. See! It couldn't live—unless you passed. If you'd passed it would have lived in you. Then I'd have had to kill you, Jim, don't you see?—or it would have killed me. But now I've killed it. [*She pats his hand*] So you needn't ever be afraid any more, Jim.

JIM [*dully*]: I've got to sit down, Honey. I'm tired. I haven't had much chance for sleep in so long— [*He slumps down in the chair by the table.*]

ELLA [*sits down on the floor beside him and holds his hand. Her face is gradually regaining an expression that is happy, childlike and pretty*]: I know, Jim! That was my fault. I wouldn't let you sleep. I couldn't let you. I kept thinking if he sleeps good then he'll be sure to study good and then he'll pass—and the devil'll win!

JIM [*with a groan*]: Don't, Honey!

ELLA [*with a childish grin*]: That was why I carried that knife around—[*she frowns—puzzled*]—one reason—to keep you from studying and sleeping by scaring you.

JIM: I wasn't scared of being killed. I was scared of what they'd do to you after.

ELLA [*after a pause—like a child*]: Will God forgive me, Jim?

JIM: Maybe He can forgive what you've done to me; and maybe He can forgive what I've done to you; but I don't see how He's going to forgive—Himself.

ELLA: I prayed and prayed. When you were away taking the examinations and I was alone with the nurse, I closed my eyes and pretended to be asleep but I was praying with all my might: O God, don't let Jim pass!

JIM [*with a sob*]: Don't, Honey, don't! For the good Lord's sake! You're hurting me!

ELLA [*frightenedly*]: How, Jim? Where? [*Then after a pause—suddenly*] I'm sick, Jim. I don't think I'll live long.

JIM [*simply*]: Then I won't either. Somewhere yonder maybe—together—our luck'll change. But I wanted—here and now—before you—we—I wanted to prove to you—to myself—to become a fullfledged Member—so you could be proud— [*He stops. Words fail and he is beyond tears*].

ELLA [*brightly*]: Well, it's all over, Jim. Everything'll be all right now. [*Chattering along*] I'll be just your little girl, Jim—and you'll be my little boy—just as we used to be, remember, when we were beaux; and I'll put shoe blacking on my face and pretend I'm black and you can put chalk on your face and pretend you're white just as we used to do—and we can play marbles—only you mustn't all the time be a boy. Sometimes you must be my old kind Uncle Jim who's been with us for years and years. Will you, Jim?

JIM [*with utter resignation*]: Yes, Honey.

ELLA: And you'll never, never, never, never leave me, Jim?

JIM: Never, Honey.

ELLA: 'Cause you're all I've got in the world—and I love you, Jim. [*She kisses his hand as a child might, tenderly and gratefully.*]

JIM [*suddenly throws himself on his knees and raises his shining eyes, his transfigured face*] Forgive me, God—and make me worthy! Now I see Your Light again! Now I hear Your Voice! [*He begins to weep in an ectasy of religious humility*] Forgive me, God, for blashpeming You! Let this fire of burning suffering purify me of selfishness and make me worthy of the child You send me for the woman You take away!

ELLA [*jumping to her feet—excitedly*]: Don't cry, Jim! You mustn't cry! I've got only a little time left and I want to play. Don't be old Uncle Jim now. Be my little boy, Jim. Pretend you're Painty Face and I'm Jim Crow. Come and play!

JIM [*still deeply exalted*]: Honey, Honey, I'll play right up to the gates of Heaven with you!

She tugs at one of his hands, laughingly trying to pull him up from his knees as

THE CURTAIN FALLS

Langston Hughes

(1902–1967)

Langston Hughes spent a lifetime trying to illuminate the "soul world" of the American black. One of the best-known Negro authors in America, Hughes wrote poetry, fiction, and nonfiction, as well as plays. A prolific artist who began to flourish as a main force in the Harlem Renaissance of the 1920's and whose reputation toward the close of his life took him on reading and lecture tours all over the world, Hughes wrote more than twenty dramas, operas, and musicals. He saw the need for a Negro National Theater, somewhat akin to the famed Abbey Players of Dublin. His own efforts toward establishing such an organization began in January, 1938, with the Harlem Suitcase Theater: a second-story loft with enough stage properties to fit into a suitcase.

Hughes's *Mulatto* had been produced in 1935 and enjoyed a successful run of 373 consecutive performances on Broadway. Nearly as melodramatic and heavy-handed as Edward Brewster Sheldon's *The Nigger, Mulatto* was even somewhat similar in theme to the Sheldon play: a white Georgia aristocrat has kept a "brown woman" mistress who has borne him a son; now that son, grown to a defiant young man, and his father must confront each other. A somewhat dated play, Hughes's study of a black-white union is less forceful than O'Neill's. A better treatment of the Negro plight is Hughes's historical play, *Don't You Want to Be Free?* (1938), depicting enslavement, emancipation, suffering, and an ultimate union of all downtrodden blacks with the white working class. The idea of blacks uniting with white proletarians had been recognized by Odets in the 1930's in *Waiting for Lefty* and by Richard Wright in many of his poems, especially those written for Communist-oriented periodicals like *New Masses:*

> *I am black and I have seen black hands*
> *Raised in fists of revolt, side by side with the white fists of white workers.*
> . . .

The plight of the black in America was made worse by the overall misery of the Great Depression, and Hughes tried in his writings to respond to this crisis.

Hughes the social commentator and Hughes the black artist were most effectively fused in *Soul Gone Home,* written in 1937, a brief, brilliant tragi-comedy: a theatrical fantasy describing the brief return to life of the corpse of a black prostitute's son before the white ambulance drivers arrive to carry him to the morgue. The dialogue between mother and son reflects the plucky vitality that Hughes once put into verse in "Mother to Son":

> *Well, son, I'll tell you:*
> *Life for me ain't been no crystal stair.*
> *It's had tacks in it,*
> *And splinters,*
> *And boards torn up,*
> *And places with no carpet on the floor—*
> *Bare.*
> *But all the time*
> *I'se been a-climbin' on. . . .*

Until Lorraine Hansberry's big commercial success and the subsequent rise of interest in a New Black Theater, Langston Hughes was the leader in black dramatic art. And while it is true that Hughes wanted a Black Theater putting on black plays by black playwrights with black actors, he was forced by the heavy expenses of the theater (the ever-present need for an auditorium, staff, advertising resources) to write of the Negro dilemmas primarily for white theater-goers.

Today there are clear signs of a new Black Renaissance, and the emergence of the Black Arts experience from the black community has brought to the off-Broadway "little theater" movement vital images of the problems of ghetto-dwelling disinherited Americans. The Revolutionary Theater (Spirit House) in Newark sponsored by controversial author-activist LeRoi Jones, the Concept East group in Detroit, the Douglass House in Watts, and the New Lafayette in Harlem are among the recently developed organizations dedicated to writing, producing, and staging plays in and about the black ghettos. It is evident that long literary strides have been taken since 1930 when Marc Connelly's successful play *Green Pastures* glibly portrayed for white audiences the drawling, Bible-quoting, fish-frying, superstitious, happy and smiling Southern Negroes in all of their stereotyped shuffling.

Soul Gone Home

Characters

THE MOTHER
THE SON
TWO MEN

Night.

A tenement room, bare, ugly, dirty. An unshaded electric-light bulb. In the middle of the room a cot on which the body of a NEGRO YOUTH *is lying. His hands are folded across his chest. There are pennies on his eyes. He is a soul gone home.*

As the curtain rises, his MOTHER, *a large, middle-aged woman in a red sweater, kneels weeping beside the cot, loudly simulating grief.*

MOTHER: Oh, Gawd! Oh, Lawd! Why did you take my son from me? Oh, Gawd, why did you do it? He was all I had! Oh, Lawd, what am I gonna do? [*Looking at the dead boy and stroking his head*] Oh, son! Oh, Ronnie! Oh, my boy, speak to me! Ronnie, say something to me! Son, why don't you talk to your mother? Can't you see she's bowed down in sorrow? Son, speak to me, just a word! Come back from the spirit-world and speak to me! Ronnie, come back from the dead and speak to your mother!

SON: [*Lying there dead as a doornail. Speaking loudly*] I wish I wasn't dead, so I *could* speak to you. You been a hell of a mama!

MOTHER: [*Falling back from the cot in astonishment, but still on her knees*] Ronnie! Ronnie! What's that you say? What you sayin' to your mother? [*Wild-eyed*] Is you done opened your mouth and spoke to me?

SON: I said you a hell of a mama!

MOTHER: [*Rising suddenly and backing away, screaming loudly*] Awo-ooo-o! Ronnie, that ain't you talkin'!

SON: Yes, it is me talkin', too! I say you been a no-good mama.

MOTHER: What for you talkin' to me like that, Ronnie? You ain't never said nothin' like that to me before.

SON: I know it, but I'm dead now—and I can say what I want to say. [*Stirring*] You done called on me to talk, ain't you? Lemme take these pennies off my eyes so I can see. [*He takes the coins off his eyes, throws them across the room, and sits up in bed. He is a very dark boy in a torn white shirt. He looks hard at his mother*] Mama, you know you ain't done me right.

MOTHER: What you mean, I ain't done you right? [*She is rooted in horror*] What you mean, huh?

SON: You know what I mean.

MOTHER: No, I don't neither. [*Trembling violently*] What you mean comin' back to haunt your poor old mother? Ronnie, what does you mean?

SON: [*Leaning forward*] I'll tell you just what I mean! You been a bad mother to me.

MOTHER: Shame! Shame! Shame, talkin' to your mama that away. Damn it! Shame! I'll slap your face. [*She starts toward him, but he rolls his big white eyes at her, and she backs away*] Me, what borned you! Me, what suffered the pains o' death to bring you into this world! Me, what raised you up, what washed your dirty didies. [*Sorrowfully*] And now I'm left here mighty nigh prostrate 'cause you gone from me! Ronnie, what you mean talkin' to *me* like that—what brought you into this world?

SON: You never did feed me good, that's what I mean! Who wants to come into the world hongry, and go out the same way?

MOTHER: What you mean hongry? When I had money, ain't I fed you?

SON: [*Suddenly*] Most of the time you ain't had no money.

MOTHER: 'Twarn't my fault then.

SON: 'Twarn't *my* fault neither.

MOTHER: [*Defensively*] You always was so weak and sickly, you couldn't earn nothin' sellin' papers.

SON: I know it.

MOTHER: You never was no use to me.

SON: So you must lemme grow up in the street, and I ain't had no manners nor morals, neither.

MOTHER: Manners and morals? Ronnie, where'd you learn all them big words?

SON: I learnt 'em just now in the spirit-world.

MOTHER: [*Coming nearer*] But you ain't been dead no more'n an hour.

SON: That's long enough to learn a lot.

MOTHER: Well, what else did you find out?

SON: I found out you was a hell of a mama puttin' me out in the cold to sell papers soon as I could even walk.

MOTHER: What? You little liar!

SON: If I'm lyin', I'm dyin'! And lettin' me grow up all bowlegged and stunted from undernourishment.

MOTHER: Under-nurse-mint?

SON: Undernourishment. You heard what the doctor said last week?

MOTHER: Naw, what'd he say?

SON: He said I was dyin' o' undernourishment, that's what he said. He said I had TB 'cause I didn't have enough to eat never when I were a child. And he said I couldn't get well, nohow eating nothin' but beans ever since I been sick. Said I needed milk and eggs. And you said you ain't got no money for milk and eggs, which I know you ain't. [*Gently*] We never had no money, mama, not even since you took up hustlin' on the streets.

MOTHER: Son, money ain't everything.

SON: Naw, but when you got TB you have to have milk and eggs.

MOTHER: [*Advancing sentimentally*] Anyhow, I love you, Ronnie!

SON: [*Rudely*] Sure you love me—but here I am dead.

MOTHER: [*Angrily*] Well, damn your hide, you ain't even decent dead. If you was, you wouldn't be sittin' there jawin' at your mother when she's sheddin' every tear she's got for you tonight.

SON: First time you ever did cry for me, far as I know.

MOTHER: Tain't! You's a liar! I cried when I borned you—you was such a big child—ten pounds.

SON: Then *I* did the cryin' after that, I reckon.

MOTHER: [*Proudly*] Sure, I could of let you die, but I didn't. Naw, I kept you with me—off and on. And I lost the chance to marry many a good man, too—if it weren't for you. No man wants to take care o' nobody else's child. [*Self-pityingly*] You been a burden to me, Randolph.

SON: [*Angrily*] What did you have me for then, in the first place?

MOTHER: How could I help havin' you, you little bastard? Your father ruint me—and you's the result. And I been worried with you for sixteen years. [*Disgustedly*] Now, just when you get big enough to work and do me some good, you have to go and die.

SON: I sure am dead!

MOTHER: But you ain't decent dead! Here you come back to haunt your poor old mama, and spoil her cryin' spell, and spoil the mournin'. [*There is the noise of an ambulance gong outside. The* MOTHER *goes to the window and looks down into the street. Turns to* SON] Ronnie, lay down quick! Here comes the city's ambulance to take you to the undertaker's. Don't let them white men see you dead, sitting up here quarrelin' with your mother. Lay down and fold your hands back like I had 'em.

SON: [*Passing his hand across his head*] All right, but gimme that comb yonder and my stocking cap. I don't want to go out of here with my hair standin' straight up in front, even if I is dead. [*The* MOTHER *hands him a comb and his stocking cap. The* SON *combs his hair and puts the cap on. Noise of men coming up the stairs*]

MOTHER: Hurry up, Ronnie, they'll be here in no time.

SON: Aw, they got another flight to come yet. Don't rush me, ma!

MOTHER: Yes, but I got to put these pennies back on your eyes, boy! [*She searches in a corner for the coins as her* SON *lies down and folds his hands, stiff in death. She finds the coins and puts them nervously on his eyes, watching the door meanwhile. A knock*] Come in.

Enter two MEN *in the white coats of city health employees.*

MAN: Somebody sent for us to get the body of Ronnie Bailey? Third floor, apartment five.

MOTHER: Yes, sir here he is! [*Weeping loudly*] He's my boy! Oh, Lawd, he's done left me! Oh, Lawdy, he's done gone home! His soul's gone home! Oh, what am I gonna do? Mister! Mister! Mister, the Lawd's done took him home! [*As the* MEN *unfold the stretchers, she continues to weep hysterically. They place the boy's thin body on the stretchers and cover it with a rubber cloth. Each man takes his end of the stretchers. Silently, they walk out the door as the* MOTHER *wails*] Oh, my son! Oh, my boy! Come back, come back, come back! Ronnie, come back! [*One loud scream as the door closes*] Awo-ooo-o!

As the footsteps of the men die down on the stairs, the MOTHER *becomes suddenly quiet. She goes to a broken mirror and begins to rouge and powder her face. In the street the ambulance gong sounds fainter and fainter in the distance. The* MOTHER *takes down an old fur coat from a nail and puts it on. Before she leaves, she smooths back the quilts on the cot from which the dead boy has been removed. She looks into the mirror again, and once more whitens her face with powder. She dons a red hat. From a handbag she takes a cigarette, lights it, and walks slowly out the door. At the door she switches off the light. The hallway is dimly illuminated. She turns before closing the door, looks back into the room, and speaks.*

MOTHER: Tomorrow, Ronnie, I'll buy you some flowers—if I can pick up a dollar tonight. You was a hell of a no-good son, I swear!

CURTAIN

Ben Caldwell

(1937–   )

"We don't want to have a higher form of white art in blackface," writes Ed Bullins, a thoughtful spokesman for the Black Arts movement; "We are working toward something entirely different and new that encompasses the soul and the spirit of black people, and that represents the whole experience of our being here in this oppressive land." Thus the new drama by black playwrights reflects the disappointments and frustrations of second-class citizenship; it reveals the essential mistrust and anger bred by racism. Ben Caldwell, whose work has been performed by LeRoi Jones's Spirit House repertory group, tries to capture the contemporary black rage provoked by years of cynical coping with "the man." In one of his short plays, *Prayer Meeting or, The First Militant Minister,* Ben Caldwell's preacher, after a symbolic, traumatic confrontation with a burglar tentatively identified as "the Almighty," sees the light and says so: "Brothers and sister, I had a talk with God last night. He told me to tell you that the time has come to put an end to this murder, suffering, oppression, exploitation to which the white man subjects us. The time has come to put an end to the fear which, for so long, suppressed our actions. The time has come. . . ." Often reminiscent of the explosive rhetoric of the Depression and of the rhythmic repetitions of black sermons, such drama takes fire as militants express their need to claim their usurped inheritance from America. Watts, Newark, Harlem, and Detroit have sadly demonstrated the major conflicts exposed by writers of the New Black Theater.

Plays reflecting the alienated black and his efforts to assess present status and subsequent strategy differ in creative range and style, and Ben Caldwell bases his "musical tragedy" *The King of Soul* on an historical event: the death of Otis Redding, a Negro rock-blues singer of considerable talent and popularity, in an airplane crash in December, 1967. Was there a white plot to eliminate Redding, to impound, as it were, his financial assets and continue filling the pockets of his white agents? Had he outlived his usefulness to the community of white exploiters? Redding was looked on as a model for black racial pride. His life and death are material for a legend. He was a hero. The concluding dialogue between two young blacks—one of them, at first, unconvinced of a white conspiracy—shows the immense gulf of suspicion and anger that must be bridged. The cagey, symbolic White Devil is omnipresent throughout Caldwell's tight action.

The King of Soul *or* The Devil and Otis Redding

A musical tragedy
A one-act play

Characters

OTIS
OTIS' MOTHER
CHURCH WOMAN
BLACK LAWYER
TWO TEEN-AGED GIRLS
BLACK EXTRAS, *scene fillers*
TWO BLACK MEN, *in bar*
PILOT, *white*
THE DEVIL, *the sequence of his disguises as the devil /A&R man/master of ceremonies/aircraft salesman/airport mechanic/policeman*

Scene I

We see a church in a Black community. Down South. A sign says, "Macon County Baptist Church." It's Sunday—services are over. We see a group of PEOPLE *going, slowly, in different directions. Walking and talking, or just standing, enjoying the sun-bright morning. We focus upon a conversation between two middle-aged* WOMEN. *One of them is the mother of a young* MAN *who sings in the church choir.*

WOMAN: It sure was a lovely service today. The reverend spoke just beautifully. You know that boy of yours sure can sing! My goodness! The sisters get happy everytime he opens his mouth! He sound like he got more God in him than all the rest of us.

MOTHER: Yes, Otis makes me so proud. I feel like I was blessed to birth him. He such a good boy, too—he worries so much 'bout me and his daddy, and his sisters and brothers—he wants so much for us. He's all the time talking about how much money he might make if he went and made some records. He wants to do so much. Well, sister, I'm gon' get on home and fix dinner for that family of mine. Give my love to all of yours.

WOMAN: Alright now.

Fade out on this screen, and we go to:

Scene II

A barely lighted room. OTIS *lays sleeping. He is startled awake [he is really dreaming] by a flash of red light that flickers like a fire. A figure, a* WHITE MAN, *is standing at the foot of his bed, like an apparition. His suit looks red, and has a high white collar like a priest's. [Throughout the play, which is* OTIS' *life, we see the same* WHITE MAN. *We witness him as he changes costumes and disguises. He is the Devil. Keep your eye on the Devil.]*

OTIS: What?! Who's there? What you' doin' in here?

DEVIL: Who I am is not important—you are the important one.

OTIS: Well, whoever you are, you got no business in here! [*Not frightened, but suspicious.*]

DEVIL: Don't be afraid, you're only dreaming—but the dream is real. I can't harm you unless you let me. I only want to make a deal with you.

OTIS: What kinda deal?

DEVIL: I'll explain. You want to do a lot of things for your family—for yourself. You want to move them out of this old house and into a new one. You want all kinds of things that you think will make you and your family happier, right?

OTIS: Yeah, you' right.

DEVIL: As I said, I wish to make a deal with you. I will see that you have all that you want, but I want something that you have.

OTIS: If you can give me everything, what could I possibly have that you want?

DEVIL: You have something I don't have . . . that's the thing I want.

OTIS: What?

DEVIL: I want your soul. Truthfully, I don't have one. And that's the only weight that will hold me here.

OTIS: That sounds stupid to me—how can I give you my soul?

DEVIL: If you agree to give it to me it's mine!

OTIS [*not serious*]: Okay, you can have my soul! Now where's the house and cars?

DEVIL: It's not that easy. We must draw up a contract. I will give you all the things you want, and when that's done (to your satisfaction) you will willingly give me your soul.

OTIS: Suppose I take what you offer and then don't give you my soul?

DEVIL: Then your life would be forfeited as payment. But you're too honorable to do that. Is it a deal?

OTIS [*mumbled in his sleep*]: Yeah, uhhuh!

The red light stops flickering, and the room is dark again.

OTIS [*loudly—now awake*]: Is somebody in here? Is somebody in here? Man, I musta been dreamin'.

HIS MOTHER'S VOICE [*calls from another room*]: Otis, is somethin' the matter?

OTIS: No, ma, I'm alright. I just had some kinda funny dream. It woke me up.

In a dim lighted corner we see the DEVIL-APPARITION *change costume and wait for the scene to change.*

Scene III

Small town "downtown" scene. Signs identify the various stores and buildings. Emerging from a store, laden with packages, is a big, young, BLACK COUNTRY BOY. *His strength is his handsomeness. He's accosted by [the Devil comes out of the shadows as] a well-dressed* WHITE MAN.

DEVIL: Say, young man, stop a moment! You're Reverend Redding's son aren't you? [OTIS *nods and says, "Yes."*] I've heard a lot about you, son. I want to do something for you. I want to help you make a lot of money.

OTIS [*anticipating a scheme*]: I don't wanna be no prize-fighter mister!

DEVIL: I don't mean fighting, boy, I mean with your voice.

OTIS [*some interest*]: How?

DEVIL: My name is Mr. Jacobs. I represent Antis Records. You have a beautiful sound, Otis. If you were singing somewhere besides church you could make a lot of money.

OTIS: My daddy says my voice is God's gift—I'm supposed to share it! They enjoy my singing like I enjoy some of theirs—it would be like selling smiles! And my daddy says it's wrong to sing anything but church music.

DEVIL: Your daddy's wrong. He just doesn't know. Anything you do with your voice will be holy and spiritual—your father just doesn't know. Furthermore you can reach more people outside the church. You'll be sharing this God-gift to a much greater extent. I'm telling you, you can make a lot of money!

OTIS [*not quite persuaded*]: I don't know. Hey, do I know you? I have the strongest feelin' that I've met you before—or somebody look 'xactly like you.

DEVIL: It wasn't me, but we're the same. But that's not important to me; the important thing is you. You can have all the things you want. Everything for your mother, and father, your brothers and sisters—see the world—you can leave this *little* town if you want to—buy a new house—a car! *Give me* your voice and I'll get you everything you want.

OTIS: I don't believe it, but I'd like to try it! It sure sounds good! What do I have to do besides say, "It's a deal"? [*They shake hands.*]

DEVIL: I'm going to have to work hard in order to sell you to the public, but we're both gonna make a lot of money—here's the deal. Our contract will state that after you've made [*He says this slowly to make the figure sound more impressive.*] *one million dollars,* all rights and royalties to your singing belong to me!

OTIS [*amazed*]: A million dollars! [*Pause.*] Wait—how come only a million for me?

DEVIL: *Only* a million! Boy, what other opportunity would guarantee you a million dollars!

OTIS: But it just don't seem sensible to sell *my* voice completely for *just* a million dollars!

DEVIL: Look, you may be screaming your lungs out in that church from now to eternity and won't make anywhere near a million dollars. [*Pause.*] Now is it a deal?

OTIS: Yeah. Okay.

DEVIL: Good. Meet me here tomorrow, six o'clock, and I'll have all the papers. You're on your way, Otis.

They part company. OTIS *right.* DEVIL *left. The* DEVIL *hurriedly changes into his next costume of deception.*

Scene IV

We hear the final strains of "Satisfaction," the bedlam of a crowd screaming its appreciation. A WHITE MAN [*the Devil in a tuxedo*] *rushes onto the stage, saying:*

DEVIL: How about that? How about that? Let's hear it! The great Otis! Let's bring him back out. Come on back, Otis!

A tall BLACK MAN, *in a bright orange suit, comes back on stage. He is glistening with perspiration from his efforts, and breathing heavily. The* WHITE MAN *puts his arm over* OTIS' *shoulder, and puts the microphone to his face. The Devil is congenial.*

DEVIL: How 'bout that, Otis? They really love you out there. How does it feel to be the hottest thing in the country?

OTIS: Oh, Jack, it feels just great! I still can't believe it! I want to thank all my people—my fans—for all they've done for me. They're the ones truly responsible for my being here today!

DEVIL [*put-on sincerity*]: I wanna tell you Otis, it's really a sign of greatness when you attribute your greatness to the people. [*Brief applause*]. Tell me, what's the secret of that special sound of yours?

OTIS: Well, Jack, I believe it's sincerity. I just sing and sound the way I feel—and that's the truth. The things I sing I really feel them from my soul on out! No secret or no trick.

DEVIL: [*put on sincerity. Pretending to understand.*] That's just beautiful, Otis. Ladies and gentlemen, Otis Redding! OTIS REDDING! One of the truly great ones.

Applause, screams, as OTIS *leaves the stage.* THE DEVIL *goes to a dark corner, changes his disguise and waits.*

Scene V

A record shop. Two teen-age GIRLS *emerge with their record purchases.*

1ST: What you buy?

2ND: I bought Otis' new side. It's baddddd!

1ST: Oh yeah, Otis is *my* man! You see that house he bought for his mother?

2ND: Yeah. You seen him in person yet?

1ST: Yeah, girl, that is one big, good-looking nigger! You know what I wish I could do?

She is telling her giggling GIRL FRIEND *her wish as they continue on their way out of sight. The* DEVIL *is in the shadows, watching and waiting.*

Scene VI

An angry BLACK MAN *is pacing the floor. He has a piece of paper in his hand.* OTIS *is seated, looking dejected. The* MAN *is saying:*

LAWYER: As your lawyer I should have known about this from the very beginning. A contract like this is not only illegal, it's immoral! How did you go for a thing like this? [OTIS *shrugs.*] Oh I know—this isn't the first time a white man has shown a poor Black boy a picture of success and made him pay a ridiculously high price for it.

OTIS: But isn't there something we can do about it? It's my voice. Mine! I can say I don't wanna sing for that m.f. no more! I can say I changed my mind. *It's my voice!* I'll keep on singing! For someone to *own* my voice is damned near as ridiculous as someone owning my sou . . . see what you can do about it, huh?

LAWYER: We'll see what the courts have to say about it.

Scene VII

Court corridor. OTIS, *his lawyer,* MR. JACOBS, *stand as a group.*

DEVIL: A bargain is a bargain—you weren't man enough to live up to it.

LAWYER: What the hell you mean! That was an unfair, unethical, contract. You were taking unfair advantage of this man!

DEVIL: If it wasn't for me he wouldn't be where he is today! I didn't twist his arm and make him sign. I explained everything to him. I performed a service in return for his agreement to the terms of the contract.

LAWYER: What the hell is your grip, Mr.? You've made a few million from singing, and you can't carry a god-damned tune! You . . . the judge allowed you the rights and royalties to *all* of Otis' past recordings! Stopped all future recordings—what more do you want? Why should you make it all?

OTIS [*interrupting*]: Well, you got the records, but the things I'm gon' do gon' make the things I've done seem like nothing. I still got my voice! You won the records, but I still got my voice!

DEVIL: The only "voice" you have is what I have on records! To me, the real value of the things you've done comes after you're gone. Remember Sam? What I have will be all that's left of you! [*The* DEVIL *rushes to a dark corner and changes his disguise.*]

LAWYER [*in disgust*]: Ain't that a bitch! Well, that m.f. has a temporary victory. You can still make plenty of money. He has no claim to your live appearances. And maybe we'll get that injunction on future recordings settled soon. A few appearances around the country and you can make enough to finance your own record company.

*They are about to leave—*DEVIL *approaches carrying attaché case.*

DEVIL: Mr. Redding! Mr. Redding! I'd like to

speak to you a moment. [OTIS *and the* LAWYER *stop to listen.*] I represent the Fall-T Aircraft Company. I have a proposition, which you'll probably find very interesting. [*Shows picture.*] Your own personal aircraft. A twin-engined jet. You no longer have to be bothered with airline schedules. You make your own schedule. A private jet is a convenience and an asset to the modern businessman. All the top names have one today.

OTIS: Sounds good. Look, contact my lawyer tomorrow and he'll take care of the deal.

DEVIL: Thank you, Mr. Redding. I think you'll be pleased. [*Smiling.*]

They leave. The DEVIL *returns to the dark corner to change again.*]

Scene VIII

We see a WHITE MAN *in a phone booth, talking to someone. We hear the airport/airplane sounds.*

PILOT: Yes. I'm at the airport now. I have to have the battery changed. No, it's just a minor thing. The mechanic, here, says he'll take care of it. It'll be ready to take off as soon as you get to the airport. Alright. Okay. Yeah, the weather's bad, but I think we'll have a good trip. [*To* MECHANIC—*who is the Devil in another disguise.*] You'll take care of Mr. Redding's plane?

DEVIL [*slightly sinister*]: Yes, I'll take care of Mr. Redding's plane.

Scene IX

The same two TEEN-AGERS *are dancing to the music from a radio—a soul station—the music is interrupted by a bulletin.*

ANNOUNCER: Rhythm and Blues singer Otis Redding was believed killed, today, when his private, twin-engine jet crashed into icy-cold Lake Monona, in Wisconsin. It's an unconfirmed report, let's hope it's not true. We'll give you details as we receive them. [*Starts playing record again. Second record finishes and the* ANNOUNCER *says, sadly:*] Ladies and gentlemen, a great voice has been silenced. The king of soul is dead. The report has been confirmed. Otis Redding was killed when his jet aircraft crashed, early today, in Wisconsin. He was truly, appropriately called "the king of soul." Otis was soul. The existence of this intangible was proven by Otis' sound. You know, like you don't believe there's a voice like Otis' til you hear it. And it sounds like what began as perfection—needed no cultivation. You got to believe in soul once you've heard Otis. He's gone, but the inspiration of his soulful voice, singing his songs, still belongs to us. It's really a great, great, and tragic loss.

The DISC JOCKEY *plays "Try a Little Tenderness." The two* TEEN-AGERS *are seated on the floor, beside the radio, showing their sorrow in silence. The lights and the sound fade, as the* DEVIL *is huddled in his corner, changing his costume for another appearance.*

Scene X

Sad, sorry PEOPLE *dressed in black. Some of them are crying. The* DEVIL *is on the scene in a policeman's uniform. We hear the people's comments.*

PEOPLE: "I ain't never seen so many flowers." "Yeah, they sure put him away nice." "I didn't know he was so big!" "He looked like that statue of that Egyptian king, Khafre."

OTIS' MOTHER [*escorted by other members of the family*]: Remember how the house used to seem just to vibrate when he use to sing. It sounds like I can still feel Otis' presence.

The DEVIL *disappears into darkness, and we don't see him again.*

Scene XI

Dimly lighted bar. Two MEN *seated on high stools, drinking. They are loudly discussing the singer's death.*

1ST MAN: That's right, man, whitey is a cold motherfucka!

2ND MAN: Aw man you' crazy! You always got some crackpot ideas! What the white man gon' kill Otis Redding for?

1ST MAN: Anytime a Black man start doing something for his people whitey kill 'im—one way or another!

2ND MAN: What was Otis Redding doing for his people? All he was doing was singing and making a lotta money!

1ST MAN: WE WAS PROUD OF HIM, IF NOTHING ELSE! Look at what they did to Muhammad Ali!

2ND MAN: They just took his title, they didn't kill him! If whitey so cold why didn't he kill him?

1ST MAN: They tryin' like hell to kill him! Financially! They cut off his livelihood! And tryin' to put him in jail! They tryin' to kill his proud, strong Black image! They tried to make it look like the white man giveth, and the white man taketh away. But the champ had enough sense to say the only way you take this title is in the ring where he won it. He made Black children say, "I'm the greatest!" He made the world realize that Black is beautiful and strong!

2ND MAN: I can't see anything they'd have to gain by killing Otis—he was making a lot of money for them.

1ST MAN: He makin' more money for them now that he's dead, cause now they don't have to pay him! That's part of their game! The white man sells *you*, and you only get a part of the money! He even got the nerve to take the lion's share! Otis was moving in the direction to get more of it—or all of it! Didn't you read where he was startin' his own record company? And he was gon' manage other talent! Now to the white man it's hard enough to take a nigger makin' *some* money, but when that nigger want *all* the money—when he start goin' for himself—competing—the white man say, "He's got to go!"

2ND MAN *is beginning to give these ideas serious consideration.*

1ST MAN: Another thing, like I say, the white man was sellin' Otis—Otis was a product to the white man—like cornflakes! That's all! He want to make as much money off his "product" as he can. What increases the value of the product more than a great demand for it? What creates more of a demand for a great singer's records than his death? And whitey has no scruples, 'specially when it comes to the dollar!

2ND MAN: You soundin' foolish again—why the man gon' get rid of somebody makin' as much money for them as Otis was? Otis was young, and still had a lotta songs in him.

1ST MAN: Man, that whitey know he can find another young, hungry, Black soulbrother, to take Otis' place! Like he change car styles every year—same quality, different body!

2ND MAN *is considering these points of view seriously again.*

1ST MAN [*reminiscing*]: Yeah, man, Otis was sayin' somethin'. I could just look at my woman, sometimes, and feel and understand what Otis meant when he sang, "I Can't Turn You Loose." I've often thought about the good and bad about my woman when he sang "Respect" and "Security."

It made me think about this jive-ass, frustrating country when he sang, "I Can't Get No Satisfaction." All Otis' music had a message. Tellin' us 'bout ourselves, in a way. Make you happy, or sad, or sorry. Made you "feel" and "think." Made you examine yourself, and try to get yourself together. Yeah, man, don't tell me whitey didn't want him out of the picture. For more reasons than one.

2ND MAN: You know, I think you right! It'd be good if we didn't have to have *no* dealings with the devil!

1ST MAN: Yeah.

They drink their drinks in silence. Jazz comes from the jukebox. The lights dim black, ending the play.

LeRoi Jones (Ameer Baraka)

(1934–   )

One historian of the Black Theater in America, Clayton Riley, has observed that "[LeRoi] Jones became the theater's first genuinely unapologetic NIGGER, as thoroughly lucid in his work to black people as he was opaque to whites."* In the early 1960's, *Dutchman* assaulted the American theater-goer with what was nervously regarded as a bitter travesty of life in which a crazy but forceful *ofay* girl taunts a puzzled, then outraged, young Negro man. It depicts in graphic metaphor the confrontation of black and white in America. Set in the subway, Lula and Clay put on a charade of lies and pretenses, aberration and violence, that ends in murder. In a ritualistic manner, Jones ironically twists the Dutchman legend, making the archetypal wanderer female and suggesting that the compulsive, bloody passion will be enacted again and again. The rage only suggested by the driven and persecuted Negroes in, say, Richard Wright's fiction, was unified by Jones into inflamed sentiments not easily forgotten:

> *If Bessie Smith had killed some white people, she wouldn't have needed that [blues] music. She could have talked very straight and plain about the world. No metaphors. No grunts. No wiggles in the dark of her soul. Just straight two and two are four. Money. Power. Luxury. Like that. All of them. Crazy niggers turning their backs on sanity. When all it needs is that simple act. Murder. Just murder! Would make us all sane.*

Such revolutionary rhetoric fused with an intense, poetized emotion launched the dramatic career of this talented artist. "Something I aspire to," Jones once wryly observed, "is the craziness of all honest men."

Early in 1968 LeRoi Jones became the leader of the BCD (Black Community Development and Defense), an organization based in Newark, New Jersey, but aspiring to create a new vision of black pride and black awareness in all the ghettos across America. The purposes of black art were only second to some very practical considerations at hand: the registration of black voters, the attraction of black capital into the communities, the full utilization of all black resources within the ghetto. Jones, assuming leadership of BCD, has adopted for himself the Arabic name of Ameer Baraka. He has become a leader and celebrity of the Black Nationalist movement in contemporary America.

A versatile artist, LeRoi Jones has achieved success as a poet, short story writer, essayist, and dramatist. He has, moreover, been a prominent supporter of black theater groups, in Newark especially; because he has reached the status of a leading spokesman for black militant causes, it is frequently difficult to determine whether Jones the celebrity or Jones the creative artist is addressing his audience; for the man speaks with several voices. In his play *The Toilet,* for example, a black and a white are unified by a compassion never suggested in *Dutchman.* The inevitable movement from innocence to experience, always painful, incorporates a journey through a universe of many shades and colors.

In *Great Goodness of Life (A Coon Show)*† Jones conducts an allegorical inquisi-

**A Black Quartet* (New York: Signet, 1970), p. xii.

†The "Coon Show" is a bitter, ironic reference to the Minstrel shows depicting foolish and subservient Negroes, anathema to the black sensibility of today.

tion into the character and sensibility of Court Royal, a middle-class Negro, who for thirty years has been a U.S. Post Office Supervisor (he has his badge to prove it), who watches television and goes bowling, and who is now facing a tribunal on charges of harboring a murderer. A voice refers to the frightened Court as a "shiny shuffling piece of black vomit." The pressures generate an existentialist confrontation much like the one Kafka pictured in his classic novel *The Trial.* It is a mystery to Royal. He is a fine, upstanding, hard-working, dependable, black, American middle class, law-abiding citizen. He is no criminal. He has killed no one. He is frightened. Confused. He is a symbol vividly and trenchantly manipulated by playwright Jones to deliver his ideas on Negritude, past and present. "I'm free," exults Royal at last. "Hey, Louise," he asks, "Have you seen my bowling bag?"

Great Goodness of Life (A Coon Show)

Characters

VOICE OF THE WHITE JUDGE
COURT ROYAL
ATTORNEY BRECK
YOUNG MAN
HOOD 1 & 3
HOOD 2 & 4
YOUNG WOMAN
LEADER

The scene: *An old house, with morning frost letting up a little.*

A VOICE: Court.

A man comes out, gray but still young looking. He is around 50. He walks straight, though he is nervous. He comes uncertainly. Pauses.

Come on.

He walks right up to the center of the lights.

Come on.

COURT: I don't quite understand.

VOICE: Shut up, nigger.

COURT: What? [*Meekly, then trying to get some force up*] Now what's going on? I don't see why I should . . .

VOICE: I told you to shut up nigger.

COURT: I don't understand. What's going on?

VOICE: Black lunatic. I said shut up. I'm not going to tell you again!

COURT: But . . . Yes.

VOICE: You are Court Royal, are you not?

COURT: Yes. I am. But I don't understand.

VOICE: You are charged with shielding a wanted criminal. A murderer.

COURT: What? Now I know you have the wrong man. I've done no such thing. I work in the Post Office. I'm Court Royal. I've done nothing wrong. I work in the Post Office and have done nothing wrong.

VOICE: Shut up.

COURT: But I'm Court Royal. Everybody knows me. I've always done everything . . .

VOICE: Court Royal, you are charged with harboring a murderer. How do you plead?

COURT: Plead? There's a mistake being made. I've never done anything.

VOICE: How do you plead?

COURT: I'm not a criminal. I've done nothing . . .

VOICE: Then you plead "not guilty"?

COURT: Of course, I'm not guilty. I work in the Post Office. [*Tries to work up a little humor*] You know me, probably. Didn't you ever see me in the Post Office? I'm a supervisor, you know me. I work at the Post Office. I'm no criminal. I've worked at the Post Office for thirty years. I'm a supervisor. There must be some mistake. I've worked at the Post Office for thirty years.

VOICE: Do you have an attorney?

COURT: Attorney? Look you'd better check you got the right man. You're making a mistake. I'll sue. That's what I'll do.

THE VOICE *laughs long and cruelly.*

COURT: I'll call my attorney right now. We'll find out just what's going on here.

VOICE: If you don't have an attorney, the court will assign you one.

COURT: Don't bother. I have an attorney. John Breck's my attorney. He'll be down here in a few minutes—the minute I call.

VOICE: The court will assign you an attorney.

COURT: But I have an attorney. John Breck. See, it's on this card.

VOICE: Will the legal-aid man please step forward.

COURT: No. I have an attorney. If you'll just call, or adjourn the case until my attorney gets here.

VOICE: We have an attorney for you. Where is the legal-aid man?

COURT: But I have an attorney. I want my attorney. I don't need any legal-aid man. I have money, I have an attorney. I work in the Post Office. I'm a supervisor, here look at my badge.

A bald-headed smiling house slave in a wrinkled dirty tuxedo crawls across the stage; he has a wire attached to his back leading off stage. A huge key in the side of his head. We hear the motors "animating" his body groaning like tremendous weights. He grins, and slobbers, turning his head slowly from side to side. He grins. He makes little quivering sounds.

VOICE: Your attorney.

COURT: What kind of foolishness is this? [*He looks at the* MAN]
What's going on? What's your name?

ATTORNEY: [*His "voice" begins sometime after the question, the wheels churn out his answer, and the deliberating motors sound throughout the scene.*]
Pul . . . lead . . . errrr . . . [*As if the motors are having trouble starting*]
Pul—pul— . . . lead . . . er . . . err Guilty! [*Motors get it together and move in proper synchronization*]
Pul—Plead Guilty, it's your only chance. Just plead guilty brother. Just plead guilty. It's your only chance. Your only chance.

COURT: Guilty? Of what? What are you talking about? What kind of defense attorney are you? I don't even know what I'm being charged with, and you say plead guilty. What's happening here? [*At* VOICE]
Can't I even know the charge?

VOICE: We told you the charge. Harboring a murderer.

COURT: But that's an obvious mistake.

ATTORNEY: There's no mistake. Plead guilty. Get off easy. Otherwise *thrrrrit.* [*Makes throat cutting gesture, then chuckles*]
Plead guilty, brother, it's your only chance. [*Laughs*]

VOICE: Plea changed to guilty?

COURT: What? No. I'm not pleading guilty. And I want my lawyer.

VOICE: You have your lawyer.

COURT: No, my lawyer is John Breck.

ATTORNEY: Mr. Royal, look at me. [*Grabs him by the shoulders*] I am John Breck [*Laughs*] Your attorney, and friend. And I say plead guilty.

COURT: John Bre . . . what? [*He looks at* ATTORNEY *closely*] Breck. Great God, what's happened to you? Why do you look like this?

ATTORNEY: Why? Haha, I've always looked like this, Mr. Royal. Always.

Now ANOTHER VOICE, *strong, young, begins to shout in the darkness at* ROYAL.

YOUNG VOICE: Now will you believe me stupid fool? Will you believe what I tell you or your eyes? Even your eyes. You're here with me, with us, all of us, and you can't understand. Plead guilty! You are guilty, stupid nigger. You'll die, they'll kill you and you don't know why; now will you believe me? Believe me, half-white coward. Will you believe reality?

VOICE: Get that criminal out of here. Beat him. Shut him up. Get him.

Now sounds of scuffling come out of darkness. Screams. Of a group of men subduing another man.

YOUNG VOICE: You bastard. And you Court Royal you let them take me. You liar. You weakling. You woman in the face of degenerates. You let me be taken. How can you walk the earttttttt . . . [*He is apparently taken away*]

COURT: Who's that? [*Peers into darkness*] Who's that talking to me?

VOICE: Shut up, Royal. Fix your plea. Let's get on with it.

COURT: That voice sounded very familiar. [*Caught in thought momentarily*]
I almost thought it was . . .

VOICE: Since you keep your plea of not guilty, you won't need a lawyer. We can proceed without your services, counselor.

ATTORNEY: As you wish your honor. Good-bye Mr. Royal. [*He begins to crawl off*]
Good-bye, dead sucker! Hahahaha . . . [*Waving hands as he crawls off and laughing*]
Hahahaha, ain't I a bitch . . . I mean ain't I? [*Exits*]

COURT: John, John. You're my attorney, you can't leave me here like this. [*Starts after him . . . shouts*]
John!

A siren begins to scream, like in jailbreak pictures . . . "Arrrrrrrr." The lights beat off, on, in time with the metallic siren shriek. COURT ROYAL *is stopped in his tracks, bent in anticipation, the siren continues. Machine guns begin to bang bang as if very close to him, cell doors slamming, whistles, yells "Break . . . Break," the machine guns shatter,* COURT ROYAL *stands frozen, half bent arms held away from his body balancing him in his terror. As the noise, din, continues, his eyes grow until he is almost going to faint.*

COURT: Ahhhhhhhgggg. Please . . . Please . . . don't kill me. Don't shoot me, I didn't do anything. I'm not trying to escape. Please . . . Please . . . PLEEEEEAS . . .

THE VOICE *begins to shriek almost as loud with laughter, as all the other sounds, and jumping lights stop as* VOICE *starts to laugh. The* VOICE *just laughs and laughs, laughs until you think it will explode or spit up blood; it laughs long and eerily out of the darkness.*

COURT: [*Still dazed and staggered. He looks around quickly, trying to get himself together. He speaks now very quietly, and shaken.*] Please. Please.

The other VOICE *begins to subside, the laughs coming sharp cutoff bursts of hysteria.*

VOICE: You donkey. [*Laughs*] You piece of wood. You shiny shuffling piece of black vomit.

The laughter quits like the tide rolling softly back to silence. Now there is no sound, except for COURT ROYAL'S *breathing, and shivering clothes. He whispers.*

COURT: Please? [*He is completely shaken and defeated frightened like a small animal, eyes barely rolling*] Please. I won't escape. [*His words sound corny, tinny, stupid, dropped in such silence*] Please, I won't try again. Just tell me where I am?

The silence again. For a while no movement, COURT *is frozen, stiff, with only eyes sneaking, now they stop, he's frozen, cannot move, staring off into the cold darkness. A chain, slightly, more, now heavier, dragged bent, wiggled slowly, light now heavily in the darkness, from another direction. Chains. They're dragged, like things are pulling them across the earth. The chains. And now low chanting voices, moaning, with incredible pain and despair, the voices press just softly behind the chains, for a few seconds, so very very briefly then gone. And silence.* COURT *does not move. His eyes roll a little back and around. He bends his knees dipping his head bending. He moans . . .*

COURT: Just tell me where I am?

VOICE: Heaven.

The VOICE *is cool and businesslike.* COURT'S *eyes, head raise an imperceptible trifle. He begins to pull his arms slowly to his sides, and claps them together. The lights dim, and only* COURT *is seen in dimmer illumination. The* VOICE *again . . .*

Heaven. [*Pause*] Welcome.

COURT: [*Mumbling*] I never understood . . . these things are so confusing.

His head jerks like he's suddenly heard Albert Ayler.[1] *It raises, his whole body jerks around like a suddenly animate ragdoll. He does a weird dance like a marionette jiggling and waggling.*

You'll wonder what the devil-meant. A jiggedy bobbidy fool. You'll wonder what the devil-sent. Diggedy dobbidy cool. Ah man. [*Singing*]
Ah man, you'll wonder who the devil-sent. And what was heaven heaven heaven.

This is like a funny joke-dance, with sudden funniness from COURT, *then suddenly as before he stops frozen again, eyes rolling, no other sound heard. Now a scream, and white hooded* MEN *push a greasy-head nigger lady across in front of* COURT. *They are pulling her hair, and feeling her ass. One whispers from time to time in her ear. She screams and bites occasionally, occasionally kicking.*

HOOD 1: [*To the* VOICE] She's drunk. [*Now to* COURT]
You want to smell her breath?

COURT: [*Frightened also sickened at the sight, embarrassed*] N-no. I don't want to. I smell it from here. She drinks and stinks and brings our whole race down.

HOOD 2: Ain't it the truth!

VOICE: Grind her into poison jelly. Smear it on her daughter's head.

HOOD 1: Right, Your Honor. You got a break, sister.

They go off.

Hey, uncle, you sure you don't want to smell her breath?

---

[1]Albert Ayler, modern jazz musician whose emotionally-charged work is specially oriented toward a primitive fantasy which evokes images of spirits and ghosts, witches and devils.

COURT *shivers "No"*

VOICE: Royal, you have concealed a murderer, and we have your punishment ready for you. Are you ready?

COURT: What? No. I want a trial. Please a trial. I deserve that. I'm a good man.

VOICE: Royal, you're not a man!

COURT: Please. . . . [*Voice breaking*]
Your Honor, a trial. A simple one, very quick, nothing fancy . . . I'm very conservative . . . no frills or loud colors, a simple concrete black toilet paper trial.

VOICE: And funeral.

Now two MEN IN HOODS, *white work gloves, and suits, very sporty, come in with a stretcher. A black man is dead on it. There is long very piped applause. "Yea. Yea."*

HOOD 1: It's the Prince, Your Honor. We banged him down.

VOICE: He's dead?

HOOD 2: Yes. A nigger did it for us.

VOICE: Conceal the body in a stone. And sink the stone deep under the ocean. Call the newspapers and give the official history. Make sure his voice is in that stone too, or [*Heavy nervous pause*]
. . . just go ahead.

HOOD 1: Of course Your Honor. [*Looks to* COURT *almost as an afterthought*]
You want to smell his breath?

They go out.

COURT: [*Mumbling, still very frightened*] No . . . no . . . I have nothing to do with any of this. I'm a good man. I have a car. A home. [*Running down*]
A club. [*Looks up pleading*]
Please, there's some mistake. Isn't there? I've done nothing wrong. I have a family. I work in the Post Office, I'm a supervisor. I've worked for thirty years. I've done nothing wrong.

VOICE: Shut up, whimpering pig. Shut up and get ready for sentencing. It'll be hard on you, you can bet that.

COURT: [*A little life, he sees he's faced with danger*] But tell me what I've done. I can remember no criminal, no murderer I've housed. I work eight hours, then home, and television, dinner, then bowling. I've harbored no murderers. I don't know any. I'm a good man.

VOICE: Shut up liar. Do you know this man?

An image is flashed on the screen behind him. It is a rapidly shifting series of faces. Malcolm. Patrice. Robert Williams. Garvey. Dead nigger kids killed by the police. Medgar Evers.[2]

COURT: What?

VOICE: I asked you do you know this man? I'm asking again, for the last time. There's no need to lie.

COURT: But this is many men, many faces. They shift so fast I cannot tell who they are . . . or what is meant. It's so confusing.

VOICE: Don't lie, Royal. We know all about you. You are guilty. Look at that face. You know this man.

COURT: I do? [*In rising terror*]
No. No. I don't, I never saw that man, it's so many faces, I've never seen those faces . . . never . . .

VOICE: Look closer, Royal. You cannot get away with what you've done. Look more closely. You recognize that face . . . don't you? The face of the murderer you've sheltered all these years. Look, you liar, look at that face.

COURT: No, no, no . . . I don't know them. I can't be forced into admitting something I never did. Uhhh . . . I have worked. My God, I've worked. I've meant to do the right thing. I've tried to be a . . .

The faces shift, a long slow wail, like moan, like secret screaming has underscored the flashing faces . . . now it rises sharply to screaming point thrusts. COURT *wheels around to face the image on the screen, directly. He begins shouting loud as the voices . . .*

COURT: No, I've tried . . . please I never wanted anything but peace . . . please, I tried to be a man. I did. I lost my . . . heart . . . please it was so deep, I wanted to do the right thing, just to do the right thing. I wanted . . . everything to be . . . all right. Oh, please . . . please.

VOICE: Now tell me, whether you know that murderer's face or not. Tell me before you die!

COURT: No, no. I don't know him. I don't. I want to do the right thing. I don't know them. [*Raises his hands in his agony*]

---

[2]Patrice: Patrice Emergy Lumumba, Congolese premier killed in 1961 by Katanga Province tribesmen.
Robert Williams: Robert F. Williams, one-time black expatriate and reported head of an insurrectionist group seeking to set up a Black Republic in five Southern states.
Malcolm; Garvey; Medgar Evers: See notes for *Angela Is Happening.*

Oh, son . . . son . . . dear God, my flesh, forgive me . . . [*Begins to weep and shake*]
my sons. [*He clutches his body shaken throughout by his ugly sobs.*]
Dear God . . .

VOICE: Just as we thought. You are the one. And you must be sentenced.

COURT: I must be sentenced. I am the one. [*Almost trancelike*]
I must be sentenced. I am the one.

VOICE: The murderer is dead. You must be sentenced alone.

COURT: [*As first realization*] The murderer . . . is . . . dead?

VOICE: And you must be sentenced. Now. Alone.

COURT: [*Voice rising, in panic, but catching it up short*] The murderer . . . is dead.

VOICE: Yes. And your sentence is—

COURT: I must be sentenced . . . alone. Where is the murderer? Where is his corpse?

VOICE: You will see it presently.

COURT: [*head bowed*] God. And I am now to die like the murderer died?

VOICE: No. [*Long pause*]
We have decided to spare you. We admire your spirit. It is a compliment to know you can see the clearness of your fate, and the rightness of it. That you love the beauty of the way of life you've chosen here in the anonymous world. No one beautiful is guilty. So how can you be? All the guilty have been punished. Or are being punished. You are absolved of your crime, at this moment, because of your infinite understanding of the compassionate God Of The Cross. Whose head was cut off for you, to absolve you of your weakness. The murderer is dead. The murderer is dead. [*Applause from the darkness*]

COURT: And I am not guilty now?

VOICE: No, you are free. Forever. It is asked only that you give the final instruction.

COURT: Final instruction . . . I don't understand . . .

VOICE: Heroes! bring the last issue in.

The last two HOODED MEN *return with a* YOUNG BLACK MAN *of about twenty. The boy does not look up. He walks stiff-legged to the center of* COURT. *He wears a large ankh around his neck. His head comes up slowly. He looks into* COURT'S *face.*

YOUNG MAN: Peace.

COURT *looks at his face; he begins to draw back. The* HOODED MAN *comes and places arms around* COURT'S *shoulders.*

VOICE: Give him the instruction instrument.

HOODED MAN *takes a pistol out of his pocket and gives it with great show to* COURT.

HOODED 1: The silver bullet is in the chamber. The gun is made of diamonds and gold.

HOOD 2: You get to keep if after the ceremony.

VOICE: And now, with the rite of instruction, the last bit of guilt falls from you as if it was never there, Court Royal. Now, at last, you can go free. Perform the rite, Court Royal, the final instruction.

COURT: What? No. I don't understand.

VOICE: The final instruction is the death of the murderer. The murderer is dead and must die, with each gift of our God. This gift is the cleansing of guilt, and the bestowal of freedom.

COURT: But you told me the murderer was dead, already.

VOICE: It *is* already. The murderer has been sentenced. You have only to carry out the rite.

COURT: But you told me the murderer was dead. [*Starts to back away*]
You told me . . . you said I would be sentenced alone.

VOICE: The murderer *is* dead. This is his shadow. This one is not real. This is the myth of the murderer. His last fleeting astral projection. It is the murderer's myth that we ask you to instruct. To bind it forever . . . with death.

COURT: I don't . . . Why do . . . you said I was not guilty. That my guilt had fallen away.

VOICE: The rite must be finished. This ghost must be lost in cold space. Court Royal, this is your destiny. This act was done by you a million years ago. This is only the memory of it. This is only a rite. You cannot kill a shadow, a fleeting bit of light and memory. This is only a rite, to show that you would be guilty but for the cleansing rite. The shadow is killed in place of the killer. The shadow for reality. So reality can exist beautiful like it is. This is your destiny, and your already lived-out life. Instruct, Court Royal, as the centuries pass, and bring you back to your natural reality. Without guilt. Without shame. Pure and blameless, your soul washed [*Pause*]
white as snow.

COURT: [*Falling to his knees, arms extended as in loving prayer, to a bright light falling on him, racing around the space*] Oh, yes . . . I hear you. And have waited, for this promise to be fulfilled.

VOICE: This is the fulfillment. You must, at this moment, enter into the covenant of guiltless silence. Perform the rite, Court Royal.

COURT: Oh, yes, yes . . . I want so much to be happy . . . and relaxed.

VOICE: Then carry out your destiny . . .

COURT: Yes, yes . . . I will . . . I will be happy . . . [*He rises, pointing the gun straight at the* YOUNG BOY'S *face*]
I must be . . . fulfilled . . . I will . . .

He fires the weapon into BOY'S *face. One short sound comes from the* BOY'S *mouth.*

YOUNG BOY: Papa.

He falls. COURT *stands looking at the dead* BOY *with the gun still up. He is motionless.*

VOICE: Case dismissed, Court Royal . . . you are free.

COURT: [*Now suddenly to life, the lights go up full, He has the gun in his hand. He drops, flings it away from him*]
My soul is as white as snow. [*He wanders up to the body*]
My soul is as white as snow. [*He starts to wander off the stage*]
White as snow. I'm free. I'm free. My life is a beautiful thing. [*He mopes slowly toward the edge of the stage, then suddenly a brighter mood strikes him. Raising his hand as if calling someone*]
Hey, Louise, have you seen my bowling bag? I'm going down to the alley for a minute.

He is frozen. The lights dim to . . .

BLACK

La Raza, La Causa

"In a Revolution, One either wins or dies"

—Graffiti of the East Los Angeles Barrio
Los Angeles Times (May 2, 1971), Section C, p. 1.

Chicanos, Puerto Ricans, and Indians—American disinherited involved in a contemporary quest for ethnic identity—are now in the process of asserting a sense of unity and a sense of pride. Driven by indignation, anger, and the passionate need to reclaim their birthright and freedom, these American peoples have so far relied primarily on journalism to express their outrage and concern. Frequently the rhetoric is inflammatory, but often it is warm and exultant, emphasizing the positive aspects of ethnic awakening: "I love that emotion which Chicano, *Movimiento, La Causa* has instilled in me. This has been one of the better parts of my life," says a letter to the editor of *La Raza.** Most articles, however, reflect the feelings of a community at odds with the mainstream of America: "What the people must understand is that without our social struggle we will continue to suffer the socioeconomic and political privation which has been our legacy since the U.S. raped and stole this land from Mexico in 1848." (*La Raza,* I, no. 4, n.p.) The symbol identified with the Young Lord's Party, a New York organization devoted to the "liberation" of Puerto Riqueños, is a circle in which are mounted a star and a machine-gun. And Indian poet Red Feather thunders:

THE LAND IS INDIAN!
THE INDIAN IS LAND!
THIS IS INDIAN LAND!!! THIS IS INDIAN LAND!!!

WHITE MAN!
DIE.

(La Raza, I, 4.)

The Brown Revolution and its red counterpart are new realities in the complex, on-going story of America's disinherited.

La Raza includes people of mixed Chicano blood—Indian, Spanish, Portuguese—as well as peoples of Spanish surnames and language. La Causa is the crusade for selfhood and for the elevation of these peoples from the tenements, barrios, and reservations to which they have been consigned by a system that has designated English as the only acceptable language and has guaranteed them the rights and privileges of scrambling about on the bottom rung of the socioeconomic ladder. Racism has stereotyped the Latino as intellectually deficient, morally warped, spiritually degenerate, and economically expendable. To combat such stereotypes and to bring unity to the new awareness of Latinos and Indians, the movement of *Carnalismo* (Brotherhood) has evolved; all are brothers in Revolución, no matter the mixture of blood—Anahuac, Toltec, Maya, Aztec, Zapatec, Mixtic—or the shade of skin: "we have begun a fight . . . all we want is justice . . . we will win . . . history is on our side." (*La Gente* [April 26, 1971], 12)

Teatro Chicano and Teatro Campesino are two groups which through improvisations dramatize the contemporary plight of being Latino in America. Their performances make the point that all of the Brotherhood share the singular important condition of poverty; all seem to share too—along with the blacks—a palpable anti-Semitism.

---

* *La Raza* is a magazine published in the Chicano community of Los Angeles; La Raza is also "the race" whose people are described below.

John Figueroa

(1936–   )

The image of the Jew as slumlord and the Jew as victim share the stage in the drama by John Figueroa. A fiction-writer and playwright of Puerto Rican descent, Figueroa has spent equal time living in Spanish Harlem and in the barrios of East Los Angeles. The patterns of Puerto Riqueño and Chicano behavior and thought form the substance of Figueroa's work: violence, prejudice, spiritual squalor—to which the Anglo remains indifferent. A symbol of wealth, freedom, and oppression, the Jew spectre haunts the minds of the Puerto Rican boys and their black companion. Figueroa's conclusion fuses all of the disinherited into an amalgam of eternal suffering and understanding; that Jew, agree the shoe-shiners, might have made a good nigger or Por' Rican.

Everybody's a Jew

A One-Act Play

Curtain: *Open on a backdrop of New York brownstone buildings, downtown. On the right is a sign with an arrow pointing "right" with "Parking. Hotel Republic" imprinted on it. We see* DAVEY*, about 15. Black, wearing faded white sneakers, army fatigue pants and a dirty t-shirt. He is in front of a homemade shoeshine box, hawking customers.*

DAVEY: Hey! Shine 'em up, shine 'em up! Two-bits . . . best shine in town! Shine 'em up!

A well-dressed man hurries across stage. Exits. Davey watches him leave; then raises his middle finger.

The hell with you, you Jew mother! I don' need yo' shoeses!

DAVEY *checks himself. Startled, he looks toward stage left. Offstage the sound of feet, running hard, is heard. Davey, surprised, picks up his box and is about to run, when enter* JOEY*, a white, Pureto Rican boy, Davey's age, dressed identical to Davey and carrying a shoeshine box.*

DAVEY [*about to run*]: Hey, man! Wha's the mattah? La JARA comin'?

JOEY [*looking over his shoulder*]: Dirty mothers . . . they kicked me.

DAVEY: They aftah ya?

JOEY: Naw, man. I think I lost 'em. [*He looks around.*] Say, man, this looks like a crazy corner. Gettin' any tricks?

DAVEY: Ain' nothin' happenin' here, Jack. Don' go gettin' any idees, man. I's my corner.

JOEY: It's a free country, ain' it?

DAVEY: I don' give no shit what kinda country it is. This my corner, man.

They glare at each other.

JOEY: Ahh, o.k., so it's your corner, man. [*He picks up his box.*] Ain' you with the Tiny Tots?

DAVEY: Yeah. Where *you* from, man?

JOEY: H'un fif'.

DAVEY [*incredulous; awed*]: You wif the Scorpions?

JOEY: I'm Joey. You heard a me?

DAVEY: Naw, man. I ain' heard nofin' 'bout no Joey. Onliest one I know f'm the SCORPIONS is BULLET HAID. He's a bad stud, Jack . . . bad.

JOEY: He's my boy. We tight, Sam, tight.

Joey starts to move off-stage.

DAVEY: Where you goin', man?

JOEY: Up on Madison. 'S your corner, man, remember.

DAVEY [*a beat*]: Say, man, you don' have ta go. I didn't know you befo'. But we's allies, man. I mean, the Tots and the Scorpions, we's together, man. You c'n stay if you wan'.

JOEY: [*comes back, sets down box, smiles*]: Crazy, man!

DAVEY: 'Sides, we c'n watch the cops better wif fo' eyes.

A beat as they look both ways for customers, and cops.

JOEY: What's y' name, man?

DAVEY: Davey. You say you Joey?

JOEY: Yeah, but tha's only 'cause tha's the way I like it. They used to call me Joey Loco when I was a kid. On another block. They used to say I was crazy when I used to fight. I'd go crazy. You know, man . . . loco crazy.

DAVEY: I talk Spik. I knows.

JOEY: You know Sonny?

DAVEY: Sonny? [*he breaks into laughter. His is a loud, whooping laugh.*] SHEEIT! Man, aint you somefin! They must be a million Sonnys roun' the neighborhood. [*counting on fingers*] I know Sonny Lobo, Sonny Chino, Sonny—

JOEY: I mean Sonny Morales, man. When I was a kid . . . we had a rumble. I almos' killed him.

DAVEY: You tryin' ta say tha's why they calls you Loco.

JOEY: Used to. I like Joey now.

DAVEY: I killed a stud once. Irish mother named Ryan. He moved on the block. He had ta fight me when he came on. I broke his head, man.

JOEY: How come you aint in jail, then. In the tombs or somethin'?

DAVEY: Aint nobody knows I done it.

Activity off-stage.

JOEY: Hey, cool it, somebody's comin'.

Before anyone appears, they begin yelling in unison, "HEY, SHINE . . . SHINE 'EM UP!"

A well-dressed man comes on stage. He is walking rapidly.

MAN [*Stopped and flanked by boys*]: Out of my way, I'm in a hurry.

DAVEY [*He steps on the man's shoes.*]: Oops. Now, lookie dere what ol' Dumb Davey did.

MAN: You did that on purpose, didn't you?

DAVEY: Who me? It wuz 'n accident, honest.

MAN: Don't you have any respect for people? I wasn't doing anything to you that you should ruin my shoes.

DAVEY: I don' tol' you, MISTER, it only wuz an accident.

JOEY: Yeah. An accident. Now how 'bout it. Shine 'em up.

DAVEY: Sho'. He know. Now, tell ya what . . . you lemme shine 'em up fo' you, I'll only charge ya twenty cents, seein's how I did that to ya, by accident I means.

MAN [*looking at his watch*]: Do you realize I had an important conference to attend . . . and now I'll be late, just because a wise kid like you thought he'd act funny?

DAVEY: Now, look. I tol' you, I di'n do it in spite. So if'n you gonna stand heah and hollah at me, you jus' best be goin' on yo' way.

MAN: There ought to be a law against you kids.

JOEY: I aint done nothing. So don't you start with me, man.

MAN: Shine them, but hurry, will you.

JOEY *and the* MAN *go into background.* DAVEY *stares at them. He turns and starts yelling his shine entreaty to unseen passersby, while* JOEY *busies himself in background. While he does this, enter* STEVIE, *dressed like* JOEY *and* DAVEY, *also wearing sneakers and carrying a homemade box.*

DAVEY [*as* STEVIE *slowly comes up*]: Corner's taken, man.

STEVIE: I'm just goin' on my way to Lexington.

DAVIE: Well, keep movin' man, keep movin!

STEVIE: I'm goin'. I'm goin'. [*He spots* JOEY, *stops*] HEY, JOEY! What you doin' here?

JOEY [*Turns*]: Hey, que pasó, cuz! I thought the jara got you.

STEVIE: Nawww, they almos' did, but I ran into a buildin'. They went right on by.

DAVEY [*to* STEVIE]: You from the Scorpions, too, man?

STEVIE: Naw, he's my cousin. [*To* JOEY] I'll wait down the block, Joey.

JOEY: Stick here.

MAN: Now, Goddamit, hurry!

JOEY: I'm hurryin', I'm hurryin'.

DAVEY [*To* STEVIE]: Move on, man, move on.

JOEY: Wait!

DAVEY: Go, man.

JOEY: He's my cousin!

DAVEY: Who axed ya?

JOEY: Hey, cool it, man. I aint takin' that kinda soundin' from you! Just get off his back . . . that's all I got to say.

MAN: Now listen! You're wasting my time. Hurry up and shine my shoes, will you!

DAVEY: Finish the man's shoes, Jack. Can't you see he in a hurry.

JOEY [*finishing*]: I'm finished, I'm finished. [*gets up*]

MAN: It's about time.

THE MAN *looks at his shoes, and is about to hurry off.*

JOEY: Hey, you aint paid me!
DAVEY: Look like yo' custumah tryin' ta run out on ya!
MAN [*Stops. To* DAVEY.]: You're a wise little punk, aren't you?
DAVEY: Who you talkin' to?
MAN: You're lucky I'm in a hurry or else I'd call the cops . . . going around bothering people in the streets.
DAVEY: You jis' go right on aheaid, man, go ahead, call them mothers! I don't give no shit about no cops!
JOEY: My quarter, mister?
MAN [*Hesitates, hands some coins.*]: You damn kids are a pain in the neck!

He walks off.

JOEY: Hey! You only gave me fifteen cents.
MAN [*Offstage*]: That's all it was worth. You gave me a bum shine!
DAVEY: Say whut? What he say? BUM?
JOEY [*a beat*]: WHY YOU NO GOOD DIRTY. . . . MOTHER. . . . JEW. . . . BASTARD!
DAVEY [*to* STEVIE]: You hear that, man? The Jew done said BUM SHINE!

DAVEY *Cracks up: his is a peculiar whooping laugh, long and high, and inherently derisive.*

DAVEY: OOOOOOEEEE, that Jew done put you down, bad . . . [*whooping*]
JOEY [*a beat; he stares from where man left, to Davey*]: Who you laughin' at, man? He was jis' a cheap Jew bastard, that's all.
DAVEY: BUM SHINE. . . . BUM SHINE. . . . BUM SHINE! [*gales of exaggerated laughter*]

DAVEY *Falls onto the stage, laughing, rolling around, hooting with laughter.*

JOEY *Picks up his box. They start to walk offstage.* DAVEY *comes upright to his knees.*

DAVEY: Hey, where you goin', man?
JOEY: Aint none o' your business.

DAVEY *Gets up, goes over.*: No need to get pissed off, man. I was only funnin'. 'Sides, I aint done nothin'. The Jew did it.

JOEY: Aint nobody makes fun a my shines.
DAVEY: Awww, c'mon, man. Aint I jis' tol' you I wuz laughin' mo' at the Jew than you, man? Ain' no reason you still gotta be mad, man.
JOEY: You laughed, man, tha's what coun'. You wanna stick, Stevie?
DAVEY: Now, wait a minute, Jack. I aint said HE c'n stay. You c'n stay if you wan', but I ain' said nofin' 'bout him.
JOEY: Let's go.

JOEY AND STEVIE *Start to go.*

DAVEY: Hey! Man, wait. How come you so up on his stayin' heah. They's plenty other corners in the city fo' him, man.
JOEY: He's my cousin, that's why. We always shine together.
DAVEY: But he ain' in the Scorpions, man. I means, how you gonna act stickin' him on the corner when he ain' even one a my allies?
JOEY: I said, man, he's my cousin.
DAVEY: SHOOT! If'n I let him stay, you probly bring yo brothers and all the rest a yo' family to my corner. You studs really tight. [*Reluctantly*] O.K. stick.

JOEY AND STEVIE *Bring their boxes back, and set them down.*

JOEY: I think now we got three of us, we better split the tricks. Stevie, you take the firs' one, I'll take the second, and-
DAVEY: Who you given' orders to 'roun' here, man?
STEVIE: I think I jus' better go, Joey.
JOEY: Hold it. Don' move. I been thinkin' somefin'. You aint got to go no place. 'S a free country, 'n if you and me wanna stay here, ain' nofin' gonna stop us. We c'n stay here jus' as much as this nigger can.
DAVEY: Huh? Say whut? Who you callin' nigger in that kinda way?
JOEY: You heard me, Jack.
DAVEY: Oh, yeah. Well at leas' I ain' no Por' Rican Marine Tiger jus' come ovah on the boat wif my shoppin' bag the otha day. [*to Stevie*] An' you bettah tell your boy there he ain' gonna call me nigger like the way he did . . . else, man, they's gonna be Por' Rican blood all ovah these streets . . .
STEVIE: But he di'n mean it. He said it only like . . . like the way you say SPIK.
DAVEY: Say whut? What you puttin' down, Jack? Ain' nothin' like the way he called me like the way I say SPIK.
STEVIE: You hate Por' Ricans?
DAVEY: Hate? Shit, no, man . . . only thing I hates is Jews.
STEVIE: So he don't hate niggers, either. I's jus' the way he talks when he gets mad . . . that's all.

JOEY *In background sees something offstage.*

JOEY: Oh, oh! H-ere comes the Jara!

He picks up his box. The others follow suit. They run together off stage, right. A cop walks on.

SCENE: *The backdrop remains the same as from stage left we hear laughing and the sound of running feet as the boys come on stage.* JOEY *leads,* DAVEY *is second,* STEVIE *last.*

DAVEY: Why'nt we move on up to that they Hotel? [*He squints in direction of stage right*] REEE . . . PUB. . . . LEEK, it say. Yeah. Why'nt we jus' go on up an' catch us some a those rich bitch Jews comin' outta theah.
JOEY: O.k. wif me. Stevie?
STEVIE: O.k. Good idea.

They move to mid-stage right.

This' good enough. We' c'n catch them as they walks out. Hey, well lookee dere. We got us a pigeon comin' out already.
JOEY: Hey, shine, mister, shine!
DAVEY: Shine . . . shine 'em up!
STEVIE: Two-bits, only twenny-fi' cents.
STEVIE: He ain' stoppin!
JOEY: Ahhh, chinga tu madre, Jew! They probly got their own per'snal shoeshine boys. An' I bet they ain't Por' Ricans.
DAVEY: Ain' gonna be no niggers, either.
STEVIE: I don't know about that.
DAVEY: Say whut?
STEVIE: It's like in the movies . . . they always use niggers for shinin' shoes and butlers and stuff.
DAVEY: Sheeit. Them's only movies, man. These Jews from these big rich bitch hotels aint no movies. They probly gots Chinamen or somefin to shine they shoes. They don't wan' no niggers here. . . . o' even Por' Ricans.
JOEY: Oh. I don' know about that . . . leas' about the Por' Ricans. I know a stud works in one a those big hotels shinin' shoes. He a Por' Rican.
DAVEY: Awww, shoot, how you gonna act, Jim? Ain' no Por' Rican workin' none a those places, man. 'N if they is . . . if you tellin' the troot . . . he probly white like you, tha's how come they let him in. Like he a Paddy o' somethin'.
JOEY [*laughs*]: He as black as you are, Jack. We ain't niggers, we Por' Ricans! We Spiks!
DAVEY: Sheeeit, man. Yo' people is just as black as me, blacker even, so don' gimme that shit 'bout not being niggers. You spik, huh? Why, cause you speak spik?
JOEY: Right, man. We speak Spanish, so we aint niggers.
DAVEY [*he pauses, looking from one to the other*]: You mean you tryin' to put down that if I learned mo' Spanish, then I could pass fo' a spik . . . that I be a Por' Rican, then? [DAVEY *cracks up with his whooping laugh at his own humor. Continues*] Ain' no two ways about it. You a spade man, just like me, even though maybe you and him white-skinned, like them Jews. Yo the same as me, Jack . . . the same . . .

Enter a doorman dressed in uniform and cap, about 45 years old.

DAVEY: Hey, hey . . . shine 'em up, General?
DOORMAN: What're you kids doin' here?
DAVEY: Whut it look like, General? We jus' waitin' here fo' customahs. It's a free country.
DOORMAN: Who do you think you're talking to?
DAVEY [*aside, but loud*]: GENERAL KINGSHIT! Tha's who.
DOORMAN: Wise guys, eh? I'm gonna call the cops.

He starts to leave. DAVEY *and* JOEY *look quickly at each other, then spring forward toward the man. They stand in front of him, their hands in their pockets.*

DAVEY: You ain' gonna do no such shit, General. Onliest thing you gonna be doin' 's maybe bleed a l'il.
DOORMAN: Get out of my way.
JOEY: You aint gonna call no cops.
DOORMAN: Move, I say!

A knife appears in DAVEY'S *hand* JOEY *follows suit.*

DAVEY: You best stay where you are, General.
DOORMAN [*frozen*]: Hey!
DAVEY: Shut up. Now, General, whut wuz that you said about cops?
DOORMAN: Now take it easy with those things, boys. . . .
JOEY: Look at 'im, man. Shittin' green.
DAVEY [*whoops*]: Yeah. man. Face these Jew mothers down, man, they turns yellow and shits green all ovah the place.
DOORMAN: Put those knives away, boys. You c'n hurt somebody.
JOEY: Yeah, you.
DAVEY: Hey! I wanna ax you something'. You got any niggers or [*Pause he turns to* JOEY, *smiling broadly.*] Spookaricans. . . . [*he whoops at his pun.*] Hey! That's what you are, Joey. SPOOKARICAN.
JOEY: Don't go startin' that shit again, man.
DAVEY: Ooooeeee, Spookarican! Tha's pretty good. Anyway, say, General, I was axin'. You

got any niggers or Por' Ricans working' at yo' hotel?

DOORMAN: I don' understand.

JOEY: Answer the man, Jack.

DOORMAN: Colored or Puerto Rican? I . . . ah . . . really don't know. I'm new . . . I don't know many of the people who work here.

DAVEY: Aint you a big shit? A general a the place or something'?

DOORMAN: No, I'm just the doorman. I mean I just started working-

DAVEY: You a Jew?

DOORMAN: Why, yes I'm Jewish, but why?

STEVIE [*retreating*]: Hey, guys, c'mon,

JOEY: Cool it.

DAVEY: See, you guys. Nothin' but Jews and those Irish mothers get to wear these kinda threads. . . .

He moves in and swipes at uniform, cutting it.

DOORMAN *flinches.*

JOEY: Easy, Davey.

STEVIE: Oh, goddamn!

DOORMAN: What's the big idea?

DAVEY: Shut up, Jew. Don' go cryin' 'bout your old uniform. You rich, you' c'n buy yo'self a whole bunch mo!

DOORMAN: But why did you do that? I haven't done anything to you.

DAVEY [*he moves at the man angrily, grabbing him.*]: You a no good, sonofabitch rich Jew, tha's why. You keep all them good threads to yo'self. You keepin' me'in Joey's people from wearin' them. That's wha's wrong.

JOEY *grabs* DAVEY.

JOEY: Take it easy, Davey. Stevie, help me!

They struggle to hold DAVEY. *The man cowers, then he starts to go away.*

JOEY: You better stay right where you are, mister.

DOORMAN: But . . . you're helping me . . . I thought.

JOEY: Never min' what you thought. I don' like you and your Jews neither. I jus' don' want Davey in trouble, tha's all.

DAVEY [*He shrugs loose from* STEVIE *and* JOEY.]: Turn me loose, man. I ain' gonna dirty my clean black hands on this dirty bastard. And you, General, you best shut yo' mouf. Don' come cryin' now . . . you ain' cryin' when you keeping my fatha from wearin' yo uniform.

DOORMAN: I won't call the cops . . . turn me loose, please. I've got a family . . .

DAVEY: Big deal!

STEVIE: What we gonna do with him then?

DAVEY: I don' know, but I sho' ain' gonna let him go to call the jaras.

DOORMAN: I won't call them . . .

STEVIE: Maybe he means it. Wanna let 'im go?

DAVEY: You ax me, I think we oughtta cut 'im up a li'l, make sho' he ain' gonna call no cops.

DOORMAN: Please. . . .

DAVEY: Ahhhh, sheeit . . . will you look at the stud, man. Scared outta his min'.

DOORMAN: But I don' understand why you want to keep me. I've told you, I won't squeal. You guys can stay here, if you want.

DAVEY: He the first Jew I ever had scared, man. I ain' never done in no Jew befo'. They don' come 'round much . . . they only in the sto's. But they's only little ol' ladies and mens. Caint do nothin' to them, 'cept rob them sometimes. But this guy, he a real life rich bitch scared mother Jew.

JOEY: We better go easy, man.

DAVEY: Awww, man, don' go stickin' up fo' the Jew. Say, General, whut you gimme I turn you loose?

DOORMAN: Give you? I . . . don't have much money, but here, you can have all I've got.

DAVEY [*Pushing his hand away.*]: I don' wan' no money from you, General. You wans it, Joey?

JOEY: Naw, man.

DAVEY: Cousin?

STEVIE: Uhn-unh.

DAVEY: Put it back, General, we aint crooks, man. We jus' innerested in findin' out why you hates us.

DOORMAN: Hate you? B–ut I don' hate you. Why I've got a son about your age. I couldn't hate you. I just don't understand why you want to hurt me, that's all.

DAVEY: 'Cause you a Jew, man. Caint you get that into yo' haid?

DOORMAN: But what have I done? I was just doin' my job. The manager doesn't want any kids hanging around in front of the hotel.

DAVEY: Tha's whut you say, man. But tha's only 'cause you scared. [*He becomes angry.*] I seen your kin', man . . . so don' go givin' me that kinda stuff. I seen you openin' up them doors, smilin' real nice and friendly like with all those rich bitches. So don' be lyin' about being nuffin 'round heere.

DOORMAN: But it's the truth. Can't you see that? I only work here. I open the door for people and be polite because it's my job. Can't you understand that?

JOEY: But you a Jew, and they're Jews, so what you trying to put down?

DAVEY: Sheeit, how you gonna act? Look at the stud, man, all dressed fancylike . . . he rich, man!

DOORMAN: But I'm not. I—

STEVIE: Hey! Somebody's comin'.

DAVEY and JOEY hurriedly flank the DOORMAN and maneuver him between them.

DAVEY: These blades gonna be pointin' right at yo' ribs, Jew. You best not say nothin' about what's happenin', else they's gonna be a stone dead Jew all over the streets.

DOORMAN: I won't. But, be careful.

Enter a well dressed, obviously well-to-do man.

MAN: Afternoon, Simon.

DOORMAN: Afternoon, sir.

The MAN looks at the boys. They smile broadly.

MAN: Friends of yours?

DOORMAN: Ah, yes, Mr. Goldman. Friends.

MAN: Sorry, boys, I can't use a shine right now. Well, good afternoon, Simon.

DOORMAN: Afternoon, sir. [*The MAN exits.*]

DAVEY: See that? See he lyin'. He knows those rich bitches, all right. See the way they talked, eh? D'jyou guys see that?

JOEY: Yeah.

STEVIE: I didn't get it that way. Sounded jus' like in the movies, when the rich bitch's got a butler. You know, that yes sir, no sir, stuff.

DOORMAN: Sure, boys, that's just what it was. He's right. I told you I have to be polite. Why that Mr. Goldman, he wouldn't even talk to me if he saw me without my uniform.

DAVEY: Aint nobody axing you.

STEVIE: It looked like the way they talked to each other the same way the guy talked to us . . . I mean, real friendly 'n all. We aint Jews, he could sure see that . . . but he used the same kinda friendly wif us he did on this guy.

DAVEY: So whut?

STEVIE: I don' know. Maybe they ain' friends, tha's all.

DOORMAN: Please, listen to him, he knows what he's talkin' about.

DAVEY: Oh, yeah? Well, you a Jew and he a Jew and I heard you studs stick together . . . that mean you the same, man, bof rich bitches. You all rich, so don' be puttin' down no mo' lies, mother, else I'm gonna cut you up inta li'l Jew pieces.

JOEY: Yeah. An' how you gonna say you ain' rich when you guys own all the stores in my neighborhood?

STEVIE: That aint true, Joey. . . . you know it. We got Chinamen, niggers, Por' Rican and everybody own them stores.

JOEY: Oh, yeah? Well they own most of them.

DAVEY: Yeah. I'm wif Joey on that, man. How come you mothers own all the stores 'n go around cheating and sticking together, huh? Cause you cheatin' us, tha's why, you don' like us.

DOORMAN: I don't know where you kids picked up those ideas. But if you'll put the knives away, maybe we can talk about it.

DAVEY: Sheeit, listen to him, man. He 'fraid to talk 'cause he scared . . . man, he shittin' green jus' THINKIN' bout talking to us. Now, you listen, General. You got somefin to say to us, maybe we gonna let you say it, but we sho' ain' gonna put away our blades and let you run 'way to call the cops. No sirreee.

JOEY: An' they best not be no more lies about you ain' rich, either.

The MAN looks from one to the other. A BEAT. He relaxes.

DOORMAN: Don't worry, boys, I'm not going any place. It's just that nobody likes to be standing at the sharp end of a knife.

DAVEY: 'Specially no Jew!

STEVIE: Let him talk, why don't you guys.

DOORMAN: I was jus' going to say that I sure don' understand what you kids are up to; I mean, it looks like all this is going on because I'm Jewish. And, well, I don't understand why . . . I mean, it's not as if I or my people have done something to you . . .

JOEY: You cheat us at the stores.

DAVEY: You weahs all the sharp uniforms.

STEVIE: Why'nt you let him finish.

DOORMAN: Maybe that's true. But then maybe it isn't. I mean, really boys, you can't go blamin' a whole race for something maybe just certain people are doing.

DAVEY: You mus' be doin' somefin, man. Ain' nobody I knows aint down on you studs. My fatha alla's saying, give a Jew an inch, he takes a mile. That mean you studs ain' to be trusted, man.

JOEY: Yeah. I don' know no Por' Rican, neither, likes you Jews.

DOORMAN: But maybe it's just prejudice?

DAVEY [*Whoops*]: Sheeit, man, I ain' prejdice . . . cept maybe 'gainst Jews, and Hunkies and Guineas and Irish . . .

JOEY [*Laughs*]: Cool, man, cool!

STEVIE: You tryin' ta say we don' like some people for no reason, mister?

DAVEY: OOOOOeee, yo' cousin pretty sharp to pick up on the shit this Jew throwin' 'roun.

JOEY: Yeah, man. . . . He still in school. He don' even play hookey.

DOORMAN: I wish I could make you kids understand.

DAVEY: Wha's to unnerstand, General. You a Jew, I'm a nigger, these two studs's Por' Rican. You don' like us, we don' like you. Tha's simple enough.

DOORMAN: Wait. I know. You remember the man that just passed, Mr. Goldman?

DAVEY: Sho', yo' brother, man. We remembers.

JOEY: What about that rich bitch sonofabitch?

DOORMAN: He IS rich. And he is Jewish. He's a rich bitch like you kids say. And maybe he's a bad man, but that isn't cause he's Jewish. Maybe he's a bad man because he's rich, and greedy and selfish and—

JOEY: Jewish!

DAVEY: OOOOOOeeeee, go get 'im, Joey. [*He suddenly looks offstage right.*] Oh, oh! Cops! Keep your cool, man. Now, you look, General, when this Jara come by, you keep real nice and quiet, man. Real nice and quiet . . . 'cause we gonna be right by you. Dig?

They flank the man again.

JOEY: Stevie, you stan' up front, real innocent-like.

Enter the Policeman.

OFFICER [*stopping; to* DOORMAN]: 'Afternoon t'ye.

DOORMAN: Afternoon, Officer.

OFFICER: Well, well, what've we got here. You boys know you aint supposed to be shining shoes around here. These boys bothering you?

DAVEY: We aint doin' nothing, Officer, honest. We just shinin' the man's shoes, 's all.

OFFICER: Be quiet. I was to talking to the gentleman. They troublin' you?

DOORMAN [*He turns and looks from* JOEY *to* DAVEY.]: Trouble? Why, ah, no, Officer, whatever gave you that idea? As a matter of fact, they're friends of mine.

OFFICER: You know they aint supposed to be here? They aint supposed to be shinin' shoes in the streets. These kids have a habit of making pests of themselves, molesting people who don't want their shines.

DOORMAN: Oh. Well, actually, I didn't know. You see, I . . . ah . . . work as a Scout leader . . . uptown? . . . and they're in my Scout troop. And about a week ago, I heard them sayin's how they'd like to make some money for the summer, you know, for the beach and all, so, not thinking, I told them to set up their boxes in front of the hotel where I work.

OFFICER: Well, they're not allowed to do that.

DOORMAN: I didn't know. They won't do it again, sir. I promise.

OFFICER: O.k. But they're warned. Don't let me catch you kids around here with those boxes, understand?

JOEY: Yes, sir!

DAVEY: No mo! Honest, Officer.

OFFICER: O.k., I'll let them off this time, 'cause they're with you. But get them off the street with their boxes.

DOORMAN: Right away.

OFFICER: And if I catch you kids shining shoes around here again, you're gonna be in a lot of trouble. O.k. Good day t'ye.

DOORMAN: Good day.

The four watch the policeman walk off.

STEVIE: Hey, thanks, mister. We coulda been in a lotta trouble.

JOEY: Yeah. Why'd you do it, anyway.

DOORMAN: I really don' know. Maybe I was shitting green, like you guys say. I sure didn't want to get stabbed.

DAVEY: OOOOOOOOeeeee, ain' he somethin! He don' shit green fo' nothin'.

DOORMAN: What's wrong?

JOEY: Sheeit, we did'n have the knives. We put them away.

DOORMAN: Somehow I'm happier you put them away more than worried about shitting green.

STEVIE: Why you say that?

DOORMAN: Well, maybe they put them away because they didn't really want to hurt me.

JOEY: I sure did'n. Tha's why I put it away. I rather run from the cop, than cut somebody up. Shoot, I even hate to kill the Goldfish I catch over at Central Park.

DAVEY: I ain' makin' no 'xcuses. I put my blade away cause I wanted to, tha's all.

JOEY: You di'n have to. You coulda kept it out and if the Jara got wise, you coulda used it.

DAVEY: I did it cause I wanted to. And don' you go saying nothin' otherwise.

DOORMAN: Enough, please, boys. I think we've had enough threats for one day, don't you.

STEVIE: We better let the man go now.

DOORMAN: Can I go? I'll be missed at the job.

I'm new and I sure wouldn't want to get fired on my first week.

DAVEY: Sho' man, go 'haid. We wuz jus' funnin' anyway.

JOEY: Sure, go ahead.

STEVIE: We're . . . ah . . . sorry about your uniform.

DAVEY: You c'n buy another one.

DOORMAN: I'm afraid I can't afford it. But don' worry, my wife'll sew this one up so's you can't notice the cut.

STEVIE: We're really sorry.

DAVEY: It ain' a big cut. Easy ta fix.

DOORMAN: Well, you kids heard what the cop said. I don't think you ought to stick around here. [*He starts to leave. The boys pick up their boxes. The man stops, turns back to them.*] Oh, say, fellas. Before you go, can I tell you something's been runnin' through my mind? You maybe won't understand it right now, but maybe someday . . . sometime, it might help you.

STEVIE: Sure. Go ahead.

DOORMAN: Well . . . it's just words . . . something' I thought of . . . and . . . well, it's this . . . when you really come down to it, everybody's a Jew.

He turns and walks slowly offstage.

DAVEY: Say whut?

JOEY: He said "Everybody's a Jew."

DAVEY: Whu's that mean? You, you smart. What he tryin' to say?

STEVIE: I don' know.

JOEY: Me neither.

DAVEY: Sheeit, man. I caint make no sense a it, neither.

STEVIE: Maybe he was tryin' to say the Jews are just like everybody else.

DAVEY: That don't make no sense.

JOEY: Well, we can't stay here all day and think about it. That Jara's liable ta come back.

They start to walk offstage.

DAVEY: Well, whatever it wuz he said, he sho' turned out to be a cool stud.

DAVEY [*starting to laugh*]: SHHHHEEEEIT, man. I caint get ovah how that Jew done backed us up. [*starts to crack up*] Say, you studs know whut?

JOEY: Wha's so funny, man?

DAVEY: Shheeit, I been thinkin', man. . . . [*more laughter*] I been thinkin' that they stud woulda made a GOOD NIGGER!

JOEY [*laughing*]: Yeah, man! O' even a Por' Rican.

All three laugh and go offstage.

CURTAIN

Louis "Studs" Terkel

(1912–   )

Louis "Studs" Terkel, radio host and social commentator from Chicago, put together a series of dramatic interviews of disinherited Americans: *Division Street, U. S. A.* It is a microcosm of the country, containing a cross section of people who are prey to vain hopes and denied access to the American dream. With the dignity of a tragic soliloquy, Benny Bearskin, American Indian, tells of his life and hopes among the men whose ancestors appropriated the land from his people and erected the reservation. The dramatic addresses of disinherited American Indians, Puerto Rican, Chicana and Chicano reflect a multiplicity of current urban dilemmas: the tensions between Latinos and police, the friction between black and Spanish communities, the sense of hopelessness pervading the lives of these harassed dispossessed. The past has been grim; the future looks forbidding.

Terkel, as reporter-dramatist, has unified "human interest" and social history with art. His people truly live—as authentically as if each of them had confidently strode across the make-believe stage, captured the spotlight, and begun to speak.

Monologues From Division Street

Benny Bearskin, 45

The American Indian Center. It is on the North Side, area of many transients—elderly pensioners, Appalachians, and many of the nine thousand American Indians who live in Chicago.

Here, on a winter's Saturday night, such as this one, are ceremonial dances, songs, and stories. We're seated in the office; families are assembling in the hall.

It is the Center's purpose, in the words of Benny Bearskin, "to preserve and foster the cultural values of the American Indian, at the same time helping him to make an adjustment to an urban society."

Getting urbanized. I like this term. It means you have to learn the ropes, just like a person moving out from prairie country into the woods. You know, there are certain dangers in such a transition, and it's the same way in a city. You have to learn the ropes. And once you become urbanized, this means to me that you're gonna settle down and you have to have a goal to look forward to. Otherwise, I think it would drive you crazy.

I'll tell you the extent to which I'm urbanized, after being here for seventeen years. Some years ago, we went back to Nebraska, to my wife's parents' place. And for three or four nights in a row, I'd wake up in the middle of the night, feeling that there was something drastically wrong. And it puzzled me until I began to realize: it was quiet, that's what was wrong. There's no fire engines or police sirens passing by, no street noises. It's funny.

I was raised all the way from the Winnebago Indian reservation in northeast Nebraska, to Iowa, Minnesota, and Wisconsin. My father was a laborer. He moved his family whenever there was employment. So I got an early introduction to the melting pot.

In those days, I didn't give discrimination

much thought. Since we moved around quite a lot. The one thing that stands out in my mind is that every new school we attended, we had to go through an ordeal. The toughest fellas wanted to see how tough we were. So we got kind of oriented that way. And if we could whip the toughest kid, why then, we had it made from then on. We had a lot of friends. Of course, that didn't always happen that way, either.

I came to Chicago in 1947, after I had been married, and later on I sent for my wife and my one child and since that time we've lived here in the city. The most important reason was that I could at least feel confident that perhaps fifty paychecks a year here . . . and you can't always get that way. Even though it might be more pleasant to be back home, for instance, Nebraska.

What do you call home? Do you call Nebraska home?

Yes, I think this is one feature most Indians have in common. They have a deep attachment for the land. This has been so for a long, long time. Many different tribes of Indians are now residing in Chicago, but most of them maintain ties with the people back home. Even in cases where the older members of their families have passed away, they still make a point to go home. Many of them make the trip twice a year to go back to the place where they were born and raised.

Some Appalachian whites in this neighborhood feel the same way. Home is not the city, but where they came from.

I guess there is that one similarity. When we were in Minnesota, we listened to the Grand Old Opry on these long winter nights. My brother and I used to play fiddle and guitar for square dances. I guess that was the only phase of my life when I was interested in music other than Indian music. As a matter of fact, I still own my violin. I kept it probably for sentimental reasons. I think the country fiddler was expressing some mood to his instrument. And Indian music is similar in that way, too. There are songs that we have which might have a sad mood to it. There are others that are very joyous and sort of lighthearted. And I found that this country and hill music had this sort of appeal for me.

. . . You know, the federal government has made mistakes . . . and one time, dating back to 1887, under the Allotment Act that Congress passed, they thought that evidently all the Indian needed was a plow and a pair of horses and harnesses and some seed and he'd become a farmer overnight. This didn't happen by any means. So judging by this, I would find it very difficult if I were used to the Southern hill country and then make an abrupt changeover and finding myself in a large city.

I was fortunate in that, as I grew up, at least part of my youth was spent in a city. I did a lot of common labor the first few years, and then the war came along, the Second World War. And I picked up the welding trade, worked in a shipyard, worked in a powder plant. And after following the welding trade for some seven years, I moved to Chicago, and I became a union boilermaker, which I am yet today.

I believe, in the long run, automation will affect my trade. Because in the length of time that I've been at it, design has changed so radically in the last few years. They can erect a powerhouse perhaps twice the size of a powerhouse that was built ten years ago, and they can do it with several thousand man-hours less. And, you know, in the long run, this process of change continues, it's gonna have a great effect on the tradesman.

On the basis of my experience, I'd say about nine out of ten companies judge you solely on your performance and only about one out of ten would have any reservation because of race. This doesn't say much, because I don't know what happens to anyone else.

The one out of ten? Well, they come up with some kind of excuse that we think you can do the work, and we'll call you whenever we have an opening, and that's the end of that.

You put down on the application: INDIAN?

Yes, always. I think that's a source of pride. I think a lot of fellas think this is a source of pride, because we enjoy the distinction that no other person has. We are at home, while everyone else came here from somewhere else.

And I believe that, as time goes on, that society becomes more and more complex, there is that need for a basic pride in order to have something on which to build character. If you don't have that pride, well, then you have no identity. We understand that all the states have these mental institutions that are bulging at the seams. This is evidence of social and psychological maladjustment. So we have to have some values, I believe.

There is possibly a class of Indian youth that doesn't have these values. I've seen signs of this in my travels. Back in 1961, I covered about ninety-five percent of the reservations to the north and a little to the west. During these times I saw the cultural deterioration that some of these children are growing up with.

There are some areas where the transition from Indian culture to white culture is going on, and some of the children are born into a situation where the old values are already lost. There being no basic economies in these areas, there's much poverty. And nothing of the white culture is available to them. So they're lost in between.

And it is this type of young Indian who is ashamed he is an Indian. Because he doesn't realize, there's nobody ever told him: his ancestors were a noble race of men, who developed over many centuries a way of life, primitive though it was; it existed without prisons, hospitals, jails, courts or anything, or insane asylums or currency or anything. Yet an Indian back in those days was able to live from babyhood till all the hair on his head became white, and he lived a life of complete fulfillment. With no regrets at the end. You rarely see that in this day and age.

Four of our children were born here in this city, and yet, I think, they're oriented as American Indians. I make it a point to take them on my vacation trips in the summer, always to a different reservation to get acquainted with the people of the tribe. We take photographs, we record the songs that are sung, we participate in dancing and compete for prizes. . . .

I have five now. My wife is a full-blooded Winnebago. I met her on the Nebraska reservation.

[*Laughs.*] Oh, one time we had a little trouble with housing. In 1960 the work was kind of slack, there wasn't anything going on about that time. So I got together with three other boilermakers, and we went up to Pierre, South Dakota, where the U.S. Army Corps of Engineers had this dam-construction project going on. While I was up there, the rents were raised where I had been living on the West Side. Well, my wife, with the help of the parish priest, found another apartment.

But I was kind of worried about being eight hundred miles from home, so I jumped on a train and came back to help her make the move. We made the move, and it happened that weekend the American Indian Center was holding a show. So after we got everything moved, we all went down to the theater. And after the show, we all went to the Center and had coffee and a good visit with everyone.

When we went back to the apartment on the West Side, the first thing we discovered that most of the windows were smashed. Well, I called the Chicago police. The police came out there, and we had a police car in front of the door for about two weeks, I guess. But . . .

I still don't know who did it, because it was done at night. They evidently thought we were Mexicans. Well, when the police asked me about this, I said I was sorry to disappoint anybody. As much as I admire Mexicans, I'm not a Mexican. I'm an American Indian.

And, well, during the following days, there were representatives of many different organizations who came out and talked to us. There was a man from the Chicago Commission on Human Relations, the Illinois Commission, from the National Conference of Christians and Jews, American Friends Service Committee, Bureau of Indian Affairs, Catholic Interracial Council. You know, there was very little that they could do.

If I didn't have any children to worry about—they would have to walk to school about four, five blocks—I think I would have stayed. It was one of those arrangements where the thing was operated by a trust. Even the newspapers couldn't find out who was the actual owner. But I found out later that this was right inside the battle lines that had already been established. It was an old Italian neighborhood, and just across the line east of us were Puerto Ricans, Southern whites, and to the South were Negroes. And since we were different, we posed a threat. They thought we were breaking the dike or something. It was kind of enlightening, really, after it was over.

The most amusing part of it was the Chicago *Defender*[1] ran a cartoon. Yeah, there was a picture of an Indian family leaving a neighborhood in an old jalopy, and the people were all shouting. And then the label said, the caption said: These fellas just got off the boat. [*Laughs*]. The fellas just got off the boat were running the first Americans out of the neighborhood.

If we go back three generations in any given family, you see that perhaps our grandfathers had no education at all. But your fathers had a little, and we've had a little more than our fathers have had, and our children are getting a college education. We also see the pattern in the last two states that granted the Indian the right to vote: New Mexico and Arizona. Strange, but these are

[1]Chicago's leading Negro newspaper.

the two areas where the Indians really get out and vote when an election comes up. They realize they can swing an election in some areas of the country.

The Indian has little in common with the Negro, other than they are both minority groups. The American Negro, according to Indian observation, is that the Negro's culture, his entire culture, is obtained from the white man. *Whereas,* the American Indian still retains his own culture. For instance, you go back to the first sit-ins at lunch counters. During these periods, Indians felt that this was kind of ridiculous, because I mean after all, what was a lunch counter from an Indian's point of view? Or the front seat of a bus? Or the freedom to sit on any railroad car you want to? The Indian, in his mind, possesses values that the white man never dreamed of, which are much more important to him.

Some Indians take a stand for or against the Negro Revolution. But there are many who do not take a stand, they want to wait and see, and watch with interest. I believe that they understand, because they have an innate sense of justice, because of their heritage.

I think those Indians who retain the greatest amount of their cultural heritage are really very fortunate, because they feel that it's more important to retain one's dignity and integrity and go through life in this manner, than spending all their energy on an accumulation of material wealth. They find this a frustrating situation. I think the Indian is the only nationality under the system who has resisted this melting-pot concept. Everybody else wants to jump in, they view this idea, jumping in and becoming American or losing identity.

I don't think the flame has ever went out. Of course, we do have exceptions. We have many Indians who have been orphaned at an early age, who have become completely acculturated and know nothing of their heritage.

No, I don't think there's much bitterness retained toward the white man. I think that certainly some of the older people can recall some of the—*many* of—the atrocities that were perpetrated against the various tribes. But they more or less view it as being part of an era.

I believe the Indian sees irony in specific situations. What appears to be ironic to him is the recent Supreme Court ruling on prayer in public schools. I think the Indians felt that we almost witnessed the white man meeting himself coming back, so to speak. Because in the beginning, the foundation of this nation is supposed to be a belief in God. I think that you read some of the historical accounts of how the Puritans wiped out whole Indian tribes, burned them out, and burnt everything to the ground, and then proclaimed to the world that this is a nation so founded under God.

We then arrived at the point where the Supreme Court said you can't do it in public schools. But whether you're an atheist or not, they put the Bible in your hotel room. Indians certainly have a view in regards to things like this. During the early periods, the main motivation in the building of these big schools was one of competition for the soul of the Indian. I was baptized a Christian. Episcopalian.

I think we all share the knowledge that the Bomb has grown all out of proportion to its creator. And certainly it's nothing like warfare in the early days when warfare was pretty much of a sporting proposition. Now it's just a matter of pressing a button. And some of the older Indians point out: in the earliest times, humility was preached and practiced, which was supposed to attain nearness to one's Creator. How in the world is a man who can kill thousands of people just by pressing a button going to be humble enough to think of his Creator? It can't be done.

It's so impersonal. I think this makes itself felt in many situations. For instance, when you become urbanized, you learn how to think in abstract terms. Now when you get here on Broadway, to catch a CTA bus going south, you subconsciously know there's a driver, but you take no interest in him at all as a person, he's more like an object. And it's the same way in schools. The teacher is there to do a certain function. And I think the teacher also feels that these pupils are like a bunch of bumps on a log. You know, this can be a difficult thing, specifically for an Indian child, who, in his family life, he learns to establish relationships on a person-to-person basis. And he finds that this is absent in the classroom. And frequently parents go to talk to the principal, to talk to the teacher; it's just like going over there talking to a brick wall. They feel you just aren't hip. Something wrong with you, and if you don't conform, it's just too bad.

It would have to be a very unusual teacher, I think, who would see the capabilities of an unusual child. Unless the child came from an acculturated family, where you go by the rules, just rules only, instead of person-to-person. Then the Indian child would sail right through without any trouble because he'd be behaving just like the rest of the kids in school.

Of course, the adults accommodate to it, they can adjust to it. But there are exceptions to that, too, and this leads to personal problems: alcoholism and other such symptoms.

Poverty is not merely the lack of wealth, a lack of money. It goes much deeper than that. There's poverty in reservations and where there are no reservations, and where there are no Indians. What we try to do here, at the Center, is to some way, somehow, get people *involved.* Most of these people are coping with their problem on a day-to-day basis. The future is something rarely enters their minds.

I think that perhaps my early training in the home impressed me with the philosophy of our forebears. It was taught to us that if one could be of service to his people, this is one of the greatest honors there is. I think this has been a strong influence on my life. I'll never know all the answers. I'm still learning the answers.

I think there will be some radical changes taking place. We have a younger generation, in the age bracket of my oldest daughter. I think in the future Indians will make a bigger contribution. It's been pointed out that Indians should feel that if it was not for the land which *they* owned, this would not be the greatest nation on earth. . . .

Molly Rodriguez, 15

Mexican; one of eight children. She is seated on the sofa with her Anglo sister-in-law, seventeen-year-old Lorna, her brother Ernie's wife.

What do I do now? Nothing but laze around the house. That's all. My thoughts? Oh, my thoughts are a lot of things. Especially about school, and how it will be in the future. There won't hardly be any work because all the machines are taking over and you have to have a high-school education for this and ya have to have a college education for another thing. And that's just it, you ain't got it—well, you're just gonna sit there and just rot away.

Any hope? Oh, maybe that I get married and I find a boy that is not that smart, but at least he went to high school and he'll know what's happening and all that.

There's some colored people that are all right and there's some that are just no good. To me, they're like dirt. I just don't go for them. I'm actually *scared.* 'Cause you walk in their neighborhoods and what do they do? They throw rocks at you and all that. But then when they come walking in ours, they just want you to sit there and do nothing about it. If it's that way, why do they do it to us? We can't go all over the world, because they're all over. I mean, we can't fly over them either.

What kind of world would I like to see? A world with all white people, no colored or nothing. That's all. I mean, I just put Mexicans and Italians and a couple of Irish people, that's all. I wouldn't put no colored people in there.

* * *

Frankie Rodriguez, 17

Molly's brother. He has been arrested several times; a dropout. In a parked car somewhere in the neighborhood, about one A.M.

Why should I worry about the world? I figure it this way: Who's gonna take care of you? Nobody! And you figure these people that don't wanna take care of you and you ain't got no education, what're you gonna do?

I wasn't learning nothing in this school, nothing at all. Just sit back, watch the teacher say something, and what not. He never asked me to say anything. He never told me to do nothing. Just as as soon as the bell rings, go to another class. That was it. I even asked one teacher, "What's this?" You know. And he wouldn't even answer me. It was a drag.

What're you gonna do? You gonna be walkin' the street? So I figure like this: If I can't make money the right way, I'm sure gonna make it the wrong way. I'll be livin' in jail. [*Half-laughs.*] That's my home, that's my next home. Because look it, if I pull a job, I have it real nice, you know. If I get away with it. If I don't get away with it, I'm in jail.

What can I do in the street? I don't wanna be walkin' the street. Because you walk the street, and you see these young guys, like they wanna go bum-huntin'. Ha. They might just grab you one of these days and beat you up. So I figure like this: Why walk the street and look for your dimes and nickels and pennies on the sidewalk, when you can be robbin'. And if you rob and get away with it, you're lucky. But you can't be robbin' all your life, an' then don't get caught. So ya figure like this: You're gonna spend a couple of times in jail. But you ain't got no education, so that's it. It don't bother me. 'Cause I don't really care about the world, and the world don't care about me.

* * *

Carlos Alvarez, 33

He had come to the United States from a small Puerto Rican village sixteen years ago. He had worked in New York and Chicago as a hat blocker, assembler in a radio manufacturing plant, waiter at a fashionable Catskill resort, and clothing salesman. "When you first come to this country, you have to learn something from people all over. I have been among people of both states, they show they are very friendly."

For the last six years, he had been a night watchman at one of Chicago's smaller museums. "I enjoy work for them, otherwise I can find a job for more money any other place."

On a pleasant autumn morning, there was an unexpected encounter.

It was about six o'clock in the morning when I was getting ready to go home. I walk out about five feet away from the back door out there, at Academy. A police was approaching to our parking lot over there. The first question he asked me was what I was doing there? I told him I work here. He asked me if I have any identification. I said no, we don't have any right now. He asked me if I had the key. I said no, I just left it with the relief man. When he don't believe me, I ask him to come in and ask the relief man. He says in a kind of very rude manner, he pushed me against the car, he said he heard that before from other people, and he pushed me against the car again and called for help.

About six other cars answer his call. Another sergeant drop in, and this man grab me and put my hands in the back, cross my hands, throwed me into that holdup car. My cheek hit the glass, the hood. And my arm was hurt by the side of the car. And they were laughing about asking what my nationality I was. They were laughing, walking back and forth, back and forth, in a way that, like making fun of me. One particular fella was laughing and walking back and forth and he was trying to show off with the sergeant. He was talking to the other guys who come to help him, and he said, "Leave this one up to me, I'm gonna get him in jail, no matter what."

When I called the relief man and asked him to call Mr. Baird, who is the curator, Mr. Baird arrived about five minutes later. And he asked the police what happened. Nobody answered him any question. They asked him if he recognized me. He says, yeah, he worked for us for many years and we know him very good. What happened? Nobody happened to answer him. He went inside to call up the director.

When he went inside, there was about seven more cars, fourteen cars altogether, about fifteen policemen were surrounding me. I was innocent, I don't know what to do with myself. They were talking there for a good half an hour before they decided to take me to the station. I told the station, I think my arm is broken. And I need medical attention. One sergeant, he pushed me and told me, he said, if you need medical attention, we'll take you to the Cook County Hospital and lock you in there until tomorrow morning and you get your attention there, and you don't gonna be in court till tomorrow. Or you gotta wait over here till nine o'clock when the judge arrive. I say I rather stay over here till nine o'clock and not wait till tomorrow.

They took my fingerprints, my name, my address, where I work, how long I been working here. They put me in a room, second floor in the back, where all the bums from Clark Street, there was about seventy-five or a hundred bums there. I was the only one in there clean and decent. Only one washroom, in the middle of the floor, for everyone to use there. I asked one of the bailiffs to please change me from this pigsty to another room, not to be between so many bums in there. I was sick in there. He said, no, here is where you belong. He pushed me against the wall and close the door.

About nine o'clock the judge arrive. Everybody in line, like a pig, went to the courtroom. The courtroom where nobody is admitted. The public is not allowed to there. Behind bars. The lawyer was not allowed to go there. My cousin was not allowed to go there, even Mr. Baird was not allowed to go in there. When I went there, they push me back into the room again because the police who was involved in my case was not there.

Once I wait there for ten minutes, they call me back again. The police was there, four policemen show up. They were the ones who talked. I wasn't allowed to say a word. When I tried to defend myself, they push me, they say, you have nothing to talk in here. When I wait for my turn to come, the judge said. They talk all they want, they said I tried to punch the sergeant in the mouth or in his face. When I was even handcuffed in the back. Which is not true, because I could do nothing myself when there is a man armed with guns, and so many men around me, for no reason at all. I was tired, nervous, exhausted, I didn't know what to do.

They talked so dirty in a way over there to the judge. And the judge, the only thing he asked me was if I have any family. And I say, yes, I have a family. He said, well, I'm gonna give you guilty with a suspended sentence. When I asked him guilty for what, he said, that's all, you're not allowed to talk any more. I say good-bye and I see you later.

My cousin drive me to the hospital and I stayed there from ten o'clock in the morning till three in the afternoon, waiting for the X rays. The doctor find out that I have a fracture in my arm, about two to three inches cracked. I came home, I don't know what to think, I don't know what to do, I don't know what to say.

Next day, what I did, I wrote to different personalities, who runs the city of Chicago. Also I wrote to Congress of the United States in Washington. I wrote the President and I wrote to the governor of Puerto Rico. I explain in three full pages what happened and how it happened. They all answered to me. It was kind of a glad lift that they answered to me and at least they did something. They wrote to Superintendent Wilson[2] and they said that he said he will do everything in his power to be sure that something has to be done to the person who was involved in my case.

How long ago was this?

Four months already. Nothing has happened so far because I'm waiting for the doctor's discharge. I will know for sure what's wrong with the arm. There's 15 to 20 percent shorter, not only shorter, but curved. It still hurts when the weather is kind of damp and it's kinda cloudy, you know.

I took three weeks off. When I came back, the assistant director calls me and he says, I'm afraid we have to tell you right in your face that you have been fired. He said, I don't know if you receive a letter or not. A registered letter. The only reason that they said is that the insurance company complained that I cost the insurance company too much trouble. To my knowledge, this is the first time I ever had trouble with an insurance company.

The first time, the director, he was very shocked about what happened. He didn't believe it. He asked me how I feel and after a while he said, this happens to you for being against the police. And I told him I have nothing against the police. And I say, you talk this way because this doesn't happen to you. And the answer he gave me, he turned his back, he said, "They do this to me and nobody will have a job at that police station." That was his answer.

One day Mr. Baird, he was talking about me, about the same case, the director said, "Well, he cannot ever deny that he's a Puerto Rican." And also one day, when the director mentioned the case to the board of directors, one of the women's board said, I should go back to Puerto Rico, what was I waiting for here in Chicago that I didn't go back to Puerto Rico where I belong. They are the biggest society in Chicago.

This situation is the one that hurt me the most. I loved walking, and I enjoy walking in summertime and wintertime, I don't care. Sometimes police follow me in cars, asking me what I'm doing that time of night. But never have any trouble. They've always been very friendly to me and very nice to me, till now. But this change in the police station, to me they are nothing but like hungry dogs looking for a piece of fresh meat. Those two hours in the police station, that's the biggest experience in my life. I have been nervous ever since.

When this happened to you, were there other people around? Did they watch?

No, they don't watch. They keep walking, because maybe they might be afraid that the police might grab them and say, well, you are involved, too. They walked by and they didn't pay much attention. Maybe they were afraid to stand by because the police might throw them in the can too.

If a person is wrongdoing, it's all right, the police should do what they're supposed to do and what the law tells them to do. But if a person is just coming out of work, minding his own business, now why do the police beat him up for no reason at all?

I think the way the police acts is a very very low way of doing. I was waiting for a bus about six weeks ago. Now a black car happened to drive north up the street. The police stopped the car. The man was well dressed; he come out of the car, he had a five-dollar bill in his hand. He just hand to the police. The police say no, I cannot do that. The guy put the money in his hand. The policeman's hand is against the handle of the motorcycle. Drove away about half a block south. He put his hand in his pocket, the money in his pocket, and the other guy drove north.

---

[2]Police Commissioner of Chicago.

Female Liberation

Out of the houses and into the
streets!
Up from down under—
*Women unite!**

It was feminist suffragette Susan B. Anthony who in 1868 observed that "There shall never be another season of silence until women have the same rights men have on this green earth." Her slogan was "Men, their rights and nothing more; women, their rights and nothing less." Now, more than a hundred years after she and Elizabeth Cady Stanton inaugurated feminist protests against the oppression of their sex by American males, contemporary Feminist Liberation (Fem Lib) groups have taken to rostrum and street in concerted efforts to deal with the "unfinished business of equality." NOW (National Organization of Women), WAR (Women Against Repression), FEW (Federally Employed Women), and WITCH (Women's International Terrorist Conspiracy from Hell), while ranging in philosophy from the tepidly conservative to the out-and-out radical, all want to erase those conventional stereotypes of women as ornamental sex objects, housewife-drudges, and scatterbrained, hyperemotional status symbols. Placards of the times read: THE AMERICAN DREAM IS FOR MEN ONLY. JAILBREAK, SISTERS. AMERICAN LADIES WILL NOT BE SLAVES. WOMEN ARE PEOPLE. TIRED OF BEING BAREFOOT AND PREGNANT: WE WANT FREE LEGAL ABORTIONS (AND SHOES).

It is clear that the Fem Lib movement of the 1970's, despite some moments of comic relief (freedom trash cans for cosmetics and bras), has roiled up far more ferment than the earlier suffragettes who espoused the cause of the New Woman at the turn of the century, agitating strictly for female enfranchisement and the simple right of women to compete with men for jobs. With the publication of books like *The Feminine Mystique* (1963) by Betty Friedan, *Sexual Politics* (1970) by Kate Millett, and *The Female Eunuch* (1971) by Germaine Greer, women have attracted a large audience for their views, grievances, and, in many instances, anger. No longer is the simple issue of working girl versus docile homebody relevant. The social confrontation today is more fundamental: many women feel that they are "castrated, deprived of their sexuality, [and] forced to become female faggots."† An articulate feminist recently asserted that "the whole childbearing function is fast becoming obsolete. We don't need men now for reproduction."‡ Female "rap groups" aimed at "consciousness raising" unleash the pent-up desperation that has haunted many women for years: "It's not just you alone fighting your mother and father and all those engagement announcements. . . ."§ A militant feminist puts it this way: "Let it all hang out. Let it seem bitchy, catty, dykey, frustrated, crazy . . . nutty, frigid, ridiculous, bitter, embarrassing, man-hating, libelous, pure [sic], unfair, envious, intuitive, low-down, stupid, petty, liberating. We are the women that men have warned us about."‖

Birth control pills, legalized abortion, free contraceptive counseling, twenty-four hour child care centers, fair employment legislation—all are current aspects of the various explosive revolutions being generated by women with feminist pride. All Americans are challenged to revaluate positions and attitudes solidly

---

*Los Angeles *Free Press,* Women's Liberation Issue (September 30, 1970), p. 1.

†*The Female Eunuch* (New York, 1971), *passim.*

‡Elizabeth Fisher, Editorial, *Aphra* I (Winter, 1970), 3.

§Who's Come a Long Way, Baby?" Time (August 31, 1970), 18–19.

‖Edythe Cudlipp, *Understanding Women's Liberation* (New York: Paperback Library 1971), p. 161. The writer quoted is Robin Morgan, a founder of WITCH.

entrenched in our national past. Love, Home, and Mother no longer command automatic allegiances. The sexual revolution is clearly a prominent part of America's current upheavals.

Myrna Lamb

(1931–   )

There is a feminist guerilla theater. And there is a Fem Lib literary wing whose significant quarterly periodical *Aphra* prints short stories, poems, essays, and an occasional dramatic snippet on the New Feminism and its directions. Some editorial views express the excitement of a potentially creative renaissance: "We must find our own language, a fresh voice, shape new myths out of old." Such a new voice belongs to Myrna Lamb, to date the leading dramatist of the Fem Lib movement in America. The disinherited woman is her concern: "the house niggers in the mansion of man."

In *The Mod Donna** and *Scyklon Z*† Myrna Lamb has tried to delineate the feminist rage as well as to make a start at shaping the "new myths." Her major aim is to try to make people understand the sincerity behind Fem Lib and to dramatize the absolute responsibility (male and female) for the making of society. As Stephen Crane once wrote, "Every sin is the result of a collaboration." And complicity transcends gender. *Scyklon Z* takes government and illustrates at one point its total control over the life of a docile soldier; a young girl—simply because she is female—may similarly be made subservient, denied control of her life and denied freedom of her body. The forces are unconscious; the moral stances embodied in our social orthodoxies of the past are unquestioned, automatically accepted. *Scyklon Z* attacks such indefensible traditions.

Myrna Lamb, from the New Feminist Repertory, is a contemporary playwright of sound experimental power. Her voice in behalf of the feminine American disinherited promises to be a powerful one for our times.

Scyklon Z

But What Have You Done For Me Lately?

or

Pure Polemic

INTRODUCTION: *When I sat down to write But What Have You Done For Me Lately?, the teeth of a long-continuing rage had found a new hold in my throat. My daughter, then nineteen, suspected she might be pregnant. I knew I could probably help her. There were numbers I could call, and I had made preliminary essays into the fund-raising part of it. My husband had to be spared this knowledge, and a friend promised cash and comfort. But what I wanted, as I wrote, was not only to tell "them" off, but to put "them" in my place and in my daughter's, make "them" understand in a way they could not escape. And so for five or more hours, I wrote a polemic, a diatribe, a piece of agitprop.*

*"Madonna" traditionally designates the Virgin Mary; hence "Mod" Donna connotes bitter parody: a modern ("mod") Virgin victimized by male chauvinism.

†"Zyklon B" was the name of the gas used in the Nazi concentration camps during World War II. *Scyklon Z* suggests the ultimate in man's cycles of destructive weaponry.

The Redstocking Rap at Washington Square Church

Time: Whenever.

Place: A space, silent, encapsulated. A man lies with his head angled up and center stage, feet obliquely toward audience. His couching, which is by all means psychiatric in flavor, should also be astronautic and should incline him acutely so that he almost looks as though he is about to be launched. An almost perpendicular slantboard comes to mind or simple sliding pond or seesaw.

There is a simple table or desk, angled away from man, and a chair placed toward desk that will keep the occupant's back toward man in orthodox (approximate) psychiatric practice, but will give profile or three-quarter view to audience.

At rise man in business suit is situated as delineated. Woman in simple smock (suggestive of surgical smock) comes on upstage and crosses without looking at man. He does not see her. He sits silently. Some time elapses. A soldier, in green beret outfit, complete with M-1 rifle, comes to stage center. He faces audience.

MAN: Where am I? What have you done to me? Where am I? What have you done to me? Where am I? What have you done to me?

SOLDIER *stands at attention.*

WOMAN: [*Her voice dehumanized by amplification.*] Don't worry. We have not done that to you.

MAN: That? What do you mean, "that"?

WOMAN: We have not taken anything.

MAN: Oh. [*Pause.*] But where am I? What have you done to me?

WOMAN: Are you in pain?

MAN: Yes. I think I am in pain.

WOMAN: Don't you know?

MAN: I haven't been able to consider it fully. The whole procedure . . . strange room—anesthetic—nurses? Sisters in some order?

WOMAN: Nurses. Sisters. In some order. Yes, that would cover it. Yes, anesthetic.

MAN: Anesthetic.

WOMAN: Yes. We didn't want you thrashing about. Or suffering psychic stress. Yet.

SOLDIER *executes left turn and salute.*

MAN: I am suffering abominable psychic stress now.

SOLDIER *stands at attention through next speeches.*

WOMAN: Yes, I know. But the physical procedure is at an end. You are in remarkably good health. Arteries. Heart. Intestinal tone. Very good. Good lungs too. Very good. I suppose that's due to the electronically conditioned air and the frequent sojourns to unspoiled garden spots of nature.

MAN: What has that to do with it? Was I too healthy? Was that it? Did some secret-society deity decide I should be given a handicap to even up the race?

WOMAN: Well, that is an interesting conjecture.

MAN: It can't be! That I was considered too healthy? That's preposterous.

WOMAN: Yes, it is. You couldn't really have been too healthy.

MAN: Then . . . what have you done? Was there a handicap?

Left turn and salute by SOLDIER.

WOMAN: To even up the race. I believe that was your phrase. I approve. Very compressed. Very dense. The race that we run . . . the race of man, as we shorthandedly express it . . . and somewhere in my memory, a line about the race going to the swift . . . yes, and then the association with handicap . . . a sporting chance for the less swift.

MAN: Handicap . . . some kind of tumor . . . some kind of cancer . . .

Young woman hereafter referred to as GIRL *crawls onstage.*

Is that it? What have you done to me?

WOMAN: No, no. Calm yourself. No cancer. No tumor. Not parasitic death, my friend. Parasitic life.

MAN: I don't understand you. What have you done to me? Parasitic life? [*Pause.*] Parasitic life. Pseudo-scientific claptrap. Parasitic life. Witch doctor mumbo-jumbo. Parasitic life. Wait a moment. There is a meaning to that phrase. It can't apply to me—not to me—not—

GIRL *pulls on* SOLDIER*'s leg. She is still in crawling position.* SOLDIER *stands at rigid attention throughout next speeches with no obvious awareness of* GIRL. *She rises and approaches him, reaching out to him.*

WOMAN: Yes, it can apply to you. We have given you an impregnated uterus. Implanted. Abdominal cavity. Yours. Connections to major blood vessels were brought in very quickly. As a matter of fact, it was destined for you. It has achieved its destiny.

MAN: I don't believe it. I can't believe this nightmare.

WOMAN: Well, that is how many people feel upon learning these things. Of course, most of those people have been considered female. That made a difference, supposedly. We've managed to attach a bit of ovary to the uterus. I don't think it will do any real good, but I will give you a course of hormonal and glandular products to maintain the pregnancy.

MAN: Maintain the pregnancy, indeed! How dare you make that statement to me!

Using outreaching arm of GIRL *and foot leverage,* SOLDIER *flips her over and throws her to floor.*

WOMAN: I dare. There is a human life involved, after all.

MAN: There is a human life involved? You insane creature, I'm fully aware that there is a human life involved. My human life. My human life that you have decided to play with for your own despicable purposes, whatever they are.

WOMAN: Do you think you are in the proper frame of mind to judge? My purposes?

SOLDIER *does pushups with sexual-soldier connotations over outstretched body of* GIRL.

Your ultimate acceptance of what you now so vociferously reject? The relative importance of your mature and realized life and the incipient potential of the life you carry within you? Your life is certainly involved. But perhaps your life is subsidiary to the life of this barely begun creature which you would seek to deny representation.

MAN: Why should I give this . . . this thing representation?

SOLDIER *rises and kicks* GIRL *aside. Walks to rifle. Walks around* GIRL, *pacing, right shoulder arms.*

It is nothing to me. I am not responsible for it or where it is nor do I wish to be. I have a life, an important life. I have work, important work, work, I might add, that has more than incidental benefit to the entire population of this world and this—this mushroom which you have visited upon me in your madness—has no rights, no life, no importance to anyone, certainly not to the world. It has nothing. It has no existence. A little group of cells. A tumor. A parasite. This has been foisted upon me and then I am told that I owe it primary rights to life, and my rights are subsidiary! That is insanity! I do not want this thing in my body. It does not belong there. I want it removed. Immediately. Safely.

WOMAN: Yes, I understand how you feel. But how would it be if every pregnancy brought about in error or ignorance or through some evil or malicious or even well-meaning design were terminated because of the reluctance or the repugnance of the host? Surely the population of the world would be so effectively decimated as to render wholly redundant the mechanisms of lebensraum, of national politics, of hunger as a method, of greed as a motive, of war itself as a method.

SOLDIER *lunges and stabs at the invisible enemy, accompanying movements with the appropriate battle grunts and cries. There is hatred and despair in the sounds.*

Surely if all the unwilling human beings who found motherhood forced upon them through poverty or chance or misstep were to be given the right to choose their lives above all else, the outpouring of acceptance and joy upon the wanted progeny of desired and deliberate pregnancies would eliminate forever those qualities of aggression and deprivation that seem so necessary to the progress of society. After all, you must realize there are so many women who find themselves pregnant and unmarried, pregnant and unprepared, with work that cannot bear interruption, with no desire to memorialize a casual sexual episode with issue. So many human beings whose incidental fertility victimizes them superfluously in incidents of rape and incestuous attack.

Following the lunges, stabs, and grunts, SOLDIER *slams the rifle against the stage in vertical butt strokes.*

So many creatures confounded by sexual desire or a compelling need for warmth and attention who find themselves penniless, ill, pitifully young and pregnant too.

Finally SOLDIER *simply stands, lifts rifle to shoulder.*

And so many women who with the approval of society, church and medicine have already produced more children than they can afford economically, psychically, physically. Surely you can see the overwhelming nature of the problem posed by the individual's desire to prevail as articulated by you at this moment. If one plea is valid, then they might all be. So you must learn to accept society's interest in the preservation of the fetus, within you, within all in your condition.

MAN: Do you know that I want to kill you? That is all I feel. The desire to kill you.

SOLDIER *points rifle at* GIRL*'s head.*

WOMAN: A common reaction. The impregnated often feel the desire to visit violence upon the impregnator. Or the maintainers of the pregnancy.

MAN: You are talking about women.

SOLDIER *spreads* GIRL*'s legs with butt of rifle. Nudges her body with rifle.*

Pregnancy, motherhood is natural to a woman. It is her portion in life. It is beneficial to her. It is the basic creative drive that man seeks to emulate with all his art and music and literature. It is natural for a woman to create life. It is not natural for me.

SOLDIER *kicks and rolls* GIRL*'s body in sharp rhythm corresponding with beginning of* WOMAN*'s sentences in next speech so that* GIRL*, in three movements, is turned from her back to her stomach to her back again.* SOLDIER *then turns away. Freezes.*

WOMAN: The dogma of beneficial motherhood has been handed down by men. If a woman spews out children, she will be sufficiently exhausted by the process never to attempt art, music, literature or politics. If she knows that that is all that is expected of her, if she feels that the fertility, impregnation, birth cycle validates her credentials as a female human being, she will be driven to this misuse of nature as a standard of her worth, as a measure of the comparative worthlessness of those who breed less successfully. That will occupy her sufficiently to keep her from competing successfully with male human beings on any other human basis.

MAN: You cannot dismiss *natural* as an inappropriate term. My body cannot naturally accommodate a developing fetus. My body cannot naturally expel it at the proper moment.

WOMAN: Females cannot always naturally expel the infant at term.

SOLDIER *turns, rests butt of rifle on* GIRL*'s stomach, and presses.* GIRL *pants.*

The pelvic span is a variable. Very often, the blood or milk of a natural mother is pure venom to her child. Nature is not necessarily natural or beneficial. We know that. We alter many of its processes in order to proceed with the exigencies of our civilizations. Many newly pregnant women recognize that the situation of egress is insufficient in their cases. In your case, there is gross insufficiency. The Caesarean procedure is indicated.

MAN: But that is dangerous, terribly dangerous even to contemplate. I tell you I am terrified almost to the point of death.

WOMAN: Others have experienced the same sense of terror. Their kidneys are weak, or they have a rheumatic heart, or there is diabetes in the family. As I have told you, you are quite healthy. And you will have excellent care. You will share with others a lowered resistance to infection. But you will not go into labor and you will not risk a freak occurrence in which strong labor produces a suction through the large blood vessels that bring particles of placental detritus and hair and ultimate suffocation to the laboring woman's lungs . . .

MAN: Your comparisons are obscene! My body isn't suitable for carrying a child. There isn't room.

SOLDIER *slams rifle between* GIRL*'s legs. Hard.*

WOMAN: Many female bodies are as unsuitable for childbearing as yours is.

SOLDIER *stands at attention again.*

Modern science has interceded with remedies. Your internal circumstances will be crowded. Not abnormal. Your intestines will be pushed to one side. Your ureters will be squeezed out of shape. Not abnormal. Your kidneys and bladder will be hard pressed. All within the realm of normality. Your skin will stretch, probably scar in some areas. Still not abnormal.

MAN: But I am a man.

WOMAN: Yes, to a degree. That is a trifle abnormal. But not insurmountable.

MAN: But why should anyone want to surmount the fact of my being a man? Do you hate all men? Or just me? And why me?

SOLDIER *executes present arms maneuver.*

WOMAN: At one time I hated all men.

MAN: I thought so.

WOMAN: I also hated you most particularly. I am not ashamed of it. [*She turns toward him.*] You may guess the reason.

MAN: I recognize you, of course.

SOLDIER *comes violently to attention and slams rifle against stage, vertical butt.*

WOMAN: And you understand a little more.

MAN: But that was so long ago. So—so trivial in the light of our lives—your life—mine—so trivial! Surely your career, your honors, the esteem in which you are held . . . surely all of this has long since eclipsed that—that mere episode. Surely you didn't spend all those years—training—research—dedication—to learn how to do this . . . to me!

SOLDIER *adopts caricature of at ease position.*

WOMAN: Surely? No, I cannot apply that word to any element of my life. Trauma is insidious. My motives were not always accessible to me. That mere episode. First. Then certain choices. Yes. Certain directions. Then, witnessing the suffering of others which reinforced memories of suffering. Then your further iniquities; educated, mature, authoritative iniquities in your role of lawmaker that reinforced my identification of you as the . . . enemy. All those years to learn how to do this . . . to you.

MAN: You really intend to go through with this, then?

WOMAN: [*Silence . . . looks at him . . . even through him.*]

MAN: What will become of me? I'll have to disappear. They'll think I've died. Absconded. My work. Believe me, lives, nations, hang in the balance. The fate of the world may be affected by my disappearance at this moment. I am not stating the case too strongly!

SOLDIER *squats, staring out at audience.*

WOMAN: I recognize that. However, those arguments are not held valid—here.

MAN: Why not? They are valid arguments anywhere. Here or anywhere.

WOMAN: I think you are rather confused.

MAN: Wouldn't you be under these circumstances? [*Realizes.*]

During speech that follows SOLDIER *and* GIRL *circle counter-directionally in blind panic, looking to see where the danger is coming from as* SOLDIER *aims rifle fruitlessly in several directions.*

WOMAN: Yes. Would be and was. So were many others. Couldn't approach friends or relatives. Seemed to run around in circles. Time running out. Tried things. Shots. Rubber Tubes. Caustic agents. Quinine. Wire coat hanger. Patent medicine. Cheap abortionist. Through false and real alarms, through the successful routines and the dismal failures, our minds resided in one—swollen—pelvic—organ. Our work suffered. Our futures hung from a gallows. Guilt and humiliation and ridicule and shame assailed us. Our bodies. Our individual unique familiar bodies, suddenly invaded by strange unwelcome parasites, and we were denied the right to rid our own bodies of these invaders by a society dominated by righteous male chauvinists of both sexes who identified with the little clumps of cells and gave them precedence over the former owners of the host bodies.

GIRL *drops to ground, her face hidden in her arms.*

SOLDIER *simply stands.*

MAN: Yes. I understand. I never thought of it in that way before . . . Naturally . . .

WOMAN: Naturally. And yet, you were my partner in crime, you had sex with me and I had sex with you when we were both students . . .

MAN: Did you consider it a crime?

WOMAN: Not at the time. Did you?

MAN: I never did.

WOMAN: When did the act between two consenting adults become a crime—in your mind?

MAN: I tell you—never.

WOMAN: Not your crime?

MAN: Not anyone's crime . . .

WOMAN: So you committed no crime. You did not merit nor did you receive punishment.

MAN: Of course not.

WOMAN: Of course not. You continued with your studies, law, wasn't it?

SOLDIER *pushes* GIRL *all the way down with rifle. He gets up and kisses rifle.*

You maintained your averages, your contacts. You pleased your family, pursued your life plan. You prospered. Through all of this, you undoubtedly had the opportunity to commit many more non-crimes of an interestingly varied nature, did you not?

MAN: Non-crimes? Your terminology defeats me. Yes. Yes to all of your contentions. I led a normal life, with some problems and many satisfactions. I have been a committed man, as you know, and have done some good in the world . . .

SOLDIER *kisses own arms.*

WOMAN: Yes. I know. Well, the non-crime that you and I shared had different results for me. Do you remember?

MAN: I do remember . . . now. But I wasn't in a position then . . . I wasn't sure. I recognize my error, my thoughtlessness now . . . but I was very young, I had so much at stake . . .

WOMAN: And I? Everything stopped for me. My share of the non-crime had become quite criminal in the eyes of the world.

There is a shot offstage. SOLDIER *cries out. He is wounded in the belly. He falls. The* GIRL *falls and cries out simultaneously.*

Wherever I went for help, I found people who condemned me and felt that my punishment was justified, or people who were sympathetic and quite helpless. I had no money, no resources. My parents were the last persons on earth I could turn to, after you. I dropped out of sight; for a while I hid like an animal. I finally went to a public institution recommended by a touch-me-not charity. I suffered a labor complicated by an insufficient pelvic span and a lack of dilation. I spent three days in company with other women who were carried in and out of the labor room screaming curses and for their mothers.

SOLDIER *and* GIRL *are lying head to head on their backs. They are wounded and they cry out inarticulately for help as the amplified voice overpowers their cries. Their downstage arms reach up and their hands clasp.*

My body was jostled, invaded, exposed as a crooning old man halfheartedly swept the filthy floor. Many of my fellow unfortunates would come fresh from their battles to witness the spectacle of my greater misfortune. Three days and that cursed burden could not be released from the prison of my body nor I from it.

The GIRL *screams. She begins to pant loudly as though she cannot catch her breath. The* SOLDIER *moans.*

Finally there was a last-ditch high forceps, a great tearing mess, and the emergence of a creature that I fully expected to see turned purple with my own terrible hatred and ripped to shreds by the trial of its birth. What I saw, instead, was a human being, suddenly bearing very little relationship to me except our common helplessness, our common trial. I saw it was a female, and I wept for it. I wept and retched until my tired fundus gave way and there was a magnificent hemorrhage that pinned me to that narrow bed with pain I shall never forget, with pain that caused me to concentrate only on the next breath which seemed a great distance from the one before. Some kind fellow-sufferer and my own youth saved me. I awoke to tubes spouting blood from insecure joins. The splattered white coats of the attendants made it a butcher shop to remember. I never held that baby.

The arms drop. They lie still to end of speech.

For some days I was too ill. And then the institution policy decreed it unwise. There was a family waiting to claim that female creature, a family that could bestow respectability and security and approval and love. I emerged from that place a very resolved and disciplined machine. As you know. I worked. I studied. I clawed. I schemed. I made my way to the top of my profession and I never allowed a human being to touch me in intimacy again.

MAN: It was—it was criminal of me to have been the author of so much suffering . . .

SOLDIER *sits up.*

to have been so irresponsible . . . but I was stupidly young. I never could have imagined such things. Believe me.

WOMAN: Yes, you say you were young. Stupidly young. But what was your excuse when you were no longer young and stupid?

MAN: I'm sorry. I'm tired. I don't understand you.

WOMAN: Your daughter and mine grew to womanhood. And she and all her sisters were not spared the possibility of my experience and those of my generation.

GIRL *sits up.* GIRL *and* SOLDIER *face each other.* SOLDIER *stands and becomes speechmaker, rifle arm behind his back, other hand "sincerely" across his heart.*

Because there you were. Again. This time, not perpetrating unwilling motherhood upon a single individual, but condemning countless human females to the horrors of being unwilling hosts to parasitic life. You, for pure expedience, making capital of the rolling sounds of immorality and promiscuity which you promised accession upon relaxation of the abortion laws. Wholesale slaughter, you said, do you remember? Wholesale slaughter of innocent creatures who had no protection but the law from the untimely eviction from their mother's sinning wombs.

GIRL *crouches at his feet, in attitude of supplication. She rests her head on his boot tops and lies still.*

You murdered. You destroyed the lives of young women who fell prey to illegal abortion or suicide or unattended birth. You killed the careers and useful productivity of others. You killed the spirit, the full realization of all potential of many women who were forced to live on in half-life. You killed their ability to produce children in ideal circumstances. You killed love and self-respect and the proud knowledge that one is the master of one's fate, one's physical body being the corporeal representation of it. You killed. And you were so damned self-righteous about it.

MAN: I cannot defend myself.

GIRL *crawls off to stage right.*

WOMAN: I know.

MAN: But, I beg you, is there no appeal from this sentence?

SOLDIER *cradles rifle.*

WOMAN: As it happens, there is. We have a board before whom these cases are heard. Your case is being heard at this moment, and their decision will be the final one. The board is composed of many women, all of whom have suffered in some way from the laws which you so ardently supported. There is a mother who lost her daughter to quack abortionists. There is a woman who was forced to undergo sexual intercourse on the examining table by the aborting physician. There is a woman who unwittingly took a fetus-deforming drug administered by her physician for routine nausea, and a woman who caught German measles at a crucial point in her pregnancy, both of whom were denied the right to abortion, but granted the privilege of rearing hopelessly defective children. There is an older woman who spent a good part of her child-rearing years in a mental institution when she was forced to bear a late and unwanted child. There are others. You won't have too long to wait, now. For the verdict.

MAN: I promise you, that if I am spared, that I will be able to do much to undo the harm I have ignorantly done. This experience has taught me in a way that no other learning process could . . . I am in a position to . . . For the first time I can truly . . . identify . . . it would be to the advantage of all . . .

SOLDIER *leaves rifle and stands as a human being, without pose.*

WOMAN: That is being taken into account.

Someone brings report or WOMAN *goes to side of stage where she emerges with it from a cubicle.*

MAN: Is that the decision?

WOMAN: Yes. The board has decided that out of compassion for the potential child—

MAN: No! They can't!

SOLDIER *turns to audience.*

WOMAN: Out of compassion for the potential child, and regarding the qualities of personality and not sex that make you a potentially unfit mother, [*Pause.*] that the pregnancy is to be terminated.

Blackout.

Monologia
or
Happiness Is a Thing Called Dough

TIME: *All time.*

PLACE: *A corner.*

PERSON: *Male or female at discretion of director. Lectern or soapbox might be useful. Hecklers might be placed in or promoted from audience or backstage.*

My God, Man! There's nothing wrong with doing things for money!

Heckling.

No! Of course not! I'd like to use an illustration from my early childhood. I like to use myself as an example. I feel it's a subject I know best, and why waste it . . . well . . . anyway, there was this mother . . .

Heckling.

Whose? Mine, of course. Pay attention. Me. My mother. All right. She was valuable to me.

Heckling.

Age; Two and a half. Yes, she fed me, washed me, amused me, and . . .

Heckling.

Yes, that too. Actually, I couldn't concentrate very well at the time, and she had to help out occasionally with [*Clears throat.*] safety pins . . . [*Gestures.*] You know?

Heckling.

Only once in a while, damn it! A slip! We're all human. Most of us, anyway! Well, anyway, once upon a time, I mean, one day she came to me . . .

Heckling.

My mother! That's what I'm talking about! She came to me, and looked me straight in the eye . . .

Heckling.

Well, of course she had to bend to do it! God made man so he could bend. Yes, yes. Women too . . .

Heckling.

Well, she looked at me and she said . . . "Jupiter," . . . That's what she called me . . . "I have an offer to work in a department store for twelve dollars a week. I would rather stay here and take care of you, for I feel that it is my motherly duty, but, on the other hand, Jupiter . . ."

Heckling.

She called me that . . . Jupiter . . . yes, she did . . . "But, on the other hand," she said . . . "Can you pay me twelve dollars a week?" Now I was only two and a half at the time . . .

Heckling.

Yes, but that was a fair question she asked me! Yes, it was. Even at that tender age, I saw where her duty lay. I was very unsuccessful at the time. I admit it. Had trouble concentrating. No discipline. None. And I knew I couldn't even pay her half of that.

Heckling.

No sentimentality! Question of economics! Why should she give her time to *me* when I couldn't pay her? The department store was the high bidder. Fair and square. Going price twelve dollars. Got a good bargain in my mother. Hard worker, that woman. Dedicated. Nowadays they couldn't get a woman like that for less than fifty and commission . . . and she'd still be worth it!

Heckling.

I know what you think! You think it was less than sweet for a woman to leave her sweet little child and go off to give her fealty and allegiance to a gross business enterprise. Let's look at some of the alternatives. Yes, we could have starved sweetly together, or gone on home relief sweetly together . . . although I think we'd have rather starved . . .

Heckling.

But you see . . . my mother lived in *this* world! And she accepted it for what it was. Consequently, I grew up with none of the troublesome conflicts that afflict people like you. I knew it wasn't that she loved the department store more than me, or that the department store was bigger and more handsome or brighter or more charming than I. I knew simply that it paid her more than I could. I knew that if I could pay her more she would very happily come back to me, and it made life amazingly simple for me.

Heckling throughout next speech.

I ask you, how many of us ever realize, how many of you have ever realized, and realize at that tender age of two and a half, that one's mother can be had! Not for the asking, but for the paying! And instead of all this terrible business of going through life searching desperately, fighting, agonizing, competing for mother or mother surrogate or mother substitute or mother transference, or going round the other end and killing these mother things inside you because she was, you believed, forever tantalizingly inaccessible; how would it have been if you had suddenly realized that mother . . . Herself! could, to be unnecessarily but enlighteningly crude about it, be bought! Was, in fact, for sale! And bought by money! Not achievement or sacrifice or castration or any of those modern gimmicks, but good, old-fashioned money, which is eminently available especially if you go at it early enough.

Driven from stage by hecklers, the next line is said over his shoulder.

Think over what I said now.

Pas De Deux
or
Te Deum Tedium

TIME: *Edge of now.*

PLACE: *A bare-minimum kind of place. Mats on the floor. Evidence of primitive food preparation.*

AT RISE: *Man and woman in bare minimum of garment, modern cave-dweller style, either verging on nudity, into it, or avoiding it, at discretion of director. Both are going about their business of preparing food, basic ablutions, lying down to rest. There might be some evidence of business or work not related immediately to them.*

MAN: Kill.
WOMAN: Kill.
MAN: Kill.
WOMAN: Kill.
MAN: Apology.
WOMAN: Still kill.
MAN: Get lost.
WOMAN: More kill.
MAN: Who asked you?
WOMAN: Kill more.
MAN: Tired.
WOMAN: Die.
MAN: Never.
WOMAN: Why?
MAN: Why me?
WOMAN: Sicker.
MAN: Still why me?
WOMAN: Older.
MAN: You die.
WOMAN: Never.
MAN: Why?
WOMAN: Why me?
MAN: Why not?
WOMAN: Because.
MAN: Not me.
WOMAN: Why not?
MAN: Because.
WOMAN: Why *not?*
MAN: Because.
WOMAN: Oh, why *not?*
MAN: No.
WOMAN: Please.
MAN: No.
WOMAN: Please. Please.
MAN: No. [*Pause.*] No.
WOMAN: No.
MAN: No.
WOMAN: No.
MAN: No.
WOMAN and MAN: No.

The Butcher Shop
or
Pas de Trop

TIME: *Now.*

PLACE: *A butcher shop. Some carcasses. Some big hooks. Some knives and cleavers.*

AT RISE: *The boss sits on a bench and the man sits at the other end of it. The man functions as a kind of mirror or echo. The cigar in the boss's mouth is lit. The cigar in the man's mouth is dead.*

THE BOSS: It's immoral.
THE MAN: What is . . . ?
THE BOSS: I say it's immoral.
THE MAN: Is it . . . ?
THE BOSS: It's you.
THE MAN: Me.
THE BOSS: You. Or something to do with you.
THE MAN: Is it my . . . ?
THE BOSS: It's your failure.
THE MAN: It's my . . . ?
THE BOSS: Failure. You've worked thirty years. Thirty years.
THE MAN: Thirty years.
THE BOSS: Yes. How can you face me? Yourself? Your wife?
THE MAN: My wife?
THE BOSS: Your wife. Immoral.
THE MAN: Immoral . . . ?
THE BOSS: Immoral.
THE MAN: My wife. . . . ?
THE BOSS: Yes. That's it. You dwell on it so.
THE MAN: I . . . ?
THE BOSS: Yes. You. You think about her all the time. You can't concentrate on your work.
THE MAN: My work . . . ?
THE BOSS: Your work. You think about . . . I know what you think about . . .
THE MAN: About . . . ?

THE BOSS: About can-can stockings.

THE MAN: Stockings . . . ?

THE BOSS: How much they cost . . .

THE MAN: They cost . . . ?

THE BOSS: Yes, they cost. Women like that.

THE MAN: Like that . . . ?

THE BOSS: I don't like that in you. In her. It's a crime.

THE MAN: A crime . . . ?

THE BOSS: When she bends over you . . . you can see her breasts . . .

THE MAN: Her breasts . . . ?

THE BOSS: They don't look much different today than they did when she was sixteen . . .

THE MAN: Sixteen . . . ?

THE BOSS: When you were sixteen you were very handsome . . .

THE MAN: Handsome . . . ?

THE BOSS: You had a magnificent body. Your hair was black. Your eyes so green, your mouth turned down a bit at the corners . . .

THE MAN: My body . . . ? My hair . . . ? My eyes . . . ? My mouth . . . ?

THE BOSS: It's indecent.

THE MAN: Indecent . . . ?

THE BOSS: Your age is no excuse.

THE MAN: No excuse . . . ?

THE BOSS: You should have kept yourself in condition.

THE MAN: Condition . . . ?

THE BOSS: Exercise. Clean living. Good food. Lots of rest. At night.

THE MAN: At night . . . ?

THE BOSS: At night. I suppose she's there sometimes. That incredible skin. I'd like to manufacture it. What quality! Skin.

THE MAN: Skin . . . ?

THE BOSS: You dwell on it so. That is your main problem.

THE MAN: Your main problem . . . ?

THE BOSS: No! Not mine. I haven't time. There's a new building going up tomorrow. My name will be seventy feet high. How high will your name be?

THE MAN: My name . . . ?

THE BOSS: Your name. Her name. Does she know it? Does she look at you? What does she see?

THE MAN: Does she see . . . ?

THE BOSS: She sees what's left of you. No hair. Cataracts. A greyness on your skin. A slackness in your flesh. Your lips sunken in, almost gone . . . No woman would want to kiss that mouth. No woman.

THE MAN: No woman . . . ?

THE BOSS: Never mind about women. Take insurance companies . . .

THE MAN: Insurance companies . . . ?

THE BOSS: Are they objective enough for you? You can't consider it my prejudice. Or hers. Can you? You can't get a policy, can you? On your life? And when ever they can, they cancel don't they? Bad risk. Ask them. They know.

THE MAN: They know . . . ?

THE BOSS: They know. Everybody knows. Your car. Just stands there, doesn't it? Legally parked. A woman sees it. She knows. She backs into it. "Didn't know it was there." Didn't she though! She knew. Or sideswipes it. Just missed you, sitting there innocently. "What were you doing there?" she yells. Well, don't worry. She knew what you were doing there. And if you stop at a red light on the way home from your father's funeral, the chief mourner knows enough to ram you from behind. They all know. But the insurance companies are objective. You can rely upon what they know. What they know, you can rely upon. And they know that you are a bad risk. Tainted. With your immorality.

THE MAN: My immorality . . . ?

THE BOSS: Look at you. You're dying, aren't you? Well, do you think it's proper to do it in that public way, in front of everyone? Dragging everyone, everything around you into your private gravepit? Decomposing before everyone's eyes? Is it right?

THE MAN: It isn't right.

THE BOSS: Darned right it isn't right.

THE MAN: No, it isn't right.

THE BOSS: I'm glad you're beginning to see the light.

THE MAN: I shouldn't be dying here in front of everybody.

THE BOSS: No, you shouldn't.

THE MAN: I shouldn't have been impotent in front of men.

THE BOSS: Never.

THE MAN: I shouldn't have disappointed women.

THE BOSS: Not that woman.

THE MAN: I shouldn't have felt or looked the way I did. When I was young.

THE BOSS: It was unfair.

THE MAN: I shouldn't have promised so much.

THE BOSS: There was your sidelong look. There was your uncompromising silence. An attenuated anticipation.

THE MAN: I didn't have to talk. They looked at men and promised themselves.

THE BOSS: But remember. It was your fault. Remember that.
THE MAN: I am remembering.
THE BOSS: Well, just don't forget it. Remember it.
THE MAN: I am remembering.
THE BOSS: Yes.
THE MAN: I am remembering.
THE BOSS [*Silence*]
THE MAN: I am remembering.

[THE MAN *executes himself on meat hook.*]

[THE BOSS *scratches a match absentmindedly on* THE MAN'S *carcass as he lights a fresh cigar.*]

The Serving-Girl And The Lady
or
Just Us and the Medium

TIME: *The present.*

PLACE: *A stage [empty or with Things.]*

AT RISE: *An androgynous figure strides on stage; slender, tall, hair slicked or pulled back tightly from face. Perhaps dressed in tights and leotards.*

Following her at some distance is a dark, short, full-figured female, maybe "natural" haircut or wig, barefoot. If Things depicted on stage, can be carrying cartons, pails or whatever. Dropping them. Picking them up.

Activity during long speeches, if preferred, can include dressing of leotarded figure by herself or "serving-girl" in wig, padded bra, waist-cincher, fluffy apron, jewelry [or whatever is deemed symbolically feminine], and/or bustling, sweeping, scrubbing, sewing [or whatever is deemed essentially female] by the serving-girl.

THE SERVING-GIRL: For the man I drew, it was the end of hope. Rigidity. Rigor Mortis before death. A decapitated chicken moving through life by reflex but never any possibility of life anymore. My marriage was weighted like some intolerable mathematical proposition, the gross weight of the injustice increasing with each area of diminished returns. [*Pause. Looks at* LADY. *Indicates her.* LADY *looks back at her.*] On the other hand, what she has, the Lady that is, is this Big Man. Big. Big enough for two was what they suggested. Big head, Big hands, Big brain, Big ambition. Big. A couple of million in five years if he lives. Instantly, if he dies. He might actually be worth more alive than dead. To replace him, what he is to his wife, you would have to hire a policeman, a babysitter, a loving carpenter, a lawn boy, a nurse, a furniture mover, a shopper, a cook, a houseboy, an escort, a circumspect frigger—and above all, a Provider. Capital "P."

THE LADY [*Looks at* SERVING-GIRL *for some time.*] The serving-girl's husband is bored by himself. He knows his own incapacity too well. Therefore, his only diversion is to never make love to her. [*Pause.*] So the lovegiver is the lovestarved. [*Pause.*] And yet the serving-girl is a very desirable woman. If I wished to solve the mystery of her desirability, among other mysteries, I might—I just might—approach her husband. Yes. If, however, he is wholly occupied in maintaining his minus manipulation—I might send my own boy to do a man's job—[*Pause.*] So what? Everyone uses these methods. We want to get the cheese without the trap springing shut, don't we? And there *are* ways to keep the trap from springing shut, are there not?

THE SERVING-GIRL: The Lady lives at some distance from most traps, with sculpture in her—kitchen, and books lining her—living room. Music is piped into bathrooms and bedrooms. The children spring gleaming from the belly of an appliance.

[*Picks up oversized telephone receiver or sense memory.*] Memo to the Spic'n' Span Accomodation Agency—Flash! Mobilize all your sensual impetuous self-destructive teen-age girls. Alert your tall-highly-intelligent-with-promising-careers-before-them-but-horny-as-hell college boys. Position them felicitously. Go! [*Stares at oversize wristwatch as nine loud clicks or bells are counted off.*] Stop!

[*Exceedingly rapid delivery from this point to indicated stop.*] Mr. and Mrs. Pure have been our acquaintances for several years and intimate friends for a few years. Stop! We have been associated with them in enterprises that reflect their highly developed social consciousness. Stop! They are outgoing, intelligent, and conscientious members of the community. Stop! They are home-oriented. Stop! Mrs. Pure is very interested in the interior of the home, implementing her creative approach with solid participation in painting of rooms and furniture. Stop! She knits and sews. Stop! Mr. Pure is a talented woodworker, able to finish off basements, install cabinets, and provide toys and furniture for cooperative nurseries. Stop! The Pures are both interested in sports and travel. Stop! Mr. Pure is an excellent squash player. Stop! Mrs. Pure is an excellent spectator. Stop! Let's hear it for the Pures! Stop! [*Stop rapid delivery. Calling.*] Raply requested! The children, a boy with muscles and a girl with charm, are given rooms appropriate to their needs. Mr. Pure kisses the little boy on the mouth. A lot. He pulls the little bugger's pants down, playfully, on almost any opportunity. Mrs. Pure watches with—triumph—as the little girl lies on her back on the pink bathinette, her little legs akimbo and a silent tiny freshet wells up *uncontrollably* from the pink little sugarplum between the plump little thighs. The kimona gets wet but Mrs. Pure doesn't care.

THE LADY: In our Bacchic rites for social fertility there was love in a cage, love in a box, love in a dirty hotel room where the sheets were only slightly used. Anything, I said. Anything to make you happy. The man was very dark and shorter than I, a croupier in Pleasureland who performed as programmed. Who delivered. Who could go on to serve my husband his propulsive reaming at the crap table. Afterwards.

THE SERVING-GIRL: Sexual fantasy, *in extremis,* should be stored like oxygen, in hospital or hotel rooms, not in the properly maintained home because of its explosive nature and potential danger to—the children.

THE LADY: My husband and I watch fondly, are fond of watching the little tiny ever-so-feminine girl as she plays enthusiastically with the green shoot on the youngbrother tree, testing its firmness and resiliency as manly little brother stands, oh so still —tolerating it.

THE SERVING-GIRL: Tolerating it.

THE LADY: That is what I said.

THE SERVING-GIRL: The children do learn by example. They are exemplary children.

THE LADY: I try.

THE SERVING-GIRL: To exemplify?

THE LADY: In a manner of speaking.

THE SERVING-GIRL: And what is the manner of your speaking?

THE LADY: That is none of your concern. Haven't you something to do?

THE SERVING-GIRL: Watch Mama now. Children, see Mama.

THE LADY: Some dusting? A seam? The dishes!

THE SERVING-GIRL: See how Mama *tolerates it,* children?

THE LADY: Hold on, there. Who are you? [*Suspiciously.*] I'm not sure I recognize you—after all.

THE SERVING-GIRL: Oh, I'm just an old—gymnasium.

THE LADY: An old—gymnasium—

THE SERVING-GIRL: A business lunch? A fraternity brother?

THE LADY: Oh, yes.

THE SERVING-GIRL: Yes?

THE LADY: Yes. Now that I've looked at you more closely, I find I do recognize you after all. But I remember you differently. I remember you as a whisper of crisis, a thrill of competition, the proof that he was attractive to someone—else.

THE SERVING-GIRL: What was it you said to your croupier?

THE LADY: Anything. Anything you want.

THE SERVING-GIRL: I said that to your husband. Anything. Anything you want.

THE LADY: And did you give it to him?

THE SERVING-GIRL: And he gave it to me.

THE LADY: Really? Anything you wanted?

THE SERVING-GIRL: I wanted what he gave me. You wouldn't understand.

THE LADY: You poor thing. I wouldn't understand?

THE SERVING-GIRL: I don't think you would.

THE LADY: Just between us girls, is the name of the game—Passion?

THE SERVING-GIRL: It can only be a joke to you.

THE LADY: And you? Are you proud? Proud of your passion?

THE SERVING-GIRL [*Pause.*]: Yes.

THE LADY: Don't be. It's only a species of myth to ensure the perpetuation of the species—A specious myth to keep you forever in a convenient position—convenient for us, the Big Man and I—on your back, on your knees—and enjoying it in the bargain.

THE SERVING-GIRL [*Pause.*]: But you've got the real bargain.

THE LADY: Yes.

THE SERVING-GIRL: Feeding. Clothing. Housing. Honoring. Not dependent on the myth of passion.

THE LADY: Definitely dependent on the myth of passion. The myth of your passion. The myth of his passion for your passion. The myth of his passion for *my* passion. Here, you naughty boy. You dear sweet naughty boy. I forgive you. I will give you some. Here, for being a good naughty boy. Here for the house. Here for the money. Here for the kitchen, the car, the trip to Puerto Rico, the insurance if you shuffle off this currency-packed coil. [*Each "here" accompanied by a "bump."*]

THE SERVING-GIRL: And he thought he was a man.

THE LADY: Yes. Didn't he though?

THE SERVING-GIRL: He thought that three times from his head to his toes—proving, proving—meant the final confirmation of his manhood. Do squirrels believe the myth too? Have you seen the female squirrel, drawn up, waiting, while the male flattens himself against a redwood bench, his caution temporarily winning over the compelling little lust? Have you heard the agony of the mythic sexual urgency propelling those sounds out of them, those attack-and-defend sounds? In sun-heated smoke have you made my body the incubator of your passionate pretense, so that it might be carried warmed and ready into your winning threshold? Artificial heat. Artificial light. Forced blooming. Wigs. False eyelashes. Fake fingernails. Padded bellies. Grafted passions. All myths. All efficacious.

THE LADY: That's really enough. Quite enough. Rather too much catharsis for one day. When you speak to me next, remember the reality. Tolerance is terminated. Come to terms. What do you say to me, Serving-girl?

THE SERVING-GIRL: I say—

THE LADY: You say what?

THE SERVING-GIRL: I say—

THE LADY: What do you say to me? Come now, you must remember—you know how to say it—you love to say it—it was only a rehearsal with him, the myth belongs to him, but this is the *real thing,* little peasant, *the real thing.*

THE SERVING-GIRL: But will you shut me out?

THE LADY: Perhaps.

THE SERVING-GIRL: No protection?

THE LADY: None guaranteed.

THE SERVING-GIRL: I won't! *I don't have to!*

THE LADY: You will. I'm the only hope you have, the only possible hope.

THE SERVING-GIRL [*Dully.*]: Anything—

THE LADY: The Big Man will love this. It's what he wanted all along—

THE SERVING-GIRL: Anything you want.

THE LADY: That's right. Louder, please.

THE SERVING-GIRL [*Shouts.*]: Anything to make you happy.

THE LADY: Oh, perfect—Just perfect—Say it—Say it again—keep on saying it—but, as I say—Perfect.

In the Shadow of the Crematoria

or

Be Heard, This Euphoria
Eu Heard, This Beforia

TIME: *The present.*

PLACE: *A representation, a caricature of a laboratory. Vastly oversized bell jars of normal and prominently displayed abnormal fetuses are deployed at several suspended levels. These are to be two-dimensional, possibly photographs including the Hiroshima malformities, or more properly black and white drawings. One table or tabletop (could be illustration board) with sketched representations of appropriate lab tools. Tilted and at oblique angle.*

AT RISE: *Female Lab Research Director, large glasses, hair severely clasped back, a la Hollywood for such creatures. Male Success, suave, attired in sport or smoking jacket, silk scarf, self-confident pompadour a la Hollywood, T. V. for such creatures. They have been caught in mid-converse.*

SHE: You say you are the greatest mind of the twentieth century, and you mysteriously managed to survive the Dachau concentration camp and your head was bashed in by a Nazi guard. [*Pause.*] You said.

HE: Yes, and mended by a Pole who managed to sew me together without anesthetic, hating me. [*Pause.*] But doing it.

SHE: Why not? The head injury that produces lifelong mania is only possible with long life. [*Pause.*] My grandfather went once to Washington to complain in his broken Russian Yiddish English to the Secretary of Labor, and he was very strong and innocent, but the trolley car was stronger and less innocent and it caught him up neatly and tossed him playfully to the cold Washington D.C. car tracks. And they sewed him up sloppily and waited for him to die. But he lived to twist his innocence into the mad guile of a child. [*Pause.*] They sew you up. Ethics? Practice? But hating you.

HE [*Oneupsmanship.*]: When you live in the shadow of the crematoria, smelling it, you see your mother killed. You see them all die, but you survive, pulling your teeth from your shrunken gums and replacing them. [*Pause.*] For amusement. [*His accent could be reminiscent of Bela Lugosi.*]

SHE [*Pause.*]: Is that a fantasy?

HE [*Looking at her steadfastly.*]: Anyway. You live in the shadow. Never knowing when it will be your turn, but managing . . .

SHE [*Stepping on his line.*]: Through what means?

HE [*Picks it up neatly.*]: Through what means, to survive.

SHE: To survive. [*Repeat ad lib by* HE *and* SHE.]

HE [*Breaking it.*]: So that death never matters again, not even the potential death of the world.

SHE: Including the children?

HE: Including the children. [*Dismissing it.*] But you come here, here where you are most needed, and at first you work to save the world. Here where it is most needed. [*Portentous.*] In the shadow of the crematoria.

SHE: In the shadow of the crematoria. And you have the greatest mind.

HE: And then you realize there is nothing to save but, for a little while, yourself, and you add yourself up candidly, the greatest mind you say . . .

SHE [*Arms folded.*]: You say. And accomplished genitals. You say. And nothing in between. I say.

HE: You mean I have no heart. In the classic sense.

SHE: Yes.

HE [*Hands upturned.*]: I am a man who adjusted to the requirements of society.

SHE: And that is the secret of your—success.

HE: Indubitably.

SHE: But it will be the secret of your failure—with me.

HE: But why? Because you think *you* have a "heart" or that it matters if you do? [*Pause.*] *Because you think you still can save the world?*

SHE [*Pause.*]: Guilty as charged.

HE: And you think that one of the ways in which you will save this world is to give yourself to a world savior?

SHE [*Pause.*]: Guilty as charged. [*Less strong.*]

HE [*Pressing his advantage.*]: But my dear girl, let me tell you. [*Pause.*] The savior may be everlastingly grateful, but the world is not going to be saved if you offer yourself to the savior. [*Pause.*] I know. You imagine that he will rise from your couch to utter messianic cries anew to a waiting populace after first, however, having uttered them pristine and whole into your devouring ear. Oh, that you should hear those cries! Hear them first, and when you hear them again, hear them unscalding the pitch of napalm! You will hear them, you imagine, sharp little commands of Jovian complexion, turn right at the next door to peace and happiness forevermore and you will gloat, oh, how you will gloat, that in the beginning *you gave tongue to the Word!*

SHE [*Turns away from him, stung; to bell jars of fetuses: despair.*]: These little embryos are very, what we like to call, human, wrapping fingers as tender as pea sprouts round the mother vine. They float forever, never doomed to grasp for things with fingers grown corrugated with dull use, to pursue endless sexual parodies of the holy grail. The big fullterm Hiroshima washouts did it quickly. But we go on, radiated slowly over scores of years until the gutting of our tender human potential is accomplished. [*Half unconsciously* SHE *partially unzips or unbuttons the long white lab coat. During this speech* HE *has been washing his hands in surgery-prep manner.*]

HE [*Puts his hand on her breast. Eagerly, pressing his advantage.*]: But don't you see, dear girl? [*Pause.*] I am offering you *love!* [HE *puts his hand on her pudenda.*] I have always determined that I should love, of course, but love in keeping with the rest of my life, and to my complete advantage.

SHE [*Continues as if in a trance to slowly remove lab coat, revealing sheer Fredericks of Hollywood slave nightgown beneath it, and through next speeches at discretion of director will remove glasses, unfasten hair, etc.*]: Sometimes I lie on the bed and talk to myself.

HE [*During next speeches, methodically removes clothes, folds them.*]: There were many women that I could have loved but the motif and the motive were missing. I recognized long ago that I must annex a woman who believes she is incorruptible. Who still believes in her own goodness.

SHE: A mythic man that I want to be real. Will he love me with these fingernails and these eyes?

HE: I have held my love in reserve for just such an occasion, dear girl. Once we have come to an agreement and it is decided that I shall love you, you will have love in such measure and compass that it will surpass the dreams you have undoubtedly set aside.

SHE: Clear small eyes. Not romantic.

HE: You see, dear girl, you will be *my* love. You will become the unique individual in all this world that I have decreed it wise and beneficial to adore.

SHE: The acoustic tile on the ceiling reminds me of my face when I look into the mirror. Pores.

HE [*Retaining his trousers,* HE *rips shirt off to reveal very large wooden cross.*]: It will be you and you with all of what you unquestionably have been conditioned to think of as your imperfections that I will make the epitome of love's perfection. [*Goes toward her.*]

SHE: But after making love I can be beautiful . . . [SHE *is wearing, finally, just the short "sexy" nightgown.*]

HE: You. Because you are small and round and fleshy and soft. You, my image of secret delight. You, because your legs are short and full and your feet wide and your shoulders broad and abdomen ample, are the image of what I have decided I have always desired. You, because your lips are big and unrouged and slightly wet, and nose generous, and eyes down-turned and hair disheveled, arouse me to a passion I can scarcely contain. [HE *takes her in his arms.*]

SHE: Will you love me? Will you?

HE [*Bends her backwards.*]: Dare you disbelieve me?

SHE [*In awkward position.*]: Will you take me to places that I've never seen? Will you love me the way that I am? Will you help me with my work? Will you be strong? Will you be wise? Will you make me value myself? Have you been waiting for me? Why will you want me? Why will you need me? *What's wrong with you?* [HE *lowers her to floor.*] Will you love my legs? And my breasts? Not always that firm and with lines you can feel? And my belly? Swollen with phantom pregnancies? And my waist not that small and round shoulders and the line of my back muscles not even and sleek and overlapping and at least three real dimples on each cheek of my behind and horizontal lines along the back of my legs and a flattened half-closed belly button and veins protruding on my feet and calves and the backs of my hands and my hair whitening and drying? And —*will you love all of that and love it with a passion that permits of no other equally satisfying image?!* [*Great agitation upon being confronted with the* Dream.]

HE [*Home free.*]: I tell you, when you have wrinkles, I shall be mad about wrinkles. They will remind me of my sacred mother and I will revere them and you with incestuous intensity. I will guard you jealously and install you in luxury in which you shall be the chief ornament. And I say ornament advisedly, because you will be absolutely nonfunctional. You will never again have to be useful in the smallest way in order to be valuable. You will be valuable because you will be my most prized possession and you will be the prized possession of a man who is himself valuable. You may eat sweets, forget to exercise, indulge yourself in clothes that are too young for you and the wrong color, throw makeup on with abandon or completely away. It will not matter. *You will be desired.* I guarantee it in a way that no other man can. I have no doubts about myself, you see. I do not allow them. Therefore, I will have no doubts about my choice. Ever.

SHE [*Puts her arms up.*]: My savior.

HE: Yes.

SHE: *And will you save the world, too?*

Lower Depths

Tennessee Williams

(1914–   )

Tennessee Williams, regarded by many as "the greatest poet-dramatist to have appeared on the American scene since Eugene O'Neill,"* has said:

> *"In my opinion art is a kind of anarchy, and the theater is a province of art. . . . Art is only anarchy in juxtaposition with organized society. It runs counter to the sort of orderliness on which organized society apparently must be based. It is a benevolent anarchy: it must be that and if it is true art, it is."*†

Williams' sense of anarchy has led him to explore the bizarre, the freakish, the disturbed behavior of disinherited Americans. Seldom has a dramatist focussed in so spectacular a fashion on the human suffering and tragic aberrations of modern man. With deep compassion and sensitivity Williams has dramatized the collisions of spiritually maimed people caught up in tragic or at least pathetic circumstances. "Disinheritance" could be the subtitle for many of his works.

Although he had been publishing since the age of sixteen, Williams' reputation was not established until after he had failed as a screenwriter for MGM and had subsequently turned his considerable talents to the writing of *The Glass Menagerie* (1944), his first major stage success. Laura, the main character, is a shy, hypersensitive, crippled young lady, whose misfortunes contribute to tensions that afflict her whole family. Williams is typically concerned with personal conflicts that reflect fundamental differences in values and needs.

In *The Glass Menagerie* he looks particularly at the subtle and then violent antagonism between Amanda, the mother, with her dreams of a genteel Southern past and her own beaus, and Laura, with no beaus, in effect imprisoned by the tenement and her leg brace. In 1947 Williams won the Pulitzer Prize for *A Streetcar Named Desire,* whose disinherited schoolteacher Blanche DuBois, driven by her loneliness and insecurity, creates a series of evasions and fictions about her recent past. When Blanche's gilded tales are exposed, she heads toward a breakdown. Assaulted sexually by her brother-in-law, she at length sinks into insanity and is taken to an institution. Tottering, trying to establish a foothold in reality, Blanche fails; and mankind fails her too. *Summer and Smoke* (1948), *Cat on a Hot Tin Roof* (1955), and *Sweet Bird of Youth* (1959) are other Williams dramas exploring contemporary sexual pathology, materialism, and spiritual poverty. Outcasts and misfits are generally the people he depicts. Painfully, Williams forces his characters to reveal the face behind the images they present to the world. He leaves them sprawled, vulnerable, dissected, perhaps, but not without the playwright's sympathy.

The collection *Twenty-Seven Wagon Loads of Cotton and Other One-Act Plays* (1946) runs the gamut of Williams' dramatic virtuosity. The dramatist reveals the tortured psyches of life's stricken from the Mississippi delta to the slums of St. Louis, as they sometimes silently, sometimes dramatically appeal for help.

---

*Signi L. Falk, *Tennessee Williams* (New York: Twayne Publishers, 1962), p. 189.

†Preface to *Twenty-Seven Wagon Loads of Cotton and Other One-Act Plays* (New York: New Directions, 1946), p. VII.

In *Hello from Bertha,* Williams studies the pathetic figure of an aging prostitute as she begins to lose her grip on the thin edge of reality. Physically defeated, Bertha frantically tries to recall the past: the gaudy life of the "red-light district" and her flashy days in the "sporting house." A victim, virtually a ghost, Bertha must now be separated even from the illusory memories of happier days.

Talk to Me Like the Rain and Let Me Listen is one of Williams' most poetic short plays; centering on the themes of love, loneliness and poverty—the great triad in Williams' art—this play dramatizes with moving language the chemistry of defeat and hope in man. Tragic nobility is not alien to the ordinary person. Love has passed; time has gone. In the works of Tennessee Williams, disinheritance transcends race, nationality, and color. It is a simple, internal condition gnawing at us all.

Hello from Bertha

SCENE: *A bedroom in "the valley"—a notorious red-light section along the river flats of East St. Louis. In the center is a massive brass bed with tumbled pillows and covers on which Bertha, a large blonde prostitute, is lying restlessly. A heavy old-fashioned dresser with gilt knobs, gaudy silk cover and two large Kewpie dolls stands against the right wall. Beside the bed is a low table with empty gin bottles. An assortment of lurid magazines is scattered carelessly about the floor. The wallpaper is grotesquely brilliant—covered with vivid magnified roses—and is torn and peeling in some places. On the ceiling are large yellow stains. An old-fashioned chandelier, fringed with red glass pendants, hangs from the center. Goldie comes in at the door in the left wall. She wears a soiled double-piece dress of white and black satin, fitted closely to her almost fleshless body. She stands in the doorway, smoking a cigarette, and stares impatiently at Bertha's prostrate figure.*

GOLDIE: Well, Bertha, what are you going to do? [*For a moment there is no answer.*]

BERTHA [*with faint groan*]: I dunno.

GOLDIE: You've got to decide, Bertha.

BERTHA: I can't decide nothing.

GOLDIE: Why can't you?

BERTHA: I'm too tired.

GOLDIE: That's no answer.

BERTHA [*tossing fretfully*]: Well, it's the only answer I know. I just want to lay here and think things over.

GOLDIE: You been layin' here thinkin' or somethin' for the past two weeks. [*Bertha makes an indistinguishable reply.*] You got to come to some decision. The girls need this room.

BERTHA [*with hoarse laugh*]: Let 'em have it!

GOLDIE: They can't with you layin' here.

BERTHA [*slapping her hand on bed*]: Oh, God!

GOLDIE: Pull yourself together, now, Bertha. [*Bertha tosses again and groans.*]

BERTHA: What's the matter with me?

GOLDIE: You're sick.

BERTHA: I got a sick headache. Who slipped me that Mickey Finn last night?

GOLDIE: Nobody give you no Mickey Finn. You been layin' here two solid weeks talkin' out of your head. Now, the sensible thing for you to do, Bertha, is to go back home or—

BERTHA: Go back nowhere!—I'm stayin' right here till I get on my feet. [*She stubbornly averts her face.*]

GOLDIE: The valley's no place for a girl in your condition. Besides we need this room.

BERTHA: Leave me be, Goldie. I wanta get in some rest before I start workin'.

GOLDIE: Bertha, you've got to decide! [*The command hangs heavily upon the room's florid atmosphere for several long moments. Bertha slowly turns her head to Goldie.*]

BERTHA [*faintly*]: What is it I got to decide?

GOLDIE: Where you're going from here? [*Bertha looks at her silently for a few seconds.*]

BERTHA: Nowhere. Now leave me be, Goldie. I've got to get in my rest.

GOLDIE: If I let you be, you'd just lay here doin'

nothin' from now till the crack of doom! [*Bertha's reply is indistinguishable.*] Lissen here! If you don't make up your mind right away, I'm gonna call the ambulance squad to come get you! So you better decide right this minute.

BERTHA [*Her body has stiffened slightly at this threat.*]: I can't decide nothing. I'm too tired —worn out.

GOLDIE: All right! [*She snaps her purse open.*] I'll take this nickel and I'll make the call right now. I'll tell 'em we got a sick girl over here who can't talk sense.

BERTHA [*thickly*]: Go ahead. I don't care what happens to me now.

GOLDIE [*changing her tactics*]: Why don't you write another letter, Bertha, to that man who sells . . . hardware or something in Memphis?

BERTHA [*with sudden alertness*]: Charlie? You leave his name off your dirty tongue!

GOLDIE: That's a fine way for you to be talking, me keeping you here just out of kindness and you not bringing in a red, white or blue cent for the last two weeks! Where do you—

BERTHA: Charlie's a real . . . sweet. Charlie's a . . . [*Her voice trails into a sobbing mumble.*]

GOLDIE: What if he is? All the better reason for you to write him to get you out of this here tight spot you're in, Bertha.

BERTHA [*aroused*]: I'll never ask him for another dime! Get that? He's forgotten all about me, my name and everything else. [*She runs her hand slowly down her body.*] Somebody's cut me up with a knife while I been sleeping.

GOLDIE: Pull yourself together, Bertha. If this man's got money, maybe he'll send you some to help you git back on your feet.

BERTHA: Sure he's got money. He owns a hardware store. I reckon I ought to know, I used to work there! He used to say to me, Girlie, any time you need something just let Charlie know. . . . We had good times together in that back room!

GOLDIE: I bet he ain't forgotten it neither.

BERTHA: He's found out about all the bad things I done since I quit him and . . . come to St. Louie. [*She slaps the bed twice with her palm.*]

GOLDIE: Naw, he ain't, Bertha. I bet he don't know a thing. [*Bertha laughs weakly.*]

BERTHA: It's you that's been writing him things. All the dirt you could think of about me! Your filthy tongue's been clacking so fast that—

GOLDIE: Bertha! [*Bertha mutters an indistinguishable vulgarity.*] I been a good friend to you, Bertha.

BERTHA: Anyhow he's married now.

GOLDIE: Just write him a little note on a postcard and tell him you've had some tough breaks. Remind him of how he said he would help you if ever you needed it, huh?

BERTHA: Leave me alone a while, Goldie. I got an awful feeling inside of me now.

GOLDIE [*advancing a few steps and regarding Bertha more critically*]: You want to see a doctor?

BERTHA: No. [*There is a pause.*]

GOLDIE: A priest? [*Bertha's fingers claw the sheet forward.*]

BERTHA: No!

GOLDIE: What religion are you, Bertha?

BERTHA: None.

GOLDIE: I thought you said you was Catholic once.

BERTHA: Maybe I did. What of it?

GOLDIE: If you could remember, maybe we could get some sisters or something to give you a room like they did for Rose Kramer for you to rest in, and get your strength back—huh, Bertha?

BERTHA: I don't want no sisters to give me nothing! Just leave me be in here till I get through resting.

GOLDIE: Bertha, you're . . . bad sick, Bertha!

BERTHA [*after a slight pause*]: Bad?

GOLDIE: Yes, Bertha. I don't want to scare you but . . .

BERTHA [*hoarsely*]: You mean I'm dying?

GOLDIE [*after a moment's consideration*]: I didn't say that. [*There is another pause.*]

BERTHA: No, but you meant it.

GOLDIE: We got to provide for the future, Bertha. We can't just let things slide.

BERTHA [*attempting to sit up*]: If I'm dying I want to write Charlie. I want to—tell him some things.

GOLDIE: If you mean a confession, honey, I think a priest would be—

BERTHA: No, no priest! I want Charlie!

GOLDIE: Father Callahan would—

BERTHA: No! No! I want Charlie!

GOLDIE: Charlie's in Memphis. He's running his hardware business.

BERTHA: Yeah. On Central Avenue. The address is 563.

GOLDIE: I'll write him and tell what condition you're in, huh, Bertha?

BERTHA [*after a reflective pause*]: No. . . . Just tell him I said hello. [*She turns her face to the wall.*]

GOLDIE: I gotta say more than that, Bertha.

BERTHA: That's all I want you to say. Hello from —Bertha.

GOLDIE: That wouldn't make sense, you know that.

BERTHA: Sure it would. Hello from Bertha to Charlie with all her love. Don't that make sense?

GOLDIE: No!

BERTHA: Sure it does.

GOLDIE [*turning to the door*]: I better call up the hospital and get them to send out the ambulance squad.

BERTHA: No, you don't! I'd rather just die than that.

GOLDIE: You're in no condition to stay in the valley, Bertha. A girl in your shape's got to be looked out for proper or anything's likely to happen.

Outside, in the reception room, someone has started the nickel phonograph. It is playing "The St. Louis Blues." A hoarse male voice joins in the refrain and there is a burst of laughter and the slamming of a door.

BERTHA [*after a slight pause*]: You're telling me, sister. [*She elevates her shoulders.*] I know the rules of this game! [*She stares at Goldie with brilliant, faraway eyes.*] When you're out you're out and there's no comeback for you neither!

She shakes her head and then slowly reclines again. She knots her fingers and pounds the bed several times; then her hand relaxes and slips over the side of the bed.

GOLDIE: Now, pull yourself together, Bertha, and I'll have you moved to a nice, clean ward where you'll get good meals and a comfortable bed to sleep in.

BERTHA: Die in, you mean! Help me outa this bed! [*She struggles to rise.*]

GOLDIE [*going to her*]: Don't get excited, now, Bertha.

BERTHA: Help me up. Yes! Where's my kimono?

GOLDIE: Bertha, you're not in any shape to go crawling around out of bed!

BERTHA: Shut up, you damned crepe-hanger! Get Lena in here. She'll help me out with my things.

GOLDIE: What've you decided on, Bertha?

BERTHA: To go.

GOLDIE: Where?

BERTHA: That's my business.

GOLDIE [*after a pause*]: Well, I'll call Lena. [*Bertha has risen painfully and now she totters toward the dresser.*]

BERTHA: Wait a minute, you! Look under that tray. The comb and brush tray. [*She sinks, panting, into a rocker.*] You'll find five bucks stuck under there.

GOLDIE: Bertha, you ain't got no money under that tray.

BERTHA: You trying to tell me I'm broke?

GOLDIE: You been broke for ten days, Bertha. Even since you took sick you been out of money.

BERTHA: You're a liar!

GOLDIE [*angrily*]: Don't call me names, Bertha!

They glare at each other. A Girl, in what looks like a satin gymnasium outfit, appears in doorway and glances in curiously. She grins and disappears.

BERTHA [*finally*]: Get Lena in here. She won't cheat me.

GOLDIE [*going to the dresser*]: Look, Bertha. Just to satisfy you. See under the tray? Nothing there but an old post-card you once got from Charlie.

BERTHA [*slowly*]: I been robbed. Yes, I been robbed. [*with increasing velocity*] Just because I'm too sick an' tired an' done in to look out for myself, I get robbed! If I was in my strength, you know what I'd do? I'd bust this place wide open! I'd get back my money you stole or take it out of your hide, you old—

GOLDIE: Bertha, you spent your last dime. You bought gin with it.

BERTHA: No!

GOLDIE: It was Tuesday night, the night you got sick, you bought yourself a quart of dry gin that night. I swear you did, Bertha!

BERTHA: I wouldn't believe your dying word on a Bible! Get Lena in here! It's a frame-up! [*She rises and staggers toward the door.*] Lena! Lena! [*Get me police headquarters!*]

GOLDIE [*alarmed*]: No, Bertha!

BERTHA [*still louder*]: GET ME POLICE HEADQUARTERS!

Collapsing with weakness against the side of the door, she sobs bitterly and covers her eyes with one hand. The electric phonograph starts again. There is the shuffling of dancers outside.

GOLDIE: Bertha, be calm. Settle down here now.

BERTHA [*turning on her*]: Don't tell me to be calm, you old slut. Get me police headquarters quick or I'll—! [*Goldie catches her arm and they struggle but Bertha wrenches free.*] I'll report this robbery to the police if it's the last thing I do! You'd steal the pennies off a dead nigger's eyes, that's how big-hearted you are! You come in here and try to soft-soap me about priests and confessions and—GET ME POLICE HEADQUARTERS! [*She pounds the wall, and sobs.*]

GOLDIE [*helplessly*]: Bertha, you need a good

bromide. Get back in bed, honey, and I'll bring you a double bromide and a box of aspirin.

BERTHA [*rapidly, with eyes shut, head thrown back and hands clenched*]: You'll bring me back my twenty-five dollars you stole from under that comb and brush tray!

GOLDIE: Now, Bertha—

BERTHA [*without changing her position*]: You'll bring it back or I'll have you prosecuted! [*Her tense lips quiver; a shining thread of saliva dribbles down her chin. She stands like a person in a catatonic trance.*] I've got friends in this town. Big shots! [*exultantly*] Lawyers, politicians! I can beat any God damn rap you try to hang on me! [*Her eyes flare open.*] *Vagrancy, huh?* [*She laughs wildly.*] That's a laugh, ain't it! I got my constitutional rights!

Her laughter dies out and she staggers to the rocker and sinks into it. Goldie watches her with extreme awe. Then she edges cautiously past Bertha and out the door with a frightened gasp.

BERTHA: Oh, Charlie, Charlie, you were such a sweet, sweet! [*Her head rocks and she smiles in agony.*] You done me dirt more times than I could count, Charlie—stood me up, married a little choir-singer— Oh, God! I love you so much it makes my guts ache to look at your blessed face in the picture! [*Her ecstasy fades and the look of schizophrenic suspicion returns.*] Where's that hell-cat gone to? Where's my ten dollars? Hey, YOU!! Come back in here with that money! I'll brain you if ever I catch you monkeying around with any money belonging to me! . . . Oh, Charlie . . . I got a sick headache, Charlie. No, honey. Don't go out tonight. [*She gets up from the rocker.*] Hey, you! Bring me a cold ice-pack—my head's aching. I got one hell of a hang-over, baby! [*She laughs.*] Vagrancy, huh? Vagrancy your Aunt Fanny! Get me my lawyer. I got influence in this town. Yeah. My folks own half the oil wells in the state of—of—Nevada. [*She laughs.*] Yeah, that's a laugh, ain't it? [*Lena, a dark Jewish girl in pink satin trunks and blouse, comes in the door. Bertha looks at her with half-opened eyes.*] Who're you?

LENA: It's me, Lena.

BERTHA: Oh. Lena, huh? Set down an' take a load off yer feet. Have a cigarette, honey. I ain't feeling good. There ain't any cigarettes here. Goldie took 'em. She takes everything I got. Set down an'—take a—

LENA [*in doorway*]: Goldie told me you weren't feelin' so good this evening so I thought I'd just look in on you, honey.

BERTHA: Yeah, that's a laugh, ain't it? I'm all right. I'll be on the job again tonight. You bet. I always come through, don't I, kid? Ever known me to quit? I may be a little down on my luck right now but—that's all! [*She pauses, as if for agreement.*] That's all, ain't it, Lena? I ain't old. I still got my looks. Ain't I?

LENA: Sure you have, Bertha. [*There is a pause.*]

BERTHA: Well, what're you grinning about?

LENA: I ain't grinning, Bertha.

BERTHA [*herself slightly smiling*]: I thought maybe you thought there was something funny about me saying I still had my looks.

LENA [*after a pause*]: No, Bertha, you got me wrong.

BERTHA [*hoarsely*]: Listen, sweetheart, I know the Mayor of this God damn little burg. Him and me are like that. See? I can beat any rap you try to hang on me and I don't give a damn what. Vagrancy, huh? That's a sweet laugh to me! Get me my traveling bag, will you, Lena? Where is it? I been thrown out of better places than this. [*She rises and drags herself vaguely about the room and then collapses on bed. Lena moves toward the bed.*] God, I'm too tired. I'll just lay down till my head stops swimming. . . . [*Goldie appears in the doorway. She and Lena exchange significant glances.*]

GOLDIE: Well, Bertha, have you decided yet?

BERTHA: Decided what?

GOLDIE: What you're gonna do?

BERTHA: Leave me be. I'm too tired.

GOLDIE [*casually*]: Well, I've called up the hospital, Bertha. They're sending an ambulance around to get you. They're going to put you up in a nice clean ward.

BERTHA: Tell 'em to throw me in the river and save the state some money. Or maybe they're scared I'd pollute the water. I guess they'll have to cremate me to keep from spreadin' infection. Only safe way of disposin' of Bertha's remains. That's a sweet laugh, ain't it? Look at her, Lena, that slut that calls herself Goldie. She thinks she's big-hearted. Ain't that a laugh? The only thing big about her is the thing that she sits on. Yeah, the old horse! She comes in here talking soft about callin' a priest an' havin' me stuck in the charity ward. Not me. None a that stuff for me, I'll tell you!

GOLDIE [*with controlled fury*]: You better watch how you talk. They'll have you in the strait-jacket, that's what!

BERTHA [*suddenly rising*]: Get the hell out! [*She throws a glass at Goldie, who screams and runs out.*

Bertha than turns to Lena.] Set down and take a letter for me. There's paper under that kewpie.

LENA [*looking on the dresser*]: No, there ain't, Bertha.

BERTHA: Ain't? I been robbed a that, too! [*Lena walks to the table by the bed and picks up a tablet.*]

LENA: Here's a piece, Bertha.

BERTHA: All right. Take a letter. To Mr. Charlie Aldrich, owner of the biggest hardware store in the City of Memphis. Got that?

LENA: What's the address, Bertha?

BERTHA: It's 563 Central Avenue. Got it? Yeah, that's right. Mr. Charlie Aldrich. Dear Charlie. They're fixing to lock me up in the city bughouse. On a charge of criminal responsibility without due process of law. Got that? [*Lena stops writing.*] And I'm as sane as you are right this minute, Charlie. There's nothing wrong with my upper-story and there never will be. Got that? [*Lena looks down and pretends to write.*] So come on down here, Charlie, and bail me out of here, honey, for old times' sake. Love and kisses, your old sweetheart, Bertha. . . . Wait a minute. Put a P.S. and say how's the wife and your—No! Scratch it out! That don't belong in there. Scratch it all out, the whole damn thing! [*There is a painful silence. Bertha sighs and turns slowly on the bed, pushing her damp hair back.*] Get you a clean sheet of paper.

Lena rises and tears another sheet from the tablet. A young Girl sticks her head in the door.

GIRL: Lena!

LENA: Coming.

BERTHA: Got it?

LENA: Yes.

BERTHA: That's right. Now just say this. Hello from Bertha—to Charlie—with all her love. Got that? Hello from Bertha—to Charlie . . .

LENA [*rising and straightening her blouse*] Yes.

BERTHA: With all . . . her love . . .

The music in the outer room recommences.

CURTAIN

Talk to Me Like the Rain and Let Me Listen . . .

Scene: *A furnished room west of Eighth Avenue in midtown Manhattan. On a folding bed lies a* MAN *in crumpled underwear, struggling out of sleep with the sighs of a man who went to bed very drunk. A* WOMAN *sits in a straight chair at the room's single window, outlined dimly against a sky heavy with a rain that has not yet begun to fall. The* WOMAN *is holding a tumbler of water from which she takes small, jerky sips like a bird drinking. Both of them have ravaged young faces like the faces of children in a famished country. In their speech there is a sort of politeness, a sort of tender formality like that of two lonely children who want to be friends, and yet there is an impression that they have lived in this intimate situation for a long time and that the present scene between them is the repetition of one that has been repeated so often that its plausible emotional contents, such as reproach and contrition, have been completely worn out and there is nothing left but acceptance of something hopelessly inalterable between them.*

MAN: [*hoarsely*] What time is it? [*The* WOMAN *murmurs something inaudible.*] What, honey?

WOMAN: Sunday.

MAN: I know it's Sunday. You never wind the clock.

The WOMAN *stretches a thin bare arm out of the ravelled pink rayon sleeve of her kimona and picks up the tumbler of water and the weight of it seems to pull her forward a little. The* MAN *watches solemnly, tenderly from the bed as she sips the water. A thin music begins, hesitantly, repeating a phrase several times as if someone in a next room were trying to remember a song on a mandolin. Sometimes a phrase is sung in Spanish. The song could be Estrellita.*

Rain begins; it comes and goes during the play; there is a drumming flight of pigeons past the window and a child's voice chants outside—.

CHILD'S VOICE: Rain, rain, go away! Come again

some other day! [*The chant is echoed mockingly by another child farther away.*]

MAN: [*finally*] I wonder if I cashed my unemployment. [*The* WOMAN *leans forward with the weight of the glass seeming to pull her; sets it down on the window-sill with a small crash that seems to startle her. She laughs breathlessly for a moment. The* MAN *continues, without much hope.*] I hope I didn't cash my unemployment. Where's my clothes? Look in my pockets and see if I got the cheque on me.

WOMAN: You came back while I was out looking for you and picked the cheque up and left a note on the bed that I couldn't make out.

MAN: You couldn't make out the note?

WOMAN: Only a telephone number. I called the number but there was so much noise I couldn't hear.

MAN: Noise? Here?

WOMAN: No, noise there.

MAN: Where was "there"?

WOMAN: I don't know. Somebody said come over and hung up and all I got afterwards was a busy signal . . .

MAN: When I woke up I was in a bathtub full of melting ice-cubes and Miller's High Life beer. My skin was blue. I was gasping for breath in a bathtub full of ice-cubes. It was near a river but I don't know if it was the East or the Hudson. People do terrible things to a person when he's unconscious in this city. I'm sore all over like I'd been kicked downstairs, not like I fell but was kicked. One time I remember all my hair was shaved off. Another time they stuffed me into a trash-can in the alley and I've come to with cuts and burns on my body. Vicious people abuse you when you're unconscious. When I woke up I was naked in a bathtub full of melting ice-cubes. I crawled out and went into the parlor and someone was going out of the other door as I came in and I opened the door and heard the door of an elevator shut and saw the doors of a corridor in a hotel. The TV was on and there was a record playing at the same time; the parlor was full of rolling tables loaded with stuff from Room Service, and whole hams, whole turkeys, three-decker sandwiches cold and turning stiff, and bottles and bottles and bottles of all kinds of liquors that hadn't even been opened and buckets of ice-cubes melting . . . Somebody closed a door as I came in . . . [*The* WOMAN *sips water.*] As I came in someone was going out. I heard a door shut and I went to the door and heard the door of an elevator shut . . . [*The* WOMAN *sets her glass down.*]—All over the floor of this pad near the river—articles—clothing—scattered . . . [*The* WOMAN *gasps as a flight of pigeons sweeps past the open window.*]—Bras!—Panties!—Shirts, ties, socks—and so forth . . .

WOMAN: [*faintly*] Clothes?

MAN: Yes, all kinds of personal belongings and broken glass and furniture turned over as if there'd been a free-for-all fight going on and the pad was—raided . . .

WOMAN: Oh.

MAN: Violence must have—broken out in the—place . . .

WOMAN: You were—?

MAN: —in the bathtub on—ice . . .

WOMAN: Oh . . .

MAN: And I remember picking up the phone to ask what hotel it was but I don't remember if they told me or not . . . Give me a drink of that water.

Both of them rise and meet in the center of the room. The glass is passed gravely between them. He rinses his mouth, staring at her gravely, and crosses to spit out the window. Then he returns to the center of the room and hands the glass back to her. She takes a sip of the water. He places his fingers tenderly on her long throat.

Now I've recited the litany of my sorrows! [*Pause: the mandolin is heard.*] And what have you got to tell me? Tell me a little something of what's going on behind your—

His fingers trail across her forehead and eyes. She closes her eyes and lifts a hand in the air as if about to touch him. He takes the hand and examines it upside down and then he presses its fingers to his lips. When he releases her fingers she touches him with them. She touches his thin smooth chest which is smooth as a child's and then she touches his lips. He raises his hand and lets his fingers slide along her throat and into the opening of the kimona as the mandolin gathers assurance. She turns and leans against him, her throat curving over his shoulder, and he runs his fingers along the curve of her throat and says—

It's been so long since we have been together except like a couple of strangers living together. Let's find each other and maybe we won't be lost. Talk to me! I've been lost!—I thought of you often but couldn't call you, honey. Thought of you all the time but couldn't call. What could I say if I called? Could I say, I'm lost? Lost in the city? Passed around like a dirty *postcard* among people?—And then hang up . . . I am lost in this—city . . .

WOMAN: I've had nothing but water since you left! [*She says this almost gaily, laughing at the statement. The* MAN *holds her tight to him with a soft, shocked cry.*] Not a thing but instant coffee until it was used up, and water! [*She laughs convulsively.*]

MAN: Can you talk to me, honey? Can you talk to me, now?

WOMAN: Yes!

MAN: Well, talk to me like the rain and—let me listen, let me lie here and—listen . . . [*He falls back across the bed, rolls on his belly, one arm hanging over the side of the bed and occasionally drumming the floor with his knuckles. The mandolin continues.*] It's been too long a time since—we levelled with each other. Now tell me things. What have you been thinking in the silence?—While I've been passed around like a dirty postcard in this city . . . Tell me, talk to me! Talk to me like the rain and I will lie here and listen.

WOMAN: I—

MAN: You've got to, it's necessary! I've got to know, so talk to me like the rain and I will lie here and listen, I will lie here and—

WOMAN: I want to go away.

MAN: You do?

WOMAN: I *want to go away!*

MAN: How?

WOMAN: Alone! [*She returns to window*]—I'll register under a made-up name at a little hotel on the coast . . .

MAN: What name?

WOMAN: Anna—Jones . . . The chambermaid will be a little old lady who has a grandson that she talks about . . . I'll sit in the chair while the old lady makes the bed, my arms will hang over the—sides, and—her voice will be—peaceful . . . She'll tell me what her grandson had for supper!—tapicoa and—cream . . . [*The* WOMAN *sits by the window and sips the water.*] —The room will be shadowy, cool, and filled with the murmur of—

MAN: Rain?

WOMAN: Yes. Rain.

MAN: And—?

WOMAN: Anxiety will—pass—over!

MAN: Yes . . .

WOMAN: After a while the little old woman will say, Your bed is made up, Miss, and I'll say—Thank you . . . Take a dollar out of my pocketbook. The door will close. And I'll be alone again. The windows will be tall with long blue shutters and it will be a season of rain—rain—rain . . . My life will be like the room, cool—shadowy cool and—filled with the murmur of —

MAN: Rain.

WOMAN: I will receive a check in the mail every week that I can count on. The little old lady will cash the checks for me and get me books from a library and pick up—laundry . . . I'll always have clean things!—I'll dress in white. I'll never be very strong or have much energy left, but have enough after a while to walk on the—esplanade—to walk on the beach without effort . . . In the evening I'll walk on the esplanade along the beach. I'll have a certain beach where I go to sit, a little way from the pavillion where the band plays Victor Herbert selections while it gets dark . . . I'll have a big room with shutters on the windows. There will be a season of rain, rain, rain. And I will be so exhausted after my life in the city that I won't mind just listening to the rain. I'll be so quiet. The lines will disappear from my face. My eyes won't be inflamed at all any more. I'll have no friends. I'll have no acquaintances even. When I get sleepy, I'll walk slowly back to the little hotel. The clerk will say, Good evening, Miss Jones, and I'll just barely smile and take my key. I won't ever look at a newspaper or hear a radio; I won't have any idea of what's going on in the world. I will not be conscious of time passing at all . . . One day I will look in the mirror and I will see that my hair is beginning to turn grey and for the first time I will realize that I have been living in this little hotel under a made-up name without any friends or acquaintances or any kind of connections for twenty-five years. It will surprise me a little but it won't bother me any. I will be glad that time has passed as easily as that. Once in a while I may go out to the movies. I will sit in the back row with all that darkness around me and figures sitting motionless on each side not conscious of me. Watching the screen. Imaginary people. People in stories. I will read long books and the journals of dead writers. I will feel closer to them than I ever felt to people I used to know before I withdrew from the world. It will be sweet and cool this friendship of mine with dead poets, for I won't have to touch them or answer their questions. They will talk to me and not expect me to answer. And I'll get sleepy listening to their voices explaining the mysteries to me. I'll fall asleep with the book still in my fingers, and it will rain. I'll wake up and hear the rain and go back to sleep. A season of rain, rain, rain . . . Then one day, when I have closed a book or come home alone from the movies at eleven o'clock at night—I will look in the mirror and see that my hair has turned white. White, absolutely white. As white as the foam on the waves. [*She gets up and moves about the room as she continues* —] I'll run my hands down my body and feel how amazingly light and thin I have grown. Oh, my, how thin I will be. Almost transparent. Not hardly real any more. Then I will realize, I will know, sort of dimly, that I have been staying on here in this little hotel, without any —social connections, responsibilities, anxieties or disturbances of any kind—for just about fifty years. Half a century. Practically a lifetime. I won't even remember the names of the people I knew before I came here nor how it feels to be someone waiting for someone that —may not come . . . Then I will know—looking in the mirror—the first time has come for me to walk out alone once more on the esplanade with the strong wind beating on me, the white clean wind that blows from the edge of the world, from even further than that, from the cool outer edges of space, from even beyond whatever there is beyond the edges of space . . . [*She sits down again unsteadily by the window.*]—Then I'll go out and walk on the esplanade. I'll walk alone and be blown thinner and thinner.

MAN: Baby. Come back to bed.

WOMAN: And thinner and thinner and thinner and thinner and thinner! [*He crosses to her and raises her forcibly from the chair.*]—Till finally I won't have any body at all, and the wind picks me up in its cool white arms forever, and takes me away!

MAN: [*presses his mouth to her throat.*] Come on back to bed with me!

WOMAN: I want to go away, I want to go away!

He releases her and she crosses to center of room sobbing uncontrollably. She sits down on the bed. He sighs and leans out the window, the light flickering beyond him, and the rain coming down harder. The WOMAN *shivers and crosses her arms against her breasts. Her sobbing dies out but she breathes with effort. Light flickers and wind whines coldly. The* MAN *remains leaning out. At last she says to him softly—*

Come back to bed. Come on back to bed, baby . . . [*He turns his lost face to her as—*]

THE CURTAIN FALLS

Bibliography

Ballet, Arthur H. *Playwrights for Tormorrow I* (Minneapolis: University of Minnesota Press, 1966). Includes Megan Terry, *Ex-Miss Copper Queen on a Set of Pills* (1965).

Brasmer, William and Consolo, Dominick. *Black Drama* (Columbus, Ohio: Charles E. Merrill, 1970).

Bullins, Ed. *New Plays from the Black Theater* (New York: Bantam, 1968).

Cerf, Bennett. *SRO: The Most Successful Plays in the History of the American Stage* (New York: Doubleday Doran, 1944). Includes Jack Kirkland, *Tobacco Road* (1933).

Cerf, Bennett and Van H. Cartmell. *Sixteen Famous American Plays* (Garden City, N.Y.: Garden City Publishing Co., 1941). Includes Sidney Kingsley, *Dead End* (1935); William Saroyan, *The Time of Your Life* (1939); Robert E. Sherwood, *The Petrified Forest* (1935).

Clark, Barrett H. *Favorite American Plays of the 19th Century* (Princeton, N.J.: Princeton University Press, 1943). Includes Charles H. Hoyt, *A Trip to Chinatown* (1890).

Clurman, Harold. *Famous American Plays of the 1930's* (New York: Dell Publishing Co., 1959). Includes John Steinbeck, *Of Mice and Men* (1937).

Corrigan, Robert W. *New American Plays* I (New York: Hill and Wang, 1965). Includes Dennis Jasudowicz, *Blood Money* (1965).

Couch, William. *New Black Playwrights* (Baton Rouge, La.: Louisiana State University Press, 1968).

Halline, Allan G. *American Plays* (New York: American Book Company, 1935). Includes Augustin Daly, *Horizon* (1885); Paul Green, *The Field God* (1927).

Hoffman, William M. *New American Plays* II (New York: Hill and Wang, 1968). Includes Tom Eyen, *The White Whore and the Bit Player* (1964); Rochelle Owens, *Futz* (1967).

King, Woodie and Milner, Ron. *Black Drama Anthology* (New York: Signet, 1971).

Kozlenko, William. *The Best Short Plays of the Social Theater* (New York: Random House, 1939).

Lahr, John. *Showcase I* (New York: Grove Press, 1969). Includes Frank Gagliano, *Father Uxbridge Wants to Marry* (1967); Israel Horovitz, *The Indian Wants the Bronx* (1968).

Locke, Alain. *Plays of Negro Life* (New York: Harper and Brothers, 1927).

Matlaw, Myron. *The Black Crook* (New York: E. P. Dutton, 1967). Includes James A. Herne, *Margaret Fleming* (1890); Bronson Howard, *Shenandoah* (1888).

Moody, Richard. *Dramas from the American Theater 1762–1909* (New York: World Publishing Co., 1966). Includes George L. Aiken, *Uncle Tom's Cabin, or Life Among the Lowly* (1852); Clyde Fitch, *The City* (1909); Bronson Howard, *Shenandoah* (1880); Charles H. Hoyt, *A Temperance Town* (1893); W. H. Smith, *The Drunkard, or, The Fallen Saved* (1844); John Augustus Stone, *Metamora, or, The Last of the Wampanoags* (1829).

Moses, Montrose J. *Representative Plays by American Dramatists,* 3 vols. (New York: E. P. Dutton, 1918; reprinted, 1964). Includes J. N. Barker, *The Indian*

Princess, or, *La Belle Sauvage* (1808); Robert Rogers, *Ponteach,* or, *The Savages of America* (1766); Augustus Thomas, *In Mizzoura* (1893); Eugene Walter, *The Easiest Way* (1909).

Parone, Edward. *Collision Course* (New York: Random House, 1968). Includes Israel Horovitz, *Rats* (1967); Adrienne Kennedy, *A Lesson in Dead Language* (1968); Harvey Perr, *Jew!* (1968).

Quinn, Arthur H. *Representative American Plays* (New York: Appleton-Century-Crofts, 1958). Includes Dion Boucicault, *The Octoroon,* or, *Life in Louisiana* (1859); George Washington Parke Custis, *Pocahontas,* or, *The Settlers of Virginia* (1830); Edward Sheldon, *The Boss* (1911).

Reardon, William R. and Pawley, Thomas D. *The Black Theater and the Dramatic Arts* (Westport, Conn.: Negro University Press, 1970). Selections and Bibliography.

Richardson, Willis. *Plays and Pageants from the Life of the Negro* (Washington, D.C.: The Associated Publisher, 1930).

Riley, Clayton. *Black Quartet* (New York: Signet, 1970).

Individual Dramatists

Albee, Edward. *The American Dream* (1961); *The Death of Bessie Smith* (1961); *The Sandbox* (1960); *The Zoo Story* (1960).

Alexander, Hartley. *Manito Masks* (1925). Indian folk-theater.

Anderson, Maxwell. *Gods of Lightning* (with Harold Hickerson, 1928); *Night over Taos* (1935).

Anderson, Robert. *Tea and Sympathy* (1953).

Baldwin, James. *The Amen Corner* (1968); *Blues for Mr. Charlie* (1964).

Boucicault, Dion. *The Poor of New York* (1857).

Bullins, Ed. *The Electronic Nigger* (1968); *Four Dynamite Plays* (1972); *Goin a Buffalo* (1969).

Chapman, Charles H. *Mormon Elder,* or, *The Triumph of Virtue. A Farce* (1912).

Crane, Stephen. *Drama in Cuba* (1898), in *The War Dispatches of Stephen Crane* (1964).

Curtis, Ariana Wormeley. *The Spirit of '76* (1868).

Duberman, Martin B. *In White America* (1964).

Elder, Lonnie. *Ceremonies in Dark Old Men* (1965).

English, Thomas Dunn. *The Mormons,* or, *Life at Salt Lake City. A Drama in Three Acts* (1858).

Gazzo, Michael. *A Hatful of Rain* (1956).

Gordone, Charles. *No Place to Be Somebody: A Black-black Comedy* (1969).

Green, Paul. *Roll, Sweet Chariot* (1934).

Hansberry, Lorraine. *A Raisin in the Sun* (1959).

Heyward, Dorothy and Dubose. *Porgy* (1927).

Heyward, Dubose. *Brass Ankle* (1931).

Hughes, Langston. *Black Nativity* (1961); *Don't You Want to Be Free* (1939); *Scottsboro Limited* (1932).

Inge, William. *Come Back, Little Sheba* (1950); *The Dark at the Top of the Stairs* (1958); *Picnic* (1953).

Jones, LeRoi (Ameer Baraka). *The Baptism* (1966); *Dutchman* (1964); *The Slave* (1964); *The Toilet* (1966).

Kingsley, Sidney. *Detective Story* (1949).

Kopit, Arthur. *Indians* (1969).

Lawson, John Howard. *Marching Song* (1937).

Maltz, Albert. *Black Pit* (1934); *Peace on Earth* (with George Sklar, 1936).

Miller, Arthur. *All My Sons* (1947); *Death of a Salesman* (1949); *A Memory of Two Mondays* (1955); *A View from the Bridge* (1955).

Odets, Clifford. *Awake and Sing* (1935); *Golden Boy* (1937); *Paradise Lost* (1935).

O'Neill, Eugene. *Anna Christie* (1922); *Desire Under the Elms* (1925); *The Emperor Jones* (1921); *The Hairy Ape* (1922).

Peters, Paul and Sklar, George. *Stevedore* (1934).

Phillips, David Graham. *The Worth of a Woman* (1906).

Rice, Elmer. *Street Scene* (1929).

Saroyan, William. *Razzle Dazzle* (1942).

Twain, Mark and Harte, Bret. *Ah Sin* (1877; reprinted, 1961).

Ward, Douglas Turner. *Day of Absence* (1965); *Happy Ending* (1965).

Wexley, John. *The Last Mile* (1929); *They Shall Not Die* (1934).

Williams, Tennessee. *The Glass Menagerie* (1945); *The Rose Tattoo* (1950); *A Streetcar Named Desire* (1947); *Summer and Smoke* (1948); *Sweet Bird of Youth* (1959).